BRITISH
CARTRIDGE
MANUFACTURERS,
LOADERS AND
RETAILERS

INCLUDING IRONMONGERS AND GUNSMITHS

BRITISH CARTRIDGE MANUFACTURERS, LOADERS AND RETAILERS

INCLUDING IRONMONGERS AND GUNSMITHS

C W HARDING

Quiller

WARNING

The loads quoted in this book were taken from original factory data where identical components used in these loads are no longer available. It is also known that the breech pressures, generated by differing brands of black powder when compared on a weight for weight or volume for volume basis, vary considerably. Based on these facts, together with the fact that neither the author, publisher, editor or distributor of this book has control over the potential users choice of such cartridge components, their individual characteristics, or their method of assembly into cartridges nor over the ability or knowledge of potential users, no responsibility either implied or expressed is assumed, should any party attempt to use the cartridge loading data which appears in this book.

Many of the calibres listed in this book are now obsolete and the weapons for which they were designed are in many instances over 100 years old. In view of this a large portion of these small arms will have been subjected to heavy usage or neglect during their working lives, potentially rendering them unsafe to be used. It should also be noted that many of them will have been made and tested solely for use with black powder and should never be used with nitro loads without being specifically reproved for that purpose. In view of this, arms of this nature should be subjected to examination by an experienced gunsmith or an independent Proof House before their owners even consider firing them and the old adage applies, "IF IN ANY DOUBT ABOUT THE GUN OR THE AMMUNITION DO NOT FIRE IT!"

First published in the UK in 2012
by Quiller, an imprint of Quiller Publishing Ltd

British Library Cataloguing-in-Publication Data
A catalogue record for this book
is available from the British Library

ISBN 978 1 84689 145 8

Printed in China

Quiller

An imprint of Quiller Publishing Ltd
Wykey House, Wykey, Shrewsbury, SY4 1JA
Tel: 01939 261616 Fax: 01939 261606
E-mail: info@quillerbooks.com
Website: www.countrybooksdirect.com

ACKNOWLEDGEMENTS

Sincere and grateful thanks are due to the following persons for the help given to the author in the preparation of this book.

Mr M. Golland, Mr C. Lewis, Mr R. Jones formerly of the National Firearms Centre, Mr J.E. Harding, Mr J. Harding, Mr R.J. Hancox, Proof Master Birmingham Gun Barrel Proof House, Mr Alec Morris, the late Mr D. Fearn, Mr J. Buchanan, Miss J. Willetts, Mr Adrian Gamble, Mr E.A. Bush, Mr D.W. Bush, Mrs J. Jarvis, Mr Peter Chapman, Mrs M. Barnett, Mr Hugh Clark, Mr Peter Bontoft, Mr David Bontoft, Mr John Wilson, Ms T. Townsend, Ms N. Skelton, Mr F. Brown, Mr T.G. Crouch, Mr Tom Grange, Mr D. Crow and Mr S. Ings and Mr D. Little, Kynamco.

Particular thanks must go to my wife Sarah who has painstakingly read and corrected the drafts which preceded this book's acceptance for publication.

Similar thanks must also be extended to the Leeds Royal Armouries Library, Birmingham Library, North East Lincolnshire Archives, Central Library Grimsby, Rio Tinto Zinc and the Birmingham Proof House Museum who permitted me to use material in their collections.

The specimens and illustrations shown in the book are owned by numerous individuals, organisations, museums and companies who allowed them to be photographed or copied and their ownership and locations have in most cases not been revealed for security reasons. Nevertheless my sincere thanks go to those parties and organisations since without their material the book would have been unworthy of publication.

CONTENTS

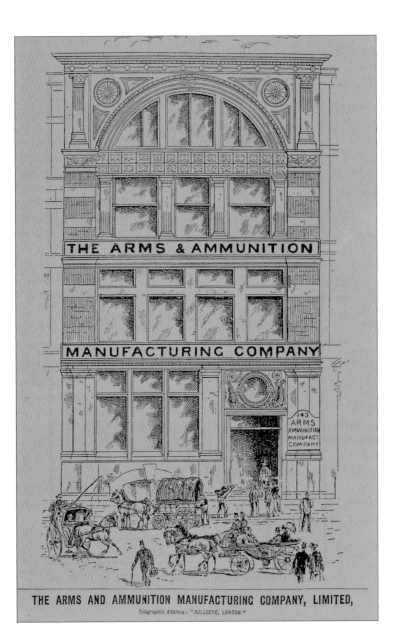

THE ARMS AND AMMUNITION MANUFACTURING COMPANY, LIMITED,

Telegraphic Address: "BULLSEYE, LONDON."

CHAPTER 1
Introduction

T he aim of this book is to attempt to record a brief history of the remaining metallic and shotgun cartridge companies which currently or once produced cartridges for both military and sporting use at home and abroad, other than those manufactured by Eley of London or by the Birmingham companies which were covered in my two former books entitled *Eley Cartridges* and *The Birmingham Cartridge Manufacturers*. The book in essence covers the four separate groups involved in this industry, namely the manufacturers who made the cases, primers and loaded the cartridges with either their own or other companies' powders; the powder companies who bought in cases from case manufacturers and then loaded and retailed these cartridges; a small group of large scale loaders and retailers who used other companies' components; and a fourth group consisting of a long list of gunsmiths, ironmongers, shops and stores who either loaded cases obtained from the large case manufacturers, or alternatively got the case makers to load them and print their name on the tube or impress it into the brass head.

The introduction of breech loading small arms generated major increases in the demand for both military and sporting cartridges of all types. This change in small arms design was also linked to their use with new nitro based propellants and this resulted in the formation of a number of new smokeless powder companies seeking to satisfy that demand fuelled by overseas wars and a huge increase in game shooting in Britain during this transitional period. By the end of the Victorian era and during the Edwardian period, which ended just prior to WWI, most members of the British aristocracy regularly held huge shoots on their estates, and these became a major part of the social calendar. This period was to mark the zenith in the demand for cartridges used for game shooting, which to date has never been surpassed.

These new powder companies offered the sportsman their new nitro based propellants for use in a range of sporting cartridges and, like today's salesman's banter, their products were always better and possessed qualities which surpassed those of their rivals. Most of these powder companies however were never to possess the requisite cartridge manufacturing equipment due to its costs and therefore initially entered into agreements with the big cartridge manufacturers, such as Eley, to load and retail their powders through the cartridge manufacturers' outlets. In the alternative camp the big cartridge manufacturing companies like Eley Bros Ltd and G. Kynoch & Co. did not initially produce their own nitro based propellants so they were initially happy with these agreements. The main reason why this situation had arisen was that the case suppliers for many years did not have the knowledge or facilities to produce the new smokeless propellants which, shortly after their invention, rapidly became the subject of patents.

During the 1890s the powder companies realised that they could generate even greater returns if they could acquire primed cases from the big cartridge manufacturers and then load and retail the cartridges themselves, and amazingly the cartridge case manufacturers initially agreed to this action. Also during this period and indeed well before in the black powder cartridge era, many gunmakers, gunsmiths, stores and ironmongers had ordered shotgun cartridge cases from the main cartridge case manufacturers bearing their individual company names which they then loaded on their own premises and retailed through their shops.

Collectively the actions of the powder companies, gunmakers, gunsmiths, stores and iron-mongers were to reduce the profits which the big cartridge companies would have been capable of achieving if they had made, loaded and retailed the cartridges themselves using their own home produced powders and shot. As a result the cartridge manufacturers responded by either buying powder manufacturing companies or by starting to produce their own in house powders. Eley Bros Ltd, for example, bought out Schultze in October 1911 by becoming their main shareholders, whilst in 1898 G. Kynoch & Co. started manufacturing their own KS shotgun powder. The reasons for their actions were obvious: they wanted to be self sufficient, not reliant on receiving the needed quantities of propellant from the powder manufacturers, and to regain their former share of the market which was under attack from all sides with each player seeking to cost cut their products to be competitive.

Finally a point was reached when the big cartridge manufacturers started to either refuse to supply the powder companies with cases or they were not prepared to provide them with the quantities requested. Alternatively they refused to print on the cartridge tubes and headstamps what the powder companies wanted and it was at this point that the smaller powder companies started to look further afield for new supplies of primed shotgun cartridge cases.

Many of the overseas cartridge manufactures also recognised the huge levels of demand for game cartridges in the UK during this period and wanted to gain entrance to this lucrative market. If these companies were sited in Europe then the transport costs of loaded shotgun cartridges were minor compared, for example, with the cost of shipping loaded cartridges from the USA. If however you were to import loaded shotgun cartridges from the USA, a major manufacturer of small arm ammunition, and offer them for sale alongside their English counterpart, the US cartridge could never be competitively priced due to the related transport costs into the UK. That equation how-ever was to be dramatically changed when only primed cases were imported, since the cartridge tube production levels in the United States were so large that the unit cost per primed case was less than those made in the UK. As a direct result REM-UMC (Remington Union Metallic Cartridge Co.), an English subsidiary of its American parent was formed and opened its Brimsdown factory in Middlesex in 1916, where it was to load primed cases made in the USA with English powders and shot. This company also offered gunsmiths etc. the opportunity to place their own name on REM-UMC cases as long as the order was for 20,000 or more, thereby satisfying the demand for primed cases from the gunsmiths etc.

The big powder companies also sought solutions to the actions of the cartridge case makers in the period prior to WWI and this resulted in the largest of these companies buying out two existing cartridge case manufacturers. One was Nobel's and their initial action was the start of the total buy out of the British ammunition and powder manufacturers. When Nobel's initially invented Ballistite which they patented in 1887 they went to Eley Bros Ltd of London for their primed case supplies for both metallic and shotgun cartridges which they loaded at the Ardeer Nobel factory. In 1897 Alfred Nobel bought the Birmingham Metal & Munitions Co. to make metallic cartridges loaded with Ballistite, then via extremely devious means in 1904 he managed to obtain a major shareholding in Joyce & Co. Ltd of London. When Eley realised the level of competition which Nobel's posed them the relationship between the two companies declined and before Nobel's were able to rebuild and modernise the Joyce factory at Waltham Abbey, they moved in 1904 to obtaining shotgun cases from the UMC (Union Metallic Cartridge Co.) which supplied them with Acme UMC cases which they loaded with Ballistite together with Magic UMC cases which they loaded with Empire powder. In due course following the rebuilding of the Joyce works, Joyce & Co. Ltd was to provide Nobel's with a shotgun cartridge manufacturing company in which they could load their Ballistite and Empire powders. The Schultze Gunpowder Co. Ltd tried the alternative route of amalgamation with the Cogswell & Harrison Manufacturing Company, which manufactured cartridge cases and primers. In 1911 the Cogschultze Ammunition & Powder Co. Ltd was formed. Cogswell & Harrison and Schultze however had a major disagreement shortly afterwards and the company broke up, resulting in Eley Bros Ltd finally acquiring Schultze later that year.

The Normal Powder Syndicate Ltd /Normal Powder Co./New Normal Ammunition Co. (this being the sequence of names used during its existence) is first mentioned in 1895, with the syndicate obtaining rights to sell their powder in Britain. It was initially loaded into metallic ammunition made by Kynoch, Eley and Greenwood & Batley. In April 1897 they were retailing their powders in Pegamoid cases, Brass Ejectors, and Nimrod brand pink paper cases which were made for them by Joyce of London, Eley Bros, G. Kynoch & Co. and Bachmann of Belgium. However by July the same year, with an order on hand for 300,000 shotgun cartridges they stated they were now obtaining cases from England, the USA and Europe. The initial supplies from the USA were from the Winchester Rifle Ammunition Co. This action reflected two changing facets, namely the reluctance of the English case makers to supply them with adequate quantities and their need to be competitively priced alongside the products of the big cartridge manufacturers.

The end of WWI brought about marked changes in the social structure created by that war in relation to both the roles and salaries allocated to the working man and woman. The former action of a large percentage of our working class population working 'in service for the aristocracy' for a mere pittance was never to be repeated. Following the war most of the large estates were unable to afford the numbers of servants they had before its outbreak and the loss to the Army of the estate game-keepers during the 1914-1918 period was reflected in the decimation of the game bird numbers, due to a lack of husbandry. The direct result of these events was that many of the families, previously in service, had migrated to the cities and towns and they were never to return to the estates. Their initial movement was engendered by the Government need to staff the munitions, armament, and aircraft factories and the many other industries associated with the 'War Effort' and it was in these new locations that these former servants discovered that they could obtain better wages than they had received whilst in service. After the war the numbers of shoots on the large estates were dramatically cut, due to the associated rises incurred in staffing costs. This in turn reflected in a huge drop in demand for game cartridges and since the same cartridge and powder companies were no longer required to manufacture military metallic ammunition and propellants, the scene was ripe for amalgamation. In November 1918 Nobel's were to amalgamate many of these former cartridge manufacturers and propellant companies into one, which in due course was to gain the name of Imperial Chemical Industries.

Following the termination of case manufacture for both metallic and shotgun ammunition by ICI/IMI only a few new cartridge manufacturing companies have emerged. As for the shotgun cartridge loading shops sited in gunmakers and ironmongers where shotgun cartridges were loaded for their customers, these started to vanish as the provisions of the Explosives Act were more rigorously applied and the licence renewal conditions were such they became financially unviable.

In today's age we have a relatively small number of companies in the UK which load imported shotgun cases and propellants. However as a result of a major rise in clay pigeon shooting over the last 20 years, the number of shotgun cartridges loaded in the UK now exceeds the quantities manufactured here in the late Victorian and early Edwardian periods for game shooting on our large estates. Unfortunately the same cannot be said about the loading and manufacture of metallic ammunition in the UK since we have only managed to retain a single rim-fire manufacturer and one large scale loader of centre-fire ammunition.

STANDING BACK ROW: *Dark Ignition flare by J. Pain & Sons and a Parachute Flare by Wilders of Birmingham, both in 1½" Eley Bros Ltd punt gun case. A 10 bore message launcher fired from a REM-UMC case, all used during WWI by British troops. A 32mm pin-fire shotgun cartridge by Gevelot made for Maharajah Duleep Singh, former ruler of the Punjab, whilst owner of the Elveden Estate in Suffolk after his enforced departure from India by the East India Company.*
STANDING MIDDLE ROW: *'Pygmy' for C. Lancaster case by Joyce, a Curtis's & Harvey's Ruby loading. 'The Priority' by W. Palmer Jones, .410" 'Comet' by J.R. Watson & Co., 'High Velocity' by Aubrey Lewis, Luton, Eley Nobel case loaded with Smokeless Diamond for H.G. Tett Ltd, Coventry, ICI loading for J. Rigby & Co.*
LYING DOWN: *'The Retriever' by ICI for W.H. Tisdall Ltd, New Zealand, 'Cosmo' for C.F. Perrins & Co. Johannesburg & Pretoria by Trent Cartridge Co., an Eley Nobel loading for Von Lengerke & Detmoid, USA.*

CHAPTER 2
George Henry Daw

2.1 Daw's history and his role in the production of centre-fire cartridges

It is believed that the centre-fire system was invented by a M. Pottett of Paris, however a more accurate description of his invention was that he introduced anvils within percussion caps. Mr F. Schneider, a French gunsmith, patented a modified and more practical form of Pottett's anvils. Mr George Henry Daw, a London gunmaker who had been born in 1830, secured the English rights to this patent. He traded from 57 Threadneedle Street in London and produced a hammerless centre-fire gun, several percussion revolvers and centre-fire ammunition which he exhibited at the International Exhibition in 1861. This system of cartridge ignition is still in use today throughout the world and was to replace the former pin-fire ignition system.

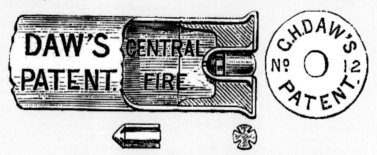

DAW'S PATENT CENTRAL-FIRE METALLIC CARTRIDGES.

The Daw Cartridge won the 400l. Prize awarded by the English Government in the recent competition at Woolwich.

They are specially adapted for Military Breech-loading Rifles (chambered), same form as the Government converted Rifles.

DAW'S PATENT CENTRAL FIRE

G.H.DAW'S No 12 PATENT.

SHAPE OF ANVIL USED IN EACH COPPER CAP.

G. H. DAW AND CO.,
PATENTEES AND SOLE MANUFACTURERS,
GREAT TRINITY LANE,
LONDON, E.C.

Until recently I have been unable to discover where and if Daw produced his own shotgun and rifle cartridges; however I have recently unearthed a source which dispels any beliefs that others produced cartridges on his behalf. The information in question is as follows:

In October 1867 several orders were placed with Greenwood & Batley of Leeds, a former huge engineering company, by L.J. Enthoven & Co. for machines designed to make cartridges for G.H. Daw. Order number 799,358 was for a machine for Daw to form the heads of cartridge cases, order number 804,359 in October 1867 was for a machine to punch holes in the base of the cup for

September 30, 1863.]

THE IRON MONGER.

577

CONVICTION UNDER THE GUNPOWDER ACT.

Mr. George Henry Daw and Mr. Frederick Joyce, gunmakers, in Threadneedle-street, were summoned before the Lord Mayor, at the Justice-room of the Mansion House, on the 25th, by Alfred Carter, inspector of the City police, for that they, on the 14th of September instant, in Sweedes-court, Great Trinity-lane, City, unlawfully, without any licence for the purpose, did carry on the manufacture of ammunition within the distance of 100 yards of divers dwelling-houses, in which persons not connected with the said manufacture were employed. Secondly, for unlawfully keeping a quantity of cartridges, containing 5 lbs. of gunpowder and upwards, in a certain place not licensed for that purpose. Thirdly, for unlawfully causing to be made a quantity of cartridges, the operation of filling and charging which was performed in a building situate at a distance less than twenty yards from other workshops connected with the same manufacture. Fourthly, for unlawfully keeping a factory for the making of ammunition, not having a magazine built with brick or stone for safely keeping the gunpowder and explosive materials used in the manufacture, and the cartridges made at such factory. And lastly, for that they, being dealers in gunpowder and manufacturers of cartridges, unlawfully had at one time in their house more than 200 lbs. of gunpowder. The City Solicitor (Mr. T. J. Nelson) appeared for the prosecution; Mr. Metcalfe (instructed by Mr. Wontner), for the defence. The respondents pleaded not guilty. After hearing the evidence in support of the charge, Mr. Frederick Alex. Preston Pigou was called for the defence. He said—I am one of the partners in the firm of Pigou and Wilks, who are large manufacturers of gunpowder. We supply gunpowder to the respondents amongst others. I have nothing whatever to do with cartridges. I am a gunpowder maker. I know gun-makers do fill cartridges very largely. I cannot say they fill them at the places where they sell. I have had orders for gunpowder with the words "For filling cartridges" upon them. I think that is quite universal among gun dealers. There is not the least danger in filling cartridges. There might be danger in removing the powder from the copper magazines or other receptacles, and putting it into the cartridge-filling machine by careless hands. I know that the Government have accepted Mr. Daw's cartridge as the safest that has yet been manufactured. I should have no hesitation whatever in holding one of his loaded cartridges—loaded with powder and shot—by one end while it was being exploded at the other. The powder would not burn my hand, and the shot would drop on the ground. I have seen it done. It is a matter of importance to the trade to know whether or not this is ammunition in law. By the City Solicitor: It is not in the least necessary that a trade of this sort should be carried on in the heart of the City of London. The City Solicitor: You have received orders, you say, from other gunmakers for powder, to be used for filling cartridges. Will you give me their names? I ask in the public interest. Witness: I have no opportunity here for looking at the orders; but I might

give you a wrong name. I should be happy to give you the information if I might refer to the orders. Mr. Metcalfe: We have heard that all gun-makers do so. The City Solicitor: It is important to know to what extent the Act of Parliament is infringed. Witness (to the City Solicitor): I saw an account in the paper of a serious explosion at Metz, at an ammunition factory. By Mr. Metcalfe: I have never heard of any accident from filling cartridges on Mr. Daw's principle. Mr. Richard Watson Smith, a partner in the firm of Messrs. Hall and Sons, gunpowder makers, said he had seen the cartridges in question, and in his judgment they were particularly safe. No more danger attended them than ordinary goods which were inflammable—cotton for instance. It was his firm belief that if one of a lot was set fire to it would not explode the rest. He had heard the Government authorities repeatedly speak of the superiority of Mr. Daw's cartridge, and that more on the ground of safety than on any other. He had read an account of the accident at Metz. It was at a manufactory for paper cartridges for Chassepot rifles. In his judgment, the machine for filling Mr. Daw's cartridges was perfectly safe. Gun-dealers almost universally filled their cartridges at their establishments, and that had been the practice of the trade ever since the Act of 1860 was passed. Nine-tenths of the trade fill cartridges on their own premises. He had never seen gas used in a manufactory of this kind. The City Solicitor: Do you think these things should be made in the heart of the City of London? Is there any necessity for it? Witness replied that they must be made somewhere, but they might just as well be made somewhere else. There was nothing in gunpowder to make it less explosive in Sweet's-court, Trinity-lane, than anywhere else. An explosion of 100 lbs. in such a place would be extremely serious, and probably be attended with great danger to life and property. In the Clerkenwell case, an application was made to them for three barrels of gunpowder, and that would be 300 lbs. Mr. Daw said the quantity of gunpowder found on the premises had been greatly exaggerated. The Lord Mayor offered the respondents, if they thought that, an opportunity to have the quantity tested; but they did not avail themselves of it. The City Solicitor withdrew one of the summonses, and eventually the Lord Mayor convicted the respondents in four others, imposing penalties amounting in the whole to £40, and directing a forfeiture of the cartridges and gunpowder found upon the premises. The Act of Parliament, he said, was clear and precise, and Mr. Daw had infringed it in every possible way. The City Solicitor said these hazardous trades would not be permitted in the City, and the police would be further instructed to aid in suppressing them. Mr. Metcalfe said his clients, after the decision which had been given, would resort to their legal rights, the more especially as there had been no desire to summon the proprietors of the other large establishments of the trade. The Lord Mayor said immediately this matter came to his knowledge, he thought it his duty to direct an inquiry, and to issue a search warrant. Mr. Metcalfe applied for, and obtained leave to state a case, by way of appeal from the decision of the bench.

cartridge heads and order number 808, 364 was for a machine to cut paper to width for the Daw's cartridge. (Although I have been unable to positively identify who Enthoven was, in 1861 a company entitled Messrs Enthoven & Sons was sited in Upper Ordnance Wharf, London and was listed as lead smelters, a company which would clearly have been of considerable use to Daw to make both shot and lead bullets.)

The second source of evidence appeared in a copy of *The Ironmonger* dated 30 September 1868 which stated that both Frederick Joyce and G.H. Daw were using the same premises in Sweedes Court, Great Trinity Lane, City to load cartridges (presumably for the London gun trade) and their action was to result in them both appearing before the court.

Between 1862 and 1867 a chain of events occurred which would have a major impact on Daw's history. During 1862, Daw alleged that a leading member of the Eley family called upon him to examine his new form of centre-fire cartridge and subsequently sought to purchase the patent relating to it. According to Daw he declined to sell the patent and for the next two years supplied cartridges incorporating the centre-fire Daw's patent to Eley. In early 1865, Daw realised that Eley Bros were manufacturing centre-fire cartridges which he believed were in infringement of his patent and he was initially successful in obtaining an injunction to prevent Eley Bros from using a triangular anvil inside their percussion caps as an alternative to Daw's tubular anvil. Although Eley Bros lost the initial court case in November 1865, their argument was that they had been approached by Charles Lancaster, in 1857, to manufacture a slightly modified version of the Pottet's patent cartridge, which Pottet had patented in France and which Lancaster purchased but never patented in Britain. Daw however had patented in Britain Schneider's modification of the Pottet design. To add to the confusion of the courts, William Thomas Eley took out two further patents on centre-fire caps. The first No. 3181 dated 9 December 1865 sought to introduce a waterproof substance between the cap and cap chamber in the form of varnish, wax etc. The second patent number 880 dated 24 March 1866 introduced a two piece percussion cap anvil aimed at making the cap chamber gas-tight.

Shortly after Eley was granted their new patents and resumed production of centre-fire cartridges and Daw took out a further injunction against them in December 1866. This time Daw failed. Not surprisingly the new patent variations imposed on the original Pottet design by both Eley and Boxer would have done little for Daw's case and Eley Bros were free to reap the benefits which the centre-fire cartridge was to afford to the company. On 1 May 1886 *The Ironmonger* reported that G.H. Daw was bankrupt. Had the court case gone in Daw's favour it is reasonable to believe his patent rights would have enabled him to dramatically extend his range of cartridges and his output would have been comparable to that of Eley Bros.

Another now long forgotten fact was that it was G.H. Daw who patented the coiled cartridge case which was to act as forerunner to the drawn brass cases used in rifle and pistol ammunition. On 8 March 1867 Daw was granted patent 660, a copy of which is shown on the following page.

In today's age very few of Daw's cartridges remain and are seldom encountered in either shotgun or metallic calibres.

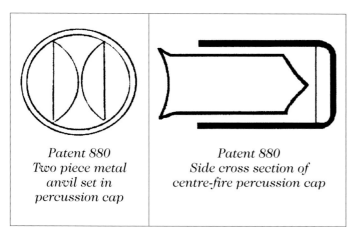

Patent 880
Two piece metal
anvil set in
percussion cap

Patent 880
Side cross section of
centre-fire percussion cap

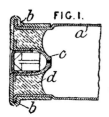

FIG.1.

The case of the cartridge is made of metal tube **a** formed from a strip bent over a mandrel, and having its over-lapping edges soldered or cemented together. At one end of the tube is fixed a base carrying a percussion arrangement **c**. Any kind of base may be used; in the form shown, a wad of paper pulp **d** is pressed in between the case and the percussion chamber **c**. The tubes are of a conical or cylindrical form, or conical and cylindrical combined; and the tube may be soldered for the whole of its length or a projecting flap only may be soldered. Alternatively a cement may be used consisting of a mixture of glue and flake white.

2.2 Examples of Daw's cartridges

Headstamp on 12 bore specimen. Although the headstamp appears indented the letters and numbers are in fact raised and this occurred on all the specimens I have seen

LEFT TO RIGHT:
.577" Snider and 12 bore shotgun cartridge. The Snider case incorporates his coiled case patent of 1867

2.3 Examples of the headstamps appearing on Daw's shotgun and metallic cartridges

1.

On 12 bore shotgun cartridge

2.

On 16 bore shotgun cartridge

3.

On .577" Snider cartridge

4.

On 17.5mm x 29R Dutch Snider cartridge Model of 1867 using a rolled foil case

5.

On .500" 2.18" cased rifle cartridge made of rolled foil

CHAPTER 3
Frederick Joyce and Company of London

3.1 The company's history

Frederick Joyce was born in 1799 in London. He initially established his business in 1820 being one of the first parties in this country to manufacture percussion caps. His first manufacturing base was sited at 55 Bartholomew Close, West Smithfield, London where he manufactured percussion caps and wadding. Shortly after establishing these premises they caught fire forcing him to move to a temporary location at 11 Old Compton Street, which the *London Trade Directories* indicates he occupied between 1823 and 1827; after which he returned to 55 Bartholomew Close between 1831 and 1833.

The 1841 census for the City of London in relation to Bartholomew Close shows he was now married, had two children named Alfred and Agnes at home, whilst his two eldest sons, Robert and Frederick, were shown to be at school at Clapham.

The huge demand for percussion caps both home and abroad, both for military and sporting purposes was to guarantee a dramatic rise in demand, however these early cap manufacturers were constantly facing a problem of explosions wrecking their premises. These problems were further added to by an ever present public outcry concerning their factory siting, since very often they were located in the heart of residential areas which posed a huge risk to their residential neighbours.

These two factors were no doubt the reason why in 1842 the company were to expand to a new factory at Waltham Abbey, a site where gunpowder had been manufactured for a number of years; and in 1846 the company opened a separate office at 57 Upper Thames Street, London, EC. The change of working premises also caused the family to move and the 1851 census shows the family home at Farmhill House, Waltham Holly Cross, Waltham Abbey. By this date the family size now consisted of four girls and three boys. Two of the boys, namely Robert George aged 20 years was now employed by the company as a clerk as indeed was his brother Frederick aged 18 years, whilst the youngest Alfred aged 15 years had been sent to boarding school at Epping. This census also revealed that the company were employing 44 members of staff.

The company was for many years to be run as a family concern and Frederick was to introduce his three sons Robert George, Frederick and Alfred to the business, who during the 1850s were to take over from him in a partnership allowing Frederick Senior to retire and move to New Road, Brighton.

In 1852 the company had expanded and started to manufacture cartridges and the letter 'J' was to become the reference mark used on their metallic ammunition.

This tin bears the date 1855. This related to Frederick Joyce's patent number 749 taken out on 3 April 1855 where he used nitrated paper or other vegetable substance as a protective covering for the fulminate

1851

FREDERICK JOYCE,

Inventor & Manufacturer of Anti-Corrosive Percussion Caps,

CHEMICALLY PREPARED GUN WADDINGS, &c.,

PATENTEE OF THE WATERPROOF PYROXYLINE PERCUSSION CAPS,

CONTRACTOR TO HER MAJESTY'S WAR DEPARTMENT,

57, UPPER THAMES STREET, LONDON, E.C.

ESTABLISHED 1820.

PERCUSSION CAPS.

Patent Waterproof Pyroxyline Caps.

Best Anti-corrosive Caps.

Treble Waterproof Central Fire Caps.

Foil-covered or Metal-lined Caps.

Waterproof Pistol Caps of all lengths and sizes.

Caps made expressly for Deane's, Adams', or Tranter's Patent Revolvers.

Do. for Colt's Patent Revolvers.

Military Caps of various kinds.

Waterproof Caps for Duck Guns, Alarm Guns, Harpoon Guns, &c.

Bulleted Caps for Saloon Pistols and Rifles.

Best 5 A Caps for Dart Guns.

Smith's Patent Caps.

Jones's Patent Caps.

Loading Caps for Stick Guns.

Needle Gun Caps, &c.

Plain and Headed Tubes.

Maroon Tubes.

Detonating Balls.

Percussion Patches.

Grain Powder for Magazine Locks.

Maroons for Alarm Guns.

Rifle Patches of two substances, from 1 to 2 in.

Clarified Oil for Gun Locks.

Cap Gauges to try the sizes of Caps.

GUN WADDINGS.

Concaved Elastic Felt Waddings.

Patent Felt Waddings in Oil Silk Bags.

Chemically-prepared Green Waddings.

Elastic White Felt Waddings with Pink edges.

Grey Felt Waddings with Prepared edges.

Indented Paper Waddings.

SHEET WADDING.

Felt Sheets from ¼ inch thick and upwards.

White Felt Sheets, 17 inches by 11 inches.

Grey Felt Sheets, 17 inches by 11 inches.

Best Paper Wadding Sheets.

Millboard Sheets.

CARTRIDGES.

Improved Wire Cartridges.

Green, for Long Distances.

Red, for Medium Distances.

Universal Shot Cartridges, for general use.

Duck Gun Cartridges made to order, of any size or weight required.

Cartridge Cases, for Breech loading Shot Guns.

Cartridges for Muzzle Loading Guns, containing Powder and Shot.

Cartridges for Deane's, Adams', or Tranter's Patent Revolvers.

Ditto for Colt's Patent Revolvers.

Ditto for Revolvers of all kinds.

Hall's Patent Chargers and Cartridge Carrier.

The 1861 census showed that the three sons were now described as Managers of the company which was employing 60 hands and that they were each living unmarried with their sister Emma at their parents' former home at Farmhill House, Waltham Holly Cross, Waltham Abbey.

Unfortunately on 14 October 1878, one son Frederick aged 45 years was killed in an explosion at the Waltham Abbey factory, leaving his brother Robert George Joyce to continue as the firm's principal, since it appeared that Alfred had decided to leave the company and live on his investment income.

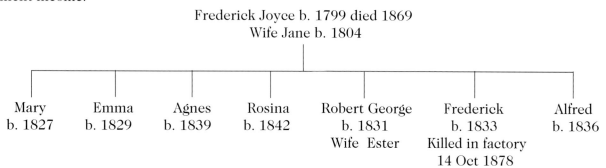

Frederick Joyce b. 1799 died 1869
Wife Jane b. 1804

| Mary
b. 1827 | Emma
b. 1829 | Agnes
b. 1839 | Rosina
b. 1842 | Robert George
b. 1831
Wife Ester | Frederick
b. 1833
Killed in factory
14 Oct 1878 | Alfred
b. 1836 |

Although the company had its main factory at Waltham Abbey it clearly still loaded cartridges within the heart of the City of London and an extract from *The Ironmonger* dated the 30 September 1868 provided evidence of two previously little known or uncirculated facts, namely:

1. The premises where Joyce was loading his cartridges, presumably for the London gun trade was situated in Sweedes Court, Great Trinity Lane, City.
2. These same premises were occupied by George Henry Daw, the famous centre-fire cartridge manufacturer.

In 1888 a company entitled F. Joyce and Company Limited was formed with Robert George Joyce initially acting as its Director. Robert George had been born in 1831 in St Johns Wood, Middlesex and the 1881 census shows him living at Farm Hill, Waltham Holy Cross, Essex with his wife Ester and his brother Alfred who by then was living the life of a Gentleman of leisure. This census also indicates the company were employing 110 staff making cartridges. For a number of years during the 1890s the annual profits of the company varied but were in the region of a few thousand pounds. Clearly such returns provided insufficient capital to enable the company to invest in new machinery or buildings in order to increase its holdings in the cartridge trade.

JOYCE'S SPORTING AMMUNITION

ESTABLISHED 1820.

F. JOYCE & CO. invited the attention of Sportsmen to the following AMMUNITION, of the best quality, now in general use throughout INDIA, ENGLAND, and the COLONIES.

Joyce's Treble Waterproof Central-Fire PERCUSSION CAPS.

Chemically-prepared Cloth and Felt Gun Wadding, Cartridge Cases of superior quality for Breech-loading Guns, Wire Cartridges for killing Game at long distances,

AND EVERY DESCRIPTION OF SPORTING AMMUNITION.

Sold by all Gunmakers and Dealers in Gunpowder.

FREDERICK JOYCE & CO.,

Patentees and Manufacturers,
57, UPPER THAMES-STREET LONDON.

On 22 December 1893 there was an explosion at their works at Waltham Abbey which killed two men. Colonel Majendie's report stated it could have been partially avoided if their employee who was mixing fulminate composition had conformed to the company's new rules. Their old hand Samuel Burton had however decided that the old system was safer and ignored the recommended new system. His work consisted of mixing the fulminate composition in a gutta-percha bottle. Once the first bottle was full he had been instructed to move the bottle to a neighbouring shed. Burton however placed the first bottle he had filled in a corner of the mixing shed and the mixture he was handling then exploded. Falling roof debris hit the second bottle, which then exploded about half a minute later. The second blast killed the second party, injured Mr Courtman the Works Manager plus two others who had hurried to the scene, having heard the first explosion. The Government Inspector had pressure put on Joyce's to adopt the jelly bag to mix these components, since it was in successful use at the Woolwich military arsenal. The bottles once mixed would contain somewhere between 15ozs to 22ozs of fulminating mixture and when filled, the accompanying instructions were that they were to be immediately removed to a safe storage area, away from the mixing area. In 1893 the company won a Gold award at The World's Fair in Chicago. In July 1896 the company opened new offices at 7 Suffolk Lane, London and during the same year Messrs Hunter & Warren were appointed to act as their sales agents in Scotland.

Robert George Joyce retired from the company in 1897, dying at the age of 72 on 23 August 1902, leaving an estate worth £143,429.

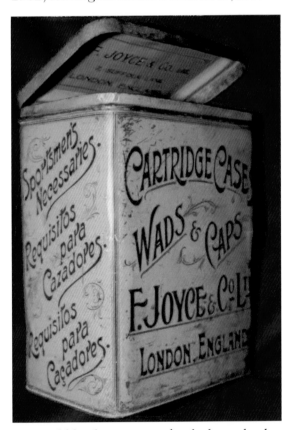

A tin sold by the company for the home loader. It will be noted that the inside lid indicates the company address of 7 Suffolk Lane
(PHOTOGRAPH COURTESY OF MR F. BROWN)

In June 1897, *Sporting Goods Review* sent one of its reporters to visit Joyce's new offices sited at 7 Suffolk Lane, where he met with Mr Percy Newton the company's Manager who was later to become the Secretary in 1904. Newton was clearly very reticent about discussing the company's manufacturing base at Waltham Abbey and stated that he had no photographs of the site. From this response linked to the company's poor profit returns, I believe we can draw the conclusion that the Waltham Abbey site was antiquated and in dire need of new equipment. Newton did however show the reporter around the offices and allowed a photograph to be taken of them. A previous article described this site as having three private rooms. One was occupied by the Company Secretary Mr Harry Rayment, the second by Mr Newton and the third acted as the main board room. The site also housed a museum of ammunition including specimens of all the cartridges produced by the company and specimens showing the evolution of the cartridge. In the basement were stored percussion caps and cartridges. The report also indicated the premises had supplies of water and electricity, which in today's age we would take for granted.

The company's AGM in April 1899 indicated an annual net trading profit of £19, compared to just over £2,000 in the previous year. This resulted in

Mr Percy Newton

the Chairman Sir John R. Heron-Maxwell and his fellow Director Colonel Ricardo resigning their posts. It was claimed that part of the problem arose since the new auditors insisted on writing off £600 of stock which previously had resulted in an over valuation of stock being passed over year by year by the old auditors. It appears however that no one had ever queried if the company was still maintaining its position in the market place and there was a strong suspicion it was facing increased opposition from other companies and losing customers and orders to them. Neither of these two concerns appears to have been addressed by the Board of Directors.

At the company's twelfth annual general meeting in 1900, a new Chairman was appointed, namely Mr William Stacey together with a fellow Director, a John Parnell. The companies' balance on hand was £2,796 and it was announced that an agreement had been reached over the selling price of cartridges with its fellow manufacturers. This same year the company appointed Messrs J.P. Clabrough & Johnstone of Price Street, Birmingham as their Birmingham agents and opened a new depot at 50 Loveday Street to stock hold ammunition for the Birmingham Gun Trade. In April 1901 Mr Percy Newton was appointed the company's General Manager.

The company continued independent production until its sixteenth AGM held on 28 March 1904 at Winchester House. The Presiding Officer Mr John Parnell stated that the year's accounts had been the most disastrous on record, with profits being just £1,856 compared with £2,104 the previous year. He stated that of the £10,000 debentures authorised by the articles of association, £6,500 of these had been issued for the purpose of paying for the enlargement of the buildings, plant and machinery most of which was nearing completion. The minutes of the meeting also revealed that a Mr W.H. Greenwood had been co-opted onto the Board of Directors. Greenwood was also a Director of Birmingham Metal & Munitions Company, a company owned by Nobel's Explosives Co. Ltd. At the former annual general meeting the company's shareholders had been asked to give up a third of their shares at 10s per share, after they had established as a result of a question posed by the Director Sir John Maxwell that this was not going to result in a contract between Dynamite Trust and Joyce's. This had resulted in the shareholders allowing B.M. & M.Co. to acquire 20,000 of the shares to provide an arrangement by which Joyce supplied B.M.& M.Co. with goods at certain agreed rates and visa versa. This event was to mark the start of what proved to be the termination of Joyce as an independent manufacturing company. On the 25 July 1904 Mr Harry Rayment, Secretary to the company died from appendicitis. He was a nephew of Robert George Joyce and proved to be the last family member to be involved with the company. Mr Percy Newton was to

The offices of Messrs F. Joyce & Co. Limited

take his post with a Mr Charles Dickens acting as Assistant Secretary. On 31 October 1906 the former Managing Director William Henry Greenwood died leaving an estate valued at £35,083.

In June 1908 the company moved their offices to Kingsway House above those occupied by Nobel's Explosives Co. Ltd but retaining their premises of 7 Suffolk Lane as a storage site.

On 15 December 1909 the *Sporting Goods Review* reported that the company of F. Joyce and Co. Ltd as from 1 January 1910 would be transferred to Messrs Nobel's Explosives Company of Glasgow, who would carry it on in conjunction with their sporting powder and ammunition trade at Kingsway House, London WC. The article also stated that the Waltham Abbey site was being equipped by Nobel's with new machinery both to modernise and increase its output capacity. In April 1910 a Mr T. Rosewell was appointed the Works Manager to replace Mr Courtman, who had recently died. During the same year Mr Percy Newton, the former Company Secretary retired. This then marked the end of Joyce as an independent cartridge manufacturer; however Nobel's were wise enough to retain the Joyce name for its subsequently produced percussion caps in the same way that Eley was to be retained by them as the brand name on shotgun cartridges and Kynoch was to be used in relation to metallic centre-fire ammunition.

3.2 The gas check patents used by the company

The most interesting features employed by Joyce's relate to shotgun cartridge patents taken out by a C.S. Bailey, the most important relating to percussion caps designed to create gas-tight seals at the base of the shotgun cartridge case. The patents in question which Bailey filed and which covered both full and provisional patents were:

496. Bailey, C. S. Feb. 1.

Cartridges, small-arm. — Central-fire cartridges specially for hammerless guns are provided with brass caps *g*, which serve as gas checks and enclose inner caps *b* made of sheet iron, as described in Specification No. 3625, A.D. 1882. The base of the cap *g* is indented to show the position of the percussion cap *d* and to hold the cap chamber *c*. The cap *b* is backed up by paper packing *f*, which fills the lower part of the paper tube *a*.

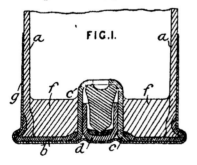

4421. Bailey, C. S. March 5.

Cartridges, ordnance and small-arm. The rear end of the percussion-cap chamber is covered with a gas-check to prevent the escape of gas into the lock of the fire-arm. This outer cap does not extend over the whole area of the base of the cartridge. When fitted to "built-up" cartridges the edges of the gas-check are turned round under the flange of the dome. When applied to solid-drawn cartridges the edge of the gas-check is turned round into an annular groove. The invention is shown applied to the cartridges described in Specification No. 496, A.D. 1882.

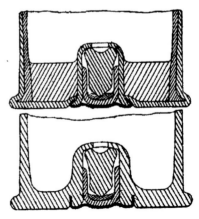

No. 3964 2 October 1879 – Provisional
No. 496 1 February 1882 – Full
No. 3625 31 July 1882 – Full
No. 4421 5 March 1884 – Full

The first patent relates to the method of attaching the paper lining in brass cartridge cases into position and the stab marks used are unique to Joyce brass cases. The last three of these patents related to Bailey's patent gas check primers.

3.3 Registered trade marks

Only two trade marks appear to have been taken out by Joyce's. The 'Stork' (No. 244984) was a joint application for this mark to be used on shotgun cartridges, taken out between Joyce and Douglas Vaughan Johnstone, which they applied for in May 1902.(J.P. Claborough & D.V. Johnstone, Gunmakers of 3 Price Street, Birmingham were appointed their Birmingham agents in 1902, when Joyce opened a new depot at 50 Loveday Street, Birmingham to supply the Birmingham trade.) The second brand name 'Sunflower' was registered to Joyce's in February 1902 and also related to shotgun cartridges but I have yet to encounter such a specimen.

3.4.1 Shotgun cartridges produced by the company

During the early period of the company's production their shot cartridges were plain with either green, blue or brown tubes. The three colours indicated the quality of the cases, green being the best quality, blue medium quality and brown the cheapest quality. All of these early cases only bore a few lines of text along the axis of their paper tubes. The wording used indicated if they were gas-tight or waterproof and when the smokeless powers emerged, the powder used. At the same time as the bulk powders appeared the range of colour codes on their cartridge tubes were extended to indicate which powder had been loaded into them. Buff was used for Schultze powders, red for EC and grey for SS. Clearly the colour coding system started to change in about 1902 when suddenly their shotgun cartridges started to gain names and vivid tube colours together with more interesting graphics, all presumably to compete with the actions of the other cartridge companies such as Eley and Kynoch and to offer a more visually appealing product to the sportsman.

By March 1897 Joyce were producing their short 2″ cases for condensed powders and in November 1898 it was reported that the company were making novelty matchboxes. It is assumed this was as a direct result of Kynoch's introducing their cartridge matchbox in March of that same year.

The 1902 Joyce catalogue showed cartridges being offered loaded with Henrite powder, Nobel's Empire powder together with two new named cartridges, namely the 'Imperial' with an orange tube and a half brass violet tubed case called the 'Coronation'. Both these two new brands were offered loaded with any bulk powder and examples will be encountered marked loaded with Schultze, Halls Cannonite, Halls Southern Cross and Walsrode.

An advert on the 15 April 1907 in *Sporting Goods Review* indicated that the company had introduced their 'Long Brass' and 'Ideal' cartridges and in the same month it was added to with their 'National' waterproof ejector which was not subject to price maintenance. By August 1908 their list included their solid drawn brass, ejector, waterproof, double brass, (sometimes marked D.B.), long brass, unlined long brass, 'Olympic', 'National' and 'Ideal'.

Two examples of the company's matchboxes. The end caps rotate revealing an opening to remove the matches. On the far side is a ribbed length to strike the matches

Like its competitors Joyce made shotgun cartridges for other companies and would merely leave the tube markings to indicate that they were the manufacturers. This practice reflects I believe their naive attitude to promoting their wares since both Eley Bros and Kynoch, although allowing companies to have their name on the headstamp of cartridges made by them, would almost always add their own name or initial.

Examples of Joyce manufactured cartridges include examples made for:

G. Bates, Birmingham
E. Distin & Son, Totnes
Charles Lancaster London including their
   2" 'Pygmies'
Joseph Lang, Cockspur Street, London
Linsley Bros, Leeds & Bradford
Schultze Gunpowder Co. Ltd
Turnbull, Bridgnorth, Shropshire
E.M. Reilly & Co.

3.4.2 Examples of shotgun cartridges produced by the company

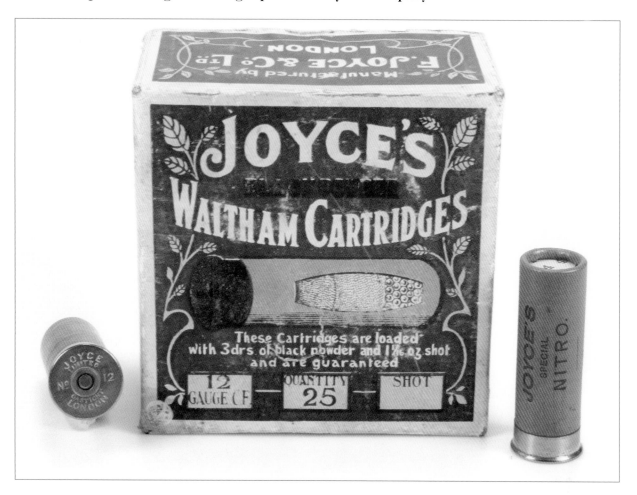

Examples of Joyce cartridges fitted with the two forms of Bailey's caps. The central specimen incorporates the first patent which covers the cap with an outer metal cover

Early specimens bear raised headstamps which appear on the pin-fire and on the sixth specimen from the left. The fifth specimen from the left has a copper rather than brass base

ABOVE:
The two blue cases are believed to have been made following the takeover by Nobel's. The cartridge on the extreme right was made by Joyce and loaded with Special Smokeless Powder

RIGHT:
Examples of rare cut away specimens by Joyce. I am certain that all these specimens were made following Joyce's takeover by Nobel's.
LEFT TO RIGHT:
Gastight, Ejector loaded with Schultze and a Special Nitro

3.4.3 Examples of shotgun cartridge headstamps used by the company

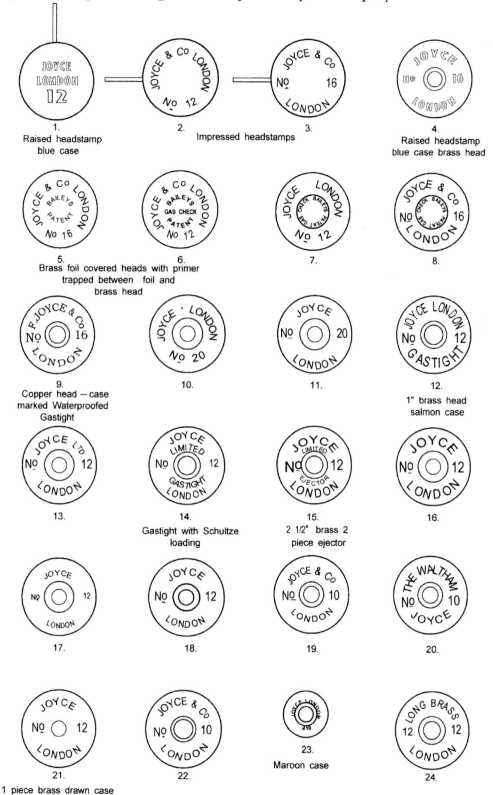

1.
Raised headstamp
blue case

Impressed headstamps

2.   3.

4.
Raised headstamp
blue case brass head

5.   6.
Brass foil covered heads with primer
trapped between foil and
brass head

7.

8.

9.
Copper head – case
marked Waterproofed
Gastight

10.

11.

12.
1" brass head
salmon case

13.

14.
Gastight with Schultze
loading

15.
2 1/2" brass 2
piece ejector

16.

17.

18.

19.

20.

21.
1 piece brass drawn case

22.

23.
Maroon case

24.

3.5.1 Metallic cartridge production

Unfortunately I have only been able to locate specimens of the 1891 and 1894 company catalogues, from which the following lists of metallic cartridge data was extracted. All the calibres below with the exception of the .300" rook rifle cartridge were listed in both catalogues, however the .300" only initially appears in 1894. It should also be noted that all these cartridges were also offered as shot and blank loads with the exception of the bulleted breech caps.

Calibre	Type	Black Powder load/Bullet weight in grains
.297/.230" Morris Short	Centre-fire	3/38
.297/.230" Morris Long	Centre-fire	5/38
.230" Short for revolvers	Centre-fire	3/30
.300" Solid for rifles	Centre-fire	10/80
.320" S&W Revolver	Centre-fire	6/85
.320" Revolver	Centre-fire	6/80
.320" Long for rifles	Centre-fire	8/80
.340" Short for revolvers	Centre-fire	8/85
.380" Smith & Wesson	Centre-fire	11/145
.380" Revolver	Centre-fire	10/124
.380" Long for rifles	Centre-fire	12/124
.410" Revolver	Centre-fire	14/160
.430" Revolver	Centre-fire	13/200
.430" Long for Rifles	Centre-fire	20/200
.442" Revolver	Centre-fire	13/220
.442" Bull Dog	Centre-fire	11/190
.442" Long for rifles	Centre-fire	20/220
.44" Winchester Model 1873	Centre-fire	49/200
.450" Revolver	Centre-fire	13/225
.450" Rifle	Centre-fire	16/225
.455" Revolver	Centre-fire	18/265
.500" Revolver & Carbines	Centre-fire	24/350
.577" Boxer for rifles	Centre-fire	70/480
7mm For French revolvers	Centre-fire	5.5/63
9mm For French revolvers	Centre-fire	8/124
12mm For French revolvers	Centre-fire	11/225
.577"/.450" Martini Henry Solid	Centre-fire	85/480
.230" (The American .220")	Rim-fire	3/30
.230" Long for rifles	Rim-fire	4/30
.297" Revolver	Rim-fire	6/70
.320" Revolver	Rim-fire	8/80

Calibre	Type	Black Powder load/Bullet weight in grains
.320" Long for rifles	Rim-fire	11/80
.340" Revolver	Rim-fire	8/85
.380" Revolver	Rim-fire	11/124
.380" Long for Rifles	Rim-fire	14/124
.410" Revolver	Rim-fire	8/140
.440" Revolver	Rim-fire	14/220
.442" Revolver	Rim-fire	14/220
.44" Henry for rifles	Rim-fire	23/235
5mm Revolver	Pin-fire	3/18
7mm Revolver	Pin-fire	5.5/63
9mm Revolver	Pin-fire	9/124
12mm Revolver	Pin-fire	11/200
15mm Revolver	Pin-fire	21/450
No 1 Bulleted breech cap	Rim-fire	Not quoted
No 2 Bulleted breech cap	Rim-fire	Not quoted
No 3 Bulleted breech cap	Rim-fire	Not quoted

In September 1898 the company were reported to be working overtime to meet demand having put a new .22" cartridge for repeating rifles into production. It was also reported that they were making a tube to fire these .22" cartridges through .303" rifles at shooting galleries. In August 1900 their new catalogue included 2" shotgun cartridge cases and the Petit Chamberettes and the related miniature ammo for use in .303" service rifles for short range practice.

3.5.2 Examples of Joyce's metallic ammunition

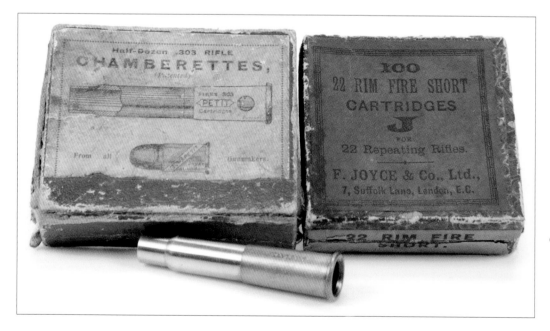

Specimen of .303" Chamberette made by Joyce and a box of their .22" short rim-fire

ABOVE:
LEFT TO RIGHT: *.410" revolver, .450" revolver, .380" Long Rifle, .297"/.230" Morris tube, .450" revolver, .320" revolver, .22" rim-fire long rifle, and .297"/.230" Morris tube*

RIGHT: Box of .297"/.230" Morris Short cartridges

3.5.3 Examples of headstamps found on metallic ammunition

NOTES: *Headstamps 1, 2 & 3 were impressed by Birmingham Metal & Munitions after Joyce was taken over by Nobel's; however Nobel's sought to confuse parties involved in placing military contracts.*

Headstamp 10 was for the Francotte carbine rifle and has a slightly different base than the normal Morris Aiming Tube cartridge.

1.
.303" Mk VII Ball
1916

2.
.303" MkVII Ball
1917

3.
.303" Mk VII
Ball with nitro
cellulose powder

4.
.38" Smith & Wesson
revolver

5.
.450" Revolver

6,
.410" Revolver

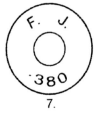

7.
.380" Long
Rifle

8.
.22" Long
Rim-fire

9.
.320" Revolver

10.
.297"/.230"
Morris Tube

11.
.450" Revolver

3.6 Examples of company advertisements

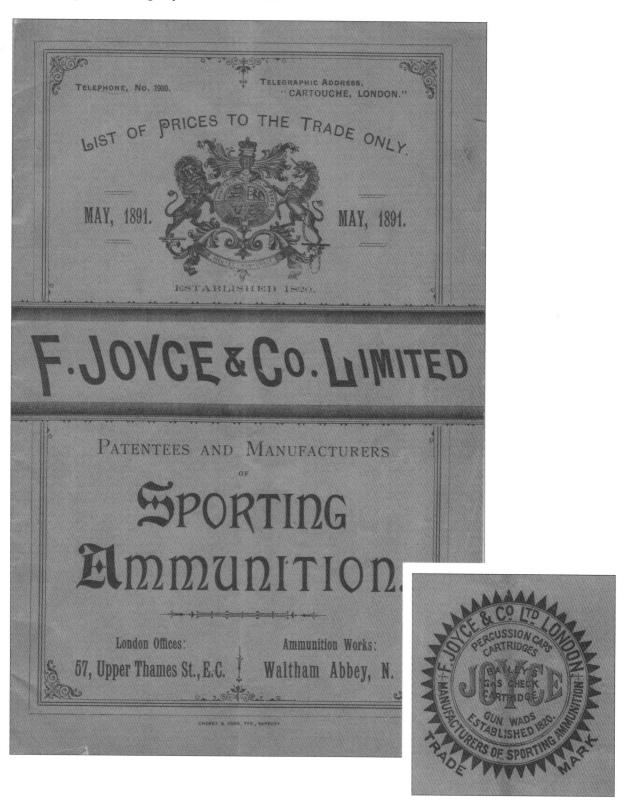

AMMUNITION for BREECH-LOADING GUNS.

JOYCE'S CENTRAL-FIRE CARTRIDGE CASES.

				£ s. d.
GREEN, Extra Quality, Stamped "JOYCE, LONDON, GAS-TIGHT."	2½ inches long	...	10 gauge	2 15 0 per 1000.
GREEN, Extra Quality, Stamped "JOYCE, LONDON, GAS-TIGHT."	2½ ,,	...	12 gauge	2 0 0 ,,
GREEN, Extra Quality, Stamped "JOYCE, LONDON, GAS-TIGHT."	2¾ ,,	...	12 gauge	2 7 6 ,,
GREEN, Extra Quality, Stamped "JOYCE, LONDON, GAS-TIGHT."	2½ ,,	...	14 gauge	2 0 0 ,,
GREEN, Extra Quality, Stamped "JOYCE, LONDON, GAS-TIGHT."	2½ ,,	...	16 gauge	2 0 0 ,,
GREEN, Extra Quality, Stamped "JOYCE, LONDON, GAS-TIGHT."	2¾ ,,	...	16 gauge	2 7 0 ,,
GREEN, Extra Quality, Stamped "JOYCE, LONDON, GAS-TIGHT."	2½ ,,	...	20 gauge	2 0 0 ,,
GREEN, Extra Quality, Stamped "JOYCE, LONDON, GAS-TIGHT."	2¾ ,,	...	20 gauge	2 7 0 ,,

Also BUFF Colour for Schultze, RED for E.C., and GREY for S.S. Powder at the above prices.

BLUE,	Best Quality, Stamped "JOYCE & CO., LONDON."	2½ inches long	...	10 gauge	2 10 0 ,,
Do.	do. do.	2½ ,,	...	12 gauge	1 17 6 ,,
Do.	do. do.	2¾ ,,	...	12 gauge	2 0 0 ,,
Do.	do. do.	2½ ,,	...	14 gauge	1 17 6 ,,
Do.	do. do.	2½ ,,	...	16 gauge	1 16 0 ,,
BROWN, Superior Quality, do.	do.	2½ ,,	...	10 gauge	2 0 0 ,,
Do.	do. do.	2½ ,,	...	12 gauge	1 11 0 ,,
Do.	do. do	2¾ ,,	...	12 gauge	1 15 0 ,,
Do.	do. do.	2½ ,,	...	14 gauge	1 11 0 ,,
Do.	do. do.	2½ ,,	...	16 gauge	1 10 0 ,,
Do.	do. do.	2½ ,,	...	20 gauge	1 10 0 ,,

JOYCE'S PIN-FIRE CARTRIDGE CASES.

GREEN, Extra quality, Stamped, "JOYCE, LONDON, GAS-TIGHT."	2½ inches long	...	10 gauge	2 15 0 ,,
GREEN, Extra Quality, Stamped "JOYCE, LONDON, GAS-TIGHT."	2½ ,,	...	12 gauge	2 0 0 ,,
GREEN, Extra Quality, Stamped "JOYCE, LONDON, GAS-TIGHT."	2½ ,,	...	16 gauge	2 0 0 ,,
GREEN, Extra Quality, Stamped "JOYCE, LONDON, GAS-TIGHT."	2½ ,,	...	20 gauge	2 0 0 ,,
BLUE, Best Quality, "JOYCE & CO., LONDON."	2½ ,,	...	12 gauge	1 17 6 ,,
Do. do. do.	2½ ,,	...	16 gauge	1 16 0 ,,
BROWN, Superior Quality, do. do.	2½ ,,	...	10 gauge	1 17 6 ,,
Do. do. do.	2½ ,,	...	12 gauge	1 10 0 ,,
Do. do. do.	2½ ,,	...	16 gauge	1 10 0 ,,
Do. do. do.	2½ ,,	...	20 gauge	1 10 0 ,,

All the Cartridge Cases of BEST QUALITY, both Pin-Fire and Central-Fire, bear the name of "Joyce London."
They are Warranted GAS-TIGHT; and being primed with DOUBLE WATERPROOF CAPS, may be kept empty or loaded for years in any climate.

N.B.—In Ordering Cartridge Cases or Cartridges, it is necessary to state the GAUGE, COLOUR, and QUALITY, and whether PIN-FIRE or CENTRAL-FIRE—This Notice is rendered necessary by these Particulars being in many instances omitted in Orders.

N.B.—CASES made with LARGE CAPS to order.

F. JOYCE & CO. LIMITED, MANUFACTURERS, LONDON.

F. JOYCE & CO. LIMITED, MANUFACTURERS, LONDON.

LOADED CARTRIDGES, containing the BEST T.S. SPORTING GUN-POWDER, in Strong Wood Boxes of 100 each. Ordinary charge—

		12 and 14 gauges.	16 gauge.	20 gauge.	
		s. d.	s. d.	s. d.	
GREEN, GAS-TIGHT, Central or Pin Fire		10 9 per 100.	10 4 per 100.	10 0 per 100.	With Shot.
Do.	do.	8 6 ,,	8 3 ,,	8 0 ,,	Without Shot.
BEST BLUE,	do.	10 0 ,,	9 8 ,,	—	With Shot.
Do.	do.	8 0 ,,	7 6 ,,	—	Without Shot.
BROWN,	do.	9 8 ,,	9 4 ,,	9 3 ,,	With Shot.
Do.	do.	7 6 ,,	7 3 ,,	7 3 ,,	Without Shot.

CARTRIDGES loaded with SCHULTZE, E.C., & S.S. GUNPOWDER. Ordinary charge—

		12 and 14 gauges.	16 gauge	20 gauge.	
		s. d.	s. d.	s. d.	
Schultze { GAS-TIGHT, Central-Fire		11 6 per 100.	11 0 per 100.	10 6 per 100.	With Shot.
& S.S. { Do.	do.	9 6 ,,	9 0 ,,	8 6 ,,	Without Shot.
E.C. { GAS-TIGHT, Central-Fire		12 0 ,,	11 6 ,,	11 0 ,,	With Shot.
{ Do.	do.	10 0 ,,	9 6 ,,	9 0 ,,	Without Shot.

CARTRIDGES LOADED with SPECIAL POWDER, from 6d. to 1s. 6d. per 100 extra, according to quality.

Joyce's Loaded Cartridges contain the most suitable charge and four wads, and are pressed separately on specially designed Lever Presses adjusted to develop the best qualities of the respective powders.

The following are the charges usually recommended and which will be sent unless otherwise ordered :—

		drams			
12	Black, 3 ~~grains~~.	Schultze and E.C., 42 grains.	S.S., 41 grains.	Shot, 1⅛
14	,, 2¾ ,,	,, 40 ,,	,, 39 ,,	.. 1⅛
16	.. 2¾ ,,	,, 38 ,,	,, 37 ,,	.. 1
20	,, 2½ ,,	,, 35 ,,	,, 35 ,,	.. ¾

WADDING FOR BREECH-LOADING CARTRIDGE CASES.

	s. d.	
Best Elastic Felt Wadding, for over Powder, in ½-lb. bags, 5/16, 3/8, 7/16, and ½-in. thick	3 4	per lb.
Improved Hair Felt Wadding, for over Powder, in ½-lb. bags	2 10	,,
Brown Felt Wadding, for over Powder, in ½-lb. bags	2 4	,,
BEST CLOTH WADS, for over Shot, numbered 4, 5, 6, or plain, in bags of 500 each	3 6	per 1000.
GREY FELT WADS, do. do. in bags of 500 each, and boxes of 250 each	2 4	,,
WHITE CARD WADS, do. do. in boxes of 500 each	1 0	,,
GREASEPROOF CLOTH WADS, to be used between the Powder and Felt Wadding, in bags of 500 each	3 6	,,
Do. CARD do. do. do. do. in boxes of 1000 each	1 0	,,

The above Wads can be put up in Bulk as follows :

If in bags of 5lbs. or 5000 each, at a reduction of 1d. per lb. on above prices.

,, 50lbs. ,, 50000 ,, ,, 2d. ,, ,, ,,

THIN CARD WADS, for over Shot, in boxes of 1000 each	0 7	,,

Waddings printed with any name and Size of Shot, Best White Cloth, 4s., Grey Felt, 2s. 10d., White Card, 1s. 9d. per 1000, in quantities of 20,000 and upwards.

MILITARY PERCUSSION CAPS.

As supplied to HER MAJESTY'S WAR DEPARTMENT, the IMPERIAL OTTOMAN, and other FOREIGN GOVERNMENTS.

MILITARY CAPS,	**TW** Treble Waterproof Central-Fire, in Boxes of 250 each	3 6	per 1000.
Do.	**FC** Foil Covered (Best Quality), do. do.	3 0	,,
Do.	**BP** Best Plain for Enfield Rifles, do. do.	2 9	,,
Do.	**FM** Foil Covered, do. do.	2 6	,,
Do.	**PM** Plain, do. do.	2 0	,,

Kept in Boxes of 100 each at 3d. per 1000 extra.

F. JOYCE & CO. LIMITED, MANUFACTURERS, LONDON.

BAILEY'S PATENT GAS-CHECK CARTRIDGE

F. JOYCE & CO. LIMITED, MANUFACTURERS, LONDON.

F. JOYCE & CO. LIMITED, MANUFACTURERS, LONDON.

HERMETICALLY SEALED.

THE "BAILEY" CARTRIDGE is an improvement on the ordinary Central-fire Cartridge. It is constructed with a thin metal envelope enclosing the cap, which constitutes the principle of the hermetically sealed base, rendering it superior to all others as an absolute Gas-Check in Hammerless Guns, and preventing all corrosion of locks and strikers.

Since 1882 many millions have been made and improvements have resulted. The improvement now introduced ensures a more certain ignition and a strong base, so arranged as to prevent the bursting force of some gunpowders being detrimental to the cap.

The "Bailey" Cartridge is equally adapted for Hammer Guns, and is made in all sizes at the usual price.

						£	s.	d.	
GREEN CASES, Extra Quality, for Black Powder,			2½ inches long,	**10** gauge	2	15	0	per 1000.
Do.	do.	do.	,,	,,	**12** gauge	2	0	0	,,
Do.	do.	do.	,,	,,	**16** gauge	2	0	0	,,
Do.	do.	do.	,,	,,	**20** gauge	2	0	0	,,
BLUE CASES, Best Quality,		do.	,,	,,	**12** gauge	1	17	6	,,
Do.	do.	do.	,,	,,	**16** gauge	1	16	0	,,

BUFF CASES for Schultze Powder and RED CASES for E.C. and GREY for S.S. Powder at the same price as Green.

BAILEY'S PATENT CARTRIDGES are loaded at the usual prices with Best Black, Schultze, E.C., and S.S. Powders.

PERCUSSION CAPS, FOR MUZZLE-LOADING GUNS.

		s.	d.	
Quality, **PW** PATENT WATERPROOF PYROXYLINE PERCUSSION CAPS, in japd. boxes of 500 and 250 each		5	0	per 1000.
Quality, **AC** BEST ANTI-CORROSIVE CAPS, in japd. boxes of 500 and 250 each		4	0	,,
Quality, **A2** EXTRA STRONG COPPER CAPS		3	3	,,
Quality, **A3** SUPERIOR PERCUSSION CAPS		2	6	,,
THIRDS, Strong Ground-edge Caps, in tin boxes of 500 and 250 each ...		1	9	,,
FOURTHS, Warranted Caps, do. do. do. ...		1	6	,,
FIFTHS, do. do. do. do. ...		1	0	,,
Quality, **TW** TREBLE WATERPROOF CENTRAL-FIRE PERCUSSION CAPS, in japd. boxes of 500 and 250 each		4	6	,,
Quality, **FC** BEST FOIL-COVERED CENTRAL-FIRE CAPS, in japd. boxes of 500 and 250 each		3	6	,,
Quality, **F2** SUPERIOR FOIL-COVERED CAPS, in tin boxes of 500 and 250 each		2	9	,,
Quality, **F3** FOIL-COVERED CAPS, in tin boxes of 500 and 250 each ...		2	0	,,
These Caps, in boxes of 100 each, 3d. per 1000 extra.				
BEST FOIL-COVERED WATERPROOF PISTOL CAPS, in boxes of 250 each		2	6	,,
SPECIAL CAPS, for Fog Signals, containing an Extra Charge of Fulminating Powder		1	10	,,

JOYCE'S SIZES OF PERCUSSION CAPS CORRESPOND WITH THOSE OF OTHER MAKERS
as follows:

JOYCE'S	C. F. Caps.	42	29	23	24	15	25	18	21	12	26	22	16s
ELEY'S	Same size.	5	7	8	24	10	11	13	12	...	13	14	26
BIRMINGHAM	..	43	46	48	50	51 52	53 54	55 56	57	...	58	...	...

Where there are two numbers of the Birmingham Sizes corresponding with only one of JOYCE'S it is in consequence of two numbers being of the same size, varying only in the length of the Caps.

F. JOYCE & CO. LIMITED, MANUFACTURERS, LONDON.

F. JOYCE & CO. LIMITED, MANUFACTURERS, LONDON.

F. Joyce & Co. Limited, Manufacturers, London.

GUN WADDINGS FOR MUZZLE LOADERS.

	s. d.	
Best White Cloth Waddings, in bags of 500 ... ... 11 gauge and smaller	3 6	per 1000.
Best White Cloth Waddings, in bags of 500 ... ... 9 and 10 gauges	4 6	,,
Best White Cloth Waddings, in bags of 500 ... ... 7 and 8 gauges	5 6	,,
Best White Cloth Waddings, in boxes of 250, at 3d. per 1000 extra.		
Grey Cloth Waddings, with prepared edges, in boxes of 250 each, 11 gauge and smaller...	2 4	,,
Grey Cloth Waddings, 9 and 10 gauges	2 8	,,
Do. do. 7 and 8 gauges	3 0	,,
Indented Paper Waddings, with prepared edges, in boxes of 250 each, 11 gauge and smaller...	1 6	,,
Indented Paper Waddings, with prepared edges, in boxes of 250 each, 9 & 10 gauge	1 10	,,
Indented Paper Waddings, with prepared edges, in boxes of 250 each, 7 & 8 gauge	2 2	,,
Patent Felt Waddings, in Oil Silk bags of 500 each	4 0	,,
Elastic Concaved Felt Waddings, in ½lb. bags	3 6	per lb.
Grey Felt Sheets, 17 in. by 11 in., in packets of 1 doz. each	6 0	per doz.
Grey Cloth Sheets, 17 in. by 11 in., in packets of 1 doz. each	5 0	,,
Best Paper Sheets, Nos. 1 and 2, in 6lb. packets	6 0	per 12 lb.

WIRE CARTRIDGES FOR MUZZLE LOADERS.

Long Distance (Green), in packets of 6 doz. each	14 0	per gross.
Medium Distance (Red), in packets of 6 doz. each	12 0	,,

These Prices to the Trade only are subject to Discount, and for large orders special quotations will be given.

F. Joyce & Co. Limited, Manufacturers, London.

BREECH CAPS FOR SALOON PISTOLS & RIFLES.

No. 1 Bulleted Breech Caps	£0 9 0	per 1000.
,, 1 ,, ,, 2nd Quality	0 7 6	,,
,, 2 ,, ,, ...	0 15 0	,,
,, 3 ,, ,, ...	1 1 0	,,
,, 1 Shot Cartridges	15 0	,,
,, 2 ,, ...	1 2 6	,,
,, 3 ,, ...	1 10 0	,,
,, 1 ,, Double Charge ...	1 4 0	,,
,, 2 ,, ,, ...	1 13 0	,,
,, 3 ,, ,, ...	2 0 0	,,

WALKING STICK GUN CARTRIDGES.

No. 1 Not Re-loading	£2 7 6	per 1000.
,, 2 ,, ...	3 7 6	,,
,, 2 Re-loading	3 12 6	,,
,, 3 ,, ...	4 0 0	,,

Any other sizes made to order.

SUNDRIES.

	s. d.	
No. 1 Air Gun Bullets...	1 0	per 1000.
,, 2 ,, ...	2 0	,,
,, 3 ,, ...	2 6	,,
,, 1 Darts	1 0	per doz.
,, 3 ,, ...	1 8	,,
,, 5A Caps, in boxes of 500 each	1 6	per 1000.
Anvils for Central-Fire Cartridge Cases ...	2 6	,,
Primers for Bailey's Patent Cases ...	10 0	,, .
Double Waterproof Caps, for re-capping Pin Cartridges, in boxes of 250 each	4 0	,,
Double Waterproof Caps, for re-capping Central-Fire Cartridges, in boxes of 250 each	4 0	,,
Cylindrical Wire Cartridges, for Breech-loading Cartridge Cases, in boxes of 100 each	9 0	per 100.
Machines for Loading Cartridge Cases, (Jeffries' Patent)	10 6	ea. nett.
Machines for re-capping Ordinary Cases ...	5 6	,,

Military and Sporting Accoutrements of all kinds at low prices.

RIFLE AND REVOLVER AMMUNITION.

CENTRAL FIRE.

Gauge.	Description.	Powder Grains.	Bullet Grains.	Loaded with Ball.	With Shot.	Blank.	Empty Cases.
297/230	For Morris' Tubes and Rifles ...	3	38	£1 7 6	£2 2 6	£1 7 6	£1 0 0 per 1000
297/230	Long, for do. ...	5	38	1 10 0	2 5 0	1 10 0	1 2 6 ,,
230	Short, for Revolvers ...	3	30	1 0 0	1 10 0	1 0 0	15 0 ,,
320	Smith and Wesson Revolver ...	6	85	1 15 0	2 10 0	1 10 0	1 2 6 ,,
320	Revolver	6	80	1 15 0	2 10 0	1 10 0	1 2 6 ,,
320	Long, for Rifles	8	80	2 0 0	2 15 0	1 15 0	1 2 6 ,,
340	Short, for Revolvers	8	85	2 0 0	2 15 0	1 15 0	1 2 6 ,,
380	Smith and Wesson	11	145	2 5 0	3 0 0	2 0 0	1 5 0 ,,
380	Revolver	10	124	2 5 0	3 0 0	2 0 0	1 5 0 ,,
380	Long, for Rifles	12	124	2 10 0	3 5 0	2 5 0	1 5 0 ,,
410	Revolver	14	160	2 5 0	3 0 0	2 0 0	1 5 0 ,,
430	Revolver	13	200	2 10 0	3 5 0	2 5 0	1 7 6 ,,
430	Long, for Rifles	20	200	3 5 0	4 0 0	3 0 0	1 15 0 ,,
442	Revolver	13	220	2 10 0	3 5 0	2 5 0	1 7 6 ,,
442	"Bull Dog"	11	190	2 5 0	—	—	,,
442	Long, for Rifles	20	220	3 5 0	4 0 0	3 0 0	1 15 0 ,,
44	Winchester (Model 1873) ...	40	200	3 10 0	—	—	2 2 6 ,,
450	Revolver	13	225	2 10 0	3 5 0	2 5 0	1 7 6 ,,
500	Revolver and Carbines ...	24	350	3 5 0	4 0 0	3 0 0	1 15 0 ,,
577	Boxer, for Rifles... ...	70	480	4 12 6	—	—	2 5 0 ,,
7 M/M	For French Revolvers ...	5½	63	1 15 0	2 10 0	1 10 0	1 2 6 ,,
9 M/M	Do. do.	8	124	2 5 0	3 0 0	2 0 0	1 5 0 ,,
12 M/M	Do. do.	11	225	2 10 0	3 5 0	2 5 0	1 10 0 ,,

F. Joyce & Co. Limited, Manufacturers, London.

RIFLE AND REVOLVER AMMUNITION *continued.*

RIM-FIRE.

Gauge.	Description.	Powder Grains.	Bullet Grains.	Loaded with Ball.	With Shot.	Blank.	Empty Cases.	
230	(The American 220)	3	30	£0 15 0	£1 5 0	£0 15 0	£0 10 0	per 1000.
230	Long, for Rifles	4	30	0 17 6	1 12 6	0 17 6	0 12 6	,,
297	Revolver	6	70	1 10 0	2 5 0	1 10 0	0 15 0	,,
320	Revolver	8	80	1 15 0	2 10 0	1 10 0	1 2 6	,,
320	Long, for Rifles	11	80	2 0 0	2 15 0	1 15 0	1 2 6	,,
340	Revolver	8	85	2 0 0	2 15 0	1 15 0	1 2 6	,,
380	Revolver	11	124	2 5 0	3 0 0	2 0 0	1 5 0	,,
380	Long, for Rifles	14	124	2 10 0	3 5 0	2 5 0	1 5 0	,,
410	Revolver	8	140	2 5 0	3 0 0	2 0 0	1 5 0	,,
440	Revolver	14	220	2 10 0	3 5 0	2 5 0	1 7 6	,,
442	Revolver	14	220	2 10 0	3 5 0	2 5 0	1 7 6	,,
44	Henry Winchester, for Rifles ...	23	235	3 5 0	—	—	—	,,

PIN-FIRE.

Gauge.	Description.	Powder Grains.	Bullet Grains.	Loaded with Ball.	With Shot.	Blank.	Empty Cases.	
5 M/M	For Revolvers	3	18	£1 5 0	£2 0 0	£1 5 0	£0 15 0	,,
7 M/M	For Revolvers	5½	63	1 5 0	2 0 0	1 5 0	0 15 0	,,
9 M/M	For Revolvers	9	124	1 12 6	2 7 6	1 10 0	0 17 6	,,
12 M/M	For Revolvers	11	200	2 0 0	2 15 0	1 15 0	1 5 0	,,
15 M/M	For Revolvers	21	450	4 0 0	4 15 0	3 15 0	2 0 0	,,

F. JOYCE & CO. LIMITED, MANUFACTURERS, LONDON.

FOR THE

"BAILEY" PATENT CARTRIDGE CASE.

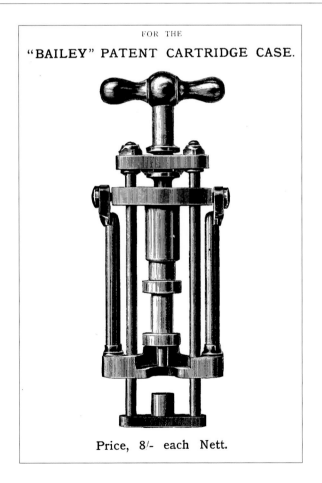

Price, 8/- each Nett.

JOYCE'S CARTRIDGES.

Unsurpassed for Excellence of Manufacture.

THE OLDEST HOUSE IN THE TRADE.

F. JOYCE & Co., Ltd., 57, Upper Thames St., E.C.

Advert in Sporting Goods Review *18 March, 1896*

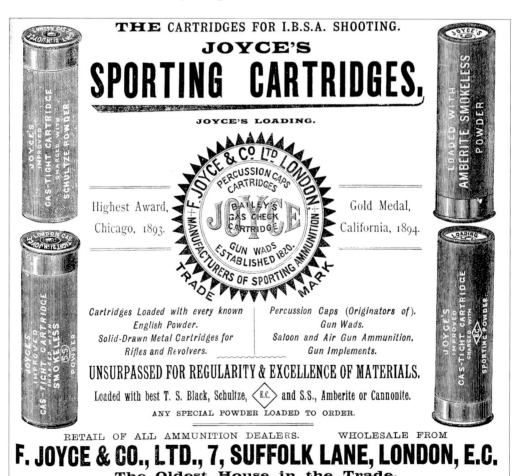

THE CARTRIDGES FOR I.B.S.A. SHOOTING.

JOYCE'S SPORTING CARTRIDGES,

JOYCE'S LOADING.

Highest Award, Chicago, 1893.

Gold Medal, California, 1894.

Cartridges Loaded with every known English Powder.
Solid-Drawn Metal Cartridges for Rifles and Revolvers.

Percussion Caps (Originators of).
Gun Wads.
Saloon and Air Gun Ammunition.
Gun Implements.

UNSURPASSED FOR REGULARITY & EXCELLENCE OF MATERIALS.

Loaded with best T. S. Black, Schultze, E.C. and S.S., Amberite or Cannonite.

ANY SPECIAL POWDER LOADED TO ORDER.

RETAIL OF ALL AMMUNITION DEALERS. WHOLESALE FROM

F. JOYCE & CO., LTD., 7, SUFFOLK LANE, LONDON, E.C.

The Oldest House in the Trade.

Advert in Sporting Goods Review *15 June, 1897*

SPORTING CARTRIDGES.

JOYCE'S LOADING.

Cartridges Loaded with every known English Powder.	Percussion Caps (Originators of). Gun Wads.
Solid-Drawn Metal Cartridges for Rifles and Revolvers.	Saloon and Air Gun Ammunition. Gun Implements.

UNSURPASSED FOR REGULARITY & EXCELLENCE OF MATERIALS.

Loaded with best T.S. Black, Schultze, E.C. & S.S., Amberite, Cannonite or Walsrode.

ANY SPECIAL POWDER LOADED TO ORDER.

RETAIL OF ALL AMMUNITION DEALERS.   WHOLESALE FROM

F. JOYCE & CO., LTD., 7, SUFFOLK LANE, LONDON, E.C.

The Oldest House in the Trade.

For all Game Shooting.

USE ONLY

JOYCE'S = = =
CARTRIDGES.

The Oldest House in the Trade.

ESTABLISHED 1820.

Percussion Caps, Gun Wadding and General Ammunition of all kinds.

F. JOYCE and CO., LTD.,

7, SUFFOLK LANE,

UPPER THAMES STREET, E.C.

ABOVE:
Advert in Sporting Goods Review *15 June, 1899*

Advert from An Illustrated Treatise on The Art of Shooting *by Charles Lancaster – 6th Edition, 1898*

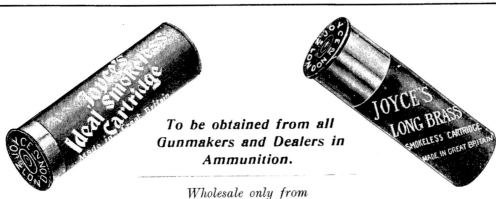
1906 advert

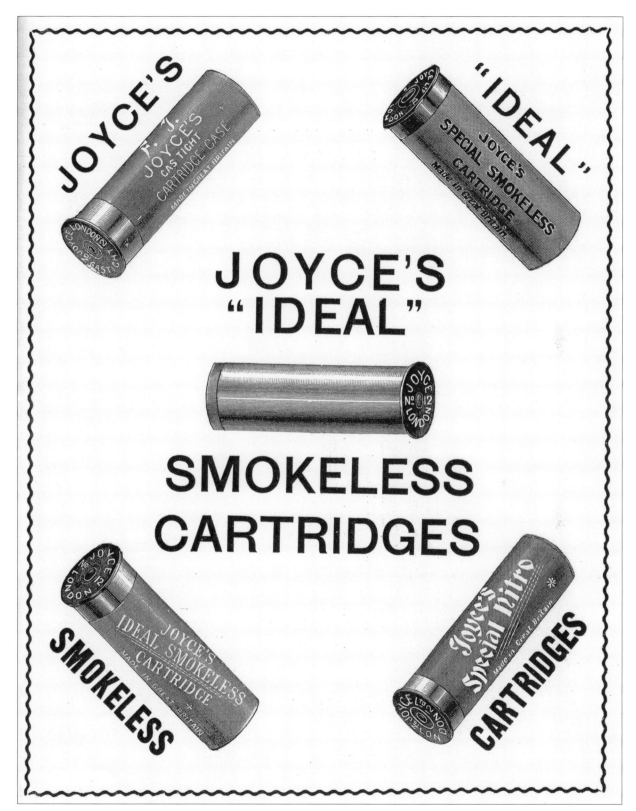

1907 advert

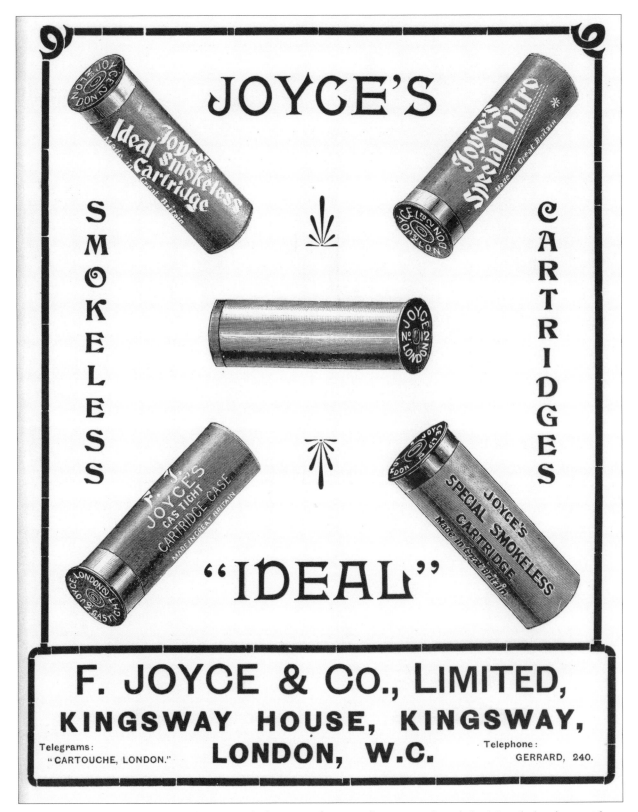

1908 advert. Note the new address and change in format of print on their 'Ideal Smokeless' cartridge

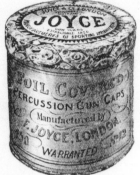

JOYCE'S PERCUSSION CAPS

For Muzzle Loading Guns and Military Rifles.

LARGEST SALE IN THE WORLD.

Manufactured only by—

NOBEL'S EXPLOSIVES CO., LTD., GLASGOW & LONDON.

A 1912 advert following the takeover by Nobel's. Note that the advert states who manufactures the caps but the Joyce name has been retained on the packaging

JOYCE'S AIR GUN SLUGS.

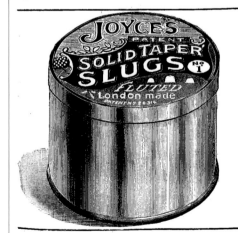

DARTS, METALLIC AIR GUN CARTRIDGES, AIR GUNS, &c.

F. JOYCE & Co., LTD., SUFFOLK LANE, LONDON, E.C.

Advert in Sporting Goods Review *15 February, 1902*

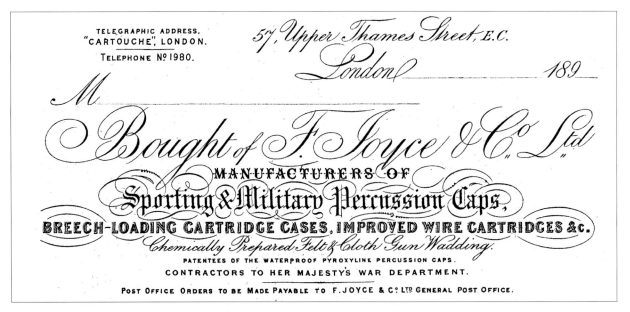

Copy of the company letterhead in the 1890s

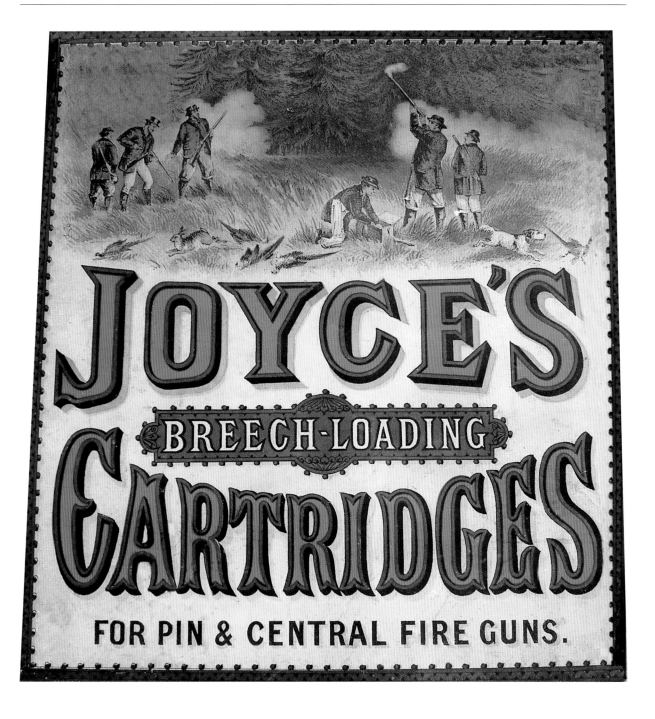

CHAPTER 4
Nobel's

4.1 The personal history of Alfred Nobel

To most readers the name Nobel immediately brings to mind two subjects, namely Dynamite and the Nobel Peace Prize and both stem from one of the most famous inventors and scientists, namely Alfred Nobel.

Alfred Nobel was one of three sons. He was born on 21 October 1833 to Immanuel Nobel (1801–1872) and Andriette Ahlsell Nobel (1805–1889) in Stockholm, Sweden. In 1833 his father's construction business went bankrupt and the father left his family and moved to St Petersburg in Russia. Later in 1842 the family joined their father at St Petersburg. Alfred, the middle of the three sons, studied chemistry at a university in Torino. The family business in Russia was initially boosted by the advent of the Crimean War but towards the end of the war Russian military orders ceased and in 1856 the company business went bankrupt for a second time. A few years later Alfred returned to Sweden where he concentrated on the production of industrial explosives, in particular the processes involved in the manufacture of Nitroglycerine (previously discovered by Ascanio Sobrero), together with the design of a detonator to initiate the explosive at a factory sited at Heleneborg. Nitroglycerine was, however, a very dangerous and unstable substance in terms of both production and handling and in the autumn of 1864 the factory blew up, killing Alfred's younger brother and four other employees. The same year as this explosion occurred Alfred continued his experiments and formed a company named Nitroglycerine AB in Stockholm, Sweden and one year later he improved the blasting cap design and moved to Germany to set up a company entitled Alfred Nobel & Co. in a factory in Krümmel, near Hamburg. Shortly afterwards in 1866 a violent explosion destroyed the Krümmel plant.

Experimenting on a raft anchored on the river Elbe, Alfred tried to make Nitroglycerine safer to handle. During his research he discovered that Nitroglycerine could be stabilised by the addition of *kieselguhr* (a siliceous deposit, also known as diatomaceous earth). The new substance was duly named Dynamite, the composition of which he patented in 1867. In 1871 Nobel established the British Dynamite Company in Ardeer, Scotland, and in 1877 its name was changed to Nobel's Explosives Company.

On reaching the age of 40 Alfred had become a wealthy man as his explosives had been used across the world for mining and construction and he moved to live in Paris, whilst at Ardeer in Scotland his company started to manufacture Nitroglycerine and Dynamite. In 1875, whilst in Paris, he invented yet another explosive named Blastine Gelatine and created a company for its manufacture in France. In 1876 Dynamitaktiengesellschaft (DAG), formerly Alfred Nobel & Co. (Hamburg, Germany) was formed. In 1880 he set up Dynamite Nobel when he merged his Swiss and Italian companies. In 1885 the German Union emerged when he amalgamated DAG and a number of German Dynamite companies. Finally in 1886 be began trading as Nobel-Dynamite Trust Co. (London, UK) by merging DAG and the Nobel's Explosives Company.

In 1887, whilst living in Paris, Alfred patented a new propellant which he called Ballistite. It consisted of Nitrocylcerine, collodion and camphor. He initially attempted to sell his patent rights to Ballistite to the French Government but they rejected his offer, since shortly before they had adopted a similar substance entitled Poudre B. As a consequence his patent on Ballistite was offered to the Italian government who accepted it, resulting in him opening a new factory for its production in Turin. Ballistite was to be used by the Italians in the cartridge for their new Model 1890 Vetterli rifle, which was to be their first military rifle designed to use a nitro based propellant rather than the former black powder. Unfortunately for Alfred, France saw Italy as a threat and the French newspapers of the day accused him of using the knowledge gained from Vielle, the inventor of Poudre B, to make Ballistite. Consequently the French Government refused him the right to undertake any further research into explosives or propellants, which resulted in him leaving Paris in 1891 to live his remaining life in San Remo, Italy where he died on 10 December 1896. His body was subsequently buried back in his homeland in Norra begravningsplatsen in Stockholm.

Alfred remained single and during his life he became a proficient linguist in six languages namely Swedish, Russian, German, French, English and Italian. In 1895, when writing his will he left the majority of his estate to found the basis of the Nobel Prize, which since 1901 has honored individuals' outstanding achievements in physics, chemistry, medicine, literature and for their work to achieve world peace.

4.2 The company's management and production sites

Ardeer was to become the company's main manufacturing base for explosives and it was here, following the invention of Ballistite, that the company started to load shotgun and metallic cartridges. Not having the equipment or machinery to manufacture cartridges, Nobel's Explosives Co. Ltd initially sought agreement with Eley Bros Ltd, of London to supply them with cartridge cases, both metallic and shotgun, which they loaded at their Ardeer site in Scotland, and numerous examples of such cartridges still exist.

A Nobel Exploder, used to discharge sticks of explosives by generating an electric current to a detonator attached to the other end of the wires, which were attached to the exploder via the two screw terminals

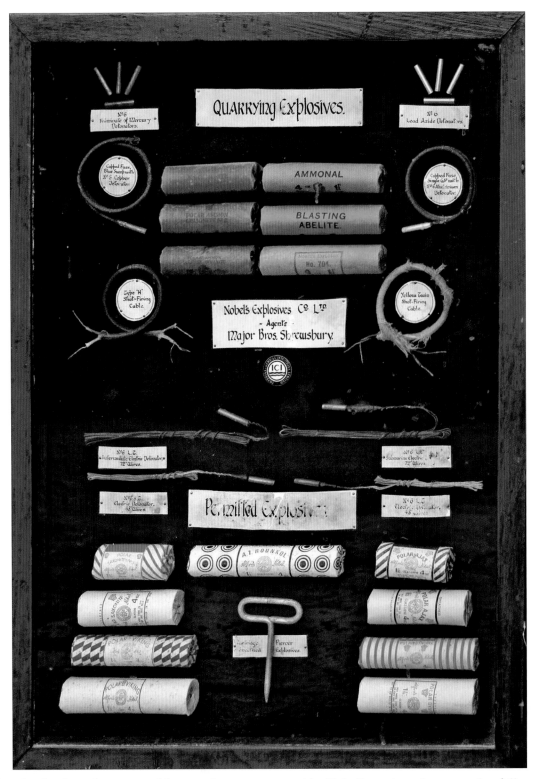

This display board originated from a shop once owned by Nobel's main salesman who, following retirement, purchased an ironmongers in Shrewsbury and sold explosives to farmers, mainly to remove tree stumps

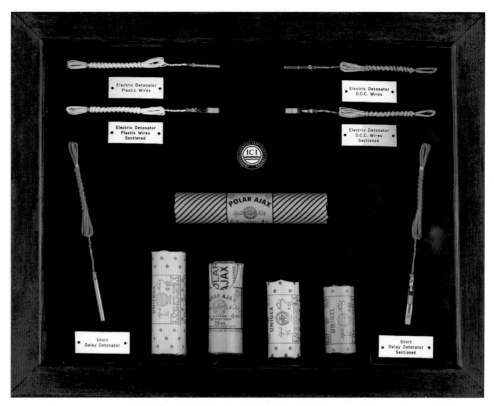

Even after Nobel's had amalgamated with the other cartridge, propellant and explosives companies to form ICI in November 1918, the sticks of explosives still bore the signature of Alfred Nobel together with the Nobel's Explosives trade mark. This display board was once housed in a Welsh coal mine

By December 1896 the demand for Sporting Ballistite shotgun cartridges could not be satisfied at Ardeer and the company acquired a further site near Bedford Row, London, which was equipped with the necessary loading equipment. The Arundel Street agency, which is referred to in numerous adverts, was by then in existence.

It was, however, only a matter of time before Nobel's were able to identify and purchase an existing cartridge manufacturing company which would enable them to produce the complete product, thereby becoming self reliant in terms of manufacture. In 1897 they started this process by acquiring The Birmingham Metal and Munitions Company which produced metallic ammunition at Adderley Park in Birmingham and at Streetly, just across the road from Sutton Coldfield Park.

Cartridge loading site for Ballistite cartridges at Ardeer

*Wet mixing house for Ballistite or
Cordite paste at Ardeer*

In June 1897 the company extended their offices at Effingham House, Arundel Street, London WC and in the same year *The Melbourne Sportsman* reported that the Nobel's Explosives Co. Ltd were purchasing a large factory at Deer Park Melbourne, near Braybrook Junction, for the manufacture of smokeless powder to supply the Australian Colonies, via a company known as the Colonial Ammunition Company. Initially it was believed it would manufacture Cordite but anticipated that this would be followed by Ballistite. In July 1897 *Arms & Explosives* reported that the Nobel's Explosive Co. had written to the Australian Government stating it would be prepared to manufacture Cordite at Braybrook instead of merely loading the Martini-Henry cartridge there with imported components and if the Australian Government were to accept the .303" calibre cartridge they would set up new plant for the complete production of .303" ammunition.

In May 1900 the company's head offices moved from 149 to 195 West George Street, Glasgow, and in November 1902 Mr H. McGowan was appointed Deputy Assistant Manager at Ardeer after working for 13 years with the company. McGowan was knighted in 1918 and progressed to the role of Managing Director of the company and following the subsequent formation of ICI he was to become Deputy Chairman and President of the Board of Directors.

A visit to Nobel's cartridge loading site in London in July 1902 revealed it was situated in 32 Union Street close to the Middlesex Hospital. Cases were being loaded using powdering machines similar to those designed by Eskine, whilst Dixon's machines were in use to load shot. The loaded shotgun cartridge cases were then placed on power driven turnover machines to achieve a crimp. The Foreman in Charge at the time of the visit was a J.C. Hamilton. The company's two specialty loads, namely, Ballistite and Empire were loaded in separate

rooms. Mr Hamilton had invented a special hopper to feed the powder so as to get the same density in each row, since there was the possibility that the first holes receiving a charge would be packed more densely than those at the rear. The aggregate of powder for each 100 cartridges was weighed before loading and specimens were being constantly withdrawn and separately tested to ensure uniformity. The turnover lathe which was being used was being driven at 1,400 rpm and the foreman claimed it was possible to achieve a throughput of 4,000 cartridges per hour with this turnover tool.

A press visit by a group to the Ardeer site in December 1902 discovered that different coloured clothing was being worn by staff in differing areas of the site so that supervisors were able to see if anyone had entered the wrong areas, an action contrary to the related site discipline regulations. Light blue garments were worn in the Cordite and Smokeless Powder areas whereas dark blue garments with no pockets were in use in the area where Dynamite was loaded into sticks. Red garments were also used in another undisclosed area.

In 1907 Nobel's acquired F.W. Joyce & Co. Ltd, a major shotgun cartridge and percussion cap manufacturer, a well respected and long established company whose factory was sited at Waltham Abbey in Essex, together with the New Explosives Company. In October 1907 Captain J.H. Hardcastle was appointed ballistic consultant to Nobel's Explosives Co. Ltd and in June 1908 the company moved its southern offices to Kingsway House London WC from College Hill Chambers, London EC. These same premises were also to act as F.W. Joyce's headquarters.

By July 1908 Nobel's had started the erection and equipping of a new factory at their Waltham Abbey site, the former home of F. Joyce and Co. Ltd for the loading of their Ballistite and Empire powder shotgun cartridges. This resulted in a complete rebuild of the site leaving but a few of the former Joyce buildings. The new layout was based on the need for cost effective and rapid production of sporting shotgun cartridges to meet the current huge demand from the sportsman and to enable it to be competitive with other English manufacturers. A visit by a writer for *Arms & Explosives* in April 1910 outlined the changes made at the premises and for the purpose of posterity an extract and resume is shown below:

The factory buildings themselves are substantially constructed of brick and reinforced concrete.

All the floors are asphalt laid over concrete, and are fireproof and dustless. The roofs are flat, and the walls have been made of such strength as to allow of another floor being carried up, should additional space thereafter be required. Communication from floor to floor is by staircases enclosed in shafts or 'towers' alongside, but not within the buildings, from which they are separated by fireproof doors. For the conveyance of goods from floor to floor automatic lifts are kept continually in operation. In all cartridge factories it is recognized as a matter of great importance that needless handling of components should be avoided. In this new factory the moving about is done by means of runways and lifts. The buildings themselves have been expressly planned with the object of arranging the several processes in orderly sequence to avoid unnecessary handling. Outside the building, as well as within, the overhead runways communicate with all parts of the factory. The runways are manipulated easily. Extending in all for over a mile, they are said to form one of the most lengthy hand-operated systems in the country.

The writer then went on to describe the water reservoirs sited on the roof of one of the main buildings used to collect soft water needed in the manufacturing process. He noticed that the whole site was fitted with a telephone communication system linked to a private exchange, whilst the magazines and danger building had been resited to safe working distances from the main buildings and the adjacent roads. He then described the process of cartridge case manufacture. He discovered that coloured sheets of paper were initially printed with the names of the firms for whom the cartridges were being made, before being made into tubes by rolling and pasting. The tubes were then dried by hot air in open racks in an area protected by fireproof doors before being cut, trimmed and burnished. In a separate area the brass heads were being prepared by stamping, annealing, sizing, cleaning and burnishing. The cap chambers were then flanged and flash holes were formed in them in the same operation. The caulk or inner wad was then wound to fit inside the head to joint it to the tube. A pressure process was then employed to amalgamate the tube, head, metal liner, inner steel head and cap chamber prior to the addition of the cap. From there it was moved into the inspection room. This housed seven separate work groups, each having within it three inspectors where reject cases are thrown out down shoots whilst those passing inspection were fed onto a constant moving band which brought down empty boxes and moved the filled boxes ready for the loading process. The site was powered by steam engines and gas engines with dynamos to provide electricity to power the motors in each shop. This had given rise to the need for a new 120 foot chimney stack. The new loading area, previously opened in 1907, was found to be equipped with automated loading machines fed with components from an upper floor. In the event of a cartridge igniting on the loading tracks the explosion was geared to be vented up a tube away from the operators, into the open air.

The former Joyce factory had produced percussion caps at this site initially in 1842 and it was to continue this process during the Nobel period of ownership. The only changes made in relation to this process were the introduction of new safety distances and the creation of a new magazine protected by earth mounds.

By 1910 the new site also housed its own comprehensive test facilities consisting of two chronographs, pressure guns and outdoor ranges with plates for pattern testing, and by February 1910 the rebuilding of Joyce's old site at Waltham Abbey was nearing completion. Almost all of the old buildings had been removed and a considerable portion of existing machinery scrapped and new plant installed.

The Nobel loading factory, although housed in entirely separate buildings, was contained within an area adjoining the ammunition factory. Clearly all these changes were a little too much for Joyce's former Manager to stomach and on 1 October 1910 Percy Newton resigned.

Prior to the major amalgamations which were to occur at the end of WWI it appears that Nobel's started a process of head hunting staff for their new cartridge business and were ruthless if parties did not match up to their needs. In January 1916 Mr F.J. Shand was appointed Managing Director of Nobel's Explosives Co. Ltd. He had previously been their General Manager and he succeeded Thomas Johnson. In January 1918 Mr Harry McGowan was appointed Managing Director of Nobel's Explosives Co. Ltd, replacing Mr Shand who resigned, who in the words of the press of the day stated that the company were replacing Mr Shand with 'a younger man invested with the vigour of youth'.

In April 1916 Mr Cecil Mack left Eley Bros Ltd as their Commercial Manager and took up employment with Nobel's Explosives Company as Assistant Manager at their Adderley Park works in August 1916.

Nobel's Explosives Company, Ltd.
(Of Glasgow).

Ammunition Manufacturers,

Waltham Abbey Factory, Essex.

Although I have been unable to establish the exact ammunition production levels for the company before WWI, from the ratio of remaining specimens encountered when compared to the two main ammunition producers in the UK, namely Eley Bros of London and George Kynoch of Birmingham, Nobel's only accounted for a small percentage of small arms ammunition made in the UK. Nobel's cartridge production was however clearly a profitable business and backed by its explosives production and other chemical products it was only a matter of time before its huge resources would swallow up its main competitors. At the end of WWI, in May 1918, Explosives Trades, a holding company, was formed; this marked the first stage of the takeover by Nobel's of the vast majority of the British cartridge manufacturers. On 29th November that year this new company achieved an authorised capital of £18,000,000 and absorbed the following companies:

Nobel's Explosives Ltd	£9,075,000
British South African Explosives	£1,533,000
Kynoch Ltd	£1,435,000
Curtis's & Harvey	£887,000
Eley Brothers Limited	£740,000
Kings Norton Metal Company	£637,000
EC Powder Co.	£119.000
New Pegamoid Limited	£75,000
Schultze	£61,000
Eley Canada	£8,000

Two years later Nobel's Industries Ltd was formed and in December 1926 it was renamed Imperial Chemical Industries Ltd. The history of Eley Bros and the products of the Birmingham cartridge manufacturers, particularly Kynoch and ICI were dealt with in my two earlier books.

4.3 The company's cartridges

4.3.1 Brand named shotgun cartridges

The main named shotgun cartridges produced by the company include the following brand names:

A Cartridge Case	Nile
Acme	Noneka
Ajax	Orion
Barwon	Parvo (2")
Belloid	Pegamoid
Boxer (Black powder loading)	Perfect
Carron	Pigeon Shooting with Cooppal No 2
Challenge (Black powder load – Mauve case)	Primeka
Clyde	Red Indian (Black powder loading)
Corio	Regent
Coronet	Reliance (Black powder loading, red case)
Derwent (Black powder loading)	Rex (Black and nitro powder loadings)
Don (Black powder loading)	Ringer (Black powder loading mauve case)
Eclipse	Ringer (Smokeless loading brown case)
Emerite	Ringtail
Empire	Sporting Ballistite
Excelsior	Starling
Field	Sun
Fox	T (for French T powder),
Gastight Waterproof (Belloid Brand Paper)	Unique (1⅞")
Hercules	Unitro
Ivil	Unity (Schultz powder loading)
Kingsway	Valeka
National	Victor
New Era (Black powder loading, fawn case)	Waltham

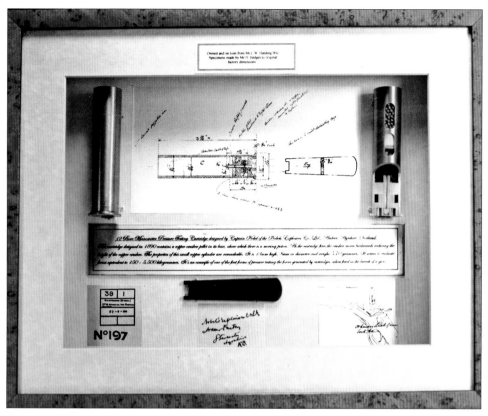

A pressure testing cartridge designed in 1890 by Captain Nobel, who I assume was a relative of Alfred Nobel. As it fires, the piston below the powder is forced down the hollow spindle through which the percussion cap flame passes to ignite the powder. The reduction in the length of the copper crusher was then compared against tables to determine how many tons per square inch were required to reduce it to its new length. These two specimens were made to the exact dimensions shown on Captain Nobel's drawing left in the factory

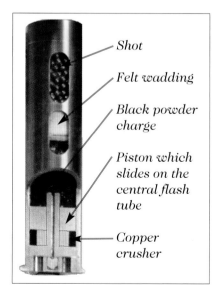

Shot

Felt wadding

Black powder charge

Piston which slides on the central flash tube

Copper crusher

The June 1904 issue of *Sporting Goods Review* revealed that Nobel's Explosives Company Ltd were loading Union Metallic Cartridge Company cases with Ballistite which were retailed under the title of Acmes together with Magic cartridges loaded with Empire powders into 2¾" and 3" 12 bore cases.

4.3.2 Known shotgun cartridge introduction dates

The majority of Nobel's shotgun cartridge brands were registered as trade marks, some gaining two different registration numbers on differing dates; however in an attempt to indicate when a given named Nobel shotgun cartridge was first placed on the market, the list of known dates has been compiled:

Parvo cartridge introduced in 1898
Nile cartridge introduced June 1901. Loaded with 25 grs
Ballistite and 1oz shot

Empire powder introduced during the 1903 season. It was a non condensed nitro cellulose powder, partially gelatinised and coloured. They loaded them into Eley cases bearing a Union Jack and the royal standard

Clyde cartridge introduced during the 1905–1906 season

Noneka Reg. Trade Mark No. 291158 granted 1907

Ajax Reg. Trade Mark No. 304090 granted 1908

Valeka Reg. Trade Mark No. 306746 granted 1908

Regent Reg. Trade Mark No. 309341 granted 1909

Primeka Reg. Trade Mark No. 314771 granted 1909

Pyramid design in circle with wording Nobel's Exp. Co. Ltd. Reg. Trade Mark No. 317098 granted 1909

N with crown above Trade Mark granted Dec. 1910

Belloid waterproof cases were first introduced in June 1910

Boxer Reg. Trade Mark No. 336016 granted 1911 (A black powder loading)

Orion introduced into their 1912 catalogue

Ringtail Reg. Trade Mark No. 336590 granted 1912

Belloid Reg. Trade Mark No. 337489 7 November 1911 granted 1912

Ajax Reg. Trade Mark No. 337487 7 November 1911 granted 1912

Clyde Reg. Trade Mark No. 337490 7 November 1911 granted 1912

Kingsway Reg. Trade Mark No. 337492 7 November 1911 granted 1912

Nile Reg. Trade Mark No. 337493 7 November 1911 granted 1912

Noneka Reg. Trade Mark No. 337494 7 November 1911 granted 1912

Empire Reg. Trade Mark No. 337491 7 November 1911 granted 1912

Regent Reg. Trade Mark No. 337495 7 November 1911 granted 1912

In February 1912 Nobel's Explosives Company applied for registration of a complete sequence of extremely colourful labels for cartridge boxes, which included a view of Dumbarton Rock with the words Nobel's Clyde and a device representing dahabeeah with the words 'Nile'.

In 1914 the company's brands of proprietary brand shotgun cartridges consisted of 'Noneka', 'Valeka', 'Nile', 'Orion', 'Kingsway', 'Regent', 'Clyde', 'National' and 'Ajax'. 'Valeka' had been removed from production due to Government demands for Cordite in September 1915.

In the Explosives Trades Ltd catalogue of 1920 a 'Waltham' brand black powder cartridge was listed.

Nobel's Industries Ltd 1923 factory notes held by Kynamco stated they were still making the following shotgun cartridge brands:

'Acme' for export only with ⅜" brass base in dark green
'Westminster'
'Green Rival' using a light orange case with 5⁄16" brass base
'Red Rival' using a dark green case with ⅜" brass base

4.3.3 Companies for which Nobel's of Glasgow loaded and which bear Nobel Glasgow headstamps

There were numerous companies and organisations which Nobel's loaded for before their amalgamation and a few of these are listed below:

Army & Navy Stores, London
E. Chamberlain, Andover & Basingstoke

William Evans, London

John R. Gow, Gunmakers Dundee (This is the only only specimen I know of to bear a Nobel London headstamp)

P.J. Harper, 59 Market Street and 44 Nantwich Road, Crewe – Ironmongers

Isaac Hollis, Weaman Street and Lench Street, Birmingham

W. Mawby & Son, Birkenhead

Midland Gun Company, Birmingham

Morrow & Co., Halifax

C. Jeffrey & Sons, Dorchester, Dorset

Page Wood

H.E. Pollard, Worcester

Purvis & Co., Alnwich

Robinson, 7 Queen Street, Hull

Shaw & Co., Mullingar

William Tarr & Son, Minehead

West London Shooting School, Perivale, Ealing

4.3.4 Examples of the company's shotgun cartridges

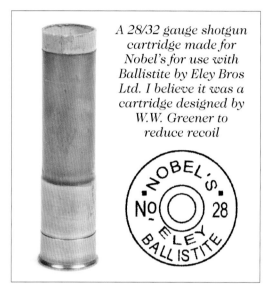

A 28/32 gauge shotgun cartridge made for Nobel's for use with Ballistite by Eley Bros Ltd. I believe it was a cartridge designed by W.W. Greener to reduce recoil

Examples of the range of Nobel's Explosives Co. 'Ballistite' cartridges loaded into both Eley Bros and UMC cases at their Ardeer factory

LEFT TO RIGHT:
*'Valeka',
'Unitro', brass
ejector, 3
'Empires', 'Clyde',
'Ballistite' and
'Noneka'*

LEFT TO RIGHT STANDING:
*Gastight with crown above N trade mark, Deep Shell, A case, Gastight Waterproof, 'Ajax', 'Ringer',
'Clyde'. LYING DOWN: 'T', 'Regent' and 'Sporting Ballistite'*

LEFT TO RIGHT:
*Unlined case for
C & H powder,
Gastight case metal
lined, Unlined Nitro
case for C & H
powder, 16 bore
believed made for
French market, 16
bore Gas-tight,
Unlined Nitro case,
20 bore Gas-tight
case*
LYING DOWN:
*Waterproof and
double headed
Gas-tight*

*A seldom encountered specimen
of the 'Carron' cartridge*

RIGHT:
LEFT TO RIGHT:
*Factory dummy window
cartridges 'Valeka',
'Ballistite', 'Empire', 'Clyde'
and lying down and half
sectioned a 'Noneka'*

BELOW:
*Interesting traveller's sample
sets made by Fiocchi of Italy
loaded with Nobel Glasgow
powders during the ICI era*

The 'Parvo' was a 2" cartridge, whilst the 'Rex', which will be encountered in both black powder and smokeless powder loadings was made for the Australian market

RIGHT:
20 bore 'Noneka'

BELOW:
Examples of further rarer Nobel's brands of cartridges.
LEFT TO RIGHT:
'Acme', 'Sun', 'Eclipse' and 'Emerite'

OPPOSITE:
Seldom encountered brands

4.3.5 Termination dates for several former named shotgun cartridges

In April 1919 Nobel's stated that they would no longer sell cartridges with retailers' names on their headstamps and that the special tube printing of retailers' names would no longer be free except for orders of 50,000 or more in one quality, gauge, length, colour and printing. Furthermore they announced that the number of available cartridge tube colours was to be considerably reduced. These statements marked the end, for many years, of the appearance of a retailer's name on the base of British manufactured shotgun cartridges.

On 20 February 1928, at the twenty fifth annual Gunmakers Association meeting, Nobel Industries announced that they were about to terminate production of the following cartridges:

> Eley Gastight proprietary cartridges in 12 and 16 bore, 'Clyde' in 16 bore, 'Noneka' in 12 and 16 bore, 'Red Rival' in 12 and 16 bore, 'Green Rival' in 12 and 16 bore, 'Zenith' in 16 bore, Kyblack in 16 bore, Kynoch Gastight quality in 12 and 16 bore, 'Eley Trapshooting' in 2¾" nitro 12 bore.

They stated that they also wished to abolish the following brands:

> Kynoch Gastight Quality in 12 and 16 bore
> Eley Nitro and Kynoch C.B. (Cone base) ⁵⁄₁₆" lined quality 12 bore 2¾" and 2½" and 16 bore
> Brown C.F. in 12 and 16 bore
> Solid Brass in 12 bore 2¾" and 2½" and 16 bore
> Kynoch 'Perfect' in 12 bore 2¾" and 2½" and 16 bore
> Gastight cone base in 16 and 20 bore
> 'Pegamoid' cone base in 12 bore

They stated they would still make 24 bore in thick and thin rim cases but asked the trade to support just the thin rim. Their new range of colours being:

> 'Pegamoid' in light maroon only
> Gastight in Indian red, blue, grey, yellow and crimson if they would take the waterproof process successfully.
> The 'Deep Shell' Lined and Nitro brands in Grand Prix quality would be made in dark green, light orange, blue, grey, yellow and crimson.

4.3.6 Headstamps on Nobel shotgun cartridges

(see illustrations opposite)

4.4.1 Metallic cartridges produced by the company

When in 1897 Nobel's Explosives Co. Ltd purchased The Birmingham Metal and Munitions Company, that company was already an established independent producer of metallic ammunition and it appears that its new owners were happy for it to continue to produce metallic ammunition at Streetly, but now using Nobel propellants. If you examine B.M. & M. Co. metallic ammunition headstamps you will discover they either carry the 'B' head mark at 6 o'clock, no headstamp or prior to ETL being formed they bear the Dominion Cartridge Company headstamp, particularly for United States rifle calibres. Following B.M. & M. Co. absorption by Nobel's in 1897, their packaging changed as shown in the following photographs. A small number of factory drawings exist

1.   2.   3.   4.   5.

6.   7.   8.   9.   10.

11.   12.   13.   14.   15.

16.   17.   18.   19.   20.

21.   22.

NOTES

No. 1. In June 1904 Nobel's were loading cartridges for the Union Metalic Cartridge Co. with Ballistite. This is an example of the related headstamp on a 2" cartridge.

Nos. 2, 3 and 10. Following the company's introduction of Ballistite and prior to acquiring Joyce of London in 1907 they used Eley Bros Ltd to manufacture their cases. These specimens therefore date between 1887 and 1907.

Nos. 4, 9, 11, 14 and 17. These specimens are all fitted with Joyce domed caps so date between 1907 an 1919.

No. 5. This specimen was made for an overseas customer. It is a typical example of an Eley Bros Ltd case loaded with Ballistite and on the side is marked Originale Della Casa Nobel's.

Nos. 5 and 6. The significance of the 'B' on the primer is unknown but was probably used to signify that the case was loaded with Ballistite.

No. 16. This specimen has the typical Joyce stab marks in the full length brass case used to hold the internal base and liner in position.

Nos. 19 and 20. These are examples of their very late markings before the ETL (Explosives Trade Ltd) mark was introduced.

No. 21. This appeared on an 'Empire' cartridge made for the West London Shooting School.

No. 22. A rare proprietary headstamp on a cartridge made for a gunmaker.

which indicate that the name Nobel appeared in certain pistol calibres; however to date no one to my knowledge has uncovered any specimens bearing these headstamps.

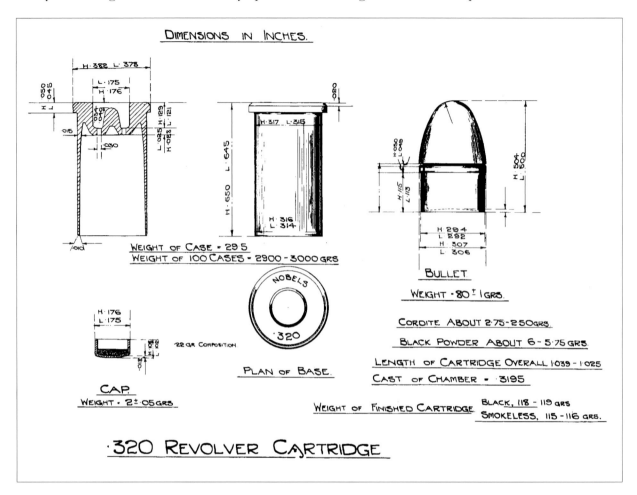

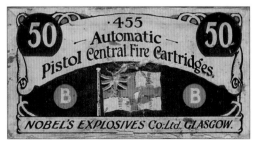

4.4.2 An unusual cartridge patented for the company by A.V. Newton in 1895

10,118. Newton, A. V., [*Nobel, A*].
May 12

Pyrotechnics. — Relates to a method of conveying a camera to a great height and suspending it there in order to obtain a photograph of the land-scape underneath. The propelling composition *d* escapes through an aper-ture in the disc *b*, and, when the combustion reaches the top of the composition *d*, a mass of guncotton is ignited through a hole in the disc *e*. The explosion of the guncotton detaches the camera *f* from the rocket and ignites a time fuse *o*. This fuse ignites an explosive charge in the cap *m* blowing off the cap and liberating a para-chute *l* which is attached to the camera. The camera is now suspended by the parachute, and after it is steady an instantaneous shutter *i* is released by another time fuse, un-covers the lens *h*, and makes an exposure.

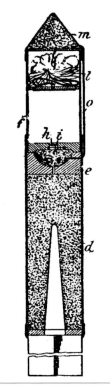

4.5 Company advertisements and display boards

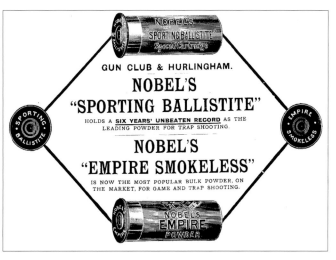

Advert in Arms & Explosives *April 1905*

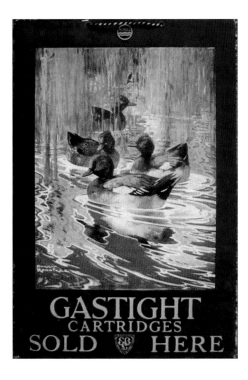

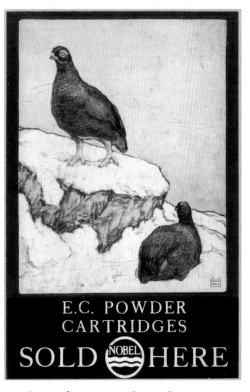

Adverts for gunsmiths and ironmongers shops, both date from post 1918

A Nobel Industries Ltd display board dating between November 1920 and December 1926. All the metallic centre-fire ammunition bears Kynoch headstamps and the shotgun cartridges are by Eley but bear Eley Nobel headstamps

A Nobel's board with cartridges bearing the headstamp Nobel-Glasgow, where the cases were made at the old Joyce factory at Waltham Abbey and loaded with Nobel powders at Ardeer. Given the introduction date of the brands displayed in the case it was assembled between 1911 and 1915 when the 'Valeka' brand was removed from production

This board like the one shown on the previous page can be dated based on its specimens as being constructed between 1911 and 1915

Prior to the formation of Explosives Trades Ltd in May 1918 Nobel's obtained their cartridge cases from Eley Bros of London and the specimens in this case bear both Eley and Nobel headstamps, the powder being loaded into this range of cases at Nobel's sites being various grades of Ballistite

NOBEL'S EXPLOSIVES CO., LTD.

NOBEL'S PROPRIETARY SHOT GUN CARTRIDGES.

Nobel's "Noneka."

Nobel's "Kingsway."

Nobel's "Valeka."

Nobel's "Regent."

Nobel's "Nile."

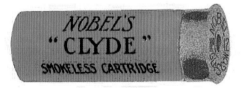

Nobel's "Clyde."

Nobel's "Orion."

Nobel's "Ajax."

Extract from Nobel's 1911 catalogue showing their proprietary cartridges

NOBEL'S ADVERTISING MATERIAL.

❡ In order to assist our Clients we shall be glad to send, post free, on request, any samples of our Advertising Literature—Showcards, Booklets, etc. An Order Form is supplied with each Price List which may be used for this purpose.

SHOWCARDS:

SHOWCARD No. 1. Size 5½ × 8½

SHOWCARD No. 2. Size 5½ × 8½

SHOWCARD No. 3. Size 5½ × 8½

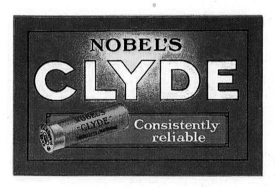

SHOWCARD No. 4. Size 5½ × 8½

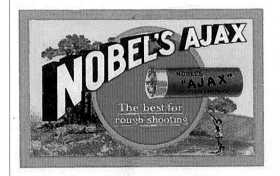

SHOWCARD No. 5. Size 5½ × 8½

SHOWCARD No. 6. Size 5½ × 8½

Extract from Nobel's 1911 catalogue

NOBEL'S EXPLOSIVES CO., LTD. 33

Central Fire Cartridges for Savage, Winchester, and Similar Rifles—Continued.

Packed in boxes of 20 unless otherwise stated.

Description.		Powder.	Bullet.	Price per 1,000.		
				Cartridges.	Shells.	Bullets.
		Grains.	Grains	£ s. d.	£ s. d.	£ s. d.
·32-20-115	(In boxes of 50)	Black	19	115	2 15 0	1 11 8	1 0 0
·32-40-165	(In boxes of 50)	Black	33	165	3 13 3	3 0 10	1 2 6
·38-55-255		Black	40	255	3 17 0	2 15 0	0 17 6
·38-56-255		Black	46	255	6 6 8	3 3 4	0 17 6
·40-60-210		Black	47	210	6 6 8	3 3 4	0 17 6
·40-82-260		Black	67	260	7 10 0	3 16 8	0 17 6

This is an extract from Nobel's 1911 catalogue. Note the metallic rifle cartridges shown on this sheet all bear Dominion Cartridge Company headstamps. This is not surprising since although they owned B.M. & M. Co. who made metallic ammunition, they only made a limited range of metallic ammunition, all of which was aimed at the military market. No doubt by 1913 Eley Bros Ltd of London had foreseen Nobel's future aims and had refused to supply them with further metallic components for sporting ammunition

4.6 Explosives Trades Ltd staff in 1919

With the formation of Explosives Trades Ltd following the takeover by Nobel's of the former British ammunition and propellant companies, it afforded them the opportunity to select the best staff available from these former companies. The people they selected were:

Arthur Chamberlain – Former Chairman of Kynoch who had trained in the cartridge trade in relation to both shotgun and metallic ammunition

S.F. Prest – Former Chairman of Eley with a cross section of knowledge

Mr W.D. Borland – Former EC Power Company chemist and Works Manager with an in-depth knowledge of finances and of the markets

F.W. Jones – Recognised within the trade as the leading British ballistician

D. J. Metcalfe – Former Managing Director of Curtis's & Harvey, a commercial man with a deep interest in sporting powders

Mr Wotherspoon – Former employee of Nobel's Explosives Company Ltd with 30 years experience in marketing sporting powders and cartridges and recent supervisor at the cartridge factory at Waltham

R.E. Fenby – Former Kynoch leading ballistician on Express rifle cartridges

Mr Ashdown – Eley's ballistician and provider of 'Proof' ammunition

Dr Tonks – Former Curtis's & Harvey specialist in smokeless powders

Dr Brownsdon – Former K.N.M.Co. specialist in cap compositions

Melville Smith – Former Abbey Wood's K.N.M.Co. specialist in .22" RF and match rifle ammunition

Mr Cowie and Mrs Lumsden – Former employees of Nobel's Explosives Co. and responsible for the production of Ballistite and Empire powders

Mr Stickland – Former New Explosives Co. employee responsible for the production of various Neonite and other nitro cellulous powders

A.R. Berry – Former New Explosives Co. Ltd specialist in cartridge components linked to powders.

CHAPTER 5
Greenwood & Batley Ltd

5.1 The company's history and its role in the production of arms and munitions machinery

Thomas Greenwood, born in 1814, first learnt his trade as an engineer in his father's machine shop in Gildersome, near Leeds, where machines were made for spinning and weaving wool. In 1833 he moved to Leeds and joined with his brother where they started a business making machinery for the textile trades. Due to a family death the enterprise terminated and Thomas moved to work for Messrs S. & J. Whitham in Leeds, a firm of engineers and tool makers. Thomas's ability and inventiveness was rapidly recognised and he devised what became known as the universal metal milling machine. His actions came to the notice of Sir Peter Fairbairn a successful Leeds engineer, who offered Thomas the role of Chief Draftsman at his Wellington Foundry. Fairbairn also engaged the services of a John Batley and the Foundry soon became known as a place where companies requiring labour saving and ingenious machine tools could be obtained.

When the Crimean War broke out this country was ill prepared in relation to armaments and a hastily formed committee, consisting of military officers was sent around the country to inspect engineering establishments to identify companies who could assist them with equipment to manufacture armaments. One place they visited was the Wellington Foundry and Greenwood's labour saving inventions were identified as an absolute need; the committee arranged for such devices to be installed at their Woolwich Arsenal. At this point Mr Greenwood became a regular consultant to the Woolwich Arsenal and designed several machines for their use. These included tools for making Boxer fuses, bushes for shells and for rocket making. He also provided the best system for shot and shell mouldings resulting in major savings in labour. Two years after Greenwood's tools had been installed at Woolwich the savings he produced covered the entire costs of the buildings, engines and plant at Woolwich Arsenal.

The late Mr Thomas Greenwood

In 1856 Thomas Greenwood and John Batley dissolved their partnership with Sir Peter Fairbairn and established their own business at the Albion Foundry. This was sited on East Street, Leeds but due to its limited size in 1859 they built a new factory in Armley Road, Leeds. By 1888 their works had expanded to cover 11 acres and they employed in excess of 1,500 staff. A rail connection with the Great Northern Railway was installed in 1890 to bring in raw materials and to deliver their finished products. Their new site and linked rail connection allowed Greenwood & Batley to rapidly expand and to manufacture an incredible range of products.

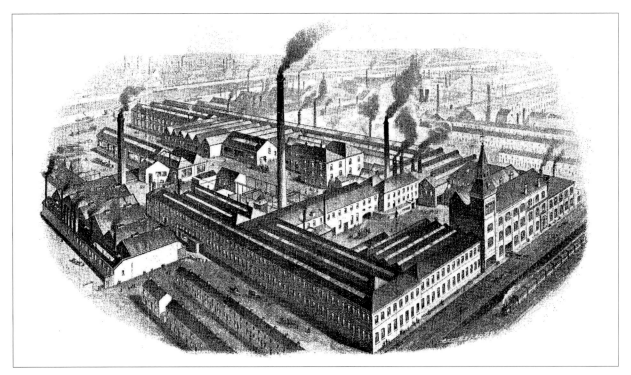

Bird's-eye view of the Albion Works

Shortly after the new company was formed the duo designed the operating machinery for the massive Armstrong guns at both Woolwich and Elswick Ordnance.

Greenwood was always ready to learn new engineering techniques and one of particular interest to him related to the work of the American James H. Burton. James H. Burton was born on 17 August 1823 in Virginia, USA. In 1844 Burton went to work as a machinist at the Harpers Ferry Armoury, where John H. Hall, the proprietor, had pioneered the mechanised production of inter-changeable rifle parts which were introduced into the breech loading Harper's Ferry Flintlock rifle. In 1854 Burton left to work at the Ames Company of Chicopee, Massachusetts, which supplied the US armouries with precision machinery for the manufacture of firearms, and in June 1855, based on his previous experience he went to work as the Chief Engineer of the Royal Small Arms Manufactory in Enfield, England where he set up newly imported production machinery from America to produce the .577" P53 Enfield muzzle loading rifle. The imported machinery proved successful and, after Burton had returned home, Enfield decided to increase the number of machines used to produce the P53 rifle and they approached Greenwood. Greenwood not only produced the machines but also applied the interchangeable system to the manufacture of bayonets, something which at the time had not been accomplished in the USA.

The sequel to this story was that in June 1862 Burton, by now a Lieutenant Colonel in the Confederate States Army and in charge of the armouries of the Southern States, was required to establish a new arms factory at Macon in Georgia and in 1863 he came to Greenwood & Batley in Leeds to acquire the machinery, tools and materials to manufacture their own arms. He returned to Macon in the autumn of 1863 and awaited the Greenwood & Batley consignments which had been shipped in late 1864 to Bermuda. Due to a blockage by the Union Forces and the fact that the American Civil War ended in 1865 he never managed to put the machinery to its intended use to manufacture arms for soldiers of the Confederate Army.

Evidence of the company's first involvement in cartridge manufacture was established from the *Proceedings of the Institution of Mechanical Engineers* Vol. 19 dated 1868, in which Thomas Greenwood outlined the then complex machinery to manufacture the Boxer .577" Snider cartridge for the British Army in conjunction with Mr Davidson at Woolwich Arsenal. In essence the Snider cartridge involved the coil winding of a thin brass sheet of metal to form the sides of the case which was attached to the cartridge base made of a steel disc, into which was seated the primer. (This concept had been patented in March 1867 by G.H. Daw, who was one of Greenwood & Batley's early customers.) This jointing of the two metals was no easy task and the complete process of manufacture of this cartridge involved 21 machines but his machines achieved their aim and this started the company on a new branch of design, namely the manufacture of cartridge producing machines with various members of the family becoming Directors, Partners or part shareholders in companies involved in cartridge manufacture.

On 9 February 1873 Thomas Greenwood died aged 65 years; he was mourned by both family members and his workforce, having been held in high esteem by all. He had been an ideal employer and was one of the first industrialists to introduce the nine hour day and five and a half day working week, reducing it from the former ten hour day and six day week. On his death management of the company moved to his two sons Arthur and George aided by Harry Greenwood, Thomas's nephew and Thomas's son-in-law, Mr J.H. Wurtzburg. Mr John Batley had retired several years previously. Mr Arthur Greenwood died in February 1910 and was replaced within the company by a second Thomas Greenwood. Thomas Greenwood the second retired to Barton Lodge, Semaphore Road, Guildford, Surrey and died on 24 October 1945.

5.2 Other unrelated machinery produced by the company

In addition to machines manufactured by the company to produce ammunition and arms it also produced a whole set of machines for unrelated industries. These included:

Cloth cutting machines
Circular power saws
Drilling and boring machines
Forging machines for use with hot and cold metals
Hydraulic and power hammers
Lathes
Leather, paper and metal punching and shearing machines
Milling machines
Printing presses
Screw cutting machines to cut parallel sided screws
Spur and bevel gear cutting machines
Textile machines for wool, jute and flax weaving
Wood and metal screw cutting machines giving threading and slotting
Woodwork machines for making casks to hold liquids
Wood planing machines

5.3 The influence which Greenwood & Batley and its company Directors had on other companies involved in cartridge manufacture

It should be noted that Greenwood & Batley were to produce and in many cases patent a complete cross section of machines used in the production of ammunition, small arms and artillery. Starting with the Boxer spiral wound foil cartridge case, it moved to make tools to manufacture the Spencer rifle solid drawn cartridge cases and then created machines to extrude and pressure form lead slugs into bullets. The company supplied its cartridge making machines not only to private British companies and the Woolwich Military Arsenal but also to overseas governments such as Austria, Brazil, China, India, France, Holland, Portugal and Turkey together with Commonwealth factories in Australia, New Zealand and Canada. One of the earliest of these was the Quebec Arsenal, which in 1878 acquired from the company a complete plant to manufacture the .577" Boxer Snider cartridge.

The inventive genius of Thomas Greenwood and his subsequent family members' involvement in the production of ammunition in other British companies was reflected in the examples below. In 1870 the company of Westley Richards Arms & Ammunition Co. was formed as a partnership between Thomas Greenwood, John Batley and Westley Richards (the son of the founder of the famous Westley Richards Company). It resulted in the emergence of the first drawn brass metallic cartridge cases for use in military small arms with the Leeds company manufacturing and installing the needed machinery.

Birmingham Metal & Munitions Co. Adderley Park, Birmingham was formed in 1871 when B.S.A. & M. Co. decided to concentrate on small arms and pedal cycle production and to sell off the ammunition side of their business, much of which was linked to large calibre shell production. The new company's registered office was at Adderley Park and its initial Directors were Mr W.H.

Major-General E. Micklem   *Mr J.H Wurtzburg*, JP   *Mr Arthur Greenwood*, M.I.C.E
(Chairman)

Lieut.-Col. Ralph Vivian   *Vice-Admiral P.H. Colomb*   *Mr Henry Greenwood*

Directors of Greenwood & Batley in 1899

Greenwood, Mr J.F. Walker, Chairman, Mr Edwin Martin Goodman, Mr Henry A. Wiggin JP, Thomas Johnston, Thomas Reid and Hugh Beckett. Once again we see Greenwood & Batley benefiting from B.M. & M. Co. decision to utilise them to manufacture the necessary machinery to produce small arms ammunition and shell cases.

In January 1872 the National Arms & Ammunition Company Limited sited in Birmingham was formed with an initial share capital of £300,000. Its Directors included Thomas Greenwood and John Batley. In essence this was a partnership between the Westley Richards Arms & Ammunition Company and a Major General W. Dixon. Dixon was previously a Colonel in the Royal Artillery and subsequently the first Superintendent of the Royal Small Arms Factory at Enfield Lock. Although the venture proved ultimately unsuccessful and started winding up procedures in 1882, in 1872 they gained an order from the Prussian Government for 150,000 Mauser action rifles and 1,000,000 rounds of Mauser 11.15mm x 60R rifle ammunition. Although the company was equipped with Greenwood & Batley machinery it only managed to complete the ammunition order and to deliver some 6,000 of these rifles; however specimens exist which bear the Greenwood & Batley name, so it would appear that they also became involved in their manufacture.

The Kings Norton Metal Company, Birmingham, was formed in 1889. The Directors of the company were Mr Arthur Greenwood (Chairman), Major General E. Micklem (both of whom were Directors of Greenwood & Batley Ltd) and Mr John Palmer Junior of London. The company's board meetings were held in the London office at 16 Great George Street; it is interesting to note that these premises were rented by the Kings Norton Metal Company from Greenwood & Batley who actually owned them. As one would expect, Greenwood and Micklem were not without influence in relation to purchases made by the new company and many of the items of equipment e.g. three sets of .303" cartridge machines and hydraulic presses needed for extruding naval shells and shell driving bands were obtained from Greenwood & Batley.

5.4 Photographs taken in the factory relating to ammunition production

Ammunition Works, East Greenwich. Cordite loading sheds

RIGHT:
Cape Mills:
Cartridge Department,
making cartridges
and bullets

BELOW:
Ammunition Works,
East Greenwich.
Loading and
completing
cartridges

*Cape Mills:
Cartridge
Department,
drawing solid
metal
cartridges*

5.5.1 Metallic ammunition production by the company from 1868 to November 1918

The first evidence of cartridge production by the company comes from company notes. On 1 June 1868 five customers ordered collectively 10,000 Spencer sporting rifle cartridges, 4,158 were delivered and the order was then cancelled. On 10 June 1868 this order was recommenced at the request of Alt. Hooper & Co. of London and a further 3,024 rounds fitted with exploding bullets were produced before the order was again stopped. This order recommenced on 24 November 1868 for Alt. Hooper & Co. of London for delivery over a 12 month period.

The next cartridge contract for ammunition components appears as factory order 808 on 14 November 1870 when a Louie Merton ordered 10,000,000 Spencer rifle cartridge cases primed ready for filling plus their related bullets with instruction to pass them to Hall & Son, Faversham for filling. On 16 December 1868 two further orders numbers 862 and 863 were placed by Louie Merton for 10,000,000 Remington drawn case rifle cartridge cases (order 862) and bullets (order 863). It appears that these were for .433" (11 x 50R) Remington Rifles and were destined for the Turkish Government. The order notes stipulated that the cases must accept 75 grains of black powder and the bullets must carry 1,000 metres. The factory notes state that the delivery rate was 500,000 per week and the price fixed was 91s 3d per 1,000 rounds.

From this point onwards Greenwood & Batley expanded their ammunition production and this table indicates their main contracts between 1868 and the end of WWI. (Note within the table the letter M after a number indicates millions.)

Yr/Month	Type	Quantity	By whom if known	Comments
1868	Spencer rifle cartridges	10,000	Alt. Hooper & Co., London	Sporting rifle version
1870	Spencer rifle cases	10 M	Alt. Hooper & Co., London	To be loaded by Hall & Son
1870	Remington rifle C/F cartridges	10 M	Alt. Hooper & Co., London	75 grn to carry 1093 yds

Yr/Month	Type	Quantity	By whom if known	Comments
1878/12	Nordenfelt M.G. cartridges	225,000		6oz steel bullet & 160+- 20 grns bp
1888/3	.303" Rubin rifle cartridges	200,000	British Government	
1889/12	.303" bullets	1 M	Woolwich Royal Laboratories	
1890*	.303" cartridges	6 M	Woolwich Royal Laboratories	Total for year
1891*	.303" Mk II Rifle cartridges	6 M	Woolwich Royal Laboratories	Yearly total for MkII Magazine Rifle
1891/9	.303" bullets	3 M	Woolwich Royal Laboratories	For MkII Magazine Rifle
1892/7	.303" bullets	2 M	Woolwich Royal Laboratories	For Magazine Rifle Mk II
1892/11	.450" Webley Pattern 994	1,083,840	India Govrn via Royal Labs	
1892/11	.303" Mk 1 Cordite rifle cases	2.8 M	Woolwich Royal Laboratories	
1892/11	.450" Webley Pattern 994	608,000	Naval Ordnance	For revolvers
1893/3	S.A. ball cases for Cordite	3 M	Kings Norton Metal Co.	Presumably .303" Mk II C
1893*	Caps for Martini Henry cartridges	602,500	Egyptian Government	Total for year
1893/9	.303" bullets for Cordite cartridges	7.5 M	Woolwich Royal Laboratories	It is assumed that these were MkIIC
1893/9	.303" cartridge cases	3 M	Woolwich Royal Laboratories	It is assumed that these were MkIIC
1893/11	.303" bullets with coated envelopes	5,000	Woolwich Royal Laboratories	With cupro nickel coated steel
1894/9	.303" cartridges	2,000	Colonial Ammunition Co Ltd	Loaded with Cannonite & Riflelite
1894/11	.303" cartridge cases MkII C	3 M	Woolwich Royal Laboratories	
1897/6	.303" bullets	20,000	Nobel's	
1897/6	.303" cartridge cases	20,000	Nobel's	
1897*	.303" cartridge cases	32,000	Maxim Nordenfelt	Total for year
1897*	.303" cartridges MkIIC	1.5 M	Maxim Nordenfelt	Total for year
1895/2	.303" cartridges	1 M	Maxim Nordenfelt	Loaded with Riflelite
1895/2	.303" Nickel envelope bullets	500,000	For Greenwood & Batley	
1895 *	.303" cartridge loaded with Riflelite	3,616,000	Maxim Nordenfelt	Total for year
1895 *	.303" cartridge loaded with Cordite	553,000	Maxim Nordenfelt	Total for year
1895 *	.303" cartridge cases	35,000	Maxim Nordenfelt	Total for year
1895*	.303" MkIC & MkIIC cartridges	7.7 M	Woolwich Royal Laboratories	Total for year
1895/9	.303" blanks	1.2 M	Woolwich Royal Laboratories	
1895*	.303" bullets	8.2 M	Woolwich Royal Laboratories	Total for year
1896*	.303" cartridge cases and bullets	20,000	Nobel's	Total for year
1896*	.303" cartridge cases	40,000	Nobe'ls	Total for year
1896*	.303" bullets	30,000	Nobel's	Total for year
1896/3	.303" cartridges	7,830	Maxim Nordenfelt	Loaded with Cordite
1896/4	.303" blanks	10,000	Maxim Nordenfelt	
1896/6	7mm Chilean Mauser cartridge	6,000	Maxim Nordenfelt	
1896/4	6.5mm Mannlicher cartridges	10,000	Maxim Nordenfelt	
1896*	.303" cartridge cases	650,000	Eley Bros Ltd	Total for year
1896/6	.303" cartridge MkII C	4 M	Admiralty	
1896/4	.303" cartridge cases	12 M	Woolwich Royal Laboratories	
1896/4	.303" bullets	5 M	Woolwich Royal Laboratories	
1896*	.303" cartridge cases	80,000	Colonial Ammunition Co. Ltd	Total for year
1896/8	.303" bullets	60,000	Colonial Ammunition Co. Ltd	
1896/8	.303" over powder wads	65,000	Colonial Ammunition Co. Ltd	
1897*	.303" cartridges	92,000	Maxim Nordenfelt	Total for year with Dum Dum bullets
1897*	.303" cartridge cases	4 M	Woolwich Royal Laboratories	Total for year
1897*	.303" cartridge bullets	5 M	Woolwich Royal Laboratories	Total for year

Yr/Month	Type	Quantity	By whom if known	Comments
1897*	.303" cartridges Cordite loaded	604,000	Colonial Ammunition Co. Ltd	Total for year
1897/7	.303" blanks	120,000	Colonial Ammunition Co. Ltd	
1897/6	.303" unnecked cases	5,000	Smokeless Powder Co.	
1897/6	.303" bullets	5,000	Smokeless Powder Co.	
1897/11	.303" Dum Dum bullets	250,000	Greenwood & Batley	
1898/1	.303" Dum Dum cartridges	205,000	Maxim Nordenfelt	
1898*	.303" Cordite cartridges	1.6 M	Admiralty	
1898/1	.303" Nickel coated bullets	5,000	Vickers Sons & Maxim	
1898/1	.303" cases	1,000	Vickers Sons & Maxim	
1898/4	.577"/.450" Martini Henry cases	50,000	Vickers Sons & Maxim	
1898/5	.577"/.450" Martini Henry	1,502,000	Vickers Sons & Maxim	Cordite loaded
1898/2	.303" cartridges Cordite	2,000	R. Crawford Pudney	
1898*	.303" cartridges Cordite loaded	4 M	Colonial Ammunition Co.	Total for year
1898/7	.303" blanks	100,000	Colonial Ammunition Co.	
1898/10	.303" cases	50,000	Colonial Ammunition Co.	plus 100,000 discs & caps
1898/11	.303" cartridges MkIV	500,000	Colonial Ammunition Co.	
1898/11	.450" Webley pistol cartridges	22,000	Colonial Ammunition Co.	
1898/6	.303" cartridge cases MkIV	2.5 M	Woolwich Royal Laboratories	
1898/6	.303" cartridge cases for blanks	250,000	Woolwich Royal Laboratories	
1898/11	.303" cartridges MkIV	4.5 M	Woolwich Royal Laboratories	
1898/1	.303" bullets	1 M	Woolwich Royal Laboratories	
1898/11	.303" cartridges MkV	4 M	Woolwich Royal Laboratories	
1899/10	.303" cartridges MkII Cordite	500,000	Colonial Ammunition Co.	
1899*	.303" MkIV bullets	360,000	Colonial Ammunition Co.	
1899*	.303" cartridge cases	60,000	Colonial Ammunition Co.	Total for year
1899/3	.303" MkIV Dum Dum bullets	5,000	Hy Birdseye & Co.	
1899*	.303" cartridge cases	82,000	Vickers Sons & Maxim	Total for year
1899/6	.577"/.450" Martini Henry	30,000	Vickers Sons & Maxim	Cordite loaded
1899*	.303" MkIIC cartridges	350,000	Vickers Sons & Maxim	Total for year
1899/12	.303" MkIIC cartridges	10,000	Colt Gun & Carriage Co.	
1899/6	.303" MkIV bullets	7,000	Smokeless Powder & Ammo	
1899/9	.303" MkIV with Dum Dum bullets	1,000	Queensland Australia	
1900*	.303" MkIIC cartridges	115,000	Colt Gun & Carriage Co.	Total for year
1900/12	.50" Colt cartridges	1,000	Colt Gun & Carriage Co.	Bullet diameter .508"
1900*	.303" MkIIC cartridges	13.2 M	Woolwich Royal Laboratories	Total for year
1900/3	.303" cartridge cases	1 M	Woolwich Royal Laboratories	
1900/3	.303" MkII bullets	1 M	Woolwich Royal Laboratories	
1900*	.303" MkIIC cartridges	17.6 M	Vickers Sons & Maxim	Total for year
1900/2	.577"/.450" Martini Henry	410,000	Vickers Sons & Maxim	
1900/2	.303" MkII cartridges	100,000	Western Australia	Does not say Cordite
1900/10	.303" blank cartridges	150,000	Colonial Ammunition Co.	
1900/10	.303" MkIIC cartridges	599,500	Colonial Ammunition Co.	
1900/11	.303" cartridge cases	50,000	Colonial Ammunition Co.	
1900/11	.303" bullets cupro nickel jackets	1 M	Kings Norton Metal Co.	To Government spec.
1900/7	.303" MkIIC cartridges	250,000	J.H. Blakesley	
1901/3	.303" cases for blank cartridges	50,000	Colonial Ammunition Co.	

Yr/Month	Type	Quantity	By whom if known	Comments
1901/5	.303" MkIIC cartridges	3 M	Colonial Ammunition Co.	
1901/11	.303" cartridge cases	500,000	Colonial Ammunition Co.	Stamped C.A.C. MkII plus caps
1901*	.303" MkIIC cartridges	17 M	Woolwich Royal Laboratories	Total for year
1901/6	.303" blanks	10,000	Colt Gun & Carriage Co.	With special wooden bullet
1901/10	.303" MkIIC cartridges	1 M	Braendlin Armoury Co.	
1901/10	.303" cartridge cases	5,000	Mills Woven Cart. Belt	See patent No. 9642 1901
1902/1	.303" cartridge cases	50,000	Mills Woven Cart. Belt	
1902/1	.303" cartridge cases capped	500,000	Colonial Ammunition Co.	
1902/1	.303" bullet envelopes	500,000	Colonial Ammunition Co.	
1902*	.303" MkIIC cartridges	1.5 M	Colonial Ammunition Co.	No headstamps on ½ million
1902/8	.303" cases cartridge cases	1 M	Colonial Ammunition Co.	Uncapped and no headstamps
1902/7	.303" blanks with wooden bullets	10,000	Colt Gun & Carriage Co.	
1902/5	.303" MkIIC cartridges	2 M	Admiralty	
1902/3	.303" MkIIC cartridges	7 M	Woolwich Royal Laboratories	
1902/6	.303" blanks with mock bullets	1 M	Woolwich Royal Laboratories	
1902/11	.303" MkIIC cartridges	500,000	Sultan of Morocco	
1903/1	.303" MkIIC cartridges	2 M	Colonial Ammunition Co.	
1903/3	.297"/.230" Morris Tube MkII	3 M	Woolwich Royal Laboratories	
1903*	.303" MkIIC cartridges	7 M	Woolwich Royal Laboratories	Total for year
1903/7	.303" blank cartridges Mk VI	4 M	Woolwich Royal Laboratories	With mock bullet
1903/3	.297"/.230" Morris Tube MkII short	500,000	Colonial Ammunition Co.	Cartridges for Francotte rifle
1903/3	.297"/.230" Morris Tube MkII long	500,000	Colonial Ammunition Co.	Cartridges for Francotte Cadet
1903*	.303" cartridge cases	2.75 M	Colonial Ammunition Co.	Uncapped un-necked no caps
1903/6	.303"MkII bullets	500,000	Colonial Ammunition Co.	
1903/12	.303" Mk V cartridges	1 M	Curtis's & Harvey	Loaded with Nitrokol powder
1903/12	.303" blanks MkV	500,000	Curtis's & Harvey	
1903/6	.303" blanks MkV	100,000	Egyptian Government	Loaded with Nitrokol powder
1903/4	.303" MkIIC cartridges	6,000	Vickers Sons & Maxim	For machine guns
1903/8	.303" cartridge cases	10,000	Vickers Sons & Maxim	Unmarked un-necked & uncapped
1903/4	.303" MkIIC cartridges	1,250,000	Colonial Ammunition Co	1 million to be unmarked
1904*	.297"/.230" Morris Tube MkII	60,000	Morris Aiming Tube & Ammo Co.	Total for year
1904/4	.303" cartridges for machine guns	200,000	Vickers Son & Maxim	Specials for use in Maxim M.G.
1904/4	.303" MkIIC cartridges	2 M	Admiralty	
1904/4	.297"/.230" Morris Tube MkII	1 M	Woolwich Royal Laboratories	
1904/5	.303" MkIIC cartridges	10 M	Woolwich Royal Laboratories	
1904/5	.303" blank cartridges	1.5 M	Woolwich Royal Laboratories	Mk VI with mock bullet
1904/5	.303" blank cartridges	10,000	Colt Gun & Carriage Co.	Mk VI with mock bullet
1905*	.303" MkIIC cartridges	750,000	Egyptian Government	Total for year
1905/5	.303" MkVIC cartridges	6 M	Woolwich Royal Laboratories	
1905/5	.303" MkVIC cartridges	1 M	Admiralty	
1905*	.303" MkIIC cartridges	20,000	Vickers Sons & Maxim	Total for year
1905/6	.297"/.230" Morris Tube MkII	500,000	Colonial Ammunition Co.	Long for Fancotte Cadet Rifle
1905/1	.303" blank MkV cartridges	500,000	Nitrokol Powder Company	
1905/2	.303" MkIIC cartridges	5,000	Greener W. W.	
1905/2	.303" MkIIC cartridges	1 M	Nitrokol Powder Company	
1905/6	.297"/.230" Morris Tube MkII	200,000	Colonial Ammunition Co.	Short

Yr/Month	Type	Quantity	By whom if known	Comments
1905/5	.303" cartridge cases	20,000	Vickers Sons & Maxim	Uncapped & un-necked
1905/11	.303" blank cartridges	250,000	Woolwich Royal Laboratories	Mk V blank without bullet
1906*	.303" MkVIC cartridges	4 M	Woolwich Royal Laboratories	Total for year
1906/5	.303" MkIIC cartridges	10,000	Greener W. W.	
1906*	.303" MkVIC cartridges	171,000	Vickers Sons & Maxim	Total for year
1906*	.297"/.230" Morris Tube MkII	750,000	Colonial Ammunition Co.	Short – Total for year
1906/1	.303" cartridges hollow nosed	50,000	Cama K.R. & Co.	
1906*	.303" MkVIC cartridges	100,000	Cama K.R. & Co.	Total for year
1906/12	.297"/.230" Morris Tube blanks	150,000	Colonial Ammunition Co.	
1906/2	.303" blank cartridges	10,000	Colt Gun & Carriage Co.	With wooden bullets
1906/2	.303" MkVC cartridges	1 M	Egyptian Government	
1906/2	.303" blank cartridges	500,000	Egyptian Government	Without dummy bullet
1906/3	.303" MkV cartridges	500,000	Nitrokol Powder Company	Loaded with Nitrokol powder
1906/9	.303" cartridge cases MkVI	1 M	Colonial Ammunition Co.	Uncapped & unnecked
1906/9	.303" MkVI bullets	500,000	Colonial Ammunition Co.	
1906/9	.303" MkVI envelopes	500,000	Colonial Ammunition Co.	
1906/9	.297"/.230" Morris Tube bullets	2 M	Stock for Abbey Wood	
1907/1	.303" MkVIC cartridges	6,000	Gambia	
1907/1	.303" MkVIC cartridges	2,520	Uganda	
1907*	.303" MkVIC cartridges	148,500	Hong Kong	Total for year
1907/1	.303" MkVIC cartridges	33,000	St Kitts	
1907/1	.303" MkVIC cartridges	6,450	Straits Settlement	
1907/1	.303" MkVIC cartridges	7,500	Penang	
1907*	.303" MkVIC cartridges	20,900	Barbados	Total for year
1907*	.303" MkVIC cartridges	118,800	Trinidad	Total for year
1907/2	.303" MkVIC cartridges	50,000	Somaliland	
1907/3	.303" blanks MkV	7,600	Trinidad	Without mock bullets
1907/3	.297"/.230" Morris Aiming Tube	10,000	Trinidad	
1907/3	.303" MkVIC cartridges	15,000	St Johns Rifle Club	
1907/6	.297"/.230" Morris Aiming Tube	60,000	Colonial Ammunition Co.	
1907/6	.303" MkVIC cartridges	52,000	Vickers Sons & Maxim	
1907*	.303" MkVIC cartridges	300,000	Cama K.R. & Co.	Total for year
1907*	.303" MkVIC cartridges	6.25 M	Woolwich Royal Laboratories	Total for year
1907/4	.303" MkVIC cartridges	33,000	Selonigor	
1908/4	.303" MkVIC cartridges	7 M	Woolwich Royal Laboratories	
1908/11	.303" MkVIC cartridges	350,000	British South Africa Co.	
1908/12	.303" MkVIC cartridges	27,500	British South Africa Co.	For N.W. Rhodesia
1908/9	.303" blank cartridges	30,000	British South Africa Co.	Without bullets
1908/4	.303" MkVIC cartridges	3,300	Crown Agents	
1908/4	.303" MkVIC cartridges	200,000	Cama K.R. & Co.	
1908/9	.303" MkVIC cartridges	50,000	Times Dharwar & Co.	
1909*	.303" MkVIC cartridges	7 M	Woolwich Royal Laboratories	Total for year
1909*	.303" MkVIC cartridges	144,100	British South Africa Co.	Total for year
1909/9	.303" MkVIC cartridges	200,000	Cama K.R. & Co.	
1909/11	7.9mm bullets	207,000	Johnson & Phillips	With cupro nickel jackets
1909/12	.303" MkVIC cartridges	100,000	Times Dharwar & Co.	

Yr/Month	Type	Quantity	By whom if known	Comments
1910/1	7.62mm Russian Nagant	100,000	Danny Nahmias	Pistol cartridges
1910/1	8mm Lebel cartridges	100,000	Danny Nahmias	Pistol cartridges
1910*	.303" MkVIC cartridges	100,000	Muscat Arabia	Total for year
1910*	.303" MkVIC cartridges	2.15 M	Woolwich Royal Laboratories	Total for year
1910/7	.303" MkVII cartridges	3,840,947	Woolwich Royal Laboratories	
1910/7	.303" blank MkV	2,818,650	Woolwich Royal Laboratories	Without bullets
1910/9	.303" experiments Mk VII	18,000	Woolwich Royal Laboratories	Developing MkVII carts
1910/12	.303" MkV C cartridges	1 M	Woolwich Royal Laboratories	
1910/12	.303" MkV C cartridges	20,000	Sudanese Government	
1911*	.303" blanks Mk V	1,085,000	Woolwich Royal Laboratories	Yearly total – w/o bullets
1911*	.303" MkVIC cartridges	1,010,000	Woolwich Royal Laboratories	Total for year
1911*	.303" MkVII cartridges	13.5 M	Woolwich Royal Laboratories	Total for year
1911/3	.303" MkVIC cartridges	14,000	H Seymour King	
1911/4	.303" MkVIC cartridges	2,000	Colonial Ammunition Co.	
1911*	.303" dummy wood bullets	355,726	Colonial Ammunition Co.	
1911/4	aluminium tips for bullets	2,000	Colonial Ammunition Co.	
1911/4	.303" bullets MkVI	2,000	Colonial Ammunition Co.	
1911/7	7.62mm Russian Nagant	10,000	Danny Nahmias	Pistol cartridges
1911/8	.310" Cadet ball rifle cartridges	2.5 M	Commonwealth of Australia	
1912/1	.303" MkV C cartridges	20,000	Egyptian Government	
1912*	.303" MkVII cartridges	14.5 M	Woolwich Royal Laboratories	Total for year
1912/7	.303" blanks with bullets	589,900	Woolwich Royal Laboratories	
1912/6	.303" MkVI bullets	50,000	Kings Norton Metal Co.	
1913*	.303" MkVI cartridges	2,106,907	Woolwich Royal Laboratories	Total for year
1913*	.303" MkV blank cartridges	4,216,200	Woolwich Royal Laboratories	Total for year
1913/4	.303" MkVII cartridges	4 M	Woolwich Royal Laboratories	
1913/11	.303" MkVII cartridges	110,000	Adgey & Murphy	
1913/12	.297"/.230" Morris tube	3 M	Australian Government	Black powder loaded
1914/3	.303" MkVII cartridges	570,000	Wm Exley & Co.	
1914*	.303" MkVII cartridges	58 M	Woolwich Royal Laboratories	Total for year
1914/11	.303" blank with boxwood bullet	1.45 M	Woolwich Royal Laboratories	
1914/11	.303" MkVII cartridges	8 M	Admiralty	
1914/12	.303" MkVI cartridges	20 M	Woolwich Royal Laboratories	
1914/11	.303" blank cartridges	2 M	Woolwich Royal Laboratories	Without bullets
1915/2	Percussion caps	5 M	Colonial Ammunition Co.	
1915*	.303" MkVII cartridge	46.85 M	Woolwich Royal Laboratories	Total for year
1915/5	.303" drill cartridges	900,000	Woolwich Royal Laboratories	With wooden bullets
1915/9	.303" cartridge cases	1.5 M	Kynoch Ltd	
1917/1	8mm Lebel rifle bullets	3.31 M	Kings Norton Metal Co.	
1916/10	.303" blanks without bullets	50,000	Ministry of Munitions	
1917/2	7.62mm Russian Nagant rifle	Unknown	Ministry of Munitions	Prod. 2M per week
1917/4	8mm Lebel rifle bullets	3 M	French Government	Pat.1898 copper bullet
1917/4	7.62mm Russian Nagant rifle	Unknown	Russian Government	Prod. 5M per week
1917/7	.303" drill cartridges	Unlimited	British Government	
1917/8	.303" capped & uncapped cases	300,000	Eley Bros Ltd	
1917/11	.303" blank cartridges	Unknown	Ministry of Munitions	Prod. 100,000 per week

Yr/Month	Type	Quantity	By whom if known	Comments
1918/1	.303" MkVII bullets	5 M	B'Ham Metal & Munitions Co.	
1918/3	.303" MkVII Z cartridges	12,000	D.I.S.A.A.	For standard proof
1918/3	.303" MkVIIZ Red Label	Unknown	Ministry of Munitions	RFC use 5M per week
1918/4	.303" MkVII proof cartridges	18,000	Ministry of Munitions	
1918/5	.303" blank cartridges MkV	Unknown	Ministry of Munitions	50,000 per week
1918/5	.303" cartridge cases	666,500	Perivale Explosives	Uncapped & unnecked
1918/6	.303" MkVII cartridges	4,000	Controller Ministry of Munits.	For waterproof tests
1918/7	.303" MkVIIZ Red Label	Unknown	Ministry of Munitions	RFC use 1.5 M per week
1918/7	.303" MkVII practice cartridges	Unknown	Ministry of Munitions	Up to 300,000 per week
1918/8	.303" MkVI cartridge cases	707,000	Perivale Explosives	Plus caps
1918/8	.303" MkVIIZ Red Label	3,000	Controller of S.A.A.	Charge weight & volume
1919/9	.300" USA ball cartridges	10,000	Controller of S.A.A.	
1919/9	.303" MkVIIZ Red Label	Unknown	Ministry of Munitions	8 million per week
1919/10	.303" MkVIIZ Red Label	10,000	Ministry of Munitions	Standard for proof
1919/10	.303" cases	2,000	Ministry of Munitions	Experimental
1919/10	.303" bullets Mk VII	2,000	Ministry of Munitions	Experimental

5.5.2 WWI cartridge production by the company

In 1915 Mr J.H. Baker, formerly of Birmingham Metal & Munitions Co. took over control of their ammunition works at Leeds and increased their staff from 300 to 700 producing an output of 6,000,000 cartridges per week. Some women were being paid between £1 and £2 per week which resulted in a court case being brought by the Home Office since their duties contravened the hours of work set by the Factories and Workshops' Act. The Judge, however, ruled against action being taken stating the contravention was in the public interests.

5.5.3 WWII and post war metallic cartridge production by the company

During WWII the company had two case and bullet factories in Leeds and two filling factories, one at Abbey Wood near Woolwich Arsenal and another at Farnham outside Knaresborough in Yorkshire. These factories produced both .303" ammunition (approximately 5,000,000 rounds per week) and 15mm Besa and 20mm Hispano Suiza cannon cartridges during WWII. Following the end of the war staff levels were dramatically cut and the few remaining staff were employed breaking down redundant ammunition. During the Korean War and the Berlin Blockade the company sprang back into action manufacturing .303" ball ammunition with production reaching some 600,000 rounds per week. This demand was short lived and after the introduction and adoption of the new 7.62mm NATO calibre and the 30mm Aden cannon they declined to go into full production of these new rounds, based, I believe, on the costs associated with retooling their production lines and the added uncertainty of receiving viable contracts from the MOD during what was predicted to be a period of military calm. The list below was compiled from company records for the period but again it is incomplete since calibres were made which were not listed. (Note within the table the letter M after a number indicates millions.)

Yr/Month	Type	Quantity	By whom if known	Comment
1922/2	.303" MkVII cartridges	3 M	War Office	Cordite
1922/10	.303" MkVII cartridges	1 M	Admiralty	Cordite

Yr/Month	Type	Quantity	By whom if known	Comment
1922/12	.303" drill cartridges	20,000	R.J. Adgey	With boxwood bullets
1923*	.303" MkVII cartridges	7 M	Director of Military Contracts	Total for year – Cordite
1923/9	.303" MkVII cartridges	2 M	Director of Military Contracts	For Admiralty – Cordite
1923/5	.303" MkVII cartridges	2 M	Director of Military Contracts	For Sudan & Egypt – Cordite
1924*	.303" MkVII cartridges	11.75 M	Director of Military Contracts	Total for year – Cordite
1924/12	.303" blanks	275,000	Director of Military Contracts	Without bullets
1925/1	.303" MkVII Red label	500,000	Finnish Government	Cordite for aerial use
1925/5	.303" MkVII cartridges	12 M	Director of Military Contracts	Cordite
1925/5	.303" blanks	3 M	Director of Military Contracts	Without bullets
1925/6	.303" MkVII cartridges	38,000	Miscellaneous orders	Cordite
1925/7	.303" MkVII cartridges	70,000	Sarawak Government	Cordite
1925/10	.303" MkVI cartridges	5 M	South Africa	Cordite
1925/12	.303" MkVII cartridges	80,000	Vickers Ltd	Cordite
1925/12	.303" MkVII cartridges	1 M	Rhodesian Government	Cordite
1926/1	.303" MkVII Z cartridges	50,000	Vickers Ltd	Red Label Air Service
1926/3	.303" MkVII cartridges	250,000	Vickers Ltd	Cordite
1926/5	.303" MkVII cartridges	9 M	Director of Military Contracts	Cordite
1926*	.303" MkVII cartridges	90,130	Miscellaneous orders	Cordite – total for year
1927/1	.303" MkVII cartridges	1 M	Rhodesian Government	Cordite
1927*	.303" MkVII cartridges	712,000	Miscellaneous orders	Cordite – total for year
1927*	.303" MkVII cartridges	1,215,900	Vickers Ltd	Cordite – total for year
1927	7.65mm Bolivian Mauser	52,000	Vickers Ltd	NC powder
1928/1	.303" MkVII cartridges	1 M	Rhodesian Government	Cordite
1928/6	.303" MkVII cartridges	9 M	Director Army Contracts	Cordite
1928/7	.5" Vickers SA ball MkIIZ	5,000	Director Army Contracts	NC powder
1928*	.303" Mk VII cartridges	76,200	Vickers Ltd	Total for year
1928*	7.65mm Bolivian Mauser	35,000	Vickers Ltd	Total for year NC powder
1929*	.5" Vickers SA ball MkIIZ	37,500	Director Army Contracts	Total for year – Cordite
1929/6	.303" MkVII cartridges	9 M	Director Army Contracts	
1929*	.303" MkVII cartridges	22,000	Miscellaneous orders	Cordite – total for year
1929/5	.303" MkVII cartridges	94,000	Vickers Ltd	Cordite
1929/5	.303" MkVII cartridges	140,000	Salter & Varge	Cordite
1930/7	.303" MkVII cartridges	300,000	Director Army Contracts	Cordite
1930/6	.303" MkVII cartridges	43,500	Vickers Ltd	Cordite
1930/6	.276" Pedersen Ball	50,000	Vickers Ltd	Streamline 126 grn bullet
1931*	.303" MkVII cartridges	4.5 M	Director Army Contracts	Cordite – total for year
1931*	.303" MkVII cartridges	20,000	Vickers Ltd	Cordite – total for year
1931*	.303" MkVII cartridges	6,000	Miscellaneous orders	Cordite – total for year
1932*	.303" MkVII cartridges	6 M	Director Army Contracts	Cordite – total for year
1933*	.303" MkVII cartridges	6 M	Director Army Contracts	Cordite – total for year
1932	.303" MkVII cartridges	5,000	Greenveld & Hicks	Cordite
1933	.303" MkVII cartridges	260,100	Vickers Ltd	Cordite
1933	.303" MkVII cartridges	20,000	Government of Sarawak	Cordite
1933*	.303" MkVII cartridges	20,000	Miscellaneous orders	Cordite – total for year
1934*	.303" MkVII cartridges	7 M	Director Army Contracts	Cordite – total for year
1934	.5" Vickers SA ball MkIIZ	350,000	Director Army Contracts	For Admiralty NC powder

Yr/Month	Type	Quantity	By whom if known	Comment
1934	.303" MkVI cartridges	28,000	Union of South Africa	Cordite
1934	.303" MkVII cartridges	40,000	Union of South Africa	Cordite
1935*	.303" MkVII cartridges	7 M	Director Army Contracts	Cordite – total for year
1936*	.303" MkVII cartridges	9 M	Director Army Contracts	Cordite – total for year
1935	.303" MkVII cartridges	2 M	Director Army Contracts	For RAF
1936*	.303" MkVII cartridges	17,000	Miscellaneous orders	Small mark
1937*	.303" MkVII cartridges	15 M	Director Army Contracts	Cordite – total for year
1937*	.303" MkVII cartridges	124,830	Miscellaneous orders	Small mark
1938*	.303" MkVII cartridges	10 M	Director Army Contracts	Cordite – total for year
1938*	.303" MkVII cartridges	33,000	Miscellaneous orders	Small mark
1939*	.303" MkVII cartridges	2 M	Director Army Contracts	Cordite – total for year
1939*	.303" MkVII cartridges	31 M	Ministry of Supply	Special for RAF use
1940*	.303" MkVII cartridges	100M	Director of Contracts	Special for RAF use
In 1940	.303" MkVII cartridges	5 M per wk	Director of Contracts	Increased to weekly output
1940	.303" cartridge cases	100,000	Ministry of Supply	Empty but necked
1940	15mm A.P. MkIZ Besa	1 M	Director of Contracts	
1940	.303" MkVII cartridges	100 M	Director of Contracts	Special for RAF use
1940	.303" MkVII cartridges	670,000	Misc & for LDV forces	LDV = Home Guard
1941	.303" MkVII cartridges	100 M	Director of Contracts	For use in machine guns
1941	.303" MkVII cartridges	14,337,000	D.O.C. Ministry of Supply	
1941	.303" MkVII cartridges	110.5 M	Director of Contracts	Special for RAF use
1941	.303" MkVII cartridges	2,658,900	Misc & for LDV forces	LDV = Home Guard
1942	.303" MkVII cartridges	240 M	D.O.C. Ministry of Supply	
1942	15mm A.P. MkIZ Besa	1,503,750	D.O.C. Ministry of Supply	Armour piercing
1942	15mm A.P. MkIZ Besa	2,660,000	D.O.C. Ministry of Supply	Tracer/armour piercing
1942	.303" Armour piercing	51 M	D.O.C. Ministry of Supply	W MkI Gomersal
1942	15mm A.P. MkIZ Besa	10,500	D.O.C. Ministry of Supply	Velocity experiments
1942	.303" MkVII cartridges	262,000	Misc & Home Guard	
1943	.303" MkVII cartridges	6 M	D.O.C. Ministry of Supply	Gomersal
1943	20mm Hispano MkIZ ball	1M	D.O.C. Ministry of Supply	
1943	15mm A.P. MkIZ Besa	527,000	D.O.C. Ministry of Supply	Amour piercing & tracer
1943	.303" MkVII cartridges	200 M	D.O.C. Ministry of Supply	
1943	.303" MkVII cartridges	560,000	Miscellaneous orders	
1943	.303" cartridges	1,236	Ministry of Supply	Experiments Guilding metal envelope
1943	20mm Hispano	3.5 M	D.O.C. Ministry of Supply	Incendiary/ high explosive
1944	.303" MkVII cartridges	6 M	D.O.C. Ministry of Supply	
1944	20mm Hispano A.P. MkIV	2 M	D.O.C. Ministry of Supply	Armour piercing
1944	20mm Hispano cases	3.5 M	D.O.C. Ministry of Supply	
1944	.303" cartridge cases	36,360	D.O.C. Ministry of Supply	Experimental tip annealment
1944	9mm bullets	5,000	D.O.C. Ministry of Supply	Experimental G&B design
1944	9mm bullets	5,340	D.O.C. Ministry of Supply	MS inside bullet tip, lead base sleeve
1945	.303" MkVII cartridges	70 M	D.O.C. Ministry of Supply	Cordite & NC
1948	.303" Mk 7 cartridges	46 M	D.O.C. Ministry of Supply	NC
1951	20mm Hispano cases	3.6 M	D.O.C. Ministry of Supply	Empty cases
1951	.303" Mk 7 cartridges	32,344,000	D.O.C. Ministry of Supply	Ball cordite
1951	.303" Mk 7 cartridges	50,000	Bisley Camp	Ball cordite

Yr/Month	Type	Quantity	By whom if known	Comment
1952	.303" Mk 7 cartridges	723,000	Bisley Camp	Ball Cordite
1953	.303" Mk 7 cartridges	20.1 M	D.O.C. Ministry of Supply	Ball Cordite
1953	.303" Mk 7 cartridges	280,000	Bisley Camp	Ball Cordite
1953	.303" Mk 7 cartridges	1 M	Canadian Government	Ball Cordite
1953	30mm Aden H.V. cases	101,004	D.O.C. Ministry of Supply	Empty cases
1954	.303" Mk 7 cartridges	32.24 M	D.O.C. Ministry of Supply	Ball Cordite
1954	20mm Hispano cases	103,460	D.O.C. Ministry of Supply	Empty cases
1954	30mm Aden H.V. cases	400,000	D.O.C. Ministry of Supply	Empty cases
1954	.303" Mk 7 cartridges	260,000	Bisley Camp	Ball Cordite
1955	D.O.C. Ministry of Supply	1.2 M	D.O.C. Ministry of Supply	Empty cases
1955	.303" Mk 7 cartridges	5,000	Canadian Government	Ball Cordite
1955	.303" Mk 7 blanks	250,000	Government of Holland	
1956	.303" Mk 7 cartridges	13,749,600	D.O.C. Ministry of Supply	
1956	7.62mm NATO ball	10,000	D.O.C. Ministry of Supply	Experimental
1957	7.62mm NATO ball	10,600	Per Mr MacLagan	
1957	30mm Aden H.V. cases	341,900	D.O.C. Ministry of Supply	
1958	.303" Proof cartridges	50,000	Birmingham Proof House	Mk 7 over pressure proof

5.5.4 Examples of metallic cartridges produced by the company

5.5.4.1 Examples of the company's rifle and light machine gun cartridges

An example of one of 200,000 Greenwood & Batley .303" Rubin cartridges made in March 1888 for the British Government. This specimen was from the former Greenwood & Batley factory collection. This was the basis on which the standard .303" cartridge was developed, a calibre used by the British Armed forces from 1889 to the 1950s when it was replaced by the 7.62mm x 51mm NATO cartridge

LEFT TO RIGHT: .303"Mk II C, .303"MkIV Dum-Dum, .30-06 Springfield, 7.62mm x 51mm NATO made in 1957
LYING DOWN: 7.62mm x 51mm NATO round made in 1958

LEFT TO RIGHT: *The first four are 8mm x 50R French Lebel rounds; the fourth specimen is fitted with a wooden bullet. Rounds 5, 6 and 7 are examples of variants by G&B of the 7.62mm x 54R Russian Mosin Nagant cartridges. Specimen 6 lying down has a rounded base with a raised headstamp*

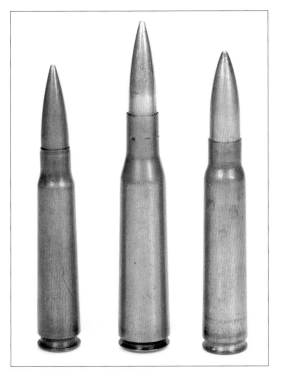

LEFT TO RIGHT: *.276" Pedersen, .276" Enfield Experimental and 7.65mm x 53mm Mauser*

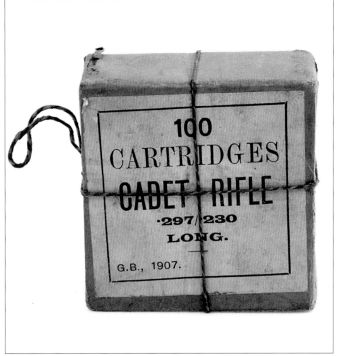

Packet of Morris tube .297"/.230" Morris Long made by G&B in 1907

5.5.4.2 Examples of the company's revolver cartridges

LEFT TO RIGHT: *.455" Mk I revolver, 8mm French Lebel revolver, 8mm French Lebel revolver and 7.62mm Russian Nagant revolver*

5.5.4.3 Examples of the company's heavy machine gun ammunition

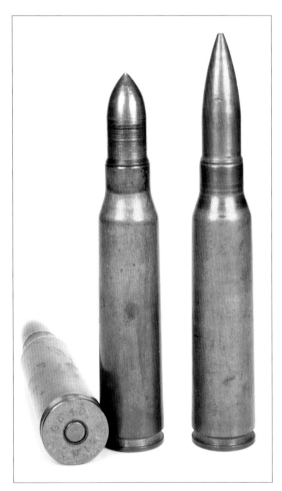

G&B 15mm Besa machine gun ammunition. The central specimen is an experimental variant

G & B produced quantities of .5" Vickers machine gun ammunition between the two world wars until final adoption by the Ministry of Defence of the .50" Browning round as a better alternative

5.5.5 Examples of their headstamps on metallic ammunition

5.5.5.1 Examples of their headstamps on pistol ammunition

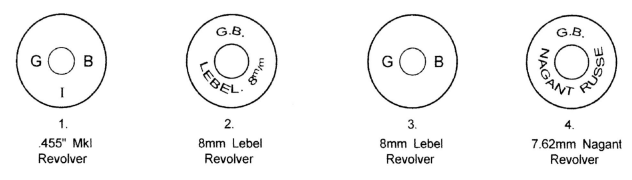

1.	2.	3.	4.
.455" MkI Revolver	8mm Lebel Revolver	8mm Lebel Revolver	7.62mm Nagant Revolver

5.5.5.2 Examples of their headstamps on heavy machine gun ammunition

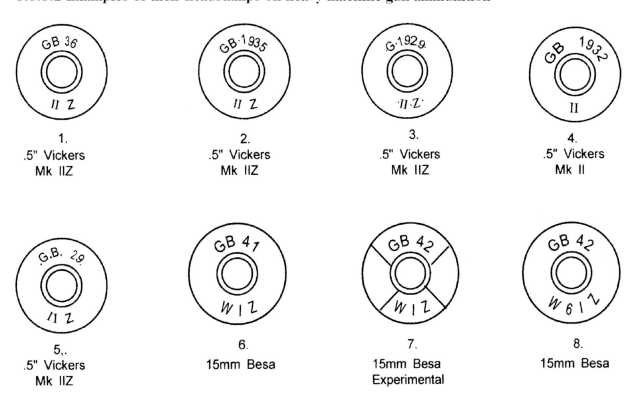

1.	2.	3.	4.
.5" Vickers Mk IIZ	.5" Vickers Mk IIZ	.5" Vickers Mk IIZ	.5" Vickers Mk II

5,.	6.	7.	8.
.5" Vickers Mk IIZ	15mm Besa	15mm Besa Experimental	15mm Besa

NOTE: 'Z' in the headstamp indicated armour piercing

5.5.5.3 Examples of their headstamps on rifle and light machine gun ammunition

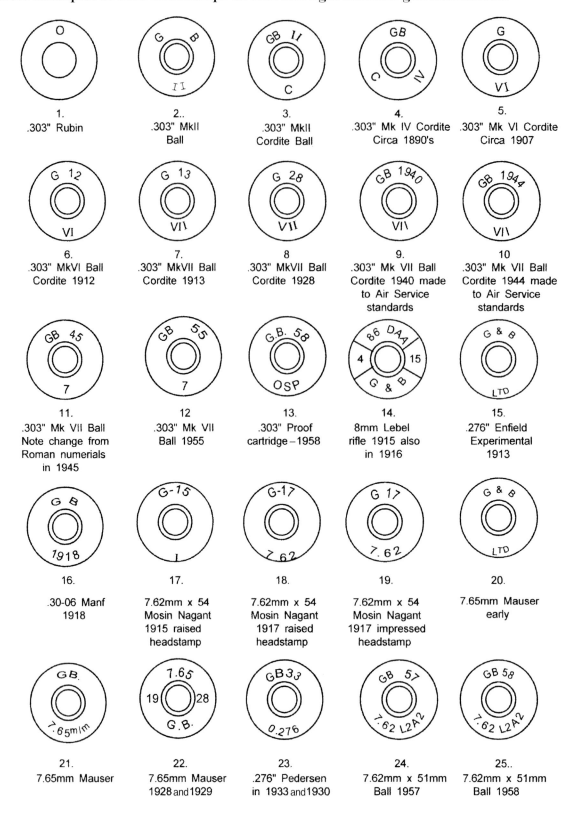

1.
.303" Rubin

2..
.303" MkII
Ball

3.
.303" MkII
Cordite Ball

4.
.303" Mk IV Cordite
Circa 1890's

5.
.303" Mk VI Cordite
Circa 1907

6.
.303" MkVI Ball
Cordite 1912

7.
.303" MkVII Ball
Cordite 1913

8
.303" MkVII Ball
Cordite 1928

9.
.303" Mk VII Ball
Cordite 1940 made
to Air Service
standards

10
.303" Mk VII Ball
Cordite 1944 made
to Air Service
standards

11.
.303" Mk VII Ball
Note change from
Roman numerials
in 1945

12
.303" Mk VII
Ball 1955

13.
.303" Proof
cartridge – 1958

14.
8mm Lebel
rifle 1915 also
in 1916

15.
.276" Enfield
Experimental
1913

16.
.30-06 Manf
1918

17.
7.62mm x 54
Mosin Nagant
1915 raised
headstamp

18.
7.62mm x 54
Mosin Nagant
1917 raised
headstamp

19.
7.62mm x 54
Mosin Nagant
1917 impressed
headstamp

20.
7.65mm Mauser
early

21.
7.65mm Mauser

22.
7.65mm Mauser
1928 and 1929

23.
.276" Pedersen
in 1933 and 1930

24.
7.62mm x 51mm
Ball 1957

25..
7.62mm x 51mm
Ball 1958

5.6.1 Post WWII shotgun cartridge production by the company

At the end of WWII it was a natural action for the Farnham factory to turn its attention to the manufacture and loading of shotgun ammunition for the sportsman, with the idle military calibre ammunition manufacturing machines sited at Armley Road, Leeds being converted to manufacture shotgun cartridge cases.

The problem faced by G&B in relation to shotgun cartridge production was the future uncertainty of supply of suitable propellants and primers, since at the end of the war the major producer was ICI which was producing Curtis's & Harvey's Smokeless Diamond, Schultze and EC powders. Although ICI was initially happy to supply these powders to G&B, since both companies were going to be in direct competitive opposition G&B made a decision to seek alternative sources of components, which initially led them to import both Belgian percussion caps and a Belgian powder called Clermonite. The cartridge cases were produced from orange coloured rolled paper tubes and passed to the Albion Works at Leeds for the brass bases to be fitted before being returned to Farnham to be loaded. Clearly there were problems with the company's early production which manifested itself in split brass base rims and the generation of a nasty kick being felt by users which was directly associated with the use of Clermonite powder.

A natural response to these problems resulted in two actions: they decided to introduce their own propellant suitable for use in shotgun cartridges which gained the name Greenbat and to manufacture their own percussion caps. The latter task was relatively simple as they had been making machinery for the manufacture of percussion caps for a number of years. The propellant name given by G&B to their shotgun powder Greenbat was odd in that it was purplish; however this was a trade mark already in use by the company and so was also applied to their powder. This powder successfully tackled the problem associated with kickback by bringing down chamber pressures and giving superior patterns.

5.6.2 Shotgun cartridges produced by the company for others

During the course of the company's production of shotgun cartridges, they, like ICI and many others, would produce loaded cartridges or primed cases for gunsmiths and ironmongers bearing the gunsmith's or ironmonger's name if the order was for sufficient quantities. This is a list of companies which are known to have used this service:

H. R Adams, Ironmongers, 120 High Street, Crediton, Devon

T. Adsett & Son, 101 High Street, Guildford

J. Bentley, 309 Halifax Road, Liversedge, Yorkshire

Bonner Williams, Tonbridge

B.E. Chaplin, Winchester

Howard A. Davies, 6 Southgate Street, Winchester, Hampshire

Elton Stores, Darlington

John H. Gill & Sons Ltd, Leeming Bar

Globemaster Arms & Ammunition, 79 Oldstead Avenue, Hull

Goughs Ironmongers of Hunsingore, Yorkshire

P.D. Malloch, Perth

Mackenzie & Duncan, Brechin, Tayside

Mullerite Cartridge Co., Birmingham

Steve Smith, 42 High Friar Street, Newcastle

T. Stensby, 12 Withy Grove, Manchester

Jas. Watson, London

A.F. Webster, 79 Oldstead Avenue, Hull

George L. Woods, Ovington, Norfolk

T. Page Wood, Bristol

Other important contracts gained by the company included contracts for shotgun cartridges for the Royal Canadian Air Force to train pilots and rear gunners in the concept of lead, and for pest control by the Ministry of Agriculture e.g. A.E.C. Grey Squirrel, A.E.C., Pest Control. (A.E.C. stood for the title Agricultural Executive Committee who controlled the issue of sporting ammunition during WWII.)

It is also clear that the company salesmen also acquired orders for overseas customers and specimens will be encountered bearing the names Komfo Anokye (imported by J. Kaddo & Bros, Gold Coast) and another imported by MY Badir, Kuwait.

The Gamemaster cartridge was made by G&B for Globemaster Arms & Ammunition, which operated from 79 Oldstead Avenue, Hull. This address was also used by A.F. Webster who also used the brand name Gamemaster

Examples of cartridges made for others. LEFT TO RIGHT: *Specimens 1, 2, 6 and 7 standing were made for Eltons Stores, Darlington. Specimen 3 was made for sale in Kuwait, specimen 4 was made for J. Kaddo & Bros, Gold Coast, specimen 5 was made for the Royal Canadian Air Force for training rear gunners and pilots and the specimen lying down was made for Howard A. Davies of Winchester*

Cartridges made for or tubes supplied to other companies. LEFT TO RIGHT: *J. Dickson, Edinburgh, 'Challenge' by Jas Watson, 'Red Seal' and 'Champion' by Mullerite Cartridge Company, Birmingham, Page Wood and J. Bentley 309 Halifax Road, Liversedge, Yorkshire* LYING DOWN: *'Aladix Ventura' for an unknown company and 'Ace Long Range' for the Mullerite Cartridge Co.*

The 'Matchless' shotgun cartridge made for P.D. Malloch by Greenwood & Batley

Elton Stores sample specimen taken from box on right

5.6.3 Examples of the company's own shotgun cartridges

LEFT TO RIGHT: *'Skyrack', 'A.E.C. Pest Control', 'Standard Load', 'Trap Shooting Load', 'A.E.C. Grey Squirrel'.* LYING DOWN: *The 'Greenwood'*

The company also had a range of their own brand named cartridges which included:

The Claybird
The Greenwood
The Skyrack
Standard Load
Trap Shooting Load

The 'Skyrack' was described as a general purpose 2¾" cartridge with a 1¼ oz load with ⅝" brass head and steel lined case; it was first listed in the companies sales catalogue in 1964 so was short lived in terms of production numbers.

The 'Claybird' was described as a trapshooting 2½" cartridge with a 1⅛ oz load with ⁵⁄₁₆" brass head and weatherproof dipped. It was first listed in the company's sales catalogue in 1964 so it too was limited in terms of the numbers produced. In the 1963 price list the identical load was allocated to their cartridge which bore the name 'Trapshooting'.

The company's 'General Purpose' cartridge was available in either 2½" or 2¾" chambering. The 2½" version had a 1¹⁄₁₆ oz load, a ⁵⁄₁₆" brass head and was waterproof dipped with a crimped closure. The 2¾" version had a 1⅛ oz load, a ⁵⁄₁₆" brass head was steel lined and was waterproof dipped with a crimped closure. Both were available in shot sizes 1–7 except No. 2.

As far as I have been able to establish the company only manufactured shotgun cartridges in 12 bore using either orange or red paper cases. The cases will be encountered with both rolled paper turnovers and star crimp closures.

The last adverts for the company's shotgun cartridges appeared during the early 1960s when the UK was hit by a myxomatosis epidemic which rapidly decimated the rabbit population. At this point sales plummeted and the company decided to terminate production.

5.6.4 Examples of headstamps which appeared on Greenwood & Batley shotgun cartridges

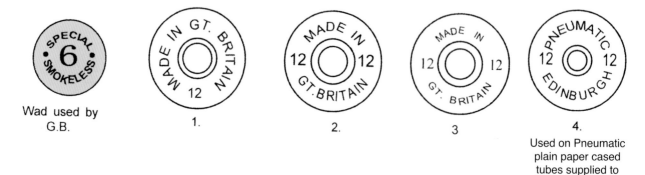

Wad used by G.B.

1.

2.

3

4.
Used on Pneumatic plain paper cased tubes supplied to Pneumatic

5.6.5 Company adverts relating to shotgun cartridges

The last advert for their shotgun cartridges appeared in *Guns Review* in March 1962, however the company's price list which used the illustrated advert as its frontispiece was still being issued in July 1964. It is also interesting to note that in the inside of this list and on its outer cover it specifically states that their cartridges can be supplied with either rolled or crimped closures, based on the customer's request, so unlike other competitors rolled turnover samples cannot be used to date specimens.

5.7 The end of the company

In the late 1960s Greenwood & Batley became part of the Fairbairn-Lawson Group. However demand for the company's products waned and in April 1980 the official receiver was called in, resulting in some 480 employees being made redundant. The company was acquired by Hunslet Holdings for £1.65 million who continued to use the Greenbat name for their battery locomotives. By 1984 the work had been transferred to Jack Lane and the Albion Works was mothballed. In 1987 the site was sold and the old works demolished.

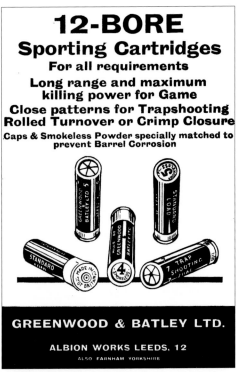

LEFT:
This type of advert
appeared in Guns Review
between September 1961
and December 1961

BELOW:
Tin plate sign designed to
be attachments to the
walls of gunsmiths' shops

CHAPTER 6
Trent Guns & Cartridges Ltd

6.1 The company's history

The first reference I can find to this company occurred in the *Sporting Goods Review* in May 1929 where it stated that Trent Guns & Cartridges Ltd had recently built a very large cartridge loading factory with up to date loading equipment in Grimsby.

The company owes its origins to a family named King. The founding member, namely Ald. Thomas King started a Liverine group of companies in the 1880s. He was a Grimsby man and by the 1930s his three sons had expanded the original business considerably. They decided to split the original company into three separate units. Clover Dairies was taken by his eldest son Harold King, the Trent Gun & Cartridge was taken over by Claude King whilst Hendric King, the youngest son, stayed with Henry Bright & Sons, who specialised in the manufacture of piccalilli and Ticklers plum and apple jam.

The cartridge company was originally situated within the Liverine companies' yard in Fraser Street, Grimsby (at the Eleanor Street and Weelsby Street corner) and this is where their shot tower was to appear, which for many years stood as a local land mark. By 1936 the main section of the factory had moved to Welholme Road, Grimsby; however the shot tower remained in situ and continued production to supply the new site.

Mr Thomas King
(Reproduced with kind permission of Mrs M. Barnett)

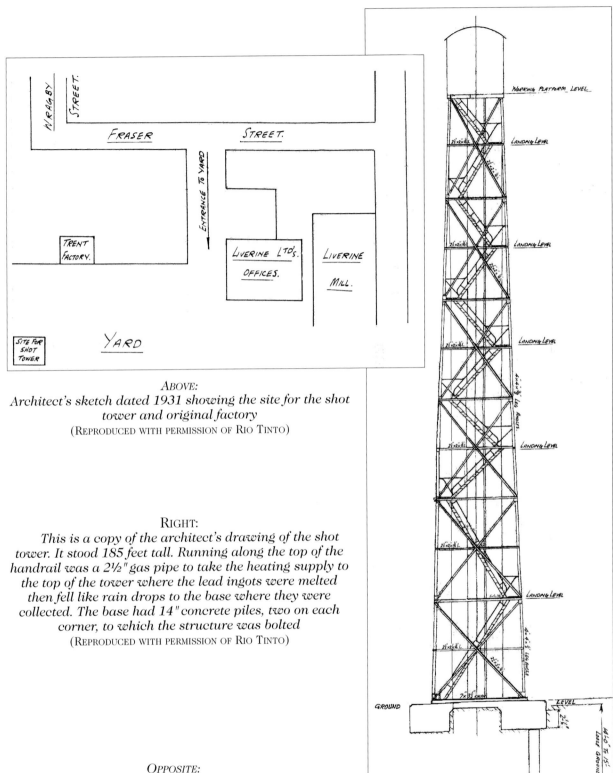

ABOVE:
Architect's sketch dated 1931 showing the site for the shot tower and original factory
(REPRODUCED WITH PERMISSION OF RIO TINTO)

RIGHT:
This is a copy of the architect's drawing of the shot tower. It stood 185 feet tall. Running along the top of the handrail was a 2½" gas pipe to take the heating supply to the top of the tower where the lead ingots were melted then fell like rain drops to the base where they were collected. The base had 14" concrete piles, two on each corner, to which the structure was bolted
(REPRODUCED WITH PERMISSION OF RIO TINTO)

OPPOSITE:
Mr Claude King, the owner of Trent Guns & Cartridge Company with his wife and children
(REPRODUCED WITH THE KIND PERMISSION OF MRS M. BARNETT)

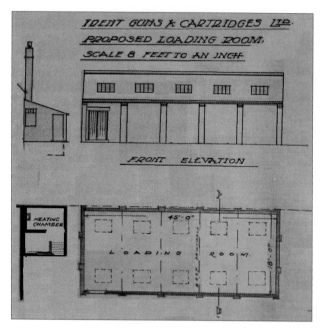

The new site where the cartridge cases where manufactured, printed and loaded was initially relatively compact as shown in the architect's drawing, however it was to be later extended by adding more bays to the original structure.

An examination of the Police Watch Committee Minutes revealed that on 9 July 1930 the company was granted a licence to keep mixed explosives at the site of Bargate Farm, Scartho which is near Grimsby. These minutes also show three separate licences being renewed in May 1932, whilst in July the same year a further application was granted for the site at Bargate Farm. From subsequent enquiries it appears that the name Bargate Farm was an erroneous title since a farm bearing this name did not exist before, during or after this period. The only evidence of the location of the company's explosives magazines was found on the planning application file dated 1934 which indicates its presence some distance off Patrick Street.

The cartridge company's site off Welholme Road
(Reproduced with the kind permission of North East Lincolnshire Archives)

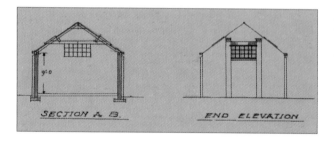

Below:
The company's site in Welholme Road
(Reproduced with the kind permission of North East Lincolnshire Archives)

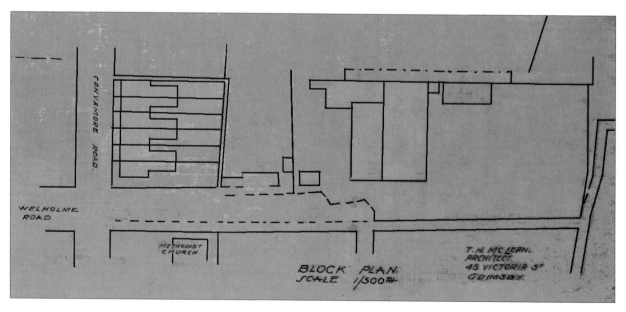

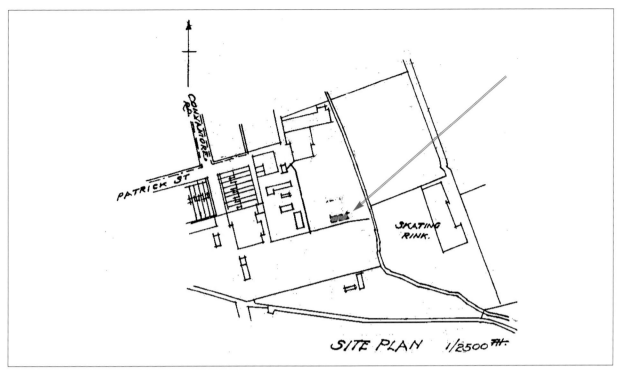

Site map of company's explosives store
(REPRODUCED WITH THE KIND PERMISSION OF NORTH EAST LINCOLNSHIRE ARCHIVES)

During WWII the company was involved in the manufacture of fuses used in mortar bombs and 35mm shells. This work employed ten female staff who were sent to replace ten men from Gateshead, who, apparently were more interested in sleeping during the night shift rather than working. Their actions resulted in the return of 10,000,000 defective fuses for the ladies to rectify.

In the spring of 1946 the company applied for an Explosives Licence to enable its cartridges to be made on the site in Welholme Road; however on 19 March just before the Watch Committee gave it their initial decision,

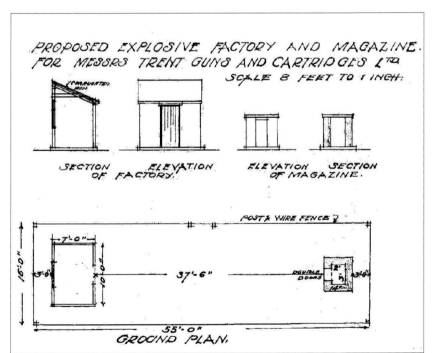

Architect's drawing of company's explosives store
(REPRODUCED WITH THE KIND PERMISSION OF NORTH EAST LINCOLNSHIRE ARCHIVES)

the Managing Director Mr Claude King, aged 62 years and who resided in Abbey Park Road, Grimsby, shot himself in the head whilst in his office at the factory. The subsequent Coroner's enquiry returned a verdict that Mr King had died of self inflicted gunshot wounds in the head, whilst the balance of his mind was disturbed through illness. Although Mr King suffered from diabetes, other witnesses stated that he had been depressed by the new restrictions imposed on this type of industry during the change over from war to peace time working and that he had been unable to acquire the new machinery he needed for cartridge production. Clearly Mr King had grounds for his concerns, since shortly afterwards the new application for an Explosives Licence for the Welholme Road site was turned down by the North East Lincolnshire Council, although it had the full backing of a Government Department.

At the end of the war the company continued to manufacture shotgun cartridges. However the drop in demand and the competition from its main rival, ICI, resulted in the company concentrating on the manufacture of lead pipes which it had been involved in for some time before WWII with a company entitled Trent Lead Pipe Co., of Welholme East, Grimsby. This company was certainly listed back in the 1936 Grimsby Directory and presumably existed before this date. Plastic and copper piping were however soon to replace lead and with that came the scare associated with lead poisoning when people drank tap water which had passed through lead piping. Finally in the spring of 1953 Trent Guns & Cartridges Limited went into liquidation and closed in 1954. The old company's site was acquired by Birds Eye Foods and the shot tower was demolished.

Abbey Park Road, Grimsby
(PHOTOGRAPH USED COURTESY OF THE EAST LINCOLNSHIRE COUNCIL LIBRARY SERVICE)

6.2 Work staff and accidents at the site

In 1936 Mabel Low, aged 29 years, of 106 Elsenham Road, Little Coates, the forewoman at the factory received a fatal injury to her stomach when a .410" double barrelled shot pistol discharged one of its barrels into her lower body. Although two other ladies were in the room at the time they did not see what happened and it was surmised that the loaded and presumably cocked pistol was under some sacks and discharged when she threw some more sacks on top of it.

At 7.45am on 12 January 1942 a violent explosion ran through the factory killing two of the female members of staff, both aged 15 years, namely Hilda Mary Baker of Wintringham Street and Pauline Lee of Lord Street, both Grimsby residents. Wartime censorship prevented the emergence of the exact cause of the explosion, however it was known that the two ladies were in the act of entering the detonator building when the explosion occurred killing them instantaneously.

A former entry in the Bygones section of the *Grimsby Telegraph* reported that in 1937 a Joan Swithinbank, aged 17 years was employed by the company as their saleswoman. Her job entailed travelling around the country on a Francis Barnett motorcycle. Her salary was £2 per week plus petrol. Her duties included visiting Customs & Excise offices in order to identify parties holding gun licences and, having obtained the information, she would send it back to the factory, where colleagues would then send details and lists of their products to these potential customers. It is also recorded that the Works Manager was a Ted Damms, whilst a Jack Sowden was in charge of the lead machine which made the material for the shot tower. By 1946 the new Works Manager was a Roy Wildman of 23 Rialto Avenue, Grimsby.

6.3 Cartridge production

6.3.1 Shotgun cartridge brands manufactured by the company and the company's related adverts

It was claimed in one of the company's adverts that at the time of its issue they were one of the only two companies making sporting cartridges cases in Britain. Although not stated in the advert the second producer must at that time have been ICI.

During the company's production period it made the following branded and unbranded shotgun cartridges: A.E.C. Rook, Best Smokeless, Deep Shell, Favourite, London, .410" Short (2"), .410" Long (2½"), unnamed, Spartan Deep Shell, Spartan, Super Range, Smokeless Air Lord, Supply Cert and Cosmo.

From remaining specimens it appears that the company mainly produced cartridges in the common calibres of 12 bore, 16 bore and .410" and to-date I have yet to encounter specimens in other gauges. Clearly the company were not averse at some period to importing foreign cases and loading them in Grimsby with their own shot.

The cartridges produced by the company were made for the cheap end of the market although their advertising material claimed some of their specimens were steel lined and were being offered at the same price as most of their competitors' unlined cartridges.

'Spartan' and 'London' brand cartridges were made by Trent for the Cartridge Syndicate Ltd, 20–23 Holborn, London EC1. An advert printed in 1935 stated that this syndicate had been formed the previous year to supply gamekeepers and sportsmen with cartridges at lower prices than they had been accustomed to.

Unlike their competitors, this company does not appear to have made many cartridges for other gunsmiths or ironmongers; or if they did they did not normally permit those parties to have their names printed on the tubes. The only examples I have encountered were A.H. Martin of Cross Ash, Abergavenny, Monmouthshire, (where his name was added under a Trent Best Smokeless marking) and one marked 'Favourite Loaded in Ireland with High Grade Smokeless Powder', where the case was made for an unknown customer, together with a specimen made bearing the name F.C. Oakey, Stafford with a trade brand name of 'The O.K.'.

During the WWII the company obtained some contracts for shotgun cartridges from the War Office; specimens will be encountered with WD arrows on their cases which were made either for issue to the Home Guard or for training RAF pilots and rear gunners.

1934
The Cheapest Cartridge in the World.
SPARTAN

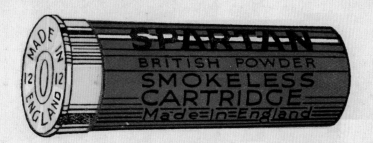

$\frac{5}{16}$ brass loaded with 33 grains of a good British Smokeless Powder and $1\frac{1}{16}$ oz. of Shot.

10/- per 100.
Sold by Cartridge Dealers all over Great Britain.

A BRITISH CARTRIDGE
British Powder, British Case, British Shot and British Wads.

CARTRIDGE SYNDICATE, Ltd..
20/23, HOLBORN, LONDON, E.C. 1.

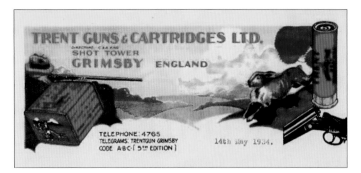

Letter heading in 1934

The "TRENT" Cartridge.

THE "TRENT" Cartridge has a $\frac{5}{16}$th inch brass head, and a metal lining. It is loaded with 33 grains of the very finest smokeless powder and 1.$\frac{1}{16}$ ounces of the best chilled shot, and has an exceedingly quick cap and is well wadded with a good quality greased felt wad.

Facts About Cartridges

A Cartridge is not a good killing cartridge at long range unless it is a fast velocity cartridge, that is to say the shot must travel at a high speed after the cartridge has been fired.

Good penetration cannot be obtained without velocity.

To get velocity a cartridge must be metal lined.

It is true velocity can be obtained by reducing the quantity of shot, but the TRENT cartridge has a standard load of the best chilled shot.

The TRENT cartridge is a high velocity cartridge.

Only 12 Bore made.

It is not the out=side appearance of a cartridge that kills, but the interior — Note the metal lining of the "TRENT."

The "TRENT" is the best killing Cartridge.

Price.
3/6 per box.
(14/- 100.)

6.3.2 Examples of the shotgun cartridges manufactured by the company

Variants of the 'Spartan' cartridge in 12 bore

Note WD marking on specimen lying down and untitled aluminium based specimen to its right

Early packaging on the 'London' cartridge

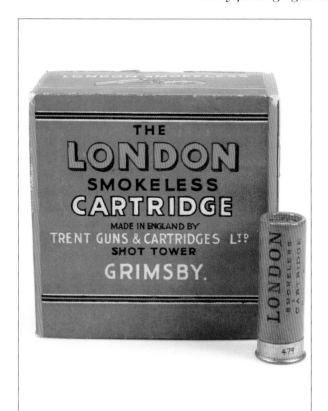

Later packaging on the 'London' cartridge

Trent .410" Long

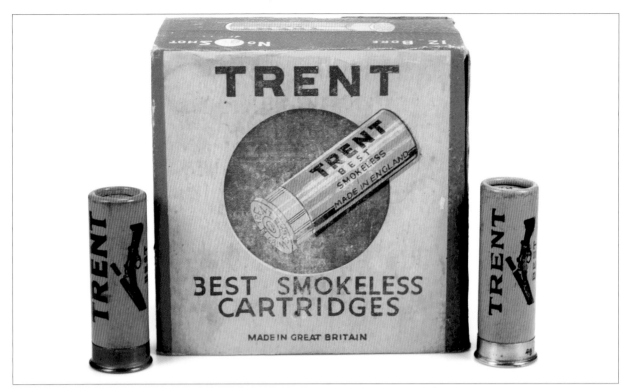

Example of 'Trent' cartridge box and cartridges

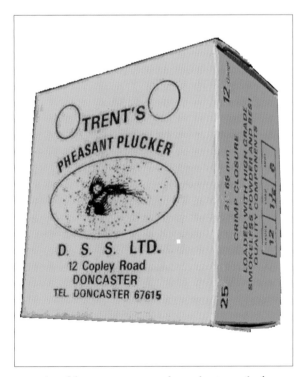

A seldom encountered product made for a second party. I have no knowledge of the identity of this company

A rare specimen box showing the tubes manufactured by the company

6.3.3 Headstamps encountered on their shotgun cartridges

1.

Found on 12 bore
Trent Smokeless

2.

Found on 12 bore London
Smokeless, 12 bore Trent,
Spartan Smokeless and on
and un-named cartridge
with an aluminium head

3.

Found on 12 bore
A.E.C. Rook

4.

Found on 12 bore
Spartan and Spartan
Deep Shell

5.

Found on 16 bore
Trent with
foreign case

6.

Found on 12
bore Trent

7.

Found on 12
bore Trent

8.

Found on 12
bore Trent

9

Found on 12 bore
Air Lord

10.

Found on pink cased
un-named .410"

CHAPTER 7
Cogswell & Harrison Ltd and the
Cogschultze Ammunition & Powder Co. Ltd

7.1.1 The company's history prior to the formation of Cogschultze

The London gunmaker Cogswell & Harrison was established in 1770 and in 1896 it became a limited company.

Clearly the company was deeply interested in designing its small arms to match the pressures generated by cartridges. In a book entitled *Sporting Gun and Gun Powder* written by Frederick Toms in 1890, a Cogswell factory advert indicated it was the manufacturer of scientific instruments for testing ammunition and explosives and gave an illustration of the below device, supplied to gunmakers by the company to test the pressures generated by their shotgun cartridges at various points down the barrel. This specimen indicates it was made by Cogswell in 1887.

Although numerous specimens of shotgun cartridges are encountered bearing the Cogswell & Harrison name, few collectors will be aware that the company once made its own shotgun cartridge cases, primers and powder and at one stage amalgamated with the Schultze Gunpowder Company to form a company named Cogschultze. This event occurred between 1906 and 1915.

On 26 February 1906 Cogswell & Harrison Ltd made an application to the Justices of the Peace at Staines to erect a powder factory on its estate at Colnbrook which it later purchased in June that year and which also housed a shooting ground for the company. The proposed site was at Poyle, Middlesex, close to Colnbrook Railway Station. The application was objected to by the local residents but was supported by evidence from F.W. Jones, one of the two leading British ballisticians and since the site met all the Home Office provisions for safety, the Justices found it no more objectionable than any other application and the Explosives Licence was finally granted on 21 August 1906.

In June 1907 the sporting press revealed that the Cogswell & Harrison Manufacturing Co., a subsidiary of the primary gun making company, had been manufacturing most of its sporting cartridge cases, primers and a powder named Vicmos (the trade name of which was first registered in 1905) at its site at Colnbrook for some considerable time. If you examine the subsequently illustrated headstamps encountered on this company's cartridges, you will find one, which at 6 o'clock bears the initials C.H.M.C. These are the initials of the subsidiary company, namely the 'Cogswell & Harrison Manufacturing Company'. The chemist employed by this company was a Vincent Harold Smith. Like many early cartridge manufacturers the company experienced manufacturing difficulties associated with the machines supplied to them and on 1 May 1914 Cogswell & Harrison brought a legal action against Messrs Taylor & Challen Limited of Birmingham in respect of a press supplied to them for making cartridge heads for shotgun cartridges. The plaintiffs alleged that by contract the press should have turned out heads of soft annealed brass but had clearly failed to do so. Taylors denied this and stated that the machine was capable of producing heads similar to the specimen submitted. A settlement was then arranged after consultation.

At the start of WWI, Mr Cogswell Edgar Harrison, the son of the Managing Director Mr Edgar Harrison who had just become 21 years of age, managed to escape from Austria and return to England. On his return he was given the task of managing the company's factory at Poyle, Middlesex, to produce explosives for the Government; however at 3pm on 16 April 1915 an explosion occurred at the site killing him and other workers. An employee named Miss Dorothy Moss, aged 17, was in one compartment of a building with Mr C.E. Harrison whilst three others, namely Frederick Donalth, aged 46, Mrs Florence May East and Mrs Emily Tilby, aged 24, were in an adjoining compartment when the explosion occurred. The blast killed Mr C.E. Harrison and Miss Moss and injured the other three parties. The house was destroyed and a fire followed, which was extinguished without any further explosions. At the time of the explosion Mr C.E. Harrison was 22 years of age. The subsequent report by Major Coningham revealed that Mr Cogswell Edgar Harrison had been Manager at the Poyle factory for eight months. The house where the explosion occurred was divided into five compartments. The first was used as a store for wet nitro-cellulose in which three were injured but this material was unconnected to the explosion. The next store was used for mixing, incorporating, granulating and sifting about 68 lbs of dry nitro-cotton. Harrison had been carrying out some experiments in connection with mixing of a nitro-cellulose powder and on the previous day had dried some nitro-cotton for this purpose. He was not satisfied that the substance was homogenous after the process had been conducted and decided to incorporate some of the remaining dried nitro-cotton with the other ingredients. The dried cotton was brought to Harrison where he and the girl were waiting and shortly afterwards the explosion occurred. Major Coningham thought the explosion may have been caused by friction whilst removing the lid from the bin containing the nitro-cotton or alternatively by dropping it. Clearly the loss of his son to Mr Edgar Harrison proved to be a turning point in the company's history and in the autumn of 1915 Messrs Cogswell & Harrison's explosives factory at Colnbrook, Staines, Middlesex was sold to the Colnbrook Chemicals & Explosives Co. Ltd, marking the end to the company's involvement in the production of propellants and explosives.

7.1.2 Cogswell & Harrison shotgun cartridge brands

In July 1898 *Arms & Explosives* reported that the company was offering for sale the following branded cartridges, namely 'Victor', 'Blagdon', 'Certus' and 2" 'Midget'. A subsequent advert in 1900 indicated no change in brand names except that the previously described 2" 'Midget' now bore the title of 'Blagdonette'. In July 1912 they introduced their 14¾ bore shotgun for 1¹⁄₁₆ oz or 1 oz shot charges using Vicmite powder.

TESTED CARTRIDGES,

WITH

SELECTED SMOKELESS POWDER.

An unbroken successful Record of 20 Years!
THE VICTOR, Standard for Price and Quality,
1900.

N.B.—The constantly increasing price of Loading Materials has been met by us by a constantly increasing output—so much so that our Selling Prices are this Season reduced, whilst quality is maintained.

Embodiment of finest materials'

Paper Cases 9/- cash per 100
Waterproof Cases 10/-   ,,
Brass-covered ,,   10/6 ,,

*Unsurpassed for efficiency
of shooting.*

8/- cash per 100.

*Reduced length Cartridge, with
1oz. shot.*

8/- cash per 100.

Reliability and economy.

7/6 cash per 100
6/6   ,,   with black
        powder.

CARRIAGE FREE for Orders of 1,000 sent in one Consignment to any Station in Great Britain by Goods Trains.
CARRIAGE PAID for consignments of less than 1,000 to Scotch Stations—Cash, 3s. 3d. To English or Welsh Stations—Cash—2s. 6d.
Cartridges by Passenger Train are generally charged the usual Parcel Rates.
CARRIAGE ALLOWANCE of 4s. on Orders of 1,000 to Ireland, Purchaser paying Carriage.
ALL WOOD PACKING CASES FREE. CHILLED SHOT, 3D. PER 100 EXTRA NET.

COGSWELL & HARRISON, Ltd.,
London: 141, New Bond Street; 226, Strand.

Advert from Shooting with Game & Gun-Room notes *by Blagdon 1900*

JULY, 1912.

Cogswell & Harrison LTD.

NEW 14¾ BORE GUN

introducing this NEW GUN a Comparison
—— is made with a MODERN 12 BORE. ——

Like a 12 Bore :—

SAME CHARGE OF SHOT.

Namely :—1 1/16 or 1 oz.

EQUAL PATTERNS.

Both Inside & Outside of
30-inch Circle.

Improvement on a 12 Bore :—

HIGHER VELOCITY.

GREATER PENETRATION.

LONGER RANGE.

SIX OUNCES LIGHTER.

The ordinary 12 Bore Cartridge of to-day is the same in general dimensions as it was 50 years ago, it was designed to shoot 3 drs. or 3¼ drs. of black powder, and 1⅛th, or rather more, of shot.

The New 14¾ Bore shoots COGSWELL & HARRISON'S Smokeless Powder, **VICMITE**, which occupies a reduced space in the cartridge and burns without residue.

—— LONDON MADE GUNS ——

The Victor. :: Crown. :: Sandhurst. :: Rover.

FIREARMS FACTORY	GILLINGHAM STREET, VICTORIA STATION, LONDON.
AMMUNITION FACTORY	COLNBROOK, MIDDLESEX.
SMOKELESS POWDER FACTORY	COLNBROOK, MIDDLESEX.

PARIS 26 AVENUE DE L'OPERA.

141 NEW BOND STREET. 226 STRAND LONDON.

An example of the company's manufactured 14¾ gauge shotgun cartridges

7.1.3 Trade marks registered by Cogswell & Harrison

The 'Zig Zag' trade mark found on Cogswell & Harrison shotgun cartridges was first registered in 1897.

277439 18 November 1905 Exceltor
273779 22 June 1905 Cosonoid
277293 14 November 1905 Vicmos
277295 14 November 1905 Vix
277437 18 November 1905 Ardit
277291 14 November 1905 Markor
293762 13 June 1907 Kelor
315474 10 August 1909 Armus
391867 1 April 1908 Markoroid
303109 15 May 1908 Konor

They also used the following brand names on shotgun cartridges: 'Blagdon', 'Blagdonette', 'Certus', 'Farmo', 'Fusilite', 'Konkor', 'Kuntic', 'Pluvoid', 'Swiftsure', 'Tower of Westminster', 'Victor', 'Victoroid' (loaded with Vicmos powder) and the 'Westro'.

334,971. Gunpowder and Cartridges. Cogswell & Harrison, Limited, 29A, Gillingham Street, Victoria Station, London, S.W. ; Fire Arms and Ammunition Manufacturers.—12th July 1911.

7.2 The Cogschultze company

7.2.1 The company's history

On 24 July 1909 Cogswell & Harrison and the Schultze Gunpowder Company submitted a joint application to register the trade mark Cogschultze relating to gunpowder, percussion caps and cartridges. This trade mark was finally registered in December 1909, registered number 315103. This was an agreement between the two companies where Cogswell would supply the shotgun cartridge cases to Schultze so Schultze would have a constant supply of cases into which it would load its powder.

In March 1911 the *Arms & Explosives* revealed that the Schultze Gunpowder Co. Ltd had issued notices calling a meeting of shareholders for 27 March to consider the sale of the company as a going concern due to it being increasingly difficult to do business without owning a plant to make cartridge cases. In April 1911 the same gun trade periodical revealed that the company's shareholders had sanctioned the sale of Schultze on 27 March. Between the decision taken to wind up the old company and the registration of a new company a case of civil litigation arose between Cogswell & Harrison over the Cogschultze agreement which had been entered into in 1909. The case was settled by mutual consent on the 5 July 1911. The Cogschultze Ammunition & Powder Co. Ltd was registered with a capital of £10,000 in £1 shares to carry on the business of manufacturers of and dealers in gunpowder, Nitroglycerine, Dynamite, gun cotton, blasting powder and other explosives, and to adopt an agreement with Cogswell & Harrison Ltd. The first Directors of the company were not named. The liquidators of the Schultze Gunpowder Co. Ltd agreed by the terms of the settlement to dispose of their former share of the trade name or brand 'Cogschultze' together the related goodwill and pass it to Cogswell & Harrison Ltd. Cogschultze had previously been owned by the Schultze Gunpowder Co. Ltd and the Cogswell & Harrison Mfg. Co.

7.2.2 Trade marks registered by Cogschultze Ammunition & Powder Co. Ltd

Cogschultze applied to register the following trade marks for cartridges and gunpowder in September 1911 which were granted in November that year: 'Bomo', 'Farmo', 'Molto' and 'Pluvoid'. In October the same year they applied to register the trade marks of 'Torro' and 'Westro', followed by 'Avlo' and 'Stelor' in November 1911. The trade marks of 'Torro', 'Westro' and 'Avlo' were granted in December 1911 followed by 'Stelor' in February 1912. The company also used the brand name 'Ranger'.

7.2.3 Cartridges made for other gunsmiths by Cogschultze

Few specimens which fall into this category still exist due to the short production period associated with the company, however I have encountered three specimens, namely: 'The Reliable', loaded by them for Heywood & Hodge, Torrington, an unnamed cartridge made for Barnard & Levet, Ironmongers sited in Lichfield in Staffordshire and another unnamed cartridge for Brassey of Eastgate, Chester.

EXPLOSIVES.   SEPT., 1911.

SCHULTZE DEVELOPMENTS.

FOLLOWING upon the settlement by mutual consent of the litigation between the Schultze Gunpowder Co., Ld., and Messrs. Cogswell and Harrison, Ld., Schultze Company, Ld., has been registered with a capital of £100,000 to adopt an agreement with the Schultze Gunpowder Co., Ld., now in voluntary liquidation. A strong and progressive board of directors has been appointed, and it is their intention further to extend the sales of the well-known and justly cele-

Extract from Arms & Explosives September 1922

Continued on next page

---

brated Schultze gunpowder, and also the popular proprietary brands of cartridges known as Rainproof, Eyeworth,
Westminster, Yeoman, and Pickaxe. These cartridges will
be loaded entirely in cases manufactured by Messrs. Eley
Bros., Ld. In addition to supplying these price-main-
tained proprietary cartridges, the Company will undertake
the supply of all the standard qualities loaded with their
well-known gunpowder. The factories remain under the
control of Capt. H. Hardy, and dealers may have every
confidence that the vigilance and forethought always associated in the past with the manufacture of Schultze gunpowder will remain a distinguishing feature in the future.
As evidence to this effect it may be stated that each day the
powder as it is finished is thoroughly tested for the three
most important requirements in a sporting gunpowder,
viz., internal pressure, rapidity of ignition, and velocity
of the shot. In addition, there are very stringent chemical
tests to verify moisture and stability. When these tests
are successfully passed the powder is ready for use, but as
an additional safeguard, a policy adopted very early in the
history of the old Company will be continued, and that is
that no powder will be issued until it has been stored for
three months in the magazines, and at the end of that period
again thoroughly tested. There is no doubt that the standard of excellence which has always been associated with
the name Schultze in the past will be realised by the new
Company. More it is impossible to say.

Circulars have recently been extensively issued to the
trade conveying the information relative to the sale of the
business to the new Company, and also enclosing lists of the
powders and cartridges to be sold. Gunmakers and dealers
who have not received a copy of the list should write to
Mr. O. G. Will, who has been appointed secretary to the new
Company, at 28 Gresham St., E.C. It may be added that
Mr. F. H. Pepper who has been associated with the old
concern for a considerable number of years, has been
retained by the new organisation.

A further development of the settlement already mentioned is the registration of the Cogschultze Ammunition
and Powder Co., Ld., with a capital of £10,000 to adopt an
agreement with Cogswell and Harrison, Ld. A circular
also issued to the trade by the last-named company announces
that by the terms of the settlement, the liquidators of the
Schultze Gunpowder Co., Ld., have disposed of their share
of the trade-name, or brand " Cogschultze " together with
the goodwill appertaining thereto, and that the whole of the
same, whether formerly belonging to the Schultze Gunpowder
Co., Ld., or to the Cogswell and Harrison Mfg. Co.,
is now vested in them.

7.3 Examples of shotgun cartridges made by the companies

LEFT TO RIGHT: *12 bore 'Victoroid', 20 bore 'Victoroid', 12 bore 'Victoroid', 12 bore Pegamoid case, 12 bore 'Exceltor', 20 bore for their Paris outlet at 26 Avenue de l'Opera, 12 bore brass Ejector.*
LYING DOWN: *12 bore 'Vicmos' and 12 bore 'Ranger' by Cogschultze (headstamp No. 3)*

LEFT TO RIGHT: *12 bore 'Konor', 12 bore Gastight, 20 bore Gastight, 12 bore loaded with Schultze (headstamp No. 2) and 12 bore black powder 'Ardit'*

Specimen of a 12 bore 'Kelor' bearing a Kynoch Birmingham headstamp

An interesting specimen made by the Cogswell Ammunition & Powder Co. for Brassey of The Eastgate, Chester. The over shot wad is marked Cogschultze. It bears headstamp No.5

| Markor | Certus | Kuntic | Victor | No brand name |

Examples of some of the range of rare Cogschultze brand named cartridges

7.4 Examples of headstamps appearing on the companies' cartridges

THESE HEADSTAMPS WERE IN USE DURING THE EXISTENCE OF COGSCHULTZE AND ALSO THE EXISTENCE OF THE COGSWELL & HARRISON MANUFACTURING COMPANY

1.
This form of headstamp appears on the 14 3/4 bore so was in use in 1912. It was also in use before this date on cartridges loaded with Cogswell's own powders

2.
This appears on headstamps during the period before 1911 following Cogswell generating the Cogswell & Harrison Manufacturing Co.to make shotgun cases which Schultze got from them to load

3.
This headstamp was used following registration of the Trade Mark Cogschultze & after the formation of Cogschultze Powder & Ammunition Co.

4.
Found on 12 bore Kuntic

On a cartridge made for Barnard & Levet. Case obtained from C&H Manufacturing Co. pre 1911 and loaded by Schultze

On a cartridge made for Bassey, Chester. The initials C.A.P.C. stand for Cogswell Ammunition & Powder Co.

5.   **6.**

IT IS BELIEVED THAT ALL THE BELOW HEADSTAMPS WERE IN USE BEFORE AND AFTER COGSWELL & HARRISON WERE MAKING THEIR OWN CASES AND POWDERS

7.
This appears on the 'Victor' and 'Kelor'

8.
This appears on Kynoch brass Grouse Ejectors

9.
This appears on untitled Eley cases

10.
This appears on the 'Victor'

11.
This appears on the 'Victor' and 'Markor'

12.
This appears on the 'Victor', 'Markor', 'Kelor' and 'Blagdon'

13.
This appears on the 'Victor'

14.
This appears on the 'Victor' made for their French outlet

15.
This appears on untitled brass, paper lined cases

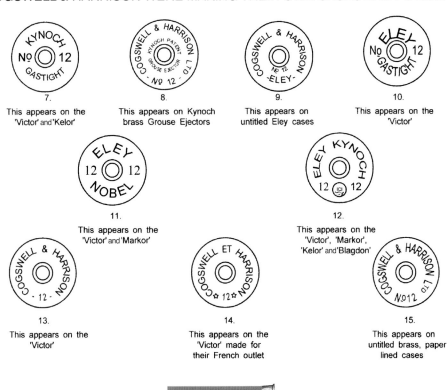

CHAPTER 8
Remington & Union Metallic Cartridge Co. Ltd, Brimsdown

8.1 The company's history in relation to Britain

The Union Metallic Cartridge Company USA had agents around the world to act as its trade outlets and London was one of the sites in question. In 1902 the Remington Arms Company merged with the Union Metallic Cartridge Company and in August 1904 the new company REM-UMC issued to the British trade its sales catalogue which indicated that the range of shotgun cartridges produced included the Arrow, Magic and Acme. Interestingly two months before in June 1904 *Sporting Goods Review* stated that Nobel's Explosives Company Ltd were loading at their premises the Acme UMC cases with Nobel's Ballistite powder and the UMC Magic cartridges with their Empire powders, both brands being in 12 bore using 2¾" and 3" cases.

In July 1911 a circular issued by Mr S.R. Hollick, which was reproduced in *Arms & Explosives*, brought to the attention of the English sportsman that the Union Metallic Cartridge Co. and the Remington Arms Co. had combined forces under the title of The Remington Arms-Union Metallic Cartridge Co. and had opened a branch office in St Stephens House, Westminster, London SW.

On 3 October 1912 the company applied to register the trade marks 'Olympic' and 'Remilion' for use on their shotgun cartridges, both of which were granted on 4 June 1913 (345976 Olympic and 345978 Remilion). The 19 October 1912 issue of *Sporting Goods Review* stated that REM-UMC had just established a loading factory near London for Arrow and Nitro Club shotgun cartridges which they would offer for sale in 12, 16 and 20 bore and by July 1913 the sporting press revealed that the company's new loading factory was now complete and in operation at Brimsdown in Middlesex.

The Remington Arms-Union Metallic Co. Ltd was registered as a private English subsidiary company of REM-UMC in August 1916 with a capital of £20,000 in £1 shares to manufacture and deal in cartridges, armaments, weapons of war and sport with its Registered Offices sited in St Stephen's House, Westminster. This registration was made with a view to putting the company in harmony with English conditions with a clear aim being for it to act as a trade outlet for its US produced small arms and cartridges into the UK market.

Although the company's production was initially restricted to loading American made shotgun cartridge cases with English powders and shot they also imported considerable quantities of metallic ammunition for use by the English sportsman, perhaps one of the best known being the Palma rifle match ammunition which found favour during the late 1920s. They were also to supply the components for US calibre metallic cartridges to Eley Bros Ltd to be made into proof ammunition for the two English Proof Houses, particularly for the more uncommonly encountered US rifle calibres where Eley were not prepared to introduce the calibre into their production lines due to lack of demand. It is also interesting to note that two of W.W. Greener's multiball loads in .30-06 and .25-25 Stevens also bear REM-UMC headstamps.

In March 1919 the company's former offices were requisitioned by the Ministry of Food so they opened temporary offices at 17 Eldon Street, London EC2. During both WWI and WWII the company's plant was engaged in wartime production for the British Government although exactly what it was used to manufacture still remains a mystery.

A fellow cartridge collector some years ago, on examining a box of ICI Bonax cartridges, where the date code indicated production during the late 1930s, noticed that one of the cartridges bore the REM-UMC headstamp but without the normal marking 'case made in the USA'. Errors of this nature are not uncommon and merely indicate a number of cartridges from one prior batch running with new tubes or heads from the subsequent batch and due to an error by the checker you encounter a mismatch of a head to tube marking. This example however is interesting in that for a period the parent company used ICI to manufacture their cases and/or possibly load them. The United States Stock Market crash of 1929 followed by the Great Depression, brought with it the imposition by the USA of import tariffs on goods entering America and as a direct response Britain imposed its own import tariffs in order to protect home industries. A situation was then reached where by adding import taxes to the cartridges cases being made in the USA, the final cartridge production costs would have been greater than the home produced products. This would have created a situation where it would have been financially unviable to continue production. As a result, during the late 1930s this state must have been reached, resulting in REM-UMC using ICI to manufacture cases for it.

By the end of WWII the British economy was in a dire financial situation created by the costs involved in the war. It had no way out other than to seek financial aid and this was granted in the form of a $4.4 billion loan from the American Government in December 1945. A natural consequence, due to the size of this loan was to increase its level of exports and reduce its levels of imports to enable the size of the deficit to decrease and thus the aim of the public was to support the concept of buying British produced goods to rebuild the UK economy. These events were to seal the fate of this company and it went into liquidation; the company's site and plant were sold at auction in November 1946.

8.2 The company's site

The Brimsdown factory was sited on what in today's age is known as the M25 London orbital motorway, relatively close to Brimsdown Railway Station which is still situated on the London to Cambridge main line.

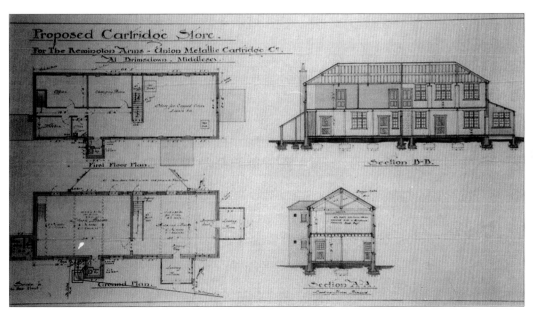

Copy 1 of a drawing of the premises at Brimsdown taken from an early Remington catalogue (COURTESY OF MR BOB CAMERON)

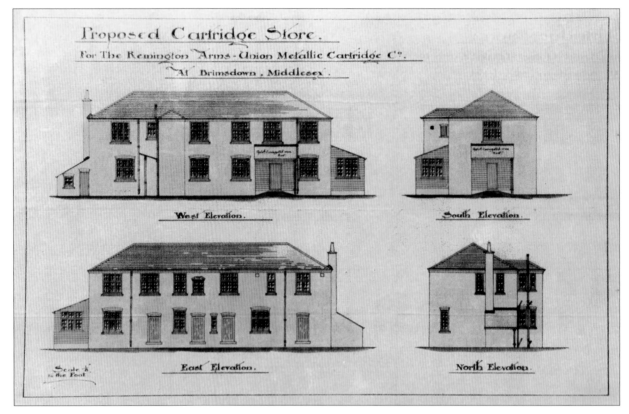

Copy 2 of a drawing of the premises at Brimsdown taken from an early Remington catalogue
(COURTESY OF MR BOB CAMERON)

8.3 Shotgun cartridges produced by the company

8.3.1 Cartridges loaded for other companies

An advert by the company in 1913 indicated that they, like their fellow competitors, were prepared to mark their cases with a customer's name on the case if they ordered 5,000 or more either loaded or empty cases.

Clearly the advert on the right proved successful since a considerable number of companies used this service and the subsequent list gives examples of some of the companies whose name appears on the sides of cartridge cases, made for them by REM-UMC:

Curtis's & Harvey of London used REM-UMC cases for use with their 'Marvel' brand powder. The cases used did not state made in the USA

Sporting Goods Review
15 March 1913

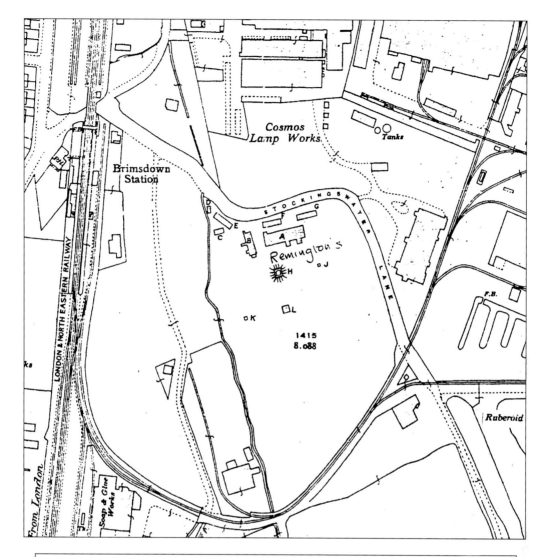

BUILDINGS - as listed in 1946 Auction Catalogue

A Single Storey Brick Building, 126ft 6in x 34ft 6in with Annexe and Boiler House.

B Two Storied Brick and Slated Building, 68ft 6in x 24ft, comprising Stores and Offices.

C Brick Built and Slated Testing House, 28ft x 15ft, single storied and divided into two rooms.

D Timber Built Stores Shed, 20ft x 12 ft, having a concrete floor and roofed in corrugated iron.

E Timber Built Canteen and Kitchen, 61ft x 16ft, sub divided into two Canteens, Kitchen and Scullery.

F Timber Built Store, 60ft x 16ft, roofed with Ruberoid and having a boarded floor.

G The "Nissen" Store Hut, 60ft x 16ft, having a concrete floor.

H, J, K & L Four Brick Built Magazines.

Albert Barnes (Gunmakers) Ulverston on 'Lonsdale Waterproof'

G.E. Bond & Son (Gunmakers) 2 Castle Street, Thetford, Norfolk on unusual yellow plain case, no brand name

Edwinson Green & Son, Cheltenham (Gunmakers) on 'Maxim' brand

M. Garnett & Son of Parliament Street, Dublin on 'Retriever' brand

Hammond Bros, Winchester (Gunmakers) on 'The Winton'

G. & A. Harris, Uttoxeter on unnamed brand

R.T. Hodgson Harrogate (Ironmonger) on unnamed brand
Lawn & Alder (Gents Outfitters) sited in Brackley Street, London on unnamed brand
J. & J. McGaldin Monaghan, Southern Ireland on 'Sure Kill' brand
New Explosives Company Ltd, on unnamed brand but loaded with NE powder
Norman & Sons, Woodbridge, Suffolk on unnamed brand
O'Riordan & Forrest, Midleton, County Cork, Southern Ireland on unnamed brand
Taylor & Son (Ironmonger), Bromsgrove, Worcestershire
Tily & Brown Ltd, Farnham and Guildford on 'Farnford'
H. Walkington, (Gun Dealer), Bridlington on 'The Reliable'
Thomas Wild (Gun Makers), Birmingham on unmarked brand
Arthur Wood Newport, Isle of Wight (Gunsmith) on 'Demon'
J. Woodward & Sons, 64 St James Street, London SW1 (Gunmakers) on 'Special Smokeless'

Examples of REM-UMC cartridges made for customers

Remington case from Brimsdown plant supplied to New Explosive Co. Ltd for loading with NE powder

Law & Alder Colonial Outfitters, Brackley Street, London – Half Brass

Taylor & Son, Ironmongers, Bromsgrove, Worcestershire

8.3.2 The company's own brand names

In September 1915 a Mr Hollicks sent in specimens of their current production to the *Arms & Explosives*, which gave a good indication of the range of production during 1915. The list in question is shown below:

'New Club' loaded with black powder
'Nitro Club' loaded with either Remington Smokeless or other first class English powders. It used a red case with a deep head
'The Remington' previously named by the company as the 'Remilion' which used a dark red case with a $\frac{5}{16}$" head loaded with the company's powder
'Arrow' a lined case with a 1" head, loaded with either Remington Smokeless or other first class English powders

To summarise it appears that the names used by the company but not necessarily marked on their tubes were:

Nitro Club
New Club
Arrow
Economy
Remilion
Remington

Many of the specimens from the factory have corrugated paper cases. This form of tube construction was patented by the company and first advertised in 1935. It was claimed corrugation produced a stronger case, enabled faster feeding and easier extraction.

8.3.2.1 Examples of the company's cartridges and boxes

LEFT:
LEFT TO RIGHT: 20 gauge smokeless, .410" case made by ICI, 12 bore case made by ICI and 16 gauge

BELOW:
STANDING LEFT TO RIGHT: 'Economy', 20 bore 'Kleanbore' and 12 bore unnamed on case
LYING DOWN LEFT TO RIGHT: 'Farnford' for Tilly & Brown of Farnham and 'L & A' for Lawn & Alder, Colonial Outfitters, Brackley Street, London

LEFT TO RIGHT: *'Arrow', 'Nitro Club', .410" 'Kleanbore' and unnamed*

8.4 Examples of the company's adverts

GOODS REVIEW   October 15, 1913.

Remington U.M.C.

NITRO CLUB   STEEL LINING

SMOKELESS POWDERS

SHOT-GUN CARTRIDGES.

REASONS why you should stock Remington U.M.C. Cartridges.

PROMPT DELIVERY.—We send you your goods without undue delay.

REPEAT ORDERS.—The cartridges are so uniformly good you avoid customers' complaints and take repeat orders.

EXTENDS BUSINESS.—The shooter always likes them, and tells his friends where he gets them.

SMALL STOCK.—We have only three grades, so the whole range of shot cartridges can be covered by a small stock.

PRINTED SHELLS.—You can have your own name and address printed on the cartridges in comparatively small quantities, and without material delay.

FULL DISCOUNTS.—We have fixed discounts irrespective of quantity, so you get your full discount on your first small order.

Write us for further particulars. We invite correspondence.

Wholesale only.

REMINGTON ARMS-UNION METALLIC CARTRIDGE CO.,

St. Stephen's House, Westminster, London, S.W.

Depot for Ireland :   Depot for Scotland :
3a, Burgh Quay, Dublin.   31, Robertson St., Glasgow.

Remington-UMC

Shot=Gun Cartridges

LOADED AT THE COMPANY'S PLANT AT BRIMSDOWN, MIDDLESEX, CAN NOW BE SUPPLIED.

They are made in FOUR STANDARD GRADES as follows :

FOR BLACK POWDER:	FOR SMOKELESS POWDER:
"NEW CLUB"	"REMINGTON"
	"NITRO CLUB"
	"ARROW"

TO GET QUICK DELIVERIES ORDER STOCK LOADS IN STANDARD CASES AS FOLLOWS :

12 ga. NITRO CLUB, 33 grs. $1^1/_{16}$ oz., in 4, 5, $5\frac{1}{2}$ and 6 Shot.

12 ga. REMINGTON, 34 grs. 1 oz., in 4, 5 and 6 shot.

12 ga. NEW CLUB, 3 drs. 1 oz., in 4, 5 and 6 Shot, or 3 drs. $1^1/_{16}$ oz. in 5 and 6 Shot.

A STANDARD CASE CONTAINS 500 CARTRIDGES, AND IS SUPPLIED FREE.

THE REMINGTON ARMS UNION METALLIC CARTRIDGE CO., LTD.,

ELDON BUILDINGS, 17, ELDON STREET, LONDON, E..C.2

Advert in Sporting Goods Review *15 January 1920*

Remington UMC Shot-gun Cartridges

LOADED AT THE COMPANY'S PLANT, BRIMSDOWN, MIDDLESEX.

"**NEW CLUB**" are warranted to give the best results with Black Powder.

"**REMINGTON**" provide Sportsmen with a reliable Smokeless Powder Cartridge at a moderate price.

"**NITRO CLUB**" have a steel-lined case of great strength.

"**ARROW**" are of the highest possible quality and are recommended for trap shooting.

All *Remington UMC* cases are waterproofed.

THE REMINGTON ARMS UNION METALLIC CARTRIDGE Co., Ltd.,
ELDON BUILDINGS, 17 ELDON STREET, LONDON, E.C. 2.

Advert in Sporting Goods Review *15 July 1920*

Remington UMC SHOTGUN CARTRIDGES

LOADED AT THE COMPANY'S PLANT, BRIMSDOWN, MIDDLESEX.

"*Remington*" provide Sportsmen with a reliable Smokeless Powder Cartridge at a moderate price.

"*Nitro Club*" known everywhere as a cartridge of superior quality and dependability.

"*Arrow*" are of the highest quality and are recommended for trap shooting.

"REMINGTON," "NITRO CLUB" and "ARROW" loaded with Remington Smokeless Powder, and "NEW CLUB" loaded with Black Powder.

All Remington UMC cases are waterproofed.

The REMINGTON ARMS UNION METALLIC CARTRIDGE CO. Ltd.,
St. Stephen's House, Westminster, London, S.W.1.

Advert in Sporting Goods Review *15 October 1921*

8.5 Examples of headstamps found on the company's cartridges

1.

On 20 gauge Smokeless
also on 12, 16 and 28 gauge
with related alteration to
gauge number

2.

3.

On 12 bore ICI
manufactured case

4.

On 12 bore loaded by
New Explosives Co. with
N E powder

5.

6.

7.

8.

On 2" Nobel's
Ballistite loading

9.

On very early loaded
case for Bond & Son
Thetford, Norfolk

10.

11.

On American
.410" case

12.

On ICI manufactured
case

CHAPTER 9
The Hull Cartridge Company Ltd and its forerunner company Turner Carbides Ltd

9.1 The company's history

Mr Sidney Bontoft, the founding member of the Hull Cartridge Company, was born in 1899 and on reaching maturity became a calcium carbide merchant in a partnership entitled Turner & Bontoft. The company's premises were sited in Posterngate, Hull where they imported and distributed calcium carbide for use in welding and as a means of generating light in early pedal cycle lamps, car lamps and in the larger homes in the rural areas. One of the company's biggest customers was the Raleigh Cycle company which used this chemical to weld tubular pedal cycle frames, since by adding water to it, oxyacetylene gas was generated.

This initial partnership broke up in 1922 leaving Mr Sidney Bontoft as its sole proprietor when it was renamed Turner Carbides Ltd and the name Bontoft was, for reasons unknown, dropped from the title. Mr S. Bontoft purchased his supplies of calcium carbide from F.A. Hughes & Co. Ltd which operated from a London address; due to the need for extra finances to run the company F.A. Hughes agreed to take a major financial interest in it.

From the advert below it would appear that F.A. Hughes & Co. Ltd was already involved in

FOR THE MOST DUCKS
AT THE
LONGEST RANGE

USE
THE WALSRODE CARTRIDGE
WITH
SINOXID PRIMING.

GREATEST
HITTING
POWER

LOWEST
RECOIL

F. A. HUGHES & CO., LTD.
ABBEY HOUSE, BAKER STREET, LONDON, N.W.1

Telephone: Welbeck 2332/6.   Telegrams: "Distancing, Norwest, London."

either the distribution or loading of shotgun cartridges. From the advert it is clear he was using the German Walsdrode powders in combination with German Sinoxid primers. Sinoxid primers were first introduced and named in 1928 and produced by Dynamit Nobel AG at Fürth (Bavaria) who claimed that the primer composition was non-rusting. I have yet to locate specimens of these cartridges and do not know if the tubes were marked with the company name.

In 1935 the company moved premises from Postern Gate to 58 De-Grey Street, Hull and this date approximately coincided with the provision by the National Grid of their extended supplies of electricity to both industry and the large country estates. This resulted in a considerable decline in the demand for calcium carbide and caused Mr Bontoft to examine what other products his major outlets for calcium carbide regularly used. The answer he arrived at was a demand for shotgun cartridges by the farming community. From remaining early specimens linked to data supplied by the company, it appears he obtained unmarked primed cases and sent them to be hand loaded by Padstone & Cox of Southampton.

During WWII the production of shotgun cartridges virtually ceased as the main cartridge tube manufacturers turned their attentions to making military small arms ammunition. During the war period Turner produced large quantities of calcium carbide for the Ministry of Defence sealed in 2 lb cans which were used for lighting, where links to the National Grid were not available, particularly for use overseas.

Early specimens of Turner's cartridges loaded by Patstone & Cox of Southampton. They also loaded a .410", and one named 'The Standard' and another entitled 'The Killer'

A very early example of their cartridges which were loaded into plain ICI cases

Immediately after the war the company recommenced its shotgun cartridge production using ICI cases, double base powders from Nobel's Ardeer factory and later single base neo disc powders from the Powfoot factory in the 1980s together with lead shot from Sheldon Bush then subsequently from Associated Lead. Their works in De-Grey Street were extended when the company acquired and demolished two houses at the rear of this site utilising the space to rebuild a new cartridge loading plant using Macrete blocks. In 1947 the Hull Cartridge Company Ltd was formed and in 1948 Mr Peter Bontoft (Sidney's son who had been born in 1927) left the Army and joined his father in the business. Initially the cartridges were loaded by hand using Dixon Loaders and the company employed some 15 ladies to undertake this work.

F. A. Hughes had some form of link with the REM-UMC factory at Brimsdown and when it closed Hughes took the machinery and a large quantity of residual Peters shotgun cases to their premises in De-Grey Street. The machinery proved too large for them to use to load cartridges and was subsequently disposed of; however they did utilise the Peters cases but experienced extreme difficulties achieving a successful crimp on the tube due to its extremely pliable nature. The closure of the Brimsdown plant also resulted in F.A. Hughes taking over as the sole UK import agent for Remington arms and ammunition. This agency was to remain with the Hull Cartridge company until 2000 when they decided to dispose of it, due to the irregularity of supply of previously ordered goods.

Mr Peter Bontoft advised me that their company had also once loaded shotgun cartridges for the New Normal Powder Company, a London based firm. This contract may have resulted from contacts held by F.A. Hughes Co. Ltd.

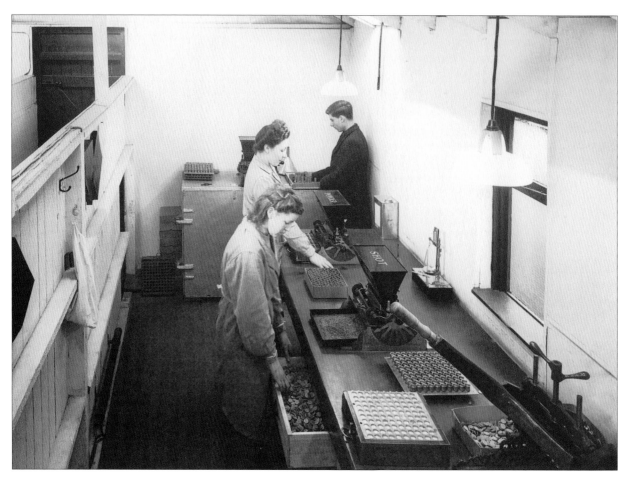

A photograph taken inside the loading room in the original factory at 58 De-Grey Street, Hull.
Note the use by the staff of the Dixon's Climax loading machines
(PHOTOGRAPH COURTESY OF MR HUGH CLARK)

After the war F.A. Hughes & Co. Ltd was still the major shareholder in this business and in due course the company was purchased by the Distillers Group which had interests in industrial concerns in addition to the drinks industry. In 1960 the Distillers Group decided to revert to its major industrial interest, namely the production of alcoholic drinks and decided to start selling off its industrial subsidiaries. This enabled Mr Sidney Bontoft (in 1965) to acquire Turner Carbides Ltd and Hull Cartridges Ltd from F.A. Hughes which in turn had been a subsidiary of the Distillers Group.

In the early 1960s, Mr Hugh Clark who was working for British Resin Products, a subsidiary of the Distillers Group was looking for new applications for his company's products. He reached the decision that plastic shotgun cartridge cases would provide an ideal outlet for use of his company's resin and since Hull Cartridge Co. Ltd were also part of Distillers Group, he obtained a patent to manufacture the all plastic shotgun cartridge case and wad, which was to gain the name of 'The Black Knight'. The application for the initial patent by Mr Clark was submitted in December 1960 and finally published as Patent No. 926196 in May 1963. It focused on providing solutions to the following foreseen problems:

a. The case had to have sufficient strength in its base to withstand the pressures generated when it was fired.

b. The technical difficulties arising from moulding plastics.
c. The need to provide an effective seal between the primer and the base of the plastic case.
d. The need to provide an effective watertight seal at the shot end of the case.
e. The need to design a special rotary injection press.

The vast majority of the problems faced by Mr Clark related to the types of plastic used in terms of their strength, melting temperatures, shrinkage upon cooling and amenability to use in injection presses. The initial problem of strengthening the base of the case to withstand ignition pressures was solved using a separate base wad which was to be inserted into the plastic tube and he successfully identified the appropriate form of plastic, which proved to be polyethylene, for use in the tube and base wads. The next problem he sought to address was the belief held by the sportsman that over shot wads interfered with the patterns of the shot after they left the muzzle of a shotgun and therefore he set out to design a wad which would disintegrate upon firing. In April 1967 Patent No. 998134, an amendment to the former patent, was taken out by Mr Clark and a Jack Walter Gordon Stapley. Mr Stapley had been tasked by the Distillers Company who owned the patent, to manufacture tools to make it a commercial success. The wad concerned had grooves running across the one face and a peripheral ridge on the other to offer a perfect watertight seal when the edge of the tube was turned over. A further amendment was the provision of a metal rim around the edge of the case head to strengthen it for use in semi automatic shot-guns. The metals used included copper and cupro nickel. Having addressed and overcome the major hurdles of the cartridge tube production, a further problem arose with primer supplies. All

Note the differences in wad colours. These were used to identify differences in the weights of loads etc. during the field trials period and specimens were made using a range of different coloured tubes and wads. Note that three of the cases have re-inforced rims for use in semi-automatic shotguns

the major primer manufacturers, with the exception of one Polish manufacturer, declined to supply them with primers. As a result they were forced to prime the 'Black Knight' with Poloxid primers imported from Poland and these proved to produce irregular results. Before the project could be effectively evaluated and the final problem relating to the primers solved, Distillers came under massive pressure arising from the thalidomide problems and the company disposed of their industrial chemical interests to British Petroleum, thus ending the project.

The company's actions however had not gone unnoticed by the trade and suddenly all the big European cartridge case manufacturers turned their attention to production of plastic cartridge cases as a substitute for the more costly paper tubed case. Although the 'Black Knight' cartridge did not prove to be a commercial success, the outcome may well have been different had the company manufactured its own primers or further time had been available to address the problems associated with their supply. These events however did provide the company with an unexpected spin off, since shortly after completion of this project Mr Bontoft asked Mr Clark if he would consider leaving British Resin Products to join the Hull Cartridge Company which he agreed to do and become their Sales Director. Mr Peter Bontoft explained to me that Mr Clark was to prove a major asset to the company, since at this time a person with a northern accent had little chance of obtaining orders from the London gunmakers or shooting schools in the southern counties. Mr Clark however possessed an accent which was far removed from Yorkshire and this was to provide the key to open the door to numerous new trade outlets in southern England. Within a short period of time the Hull Cartridge Company was loading for a considerable number of the large gun companies using plain ICI cases onto which they printed their clients' names using their own rollers. At this point in time, i.e. the 1960s, the ICI paper case was the best quality cartridge case available on the market, however the actions of the Hull company had started to affect the trade of ICI in terms of their sales of loaded cartridges. As a consequence in the late 1960s Mr Richard Van Oss, ICI's Ammunition Sales Director directed that a list be sent to the Hull Cartridge Company of gunmakers, gunsmiths and shooting schools who ICI manufactured for and they were advised not to approach these companies, otherwise ICI would refuse to supply the Hull Cartridge Company with their primed cases. Mr Clark and Mr Peter Bontoft were extremely pleased to receive this list since it was to afford them a major opportunity to expand their business. They did this by moving to the use of paper cartridge cases made by Fiocchi of Italy and then successfully targeting the companies on the list supplied by ICI which ended up with the Hull company loading and supplying all the major gunmakers and gunsmiths in southern England, with the exception of James Purdey & Sons Ltd. Their extended list now included such companies as Holland & Holland, Cogswell & Harrison, Atkin Lang & Grant and Crudg-

LEFT TO RIGHT:
Mr Peter Bontoft,
Mr Hugh Clark and Mr Sidney
Bontoft

ington. Shortly afterwards the Hull Cartridge Company gained the British agency for Fiocchi, however the Italian company changed their mind after a short period of time and started supplying anyone in Britain with their cases.

Mr David Bontoft (Peter's son) was born in 1958 and joined his father in the business in 1979. In 1980 the company moved premises to a new industrial estate to enable the company to expand. Since the Hull Cartridge Company was to permit their premises to act as what could be described as a 'Show House' for other potential factories, the road leading to it was named Bontoft Avenue after this long serving local industrial family. When the factory was purchased the company shares were split between Sidney Bontoft, Peter Bontoft and Peter's brother, Ken who had been an engineer in the Royal Air Force and had subsequently run a Post Office. Although Ken was to spend a considerable time in Spain, his engineering expertise was put to good use in introducing the installation of automatic cartridge loading machines which enabled production to expand rapidly. In 1984 the Carbide side of the company was finally disposed of and since that date it has concentrated on shotgun cartridge production and acting as the

LEFT TO RIGHT:
Mr Ken Bontoft, Mr Sidney Bontoft and Mr Peter Bontoft

UK's agent for Weihrauch air weapons, an additional role it took up in 1978 when Hull became their main factory distributor. The company's originator, Mr Sidney Bontoft, finally died aged 84 years in 1983 and Mr Ken Bontoft died in 2005 leaving Mr Peter Bontoft and Mr David Bontoft as Managers of the company.

I recently had the pleasure of visiting the company's premises, where I met Mr Peter Bontoft who still attends the premises daily to aid his son Mr David Bontoft. The subsequent visit around the site proved extremely revealing as to how the company operates. The first and very obvious feature is that it is a family run and operated company whose staff are in many instances long term employees. In respect of the manufacturing processes it was quite clear that the company, without in any way revealing the techniques used, is geared to high quality control systems being constantly applied to modern equipment, aimed at eradicating potential errors occurring in these automated loading systems. Such techniques/systems however involve additional staffing and research and development costs and all too often in today's age many manufacturers are loath to provide these needed funds, since their sole aim is to maximise returns in order to satisfy the demands of shareholders in terms of annual dividends and produce a product at the absolute minimum cost. Hopefully this company will continue to remain under family ownership and management, dedicated to continue to produce high quality cartridges. From my conversations with them it seems extremely likely that the company will in due course continue under the management of the female line of the family when both Peter and David Bontoft finally leave the workplace by nature's forces rather than retirement, since it was apparent that retirement is not a word occurring within the family's vocabulary.

It should also be mentioned that this company holds the accolade of being the official supplier of shotgun cartridges to Her Majesty the Queen. This Royal Appointment was originally granted to Mr Peter Bontoft in 1992 for a period of ten years and is periodically renewed. The grantee is now Mr David Bontoft.

The administration offices of the company

9.2.1 The company's cartridges

Below is a list of companies they produced bespoke loads for which they formerly loaded into ICI manufactured paper cases and onto which they printed their customer's name and address. They continued this process initially moving to using Fiocchi paper cases and finally into their use of plastic Fiocchi cases. The process of producing bespoke loads for customers has continued and forms a considerable proportion of the company's business. The company switched case suppliers in 2007 and now use both paper and plastic Cheddite cases made by a company based in France.

Some of the companies who they loaded for during the period they used ICI cases	Cartridge name if appropriate
Barham's, 95 Tilehouse Street, Hitchin	The Challenge
Chubbs, London, Gunmakers	Hawker
Collins Bros Ltd, The Southern Armoury, London	Special Load
Continental, 22 Cromwell Road, Redhill, Surrey	
D.C.W.	
Francis & Dean, 8 St Mary's Hill, Stamford	Hi-Bird
Horace Fuller Ltd, 72 Park Street, Horsham	The Stally
John H. Gill & Sons (Leeming Bar Ltd)	The Sproxton
H.S. Greenfield & Son, Canterbury	The County
Greenfields, Canterbury	Kentish Fire and The Wessex
Hammants, Henley on Thames, Gunmakers	Blue Rock
Hawkes of Headcorn, Kent, Gunmaker	The Yeoman
H.G. Hopkins, Sandbatch	Mk 1, Mk 2, and Mk 3

Some of the companies who they loaded for during the period they used ICI cases	Cartridge name if appropriate
Leech & Son, Chelmsford	Leechs Special Load
Little Mill Shooting Ground, Rowarth, Stockport	The High Peak
N.W.R.C.S.	
Patstone & Cox, Southampton	Bargate International
Potters, Thame	Special Load
Richardson, Halesworth	Style
A. Sanders (Maidstone) Ltd, 79 Bank Street	Long Tom
J. Venables & Son, 99 Aldates, Oxford	The Oxford
J. Wheater, Gunmaker, Hull	The Humber
John Wilkes, 79 Beak Street, London	The Doughty

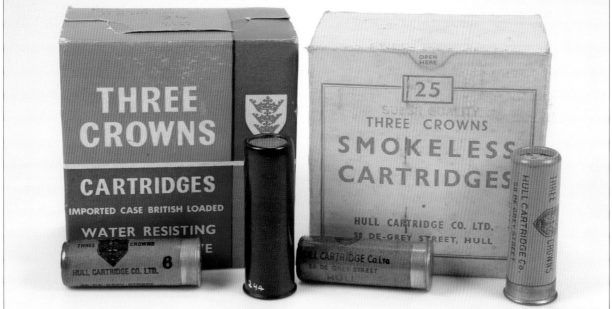

ABOVE:
LEFT TO RIGHT:
16 bore 'Three Crowns' loaded into a Fiocchi case, 'Black Knight', 16 bore 'Three Crowns' loaded into a ICI produced case and a 12 bore 'Three Crowns' loaded into a ICI produced case, the last two items bearing the De-Grey Street address

LEFT:
Very few Hull cartridges bear a specific title, this being one of them, namely the 'Standard'

143

9.2.2 Examples of headstamps which have appeared on the company's early cartridges

1.

This headstamp appeared on the early 16 and 12 bore cases loaded for the company by Padstone & Cox

2.

An early headstamp used whilst this country was still entitled Great Britain. Case made by ICI

3.

The subsequent headstamp after the U K politicians had relagated this country to second division. Case made by ICI

4.

5.

The headstamp used on the 'Black Knight' all plastic cartridge

6.

The headstamp appears on their paper case tubes imported from Fiocchi of Italy

CHAPTER 10
Messrs Jas. R. Watson & Co.

10.1 The company history

A letter written by Watson seven years prior to his death outlining his links with the Belgian powder

J. R. Watson was a successful City Merchant and proprietor of the Bear Hotel at Esher in Surrey. He had also been involved in a business relating to the supply of explosives at a point in time when the Transvaal Dynamite Concession was being organised in 1887, this was to generate a monopoly situation for the supply of explosives for a period of 15 years into the mines of South Africa. In 1891 he became the English agent for the Cooppal Smokeless Powder Co. Ltd of 35 St Victoria Street, London EC and this Belgian powder was to be offered as one of the smokeless powders used by Eley Bros Ltd in 1898 in their shotgun cartridges.

Watson's career however terminated on the 28 May 1899, when he leapt from his Brougham, a horse drawn vehicle. Apparently his horse bolted and Watson jumped out and landed on his head. On Watson's death the company continued to trade being run by his former business manager, a Mr Robert Joseph Harmer.

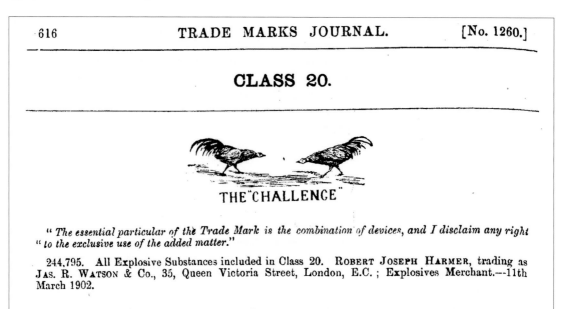

In March 1902 R.J. Harmer, trading under the title of J.R. Watson & Co. applied for the registration of the trade mark of 'The Challenge' linked to a sketch of two fighting cocks for use on shotgun cartridges and this was subsequently granted.

In July 1902 a court case commenced between Lionel Watson and R.J. Harmer over who held the official agency for the Cooppal Powder Co. Ltd. Harmer was a proprietor in the firm of J.R. Watson & Co. which had been set up under a trust created by the will of the late J.R. Watson. He won the court case and J.R. Watson & Co. remained the sole agent for Cooppal powders.

The November issue of the *Arms & Explosives* in 1903 stated that Watsons were loading Cooppal powders solely into English cases exclusively provided to them by Eley Bros Ltd, but that situation was soon to change.

On 15 March 1904 the *Sporting Goods Review* reported that J. R. Watson & Co. had purchased the Arms and Ammunition Manufacturing Co. Ltd, previously of 143 Queen Victoria Street and 140 Southwark Street, London SE. The new owners stated they would continue to supply the brands of cartridges previously made by the Arms and Ammunition Manufacturing Co. Ltd and would supply empty cartridge cases of all descriptions but that they would not trade in guns, rifles or revolvers.

The company loaded the majority of their cases in Britain as borne out on the printing encountered on their tubes and although early specimens exist bearing English manufacturers' headstamps e.g. Nobel's of Glasgow, Eley Nobel, ICI and much later Greenwood & Batley, the vast majority of remaining specimens bear evidence of case manufacture in Belgium with loading conducted in Britain. An advert relating to the company in the *Sporting Goods Review* on 15 October 1920 stated 'Our works in Belgium have practically been rebuilt since the German invasion and we are again in a position to supply "Cooppal" No. 2 powder in canisters or loaded into cartridges.' Watsons held the agency for the Belgian Cooppal powder but in order to be really competitive with companies such as ICI, they also needed to manufacture their own cases and one of their specimens of 'The Britannia' bears their evidence of case manufacture. Printed around the edge of the Britannia motif, were the words 'Manufactured at our Works in Belgium Loaded in London'.

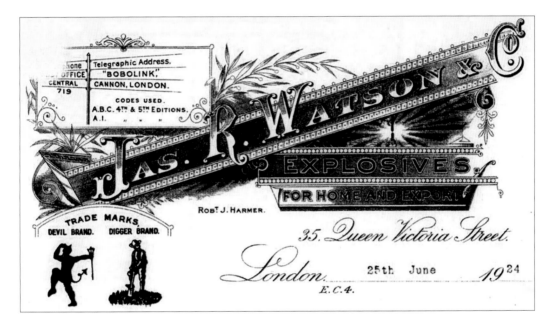

The company's London address of 35 Queen Victoria Street, London, EC4 was destroyed by German bombing during WWII and the company subsequently occupied various other London addresses, finally closing in 1976. Specimens of their 'Challenge' brand exist loaded into Greenwood & Batley cases. Greenwood & Batley manufactured shotgun cartridge cases after WWII and terminated production of cartridge tubes in the 1960s.

10.2 Known dates when cartridge brand names were introduced by the company

In June 1904 they introduced their versions of the 'Monkey', 'Dagger' and 'Britannia' brands of shotgun cartridges previously manufactured by Arms and Ammunition Manufacturing Co. Ltd.

In 1907 the company's list of cartridges included 'Gastights', 'Deep Head', 'Britannia', 'Monkey', 'Challenge' and 'Albion' which were loaded with nitro powders and 'Dagger' and 'Popular' brands which were loaded with black powder.

In July 1909 their main lines of cartridge were loaded with either 42 grains of Cooppal No. 1, 27 grains of Cooppal No. 2 or 33 grains of Emerald powder.

Adverts in 1920 indicate the company loading the Britannia cartridge and unnamed cartridges with Cooppal No. 2 powder and in 1929 the 'Sureshot' brand had been added to their range.

Further brand names used by this company included the 'Lilliput', 'Wettern', 'Warrior', 'Enterprise' – Leaflet powder, 'Hi Speed', 'Comet' in .410" and 'Fullpower No Recoil'.

10.3 Companies for which Jas. R. Watson loaded cartridges

Like all the large manufacturers Watson would load cartridges for other companies, these included:

William Garden (Gunmaker), Aberdeen – no brand name
M. James & Sons (Ironmonger), Newcastle Emlyn, Carmarthen, Dyfed – brand name 'The Gwalia'
S.A. Nobbs (Ironmonger), Norman Street, Lincoln – brand name 'The Sureshot'
Smallwoods (Gunsmiths), Milk Street, Shrewsbury – brand name 'Kleankiller'

10.4 Examples of the company adverts

Sporting Goods Review *15 November 1920*

Sporting Goods Review *30 April 1929*

Sporting Goods Review *15 October 1920*

Sporting Goods Review *5 August 1923*

510

GAME AND GUN AND THE ANGLER'S MONTHLY—August, 1935

SURESHOT ... BRITANNIA

SHOTGUN CARTRIDGES LOADED WITH "COOPPAL" LEAFLET POWDER

Major Burrard, well-known in sporting circles, and one of the greatest authorities on shotgun cartridges, tested "SURESHOT,"
"BRITANNIA" and other cartridges loaded with "Cooppal" leaflet powders and reported upon them in the September, 1934,
issue of "Game and Gun" as follows :—

"Of the efficiency of these cartridges there is no need to say anything—they must obviously be most effective against game."

LOADED WITH
"COOPPAL
EXCELSIOR"
Leaflet and Waterproof
SMOKELESS
POWDER

⅝" Gastight. Metal lined. CASH PRICE **14/-** per 100
(Chilled Shot)

₁₆⁵" Reinforced.　CASH PRICE **13/6** per 100

THESE AND OTHER CARTRIDGES LOADED WITH "COOPPAL" LEAFLET POWDER ARE
OBTAINABLE FROM ALL DEALERS.　*If there is any difficulty please apply to the Sole Distributors*

JAS. R. WATSON & CO. (Trade Enquiries Invited)

CORNWALL BUILDINGS · 35 QUEEN VICTORIA STREET · LONDON · E.C.4.

Established 1889　　[Cartridges, Guns, and all Sportsmen's Requisites]　　Telephone : City **6819**

A page from the company's 1923–24 catalogue showing the three brands of cartridge then available

10.5 Specimens of the company's cartridges

RIGHT:
Three varieties of cases made for use with
Cooppal No. 2 powder

BELOW:
LEFT TO RIGHT: *'Sureshot', 'Britannia', 'Enterprise', 2″*
' Lilliput', unnamed and 'Enterprise'
LYING DOWN: *'Britannia' and' Warrior'*

LEFT TO RIGHT: *'Warrior', 'Sureshot' 2 varieties, 'Challenge' 3 variants* LYING DOWN: *'Lilliput'*

10.6 Examples of the company's headstamps

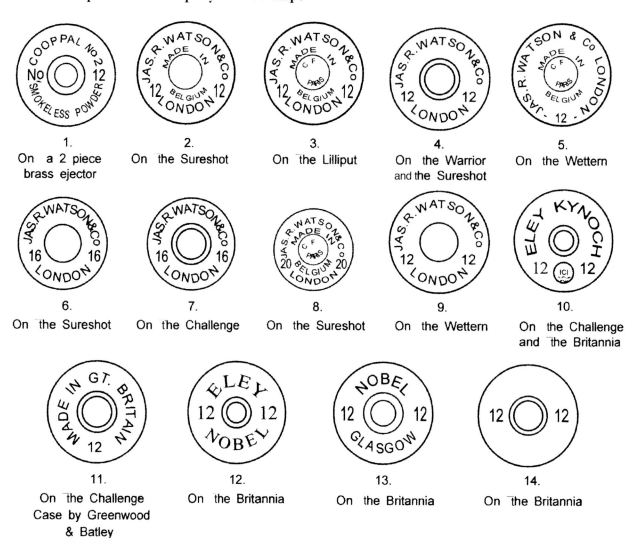

1.
On a 2 piece
brass ejector

2.
On the Sureshot

3.
On the Lilliput

4.
On the Warrior
and the Sureshot

5.
On the Wettern

6.
On the Sureshot

7.
On the Challenge

8.
On the Sureshot

9.
On the Wettern

10.
On the Challenge
and the Britannia

11.
On the Challenge
Case by Greenwood
& Batley

12.
On the Britannia

13.
On the Britannia

14.
On the Britannia

CHAPTER 11
Pneumatic Cartridge Company Ltd

11.1 The company's history

In March 1907 Bathgate & Company of Edinburgh applied to register the trade mark 'Pneumatic' and this was granted in June 1907. In June 1907 Bathgate and Company applied for the trade mark 'Pneumatic' to be applied to wads used in shotgun cartridges. This then was the founding company from which the Pneumatic Cartridge Co. Ltd was to emerge. In essence the over powder wad was made of cork with a hole cut through its central axis and a solid cork plug less than half the thickness of the hollow was placed into the hole. The aim of this system was to absorb part of the recoil within the wad to reduce recoil on the shoulder of the shooter, whilst still creating a successful gas-tight seal.

The Pneumatic Cartridge Co. Ltd was a private company registered in Edinburgh on 12 August 1909 with a share capital of £5,000 in £1 shares to acquire the company of the Pneumatic Cartridge Co., together with their patents and trade marks and to carry on business as dealers and manufacturers of shotguns, rifles, pistols, cartridges and cartridge cases with their registered offices in 65 Albert Street, Edinburgh.

In the 1950s the company moved to Bristol and was last listed in trade directories in the late 1960s.

11.2 Patents and trade marks taken out by the company

Patent No. 288783 12 Dec 1906 Pneumatic (re. cartridges) Bathgate & Co., 65 Albert Street, Edinburgh.

Patent No. 290283 9 Feb 1907 Pneumatic (re. wads) by Bathgate & Co., 65 Albert Street, Edinburgh.

Application made for trade mark 'Pneuma' for wads & cartridges by Pneumatic Cartridge Co. Ltd, Leith in June 1919 and granted in August 1919.

Advert in Sporting Goods Review *20 October 1921*

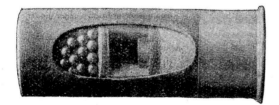

Messrs. *BATHGATE & CO., Gun Wadding Manufacturers, 360, Leith Walk, Edinburgh,* are sole licencees for the manufacture and sale of *"Pneumatic" Wadding.* They have been makers of Cork Specialities since 1894. In response to numerous enquiries and requests they are now offering *"Pneumatic" Wadding to the Trade.*

" Pneumatic " Wadding
Patented, Registered.
SECTION OF " PNEUMATIC " WAD

Highest Velocity.	Low Gun-Barrel Pressure.
Cushioned Recoil.	Perfect Patterns.

No Gun Headaches.

The pneumatic action of the Wad takes up the shock of the explosion, and "gives to the Sporting Cartridge all the advantages which the Pneumatic Tyre gives to the Bicycle and Motor Car."

PRICES :

| No. 1 Quality | ... | 7/6 per thousand. |
| No. 2 ,, | ... | 6/6 ,, ,, |

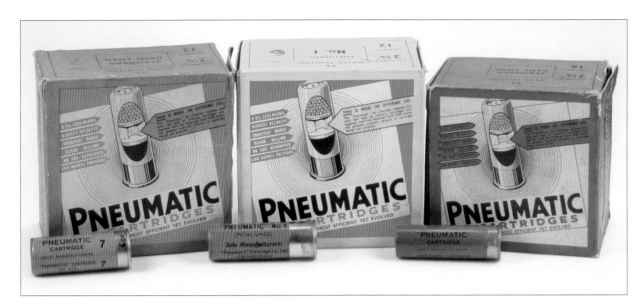

11.3 Specimens of cartridges produced by the company

The company produced a range of differing print cartridges in 12 bore, 16 bore, 20 bore, 28 bore and .410". There are five main brand identifiers namely their Number 1, Number 2 and Number 3, Pneumatic Special and Pneuma. Additional case markings indicate metal linings and in some cases damp proof.

LEFT: A seldom encountered clay pigeon version of the Pneumatic range of cartridges. It bears the Eley Kynoch headstamp which I believe dates it to between 1949 and 1950s since the over shot wad indicates their Edinburgh address and in the 1950s they moved to Bristol whilst their pre 1949 adverts fail to list it

RIGHT: This is the rare No. 2 Pneumatic. It bears the address 65 Albert Street, Edinburgh. It appears that few were made. Its headstamp indicates it was made by Eley Bros Ltd before 1926

LEFT TO RIGHT: 16 bore No. 3, .410" no tube markings and 16 bore 'Special'

LEFT TO RIGHT: No. 3, 'Special' in 16 bore, 'Special' in 12 bore, 'Special' in 16 bore, No. 1 Damp Proof
Metal Lined in 20 bore, unnamed in 20 bore, 'Pneuma' in 16 bore
LYING DOWN: 16 bore unnamed, No. 3 in 20 bore and No 3. in 16 bore

LEFT TO RIGHT:
No. 1 Damp Proof
Metal Lined, No. 1
Water Resisting
Metal Lined, No. 1
Best Quality, No. 3
Best Quality and
'Pneumatic'
LYING DOWN:
'Pneumatic'

FACTORY AND WAREHOUSES:—
90-98 HOLYROOD ROAD AND
WATERSTON AVENUE
EDINBURGH

CLOSED ON SATURDAYS

Registered Office :

96 Holyrood Road
EDINBURGH 8

TELEPHONE
EDINBURGH · 30892
AND BYPASS · 4020
PRIVATE BRANCH EXCHANGE

CABLES
"PNEUMA, EDINBURGH"

"PNEUMATIC" CARTRIDGES

EXPORT PRICE LIST No. 3

(As from 1st MARCH 1949)

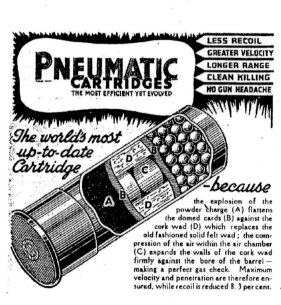

LESS RECOIL
GREATER VELOCITY
LONGER RANGE
CLEAN KILLING
NO GUN HEADACHE

PNEUMATIC CARTRIDGES
THE MOST EFFICIENT YET EVOLVED

The world's most up-to-date Cartridge

—because the explosion of the powder charge (A) flattens the domed cards (B) against the cork wad (D) which replaces the old fashioned solid felt wad ; the compression of the air within the air chamber (C) expands the walls of the cork wad firmly against the bore of the barrel — making a perfect gas check. Maximum velocity and penetration are therefore ensured, while recoil is reduced 8.3 per cent.

Description	Gauge	Length of Cartridge Case (inches)	Trade Price per 100
PNEUMATIC No. 3	12	2½	**29/6**
PNEUMATIC No. 3	16	2½	**28/9**
PNEUMATIC No. 3	20	2½	**28/6**
PNEUMATIC No. 3 WILDFOWL LOAD	12	2½	**29/6**
PNEUMATIC No. 3 TRAPSHOOTING LOAD—1¼ oz.	12	2½	**29/6**
PNEUMATIC No. 3 SKEET LOAD—1 oz.	12	2½	**29/6**
PNEUMATIC No. 1 GASTIGHT WATER-RESISTING	12 & 16	2½	**34/9**
PNEUMATIC No. 1 GASTIGHT WATER-RESISTING	20	2½	**34/3**
PNEUMATIC No. 1 GASTIGHT WATER-RESISTING	12 & 16	2¾	**36/9**
PNEUMATIC No. 1 GASTIGHT WATER-RESISTING	20	2¾	**36/3**
PNEUMATIC No. 1 GASTIGHT WATER-RESISTING	12	3	**41/-**

Figure Shot sizes including B.B. at above prices
Letter sizes of Buckshot 2/- per 100 extra

PNEUMATIC No. 3	Orange card tubes with $\frac{5}{13}$" brass heads.
PNEUMATIC No. 1	Gastight steel lined water-resisting Indian red card tubes with $\frac{5}{8}$" brass heads.
PACKING	In decorated cartons of 25 Cartridges and packed 1000 Cartridges in waterproof paper-lined strong export wood cases free.
TERMS	Strictly nett.
PAYMENT	Cash against Proforma Invoice or Irrevocable Letter of Credit in our favour to be sent to our Bankers, The Commercial Bank of Scotland Ltd., North Bridge, Edinburgh, against delivery of shipping documents.
DELIVERY	Consignments of 10,000 Cartridges and upwards delivered F.O.B. Glasgow or Leith, lesser quantities F.O.R. Works.
CONDITIONS	All prices are subject to alteration without notice, and orders are accepted on the understanding that they will be invoiced at the prices and terms current at date of despatch from Works.
IMPORT LICENCES	Particulars of Import Licence must be received before orders can be prepared.
WEIGHT AND MEASUREMENTS.	Shipping particulars for each Case containing 1000 12 Gauge 2¼" Cartridges are approximately :—

Nett Weight—3 qrs. 12 lbs.   Gross Weight—3 qrs. 25 lbs.   Measurements—18⅜" × 13¾" × 9¾"

D /500/3/49 (incl. 200 n.m.)

THE PNEUMATIC CARTRIDGE CO. LTD.

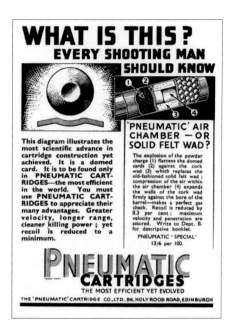

11.4 Examples of the company's headstamps

1.

Early headstamp, case by Eley Bros Ltd, London pre 1926

2.

Early headstamp, case by Eley Bros Ltd, London pre 1926

3.

4.

5.

Case by ICI between 1926 and 1953

6.

Used on Pneumatic plain paper cased tube supplied to Pneumatic

CHAPTER 12
Page-Wood & Co., T. Page-Wood, T. Page-Wood Ltd and the Patent National Cartridge Co. Ltd

12.1 The companies' histories

T. Page-Wood was established as a gunmaker in 1876 at 29 Nicholas Street, Bristol, an address they occupied until 1883. They also had premises at 13 Market Place, Frome in Somerset and 1 Westgate, Cardiff, Glamorgan. By 1894 they had premises at 39/40 Walcot Street, Bath, 21 Castle Street, Cardiff and in 19 High Street, Shepton Mallet. When exactly the company started shotgun cartridge production is unknown; however by 1887 they had patented a machine for this purpose.

The Patent National Cartridge Co. Ltd of Bristol was registered in the spring of 1894 with a capital of £15,000 in £1 shares to acquire from Messrs Page-Wood & S. Chambers two inventions for improvements in cartridges for breech loading shotguns. The company's first Directors were R.G. Webster, J. Sinnott, T.W. Jaques, S.E.H. Chambers and T. Page-Wood. As a result in 1894 the partnership of Messrs Page-Wood & Co. who then occupied premises of 26 High Street, Bristol, 21 Castle Street, Cardiff and 19 High Street, Shepton Mallet was dissolved. However the business continued to operate under the management of a Mr S.E.H. Chambers. It will be noted that S.E.H. Chambers was, in fact, Septimus Chambers who in 1888 was a gunmaker operating from 63 Broad Street, Bristol. On 15 October 1895 *Sporting Goods Review* reported that the company's affairs were too complicated and so no dividend was declared and in June 1897, the new company had wound up.

Two years later in 1899 the company was resurrected under the title of T. Page-Wood Ltd and continued to manufacture shotgun cartridges until purchased by the Sheldon Bush Company in 1961.

T. Page-Wood Junior opened a gun department at 17 Nicholas Street, Bristol in July 1901 and the com-

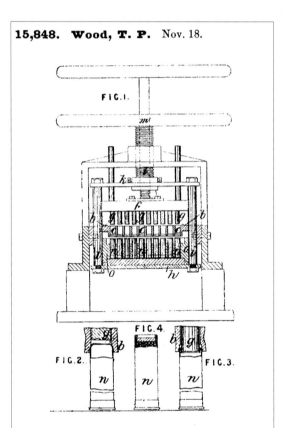

15,848. Wood, T. P. Nov. 18.

Cartridge-loading machines. — Relates to the crimping of shot cartridge cases. The table *b* has a series of perforations *c*, which are bell-mouthed at their lower ends. The cartridge cases *n* are carried in the frame *o* on the plate *h*, which is attached by the bolt *i* to the upper plate *k*. As soon as the powder charges and wads have been inserted in the cartridge cases, the screw *l* is rotated by the wheel *m*, and the cases are forced into the bell-mouths of the openings *c*, as shown in Fig. 2. The plate *f* carrying the concave plungers *g* is then forced down, and the cartridge cases crimped as shown in Fig. 3. The shot and wads are then inserted and rammed, and the cartridges finished, as shown in Fig. 4, by further pressure into the bell-mouthed openings *c*.

pany remained trading at this address until it too formed part of the purchase by the Sheldon Bush Company in 1961.

12.2 Company loading machines

The vast majority of shotgun cartridges loaded by these companies have an unusual turnover, where the muzzle end of the cartridge has been reduced. In the case of the 12 bore cartridge the nose end was reduced to 16 bore. Many claims were made by the company in terms of the cartridges' performance, the most salient claim being that the cartridge was designed to reduce recoil but there appears little factual evidence to support this statement. From the large numbers of remaining specimens they must however have found favour with numerous sportsmen.

Although the company never manufactured their own cases, unlike many of the smaller loaders they were one of the first English companies to patent early automated machines to crimp and load shotgun cartridges. Their first machine was patented in November 1887 by T.P. Wood and was designed to generate the coned crimped shotgun cartridge.

In May 1892 T.P. Wood patented a second machine which was clearly a major movement towards the fully automated loading systems we encounter today.

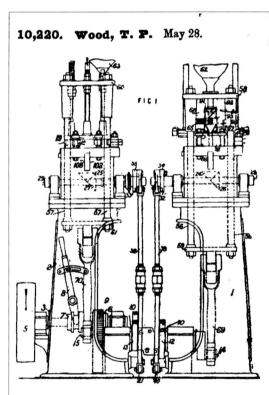

10,220. Wood, T. P. May 28.

connected by rods 69, 70 to vertically-sliding frames. One frame consists of plates 58, 59, connected by rods 56, and the other of plates 60, 61, connected by rods 57. The powder hopper 62 is carried on the plate 58, and the shot hopper 63 on the plate 60. The powder descends the shoot 66 into the horizontally-sliding block 65, which by its movement cuts off and delivers the powder charge to the shoot 67, from which it descends into a cartridge case. The reciprocating motion of the powder slide 65 is effected by one arm 91 of a three-armed lever pivoted at 92, the other arms 93, 94 of which are operated by the projection 95 on the sliding frame 56, 58, 59. The shot-charging device on the pedestal 2 is operated in a similar manner. The crank shaft 10 carries two cams 12, 13, each of which performs a double function. The cams act on the levers 40, 41 to impart a reciprocating motion to the rods 38, 39 for giving, through ratchets 32, 33 and pawls 34, 35, a step by step motion to the shafts 28, 29, and these, through the mitre-wheels 24, 26 and 25, 27, rotate the plates 18, 19, which receive the cartridge cases. The cams 12, 13 also actuate levers which bring the wads from their tubes and place them in position for being loaded into the cartridges by plungers on the plates 58 and 60. The empty cases are brought, automatically or by hand, into the recess 88, from which they are raised by a plunger on the plate 59 into position in the rotating plate 18, where they are loaded, wadded, and discharged into a bucket chain which delivers them to the recess 108 in the second pedestal, similar mechanism being then employed for charging them with shot, wadding, crimping, marking, and discharging them. The mechanism is specially adapted for crimping the cartridges into the form described in Specification No. 15,848, A.D. 1887. The apparatus may be adapted for charging the cartridges with bullets.

Cartridge-loading machines.—The Figure shows a front elevation of the machine. The cartridge cases are loaded with powder and wadded on the pedestal 1, and are then loaded with shot or bullets on the pedestal 2. The shaft 3 is rotated by the pulley 5, and is connected by the clutch 7 to the pinion 6. Upon moving the clutch 7 by the lever 8 the pinion 6 gives motion to the spur-wheel 9 on the shaft 10. This shaft has cranks 14, 15

12.3 Shotgun cartridges loaded by the company

The following is a list of brand names used by the company:

Anti-Recoil
Anti-Recoil Economic
Bristol
Climax
Double Crimp
First Quality
Imperial Crown
Lion
National Choke Cartridge
Park Row
Second Quality
Shield
Special .410
The Page-Wood DS
Wildfowler

An advert in *The Gamekeeper* in 1938 stated that they were loading the following brand names: 'The Bristol', 'Climax', 'Double Crimp', 'Park Row' and 'Wildfowler'.

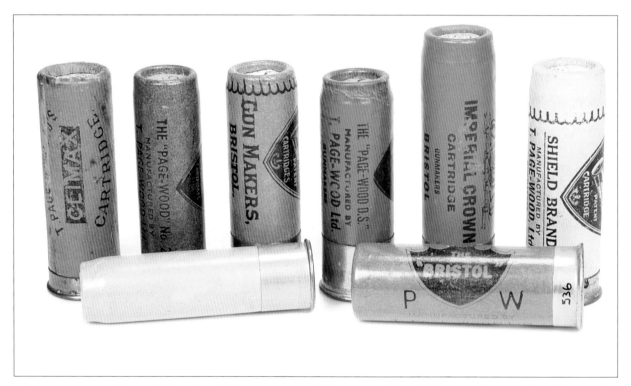

LEFT TO RIGHT: *'Climax', No. 2 in 16 bore, unnamed, 'Page-Wood D.S.', 'Imperial Crown' and 'Shield'*
LYING DOWN: *unnamed 20 bore and 'The Bristol' – note this is not cone crimped and bears a*
Greenwood & Batley headstamp

LEFT TO RIGHT: *Second Quality, First Quality, 'Shield', unnamed, 'Anti-Recoil'*
LYING DOWN: *'Double Crimp'*

It is interesting to note that when you examine later production specimens they often bear the words 'Hand Loaded' and have star crimps rather than the early rolled turnover.

12.4 Advert used by the company

12.5 Examples of headstamps which appear on the companies' cartridges

1.

2.

3.

4.

This headstamp appeared on early 12 bore case - maker unknown. The address indicates production in the 1880s/1890s

This headstamp appeared on early 12 bore case - maker unknown. The address given is A Page Wood, Baldwin Street, Bristol on a 'Lion Brand' cartridge

This headstamp appears on a 'Shield' brand 12 bore cartridge maker unknown.

This headstamp appears on a specimen marked 'Second Quality'. The Nobel headstamp was in use between 1907 and 1919

5.

6.

7.

Headstamps 5, 6 and 7 indicate the cases were manufactured by Greenwood & Batley of Leeds. Greenwood & Batley cases were made from the end of WWII to the 1960s

8.

9.

10.

Headstamps 8, 9 and 10 indicate the cases were manufactured by ICI between 1926 and 1953

11.

12.

This appears on tubes used by the company which were in production between 1919 and 1926

This headstamp appears on the Climax by T. Page-Wood Ltd

CHAPTER 13
Schultze Gunpowder Co. Ltd

13.1 The company's history

In about 1846 a German Chemist by the name of Herr Schönbein discovered the explosive qualities of cotton wool after it had been soaked in nitric acid. Some time afterwards a German officer named Captain Schultze discovered a similar effect was created by soaking wood chippings in nitric acid. The resultant material was then washed and dried and its end form was a powder resembling sawdust. Although initially tried by English sportsmen and found to be smoke free and giving less recoil than black powder it found little initial support.

In 1865 a Lt. Col. Sampson Gompertz, a former officer in the East India Company brought this powder to the attention of a Mr J.D. Dougall senior. Dougall was the senior member of a Glasgow gun and fishing tackle maker, and he was to act as its promoter on behalf of Captain Schultze. Mr Dougall introduced this powder to the British shooting fraternity and on the 22 July 1868 a new British company was formed entitled the Schultze Gunpowder Company Limited. I have been unable to trace any photographs of Captain Schultze and little is known about his background, however it appears that he returned to Europe and was subsequently associated with another set of powder companies, namely Lichtenbergar & Komp of Germany and the Belgian powder manufacturers Poudrerie de Wetteren. It is known that Captain Schultze was jointly involved with a company in licensing this new powder to the Schultze Gunpowder Company, since mention is made in the Memorandum of Association to a former agreement reached on 17 March 1868 between Schultze and Gompertz.

Subsequently the Schultze powder was defined as consisting of a base of wood fibre impregnated with nitric and sulphuric acids. The resultant nitrated base pulp was then mixed with various salts which they discovered regulated the rate of combustion and therefore controlled the explosion. Schultze was therefore the first smokeless powder made for sporting purposes in Britain.

13.2 The origins of the original factory site at Eyeworth

Eyeworth Lodge was sited in a remote part of the New Forest close to Fritham, at what was to become the centre of the Schultze factory site. It had been built to house New Forest deer keepers whose role was to control the deer herds. It came under the control of the Office of Woods, a Crown agency. In 1851 The Deer Removal Act was introduced to enable new saplings to be planted for timber, thereby removing the deer herds from the New Forest. As a direct result the deer keepers' former roles and homes became redundant and by 1852 Eyeworth Lodge was vacant. After a short period of occupation by a retired London publican, in 1859 it was to be leased to a man named Drayson, another Londoner who was to open a black powder mill on the site. During the course of the next ten years Drayson had two partners. The first partner left him in 1866 and the second partner named Brodrick described him as a rascal after Drayson absconded leaving him with substantial debts. As a direct result Brodrick, in May 1869, sought authority from the Office of Lands to dispose of the lease.

During the period this site was used to make black powder, its output was extremely limited and one of the related reasons was the distance between the Eyeworth site and the nearest railway station at Totton, some 12 miles away with transportation of the powder initially being effected by wheelbarrow.

13.3 The Schultze factories and their management

A copy of the Memorandum of Association showing the formation of the initial company in July 1868 shows that the initial shareholders were William Henry Bailey, a Gentleman resident at Cambridge Square, Hyde Park, London, Lt. Col. John Smith, James Cheny a Barrister, William Shaen a London Solicitor, Lt. Col. S. Gompertz of Bedford, George Dorman Tyser a Merchant resident at 3 Cosby Square, London EC and a Henry Stead the Secretary to the Liquidators of the London, Bombay and Mediterranean Bank.

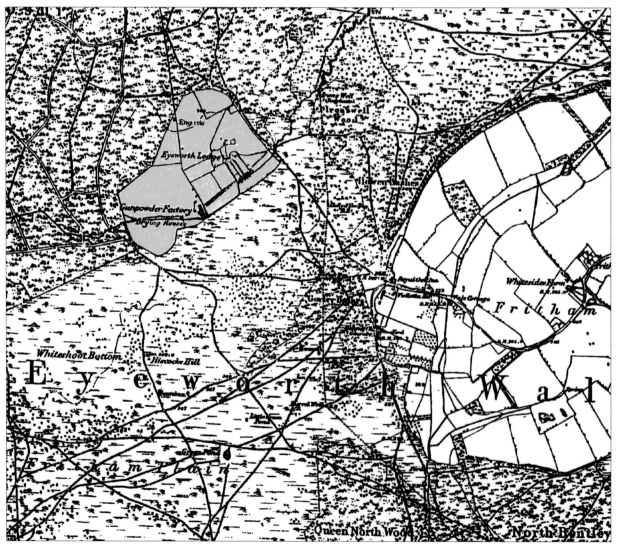

1869 map showing the remoteness of the manufacturing site at Eyeworth and the site layout prior to its development by Schultze

Memorandum of Association

OF THE

SCHULTZE GUNPOWDER COMPANY,

LIMITED.

1. The name of the Company is "THE SCHULTZE GUNPOWDER COMPANY, LIMITED."

2. The Registered Office of the Company will be situated in England.

3. The objects for which the Company is to be established are :—

(a) To import, manufacture, and sell Captain Schultze's Wood Gunpowder, and other explosive compounds, as exclusive Licensees of the said Captain Schultze, in accordance with the agreement of the seventeenth day of March, 1868, between Captain Schultze, of the one part, and Lieut.-Colonel Sampson Gompertz, of the other part.

(b) To import, manufacture, and sell all other inventions and improvements in explosive compounds made, or to be hereafter made, by Captain Schultze, or by any other person, and to take out or to purchase patents for any such inventions or improvements, and to import, manufacture, and sell any articles manufactured in connection with the said inventions and improvements, or any of them, and any apparatus which may be used with the said inventions and improvements, or any of them.

(c) To work under any patent, or under any licence or agreement with the owner of any invention, whether patented or not, having reference to the objects of the Company.

(d) To purchase or acquire land, whether freehold, copyhold, or leasehold, or to take on lease land and premises for the purposes of a manufactory for the objects of the said Company.

(e) And to do all such other acts as are usual in, or incidental to, or conducive to the attainment of the above objects.

4. The liability of the ~~Shareholders~~ *Members* is limited.

5. The capital of the Company is £10,000, divided into 100 Shares of £100 each, with power to increase.

We, the several persons whose names and addresses are subscribed, are desirous of being formed into a Company, in pursuance of this Memorandum of Association; and we respectively agree to take the number of Shares in the Capital of the Company set opposite our respective names.

Names and Addresses of Subscribers. *and description*	No. of Shares taken by each Subscriber.
W. H. Bayley. 25 Cambridge Square Hyde Park Middlesex Gentleman	Five
J Hewett Colonel Old Road Lee Kent	Three
T. Henry Clarke Temple Barrister Gentleman	Three
William Shaen 8 Bedford Row Middlesex Solicitor	Two
S Gomperts Colonel Bedford Lieut Colonel	Five
G. D. Tyser 3 Crosby Square London E.C. Merchant	Five
Henry Stead — 18 Old Broad Street London — Secretary of liquidator of London Bombay & Mediterranean Bank	Three

Registered with Articles of Association.

Dated this 18th day of July 1868

Witness to the signatures of the abovenamed William Henry Bayley, John Thomas Smith, James Henry Clarke, William Shaen, Sampson Gomperts, George Dorman Tyser and Henry Stead

William Wallett West Clerk to Messrs Shaen Solicitor 8 Bedford Row

This agreement gave the company the exclusive licensing rights to manufacture the new type of smokeless powder. The shareholder capital was put to immediate use and a lease was obtained by July 1869 for the Eyeworth site.

"SCHULTZE"
OLDEST & BEST
SPORTING POWDER

The company faced difficulties in the first decade of its existence due to many sportsmen rejecting the new smokeless powder. Part of the problem was based on the fact that radical new inventions were often treated with an element of suspicion but a secondary problem arose when users ignored the powder manufacturer's instructions and the resultant overload created breech pressures well above those which this early black powder proved shotgun had been tested to withstand. A further problem faced by the company was the lack of sufficient water, since the powder manufacturing process needed a constant supply and as output increased, so did the demand for water. In April 1871 permission was granted to build a small dam to the east of Eyeworth Lodge but one month later the project was stopped when it became clear to the authorities that the scheme was much larger than they had envisaged.

THE SCHULTZE GUNPOWDER

Labor fulmina securus

OFFICES
32 GRESHAM STREET.
LONDON. E.C.

SCHULTZE GUNPOWDER
Oldest and Best

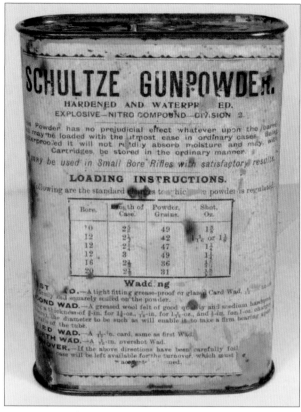

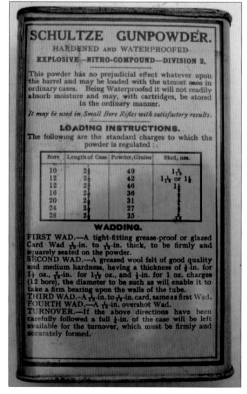

Like most powder manufacturers fatal accidents were a common problem and on 11 August 1871 a man was killed when the powder mill blew up and this was followed on a second occasion on 13 January 1873 when a second explosion injured three men.

In 1873 the company increased its capital from £10,000 to £100,000 with the issue of 10,000 shares at £10 each.

In 1874 the company gained a new employee namely Mr Richard William Smith Griffith, aged 23 years. He had trained as a chemist and for the next 32 years was to be associated with the Schultze powders. In due course he became regarded as the leading English pioneer in the development of smokeless powders and during his career he gained the satisfaction of seeing his ideas on this subject adopted throughout many areas of the world. From an initial post as the company Chemist he became a Director and Superintendent in charge of what was later to be the two factories occupied by the company.

Richard William Smith Griffith was born in Slough in 1851. The Salisbury Journal *on 7 April 1906 stated it was intended he should enter the medical profession, but he showed no aptitude and chose to devote his life to chemical research. In 1874 at the age of 23 he joined Schultze to manage the works with no real experience as a chemist, so it is assumed that his choice was a result of his social background and contacts.*

Based on his work the Schultze powders came to prominence at the Field trials of 1878 and the success of the company was down to his research into propellants. In due course he was to become the leading expert in the ballistics of shotgun cartridges and undertook the setting of related proof charges for the English Proof Houses, working alongside F.W. Jones who was the then leading authority on metallic cartridges. Griffith died on 28 March 1906.

He was a married man and lived for several years whilst working for Schultze in Eyeworth Lodge, which still exists today. He was a JP and a friend of the Romany tribes who frequented the forest

The turning point in the company's fortune came as a result of the *Field* trials of 1878 when black powder shotgun cartridges were put to the test against the new smokeless powder. The favourable results obtained with the Schultze powder were to change the old embedded beliefs held by many sportsmen of the day and there was a rapid move toward use of the new propellant. Unfortunately as a result of advice from an unknown

*Eyeworth Lodge believed taken just before 1899
when it was improved and extended as part of
the lease which stipulated that £300 had to be
spent improving it*
(Photograph courtesy of Mrs J. Jarvis)

*Eyeworth Lodge at it was during its occupation
by R. W. S. Griffith and family*
(Photograph courtesy of Mrs J. Jarvis)

Below:
Eyeworth Lodge as it appears in recent years
(Photograph courtesy of Mrs J. Jarvis)

gunmaker, Griffith was induced to make his batch of 1879 quicker in ignition which caused several actions and barrels to burst so he immediately returned to the previous formula which eradicated this problem.

In 1882 a new powder magazine was built together with three more cottages for staff. By 1891 the number of magazines had grown to six. During September 1883 a new application was made by the company to build a reservoir and in March 1884 permission was granted. However it was delayed when concerns were expressed over its proximity to Irons Well and the possible effects it may have on it. As a result in August 1888, during the negotiations over lease renewal, the Schultze company sought a reduction in rent in relation to the poor water facilities afforded to it. After some deliberation the Verderers of the Forest met and proposed no further objection to the reservoir resulting in its completion in August 1889. Also in 1883 a new road was sought by the company to carry their powder to Totton railway station. This was due to the problem that on passing through Fritham the horse drawn carts had to climb two steep hills resulting in an additional horse having to be picked up at the stables at the Round House to get up the inclines. The Crown authorised their request and a new road was built which, on leaving the works, passed through Ironswell Wood sited on a more gradual incline which offered them access to the road from Fordingbridge to Cadnam and then onto Totton. James Bush Jnr was one of the carriers who moved the powder in lead lined carts between the two sites and at peak some 30 to 40 horses per day were being used to transport the powder to the station.

A rear view of Eyeworth Lodge showing the retention of former stables once used to house the cart horses employed to move powder from the site to the railway station

James Bush Junior – one of the company's carriers (PHOTOGRAPH COURTESY OF THE BUSH FAMILY)

During the early 1880s there was a rapid expansion in the demand for Schultze powders but by 1884 it was reported in trade journals of the day that the company was not doing well and the Managing Director, Mr Clemont Dales, agreed to take a drop in salary to £100 per annum from the former £400 until the company was in a better state. Things did not improve and on the 17 March 1892 the shareholders held an extraordinary general meeting in Gresham Street, London resulting in it passing two major resolutions namely that the company should be voluntarily wound up and that George W. M. Dale and Walter F. Smith be appointed as liquidators. (Dale was a Barrister and Smith later became a Director.) These two parties were also set the task of registering a new company under the same name as the old one and they were empowered to transfer the assets of the former company to the new one, associated with which was a licence to produce a wider range of products including Dynamite, gun cotton and blasting powder.

By 1891 Griffith had been made Superintendent of the company. As he had a manager and foreman his main roles were devoted to experiments linked to the powder refining process and to establishing trade links for the company's products abroad. By now he was recognised as the leading British shotgun cartridge ballistician, which enhanced the reputation of the company. During his time with the company he had devised and experimented with equipment to determine from crusher gauges the internal pressures generated within a shotgun barrel and linking this with his use of chronographs he had studied the effect of pressure and velocity, both in terms of chamber and down barrel pressures and also in relation to produced shot patterns. Such was his and the company's standing that in 1896 60 famous gunmakers of the day, all members of the Gun-makers Association, came to the works by train from Waterloo then by road from Totton, where following a visit around the works, they received a lecture from Griffith on how the powders were manufactured and tested. The lecture was subsequently published in *Arms & Explosives* which indicated just how far forward his research had progressed in what could be regarded as a very short period of time. The visit also left a legacy of photographs of the factory recorded in a small booklet produced for the visitors, which are subsequently shown.

On the 10 December 1896 shareholders of the Smokeless Powder Company agreed to a takeover by Schultze since they found it expedient to do so, due to litigation between the two companies and Mr Heideman of the Rottweil Powder Co. of Germany over infringements of the Engel Patent by the Smokeless Powder Co. of Riflelite powder, and announced that Schultze would continue its defence to the legal proceedings taken against it.

Mr R.W.S. Griffith's office and chronograph room

The company's research laboratory

On 22 March 1897 The New Schultze Gunpowder Co. Ltd was incorporated with a capital of £325,000 divided into 32,500 5% cumulative preference shares and 32,5000 ordinary shares of £5 each, where the shareholders of the old company took £100,000 of each class of shares in part payment. The properties acquired include the leasehold land, buildings and plant etc. at the Eyeworth factory in the New Forest and also the recently acquired leasehold site at Redbridge, at which extensive works were being constructed to equip it with a nitrating plant. Directors of the new company were the Hon. John Douglas-Scott-Montagu, MP, Chairman, Mr Archibald Stuart Wortley, Mr Walter F. Smith, Managing Director, Mr G.W. Melville Dale and Mr R.W.S. Griffith, Superintendent of Works. Smith and Dale were Directors of the former named company where Griffith for 24 years had been in charge of the works. This additional finance enabled the company to manufacture gun cotton at the new Redbridge site. The Redbridge premises were previously occupied by Empire Chemical Works which

Grinding house

Purifying room

Powder hardening house

Nitrating tanks

was duly licensed by Colonel Sir Vivian Majendie, one of Her Majesty's Inspectors of Explosives in 1897.

In September 1898 the *Sporting Goods Review* reported that Mr F.C. Borer met the press in their London Gresham Street offices to announce that the Schultze company were applying for permission to erect a new factory at Totton in Hampshire. By October they reported that they had secured the lease to the Totton site and that the Redbridge factory was operational.

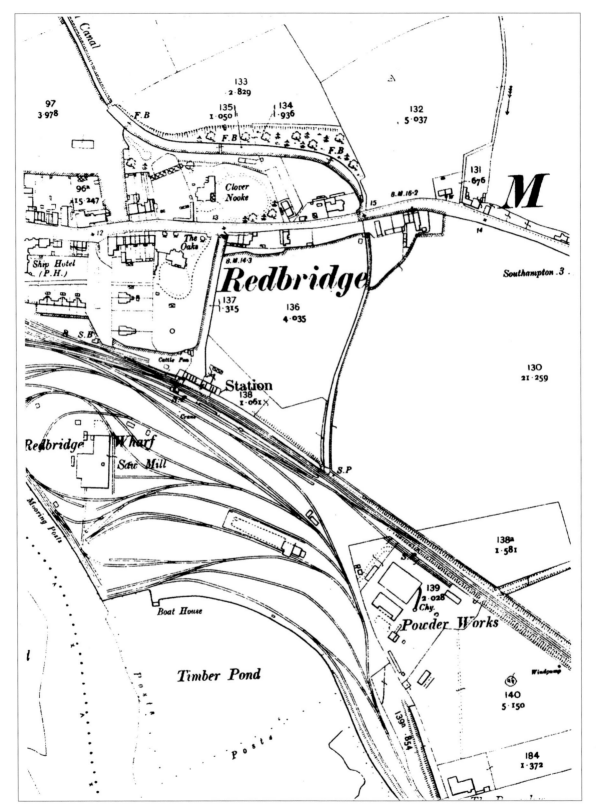

Schultze Redbridge site circa 1908

13.4 Name change to the Smokeless Powder & Ammunition Co.

On 8 November 1898 the firm of Shaen Roscoe & Massey, London Solicitors, received a letter from the Board of Trade approving a change of name of the Schultze Gunpowder Co. Ltd to the Smokeless Powder & Ammo Co. No further reference is made subsequently in any of the recorded minutes of the Schultze Co. to this company until 1912 when Schultze was being wound up and a liquidator wrote to the registrar of joint stock companies stating that the S. P. & A. Co. had no assets, had not conducted business for several years and the name had been retained solely for its commercial value.

In March 1899 an extraordinary meeting of the company was called, presided over by the Hon. J. Douglas-Scott-Montagu MP, where a resolution was passed to alter the company name back to its former title the 'Schultze Gunpowder Company Limited'. Later that year at the company's AGM in October it declared small returns and advised the shareholders that £7,000 had been spent on the new works and sought to create new capital by raising 24,000 £5 shares. This proposal was agreed and adopted.

In April 1902 the *Sporting Goods Review* reported that the company was creating considerable extensions at their cartridge loading department. The report stated that the turnover machines in use were now motor operated and totally automated providing a square turnover to the end of their cases.

Mr F. C. Borer, one of the company's Directors, retired in October 1904 and was given a pension for life having served almost 25 years with company. Borer was one of the initial founders of the Clay Bird Shooting Association.

On 15 April 1905 reports in the trade press indicated the failure of the rifle powder business of the Smokeless Powder & Ammunition Co. and depreciation in the £1 shares of American EC & Schultze Gunpowder Co. which this company held which resulted in a depreciation in the value of the main shares of the parent company.

On 10 January 1906 Griffith left Eyeworth with his wife Ellen Louisa for Cairo. By this time it was believed his health was deteriorating and after treatment for rheumatism he proceeded on a tour of the Holy Land. He subsequently contracted pneumonia and died on Ramleh near Alexandria on 28 March 1906 where he was buried. In May that year a former colleague of the late R. W. S. Griffith, Mr E.H. Durnford, was appointed Works Manager whilst a Mr Wadsworth was in charge of the company's chemical and technical departments. At the AGM in May 1906 the Hon. J. Douglas-Scott-Montagu (now Lord Montagu) was re-elected Chairman, Walter Smith was appointed Managing Director and Mr G. W. M. Dale was re-elected as a Director. At the subsequent year's AGM the company's profits had plummeted to £700 from a figure of £9,000 in 1905 and it was claimed that part of problem had arisen as a result of a faulty batch of Imperial Schultze powder which had resulted in adverse publicity.

In 1907 H. Doughty Browne, a former Chairman of the company and Mr E. M. Bristowe were elected to the Board of Directors.

13.5 The company's links with the EC Powder Company

In 1883 the EC Powder Co. was formed and created a new factory at Dartford in Kent. Like most English powder companies both Schultze and the EC Powder Company sought to penetrate the American market where the demand for propellants was massive. In March 1897 *Arms & Explosives* reported the cut throat competition which was occurring within the USA in relation to the sale of smokeless powders which had resulted in sale prices being so low than remuneration had become almost non existent. This competition led to a meeting being held on 8 February 1897 in London, to amalgamate Schultze's American market interests with those of the American EC Powder Company. The management decision resulted in the Schultze powders manufactured for the US trade being made alongside EC powder in the American EC factory sited in Oakland with the two powders subsequently being marketed side by side. Each company owned a proportional holding in the total capital of the American EC company, thus giving Schultze a half interest in its American competitor.

R. W. S. Griffith left England for America in early May 1897 and returned in July satisfied with the future prospects of the American EC and Schultze Gunpowder Co. Ltd. The initial amalgamation seems to have brought excellent results and Griffith reported that the trade in sporting powder trade 'is brighter than ever'.

The first AGM of the American EC and Schultze Gunpowder Co. was held on 26 April 1898, nine months after its formation. Walter F. Smith was appointed Chairman and Managing Director. The company's General Manager was Captain Money, the American Secretary was a Mr E. Banks and Messrs Von Lengerke and Detmold of New York were appointed to act as their business agents. Mr Hawkins had been appointed Superintendent of their Oakland Factory and Mr Charles Borland had been put in charge of their laboratory. The new company reported net profits for the nine months period of £3,093.

In 1904 the English offices of the American EC and Schultze Gunpowder Co. Ltd moved to Dashwood House, 40 New Bond Street, London EC where Mr L.G. Duff Grant has been appointed Secretary. In May 1904 the Hon. John Douglas-Scott-Montagu, MP, presided at the company's annual AGM where an agreement was reached with the English Schultze company that the American Schultze and EC Powder Co. was to supply the English company with £1,500 per annum in lieu of their interests given that the American factory had been leased to the E.I. Dupont de Nemours Company.

13.6 The company's links with Cogswell & Harrison and the emergence of Cogschultze

From about 1908 the company started encountering problems associated with Eley Bros Ltd failing to supply them with sufficient cartridge cases. This resulted in Schultze approaching Cogswell & Harrison, another cartridge case manufacturer, and they applied for the trade mark 'Cogschultze' in October 1909 in the *Trade Marks Journal*. This name was to be applicable to gunpowder, percussion caps and cartridges as a joint application between the two companies. The trade mark 'Cogschultze' was finally granted by December 1909. At the Schultze AGM in 1910 the company Directors reported problems with certain cartridge case suppliers. The name of this supplier was not quoted but this clearly related to their supplies from Cogswell & Harrison. At the same meeting mention was made of a problem associated with the lease related to the nitrating factory at Redbridge. This site was owned by the former King Edward VII and the Directors reported that they were attempting to get a temporary renewal of this lease.

On 27 February 1911, at an extraordinary meeting (held in the Cannon Street Hotel) of the Schultze company, it was agreed that the business should be wound up. Lord Montagu of Beaulieu, the Chairman was absent due to bronchitis. On the 27 March 1911 the Schultze Gunpowder Co. Ltd issued notices indicating it intended to sell up since they stated there was no point manufacturing powder without the necessary plant for making cartridge cases. Clearly others thought its demise had been due to poor management and this was expressed in a letter written by a Gerald Lascelles to the Office of the Woods in which he stated:

Formerly the Schultze Co was a most thriving and prosperous concern. But when it was bought up by the New Schultze Co under the chairmanship of Lord Montagu, and with a new board of directors, with an enormous and useless amount of capital its history has been a sad one. It had paid no dividends for some five years past. It makes no profits and is now proposing to wind up at a loss of considerably over £200,000 – more than four fifths of its subscribed capital.

Between the decision taken to wind up the old company and the registration of a new company a case of civil litigation arose between Cogswell & Harrison over the Cogschultze agreement which had been entered into in 1909. The case was settled by mutual consent and on 5 July 1911 the Cogschultze Ammunition & Powder Co. Ltd was registered with a capital of £10,000 in £1 shares to carry on the business of manufacturers of and dealers in gunpowder, Nitroglycerine, Dynamite, gun cotton, blasting powder and other explosives, and to adopt an agreement with Cogswell &

Harrison Ltd. The liquidators of the Schultze Gunpowder Co. Ltd had agreed by the terms of the settlement to dispose of their former share of the trade name or brand 'Cogschultze' together with the related goodwill and pass it to Cogswell & Harrison Ltd. 'Cogschultze' had previously been owned by the Schultze Gunpowder Co. Ltd and the Cogswell & Harrison Manufacturing Company.

13.7 Acquisition of the company by Eley Bros Limited and its final absorption into the Nobel owned group of companies

In 1911 Eley Bros Limited offered £39,098 for the company together with a further £10,800 for the properties owned by Ellen Griffith (the wife of R.W.S. Griffith) which she had sold to Schultze in 1909. The assets of the company were finally acquired by Eley on 2 August 1911. The other new shareholders were Stanley Faber Prest, an engineer, Charles Cuthbert Eley, a member of the Eley family and Kenneth Loder Cromwell Prescott, a London banker, all of whom obtained 100 £1 shares, and Gerald Lascelles (who on the share certificates is recorded as an Accounts Clerk, however he was better known locally as the Honourable Gerald Lascelles, Deputy Surveyor to the Verderers of the Forest) and Archibald Hamilton Cullen a chartered accountant both of whom obtained one £1 share.

The new company, entitled Schultze Co. Ltd was registered in July 1911 with a capital of £100,000 in £1 shares to carry on the business of manufacturers of gunpowder, Nitroglycerine, Dynamite, gun cotton, blasting powder explosives for military and mining purposes, cartridges, detonators, fuses etc. and to adopt an agreement with the existing Schultze Gunpowder Co. Ltd (on voluntary liquidation). The company's shotgun cartridges with brand names 'Rainproof', 'Eyeworth', 'Westminster', 'Yeoman' and' Pickaxe' were now loaded in Eley Bros cases at the Schultze Westminster site. The former Works Manager Captain H. Hardy was retained by the new owners as were the works premises at Eyeworth, Redbridge and Totton. In October 1911 the Schultze main offices moved from Gresham Street to 254A Gray's Inn Road, London WC, the home of Eley Bros Ltd, their new owners.

On 15 October 1914 Schultze Co. Ltd issued a series of special notices which stated that its products and the company were entirely British. This was a response to the public backlash to anything or anyone associated with Germany, a country with which Great Britain was now at war. Clearly this did not totally satisfy the Eley management and in December 1914 the Schultze Co. moved offices from those of Eley's in Gray's Inn Road to 40 New Bond Street. In January 1916 it went a stage further when its name reverted to the Schultze Gunpowder Co. Ltd, with its offices at 40 New Bond Street, London EC. The change in title involved no alteration to its Directors, staff, capital or shareholders and was aimed solely at dissipating any alien suggestion that the name Schultze may convey when used, apart from its connection with the typically English association of Schultze gunpowder.

In October 1915 the *Arms & Explosives* journal mentioned that the company had announced two new powders, 'Frankite' and 'Gallite', but I have yet to find any shotgun cartridges indicating they are loaded with either propellant.

In January 1920 an advert taken out by the company stated that the sales department had transferred to Explosives Trades Ltd, Angel Road, Edmonton, N18 following its absorption together with Eley Bros Ltd into the Nobel company.

13.8 Plans of the Schultze site at Fritham and the only remaining evidence of its former existence

If you were to visit the land on which the Schultze factory site was once sited at Fritham you

SCHULTZE.
SMOKELESS
GUNPOWDER & CARTRIDGES.

On and after 1st January, 1920, the Sales of our Powders and Cartridges will be conducted by Explosives Trades Ltd., and all orders and enquiries for our products should be addressed to :

EXPLOSIVES TRADES Ltd.,
Ammunition Sales Dept.,
Angel Road, Edmonton,
London, N. 18.

The Schultze Gunpowder Co., Ltd.,
LONDON.

Advert from Sporting Goods Review *15 January 1920*

The old post box for the factory. It was sited some distance from the factory confines to prevent postmen inadvertently bringing in material capable of generating sparks, for example, steel studs on boots or matches

A former Schultze factory powder store

would find little left to indicate its former existence with the exception of Eyeworth Lodge, whose frontage is just visible as a distant landmark from a track within the forest. There are however, two remaining features which can be seen: the former post box for the company which has been retained (although I believe it has been re-sited from its original position) and one remaining powder store which has apparently subsequently served as an animal shelter.

The only photograph I could find of this site was on a picture postcard. I believe the house in the far right sector is Eyeworth Lodge with the buildings behind and to the right being the stables.

Powder Mills, Fritham.

13.9 Work staff and recorded accidents at the site

The gatekeeper John Gage.
Albert Taylor in the Hampshire *said:*
'He was the man to watch out for. He blew his whistle at 7 o'clock and if you weren't ready to go straight in you had to wait outside until 8.30am and lose a quarter of a day's pay. Some of those who had to walk six miles or more would always be there in good time, sitting smoking a pipe and chatting whilst they waited for the whistle it was us youngsters who had no distance to travel who were always later to arrive. I never even used to leave myself time to tie up my laces until one morning I was going full tilt down the hill lost my boot in the bog. By the time I had hopped back and got it again I was too late for the whistle.'

There are a number of old maps of the site at Eyeworth and two of these are shown.

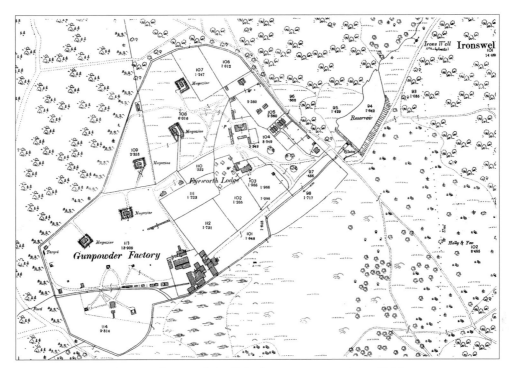

Eyeworth site of the Schultze company circa 1909

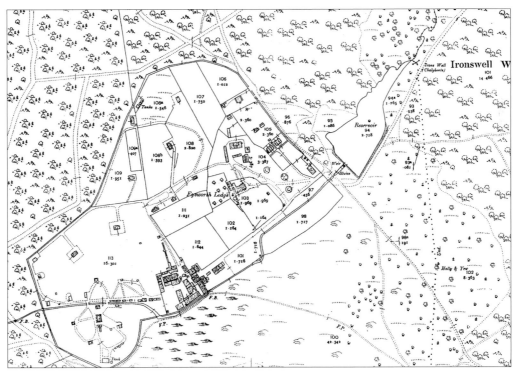

Map of Schultze factory at Eyeworth sometime after 1909 – note the new size of the reservoir and the presence of new buildings and roadways

A tradition existed where some of the workmen who owned ponies were allowed to bring them to the factory provided that they were made available to transport material around the site. One employee named Jack Batten had a particularly fast horse and on the strength of this he was sent to collect the workers' wages using a whistle for protection.

On 10 February 1908 Arthur Stainer a 26 year old blacksmith was hammering a revolving shaft and it appears he was doing this whilst it was in motion. There were hooks on the wall behind the shaft and Stainer was repeatedly struck against these which tore into his back and removed part of his skull, killing him.

On 1 March 1915 an explosion on the site killed two men and seriously injured a third. Albert Deacon an 18 year old and a James Hiscock aged 57 were working on the Poaching House taking up the flooring in two old boilers when powder that had got under the flooring ignited killing the two men. The end of one boiler was blow out and the shed wrecked. Hiscock was found dead alongside one of the boilers, Deacon was found inside one of the boilers and a Howard Webb was found some distance outside the shed suffering from major injuries. The two deceased had been given instructions to remove two old boilers from the site by road. The boilers had previously been used in the Purifying House where nitrated grain was washed within them and had been last utilised some seven years before. Although the exact cause of the accident was never established, alternative theories revolved around a spark being generated from the steel boot studs or an iron crow bar which ignited the residual powder; however with hindsight the area should have been flooded with water before this removal occurred.

At some point during the life of the company its staff formed a works band which was in existence by 1904. From a photograph I have seen it consisted of 11 men equipped mainly with wind instruments and a single base drum. The band wore extremely smart uniforms and obviously acted as ambassadors for the company.

Staff from the day shift

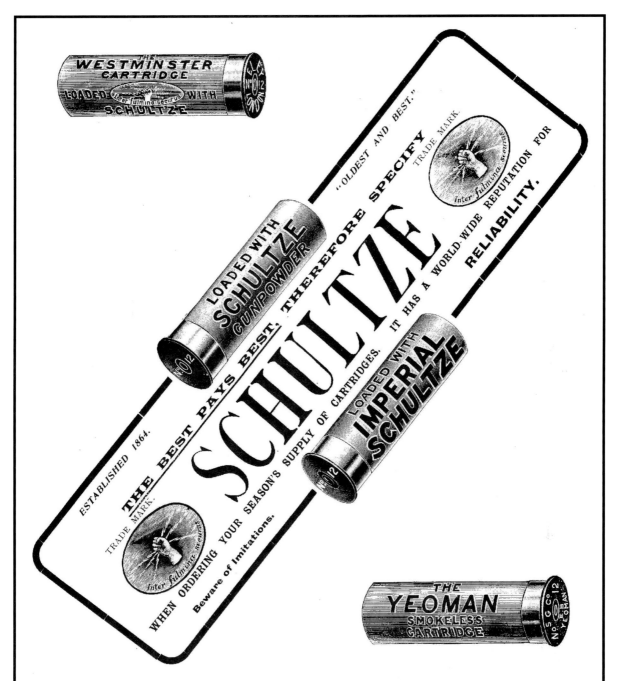

GUNMAKERS & AMMUNITION DEALERS

will be supplied with Price Lists and full particulars on application to

THE SCHULTZE GUNPOWDER COMPANY, LIMITED,

28 Gresham Street, London, E.C.

Advert in Arms & Explosives *June 1905*

13.10 Examples of adverts used by the company

Sporting Goods Review *advert 1898*

Advert in Arms & Explosives *December 1905*

SCHULTZE

GUNPOWDER

AND

CARTRIDGES

TRADE  *MARK.*

Inter fulmina securus

PRICE MAINTAINED.

USED IN EVERY QUARTER OF THE GLOBE.

=== SOLE MANUFACTURERS: ===

The Schultze Gunpowder Co. Ltd.

28 GRESHAM STREET, LONDON, E.C.

Advert in Arms & Explosives *November 1907*

Advert in Sporting Goods Review *15 September 1913*

SEASON 1914-1915.

THE

SCHULTZE COMPANY

LIMITED.

PRICE LIST

OF

CARTRIDGES

Gunpowder Factories at EYEWORTH and REDBRIDGE, HAMPSHIRE.

Head Office :

254a, GRAY'S INN ROAD, LONDON, W.C.

Cables :	EYEWORTH, LONDON.
Telegraphic Address :	EYEWORTH KINCROSS, LONDON (Two words).
Telephone Number :	HOLBORN 20.
Codes used :	A.B.C., 5th Edition.
	WESTERN UNION.

THE SCHULTZE COMPANY LTD.

PIGEON SHOOTING

SCHULTZE has Won all existing Championships

viz :—

Triennial Championship, Monte Carlo (held nine years continuously), viz :—	1889– 1898
The Amateur Championship of America	1895
The Professional Championship of America ..	1895
The Championship at Spa	1895
The Championship at Aix-les-Bains	1895
The Championship at Bosnia	1896
The Championship at Spa	1896
The Championship Medal, Rome	1896
The Championship Sweepstakes, Hurlingham ...	1896
The Champion Stakes (Gun Club) divided... ...	1896
The Championship of America, won at Larchmont, U.S.A. ... ... Jan.,	1897
The Championship at Ostend...	1897
The Championship at Cannes	1897
The Gun Club £100 Challenge Cup (won outright), International Meeting	1897
The Challenge Cup, Melbourne	1897
The Grand Prix du Casino, Monte Cralo	1898
The Grand American Handicap, 197 competitors...	1898
(1st, 2nd and 3rd used Schultze.)	
Championship of New South Wales	1903
Championship at Florence	1904
Triennial Championship, Monte Carlo	1904
Championship of New South Wales	1904

CONTENTS.

THE SCHULTZE COMPANY LTD.

THE DIRECTORS of the Schultze Company Limited have pleasure in presenting their Cartridge Catalogue for 1914, and venture to hope that they may be favoured with a continuance of the patronage extended to them in the past by their numerous customers.

The ruling principle of the Schultze Company will always be to supply the very best article that skill and money can produce, and this policy will be rigidly adhered to. All Cartridges will be loaded with the Company's powders in cases of "Eley" manufacture.

The powders manufactured and recommended by the Company are as follows :—

(1) "**SCHULTZE**" (Ordinary)—the pioneer smokeless powder—of world-wide repute. "Schultze" was the first nitro-compound powder manufactured in this country; it has been prominently before the public for nearly half a century, and is still the best; it is always regular, and thus has rightly earned a character for being absolutely reliable. It is essentially a game-shooting powder, and is expressly designed and adapted for use in the field, being standardized to give the best results with medium loads at sporting ranges, and to combine regularity of pattern and effective penetration, with due regard to safety and comfort.

The standard charge for a 12-bore gun is 42 grains.

THE SCHULTZE COMPANY LTD.

(2) "**LIGHTNING**" Powder—the latest development of Smokeless Shot Gun Powder. It is absolutely free from either smoke or "blow back" and leaves a very slight residuum in the barrel after firing. It contains no nitro-glycerine and has no prejudicial action on the gun barrels. It cannot deteriorate by age or keeping, as it is waterproof and is not affected by atmospheric changes.

"LIGHTNING" is very quick in its action and gives a uniformly high velocity with even patterns. Its recoil is less than that of any other powder of equal strength It gives very little report, and in consequence is not likely to produce gun-headache.

"LIGHTNING" is well adapted for light charges of shot owing to the regularity of the patterns produced.

The standard charge for a 12-bore gun is 33 grains.

(3) "**POPULAR**" and "**FULMEN**" Powders are very moderately priced explosives, but their shooting qualities are good, and will be found to give satisfaction.

The standard charges for a 12-bore gun are : "Popular," 42 grains; "Fulmen," 33 grains.

NOTE.—All these powders are supplied in bulk to those who wish to load their own ammunition.

THE SCHULTZE COMPANY LTD.

PROPRIETARY CARTRIDGES.—With a view to assisting our customers to compete with Continental Manufacturers' Ammunition, reductions have been made in the prices of the cheaper grades of Cartridges, and two new Proprietary Cartridges have been introduced. These are the "Conqueror" and the "Captain" Cartridges, the former being loaded with "Lightning" and the latter with "Fulmen" Powder.

Quotations for Cartridges or Cases not described in the List, or for Loading Customers' own named Cases, will be given on application.

CUSTOMERS' NAMED CARTRIDGES.—The minimum number of Cartridges on which customers' names will be printed on the tubes at list prices is: 20,000 of one quality, colour and print. For orders of between 10,000 and 20,000, however, we shall be pleased to print customers' names on the tubes at an additional price of 1s. 6d. per 1000 over and above the list price, subject.

All orders for named Cases or Cartridges are taken on the understanding that customers agree to accept in execution of their orders, plus or minus 10% of the quantity ordered.

Delivery of every order for named Cases or Cartridges must be taken within twelve months of date of order.

THE SCHULTZE COMPANY LTD.

Prices for Special Loading

FOR ALL QUALITIES OF CARTRIDGES.

The following are the MAXIMUM loads supplied at the prices shewn in this list. (*Note :—The loads recommended are shewn on pages 16 and 17.*)

Case.	SCHULTZE & POPULAR "42 Grain."		LIGHTNING & FULMEN "33 Grain."	
	Powder Grs.	Shot Ozs.	Powder Grs.	Shot Ozs.
12×2½″	42	1⅛	33	1⅛
12×2½″	44	1 1/16	34	1 1/16
12×2½″	46	1	36	1
12×2¾″	47	1¼	38	1¼

Variations from above loads will be charged as follows:—

	Extra per 100.
For each grain of Powder over maximum	2d.
For each 1/16 oz. Shot over maximum	2d.
Chilled Shot	3d.
Letter Shots, excluding S.S.G. series	6d.
S.S.G. series Shot	9d.

THE SCHULTZE COMPANY LTD.

Proprietary Cartridges.

PRICE MAINTAINED.

Loaded with **"Schultze"** Powder.

Packing: In Boxes of 100 or 25. — Price per 100. s. d. — Maintained Price per 100. s. d.

"SCHULTOID"
WATERPROOF
CARTRIDGE
SCHULTZE

13 8 — 11 0

BEST QUALITY METAL LINED GASTIGHT.
WATERPROOF PEGAMOID PAPER.
Colour: Indian Red
Gauge: 12 only.

EYEWORTH
METAL LINED
CARTRIDGE

12 8 — 10 6

BEST QUALITY METAL LINED GASTIGHT.
Colour: Buff
Gauge: 12, 16 and 20.

WESTMINSTER
CARTRIDGE

11 8 — 9 6

METAL LINED 5/16 INCH BRASS HEAD.
Colour: Buff.
Gauge: 12, 16 and 20.

The above Cartridges are sold on the understanding that they are not sold nor offered for sale below the maintained prices shewn above.

THE SCHULTZE COMPANY LTD.

Proprietary Cartridges.

PRICE MAINTAINED.

Loaded with **"Lightning"** Powder.

Packing: In Boxes of 100 or 25. — Price per 100. s. d. — Maintained Price per 100. s. d.

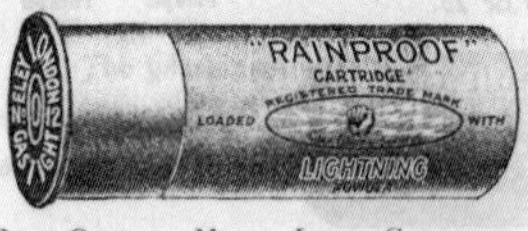
"RAINPROOF"
CARTRIDGE
LIGHTNING

13 8 — 11 0

BEST QUALITY METAL LINED GASTIGHT.
WATERPROOF PEGAMOID PAPER.
Colour: Amethyst.
Gauge: 12 only.

"CONQUEROR"
LOADED WITH
LIGHTNING POWDER

12 2 — 10 0

⅜ INCH DEEP BRASS HEADS.
Colour: Amethyst.
Gauge: 12 only.

"ALBION"
CARTRIDGE
LIGHTNING

10 8 — 9 0

5/16 INCH BRASS HEADS.
Colour: Dark Orange.
Gauge: 12 only.

The above Cartridges are sold on the understanding that they are not sold nor offered for sale below the maintained prices shewn above.

THE SCHULTZE COMPANY LTD.

Proprietary Cartridges.

PRICE MAINTAINED.

Loaded with **"Popular"** Powder.

Packing: In Boxes of 100 or 25. — Price per 100. s. d. — Maintained Price per 100. s. d.

THE
RUFUS
SMOKELESS
CARTRIDGE

11 0 — 9 6

⅜ INCH DEEP BRASS HEAD.
Colour: Deep Crimson.
Gauge: 12, 16 and 20.

YEOMAN
SMOKELESS
CARTRIDGE

9 6 — 8 6

5/16 INCH BRASS HEADS.
Colour: Indian Red.
Gauge: 12, 16 and 20.

THE
"PICKAXE"
SMOKELESS
CARTRIDGE

8 6 — 7 6

5/16 INCH BRASS HEADS.
Colour: Pale Green.
Gauge: 12 only.

The above Cartridges are sold on the understanding that they are not sold nor offered for sale below the maintained prices shewn above.

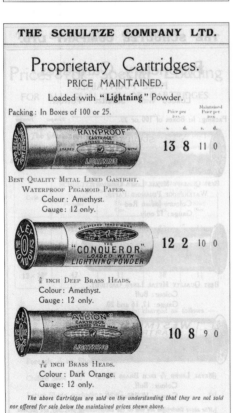

THE SCHULTZE COMPANY LTD.

A New Proprietary Cartridge.

SPECIAL CHEAP QUALITY.

Loaded with "Fulmen" Powder.

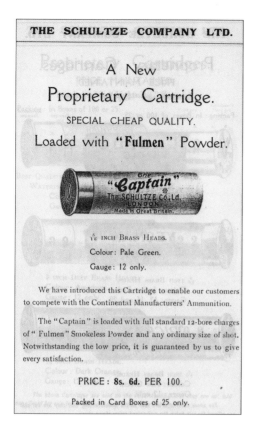

$\frac{7}{16}$ INCH BRASS HEADS.

Colour: Pale Green.

Gauge: 12 only.

We have introduced this Cartridge to enable our customers to compete with the Continental Manufacturers' Ammunition.

The "Captain" is loaded with full standard 12-bore charges of "Fulmen" Smokeless Powder and any ordinary size of shot. Notwithstanding the low price, it is guaranteed by us to give every satisfaction.

PRICE: 8s. 6d. PER 100.

Packed in Card Boxes of 25 only.

THE SCHULTZE COMPANY LTD.

"EJECTOR" Cartridge Cases.

SEAMLESS METAL COVERING.

Loaded with "Schultze" or "Lightning" Powder.

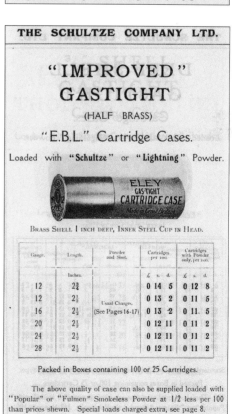

STANDARD LENGTH OF BRASS 2$\frac{1}{4}$ INCH.

INNER STEEL CUP IN HEAD.

Gauge.	Length.	Powder and Shot.	Cartridges, per 100.			Cartridges with Powder only, per 100.		
	Inches.		£	s.	d.	£	s.	d.
12	2$\frac{3}{4}$		0	17	8	0	15	11
12	2$\frac{1}{2}$		0	15	2	0	13	5
14	2$\frac{1}{2}$	Usual Charges. (See pages 16-17)	0	15	2	0	13	5
16	2$\frac{1}{2}$		0	15	2	0	13	5
20	2$\frac{1}{2}$		0	14	11	0	13	2
28	2$\frac{1}{2}$		0	14	11	0	13	2

Packed in Boxes containing 100 or 25 Cartridges.

The above quality of case can also be supplied loaded with "Popular" or "Fulmen" Smokeless Powder at 1/2 less per 100 than prices shewn. Special loads charged extra, see page 8.

THE SCHULTZE COMPANY LTD.

"PEGAMOID"

Waterproof Cartridge Cases.

Loaded with "Schultze" or "Lightning" Powder.

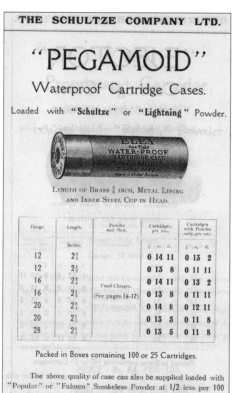

LENGTH OF BRASS $\frac{5}{8}$ INCH, METAL LINING AND INNER STEEL CUP IN HEAD.

Gauge.	Length.	Powder and Shot.	Cartridges, per 100.			Cartridges with Powder only, per 100.		
	Inches.		£	s.	d.	£	s.	d.
12	2$\frac{3}{4}$		0	14	11	0	13	2
12	2$\frac{1}{2}$		0	13	8	0	11	11
16	2$\frac{3}{4}$		0	14	11	0	13	2
16	2$\frac{1}{2}$	Usual Charges. (See pages 16-17)	0	13	8	0	11	11
20	2$\frac{3}{4}$		0	14	8	0	12	11
20	2$\frac{1}{2}$		0	13	5	0	11	8
28	2$\frac{1}{2}$		0	13	5	0	11	8

Packed in Boxes containing 100 or 25 Cartridges.

The above quality of case can also be supplied loaded with "Popular" or "Fulmen" Smokeless Powder at 1/2 less per 100 than prices shewn. Special loads charged extra, see page 8.

THE SCHULTZE COMPANY LTD.

"IMPROVED" GASTIGHT

(HALF BRASS)

"E.B.L." Cartridge Cases.

Loaded with "Schultze" or "Lightning" Powder.

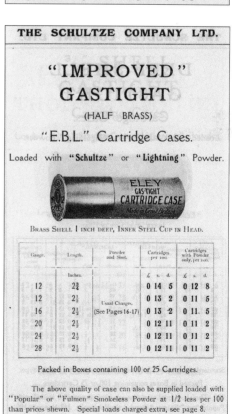

BRASS SHELL 1 INCH DEEP, INNER STEEL CUP IN HEAD.

Gauge.	Length.	Powder and Shot.	Cartridges per 100.			Cartridges with Powder only, per 100.		
	Inches.		£	s.	d.	£	s.	d.
12	2$\frac{3}{4}$		0	14	5	0	12	8
12	2$\frac{1}{2}$		0	13	2	0	11	5
16	2$\frac{1}{2}$	Usual Charges. (See Pages 16-17)	0	13	2	0	11	5
20	2$\frac{1}{2}$		0	12	11	0	11	2
24	2$\frac{1}{2}$		0	12	11	0	11	2
28	2$\frac{1}{2}$		0	12	11	0	11	2

Packed in Boxes containing 100 or 25 Cartridges.

The above quality of case can also be supplied loaded with "Popular" or "Fulmen" Smokeless Powder at 1/2 less per 100 than prices shewn. Special loads charged extra, see page 8.

THE SCHULTZE COMPANY LTD.

DEEP-SHELL GASTIGHT
Cartridge Cases.

Loaded with "**Schultze**" or "**Lightning**" Powder.

LENGTH OF BRASS ⅝ INCH. METAL LINING AND INNER STEEL CUP IN HEAD.

Gauge.	Length.	"SCHULTZE."		"LIGHTNING."		Cartridges, per 100.			Cartridges with Powder only, per 100.		
		Powder.	Shot.	Powder.	Shot.	£	s.	d.	£	s.	d.
	Inches.	Grs.	Ozs.	Grs.	Ozs.						
8	3¼	77	2¼	60	2	1	5	2	1	3	5
10	2⅞	49	1⅜	39	1¼	0	17	2	0	15	5
12	2⅝	47	1⅜	37	1⅛	0	13	11	0	12	2
12	2½	45	1⅛	35	1 to 1⅛	0	13	2	0	11	5
12	**2½**	**42**	**1 to 1⅛**	**33**	**1 to 1¹⁄₁₆**	**0**	**12**	**8**	**0**	**10**	**11**
14	2½	39	1	31	⅞	0	12	8	0	10	11
16	2½	36	1¹⁄₁₆	28	1	0	13	11	0	12	2
16	**2½**	**36**	**⅞**	**28**	**⅞**	**0**	**12**	**8**	**0**	**10**	**11**
16	2½	33	⅞	26	¾	0	13	8	0	11	11
20	**2½**	**31**	**⅞**	**25**		**0**	**12**	**5**	**0**	**10**	**8**

Standard charges for 12, 16 and 20 bore shewn in thicker type.

Packed in Boxes containing 100 or 25 Cartridges.

The above quality of case can also be supplied loaded with "Popular" or "Fulmen" Smokeless Powder at 1/2 less per 100 than prices shewn. Special loads charged extra, see page 8.

THE SCHULTZE COMPANY LTD.

³⁄₈"-SHELL GASTIGHT
Cartridge Cases.

Loaded with "**Schultze**" or "**Lightning**" Powder.

LENGTH OF BRASS ⅜ INCH. IRON LINING AND INNER STEEL CUP IN HEAD.

Gauge.	Length.	"SCHULTZE."		"LIGHTNING."		Cartridges, per 100.			Cartridges with Powder only, per 100		
		Powder.	Shot.	Powder.	Shot.	£	s.	d.	£	s.	d.
	Inches.	Grs.	Oz.	Grs.	Oz.						
12	2½	42	1 to 1⅛	33	1 to 1¹⁄₁₆	0	12	2	0	10	5
16	2½	36	1¹⁄₁₆	28	⅞	0	12	2	0	10	5
20	2½	31	1¾	25	¾	0	11	11	0	.10	2
24	2½	28	1¹⁄₁₆	22	⅔	0	11	11	0	10	2
28	2½	26	⅞	20	½	0	11	11	0	10	2
32	2½	20	⅔	16	⁷⁄₁₆	0	11	11	0	10	2

Packed in Boxes containing 100 or 25 Cartridges.

The above quality of case can also be supplied loaded with "Popular" or "Fulmen" Smokeless Powder at 1/2 less per 100 than prices shewn. Special loads charged extra, see page 8.

THE SCHULTZE COMPANY LTD.

DEEP-SHELL
UNLINED GASTIGHT
Cartridge Cases.

Loaded with "**Schultze**" or "**Lightning**" Powder.

LENGTH OF BRASS ⅝ INCH. INNER STEEL CUP IN HEAD.

Gauge.	Length.	Powder and Shot.	Cartridges, per 100.			Cartridges with Powder only, per 100.		
	Inches.		£	s.	d.	£	s.	d.
12	2½	Usual Charges. (See pages 16-17)	0	12	2	0	10	5
16	2½		0	12	2	0	10	5
20	2½		0	11	11	0	10	2

Packed in Boxes containing 100 or 25 Cartridges.

The above quality of case can also be supplied loaded with "Popular" or "Fulmen" Smokeless powder at 1/2 less per 100 than prices shewn. Special loads charged extra, see page 8.

THE SCHULTZE COMPANY LTD.

"E.B. NITRO"
Cartridge Cases.

Loaded with "**Schultze**" or "**Lightning**" Powder.

LENGTH OF BRASS ¹⁄₁₆ INCH. IRON LINING AND INNER STEEL CUP IN HEAD.

Gauge.	Length.	Powder and Shot.	Cartridges, per 100.			Cartridges with Powder only, per 100		
	Inches.		£	s.	d.	£	s.	d.
12	2¾	Usual Charges. (See pages 16-17)	0	12	11	0	11	2
12	2½		0	11	8	0	9	11
16	2½		0	11	8	0	9	11
20	2½		0	11	5	0	9	8

Packed in Boxes containing 100 or 25 Cartridges.

The above quality of case can also be supplied loaded with "Popular" or "Fulmen" Smokeless powder at 1/2 less per 100 than prices shewn. Special loads charged extra, see page 8.

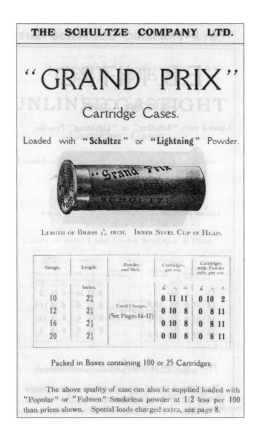

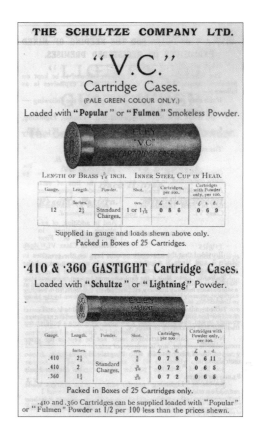

13.11 Notes on the company's cartridge production

In August 1899 it was announced that the Schultze Gunpowder Co. had started to load and retail their own cartridges and in the *Sporting Goods Review* it was reported that the Schultze Gunpowder Co. Ltd had secured offices above their main offices at Gresham Street to load cartridges. In February 1900 it was reported that the company had established a loading site at York Place, Westminster and not at Gresham Street, so presumably the initially targeted site had proved unacceptable.

In June 1900 it was reported that their new powder called Imperial Schultze would not be available until September 1900, its main characteristics being the elimination of smoke, absence of blow back and perfection of pattern.

In December 1904 the company applied for registration of its famous trade mark 'Inter Fulmina Securus' for cases and cartridges. This Latin expression can be interpreted as 'safe between bolts of lightning'. On the 28 December 1904 they applied to use the trade mark 'Westminster', which was granted Registered No. 268875 in 1905. The significance of the name was its association with where the cartridges were being loaded. By February 1905 the company were loading at their premises in Westminster the following branded cases, supplied to them by Eley Bros Ltd: Eley EB, Gastight, Improved Gastight, Ejector and Pegamoid. In January 1905 the company announced their new brand of cartridge named 'Yeoman' which was not to be retailed at less than 7s per 1,000. This trade name was registered to Schultze as trade mark No. 296921 in 1907.

In April 1907 they advertised that they were offering deep base cartridges and in July 1907 they introduced three new brand names, the 'Pickaxe', 'Rainproof' and 'Eyeworth'. Their light load cartridge named 'Pickaxe' was a cheap brand aimed at competing with the low price foreign imports.

Their 1908 catalogue showed them retailing the 'Westminster', 'Eyeworth' and 'Yeoman' in 12, 16 and 20 2½" and the 'Pickaxe' solely in 12 bore 2½". In addition they offered Ejectors, Pegamoids and Gastights in gauges from 8 bore down to .410".

Following their takeover by Eley Bros Ltd in 1911 we see an explosion of new brand names. Since WWI effectively stopped the vast majority of shotgun cartridge production, and Nobel's takeover in November 1918 of Eley Bros Ltd ended large numbers of former cartridge brand names, most of the cartridges and powder brands listed below are seldom encountered except in the large collections. The brands in question were:

'Schultoid' – This trade mark was granted Registered No. 335927 in November 1911
'Rufus' – This trade mark was granted Registered No. 337170 in February 1912. It was loaded into a red case with a ⅝" head and retailed at 9s per 100
'Albion' – This trade mark was applied for 4 December 1912 and Registered No. 347696 was granted to it on 19 March 1913
'Fulmen' powder – This trade mark was applied for 2 January 1913 and Registered No. 347696 was granted to it on 9 April 1913
'Lightning' powder – This trade mark was applied for 2 January 1913 and Registered No. 348741 was granted to it on 18 April 1913
'Captain' – This trade mark was applied for in January 1914 and granted in March 1914
'Conqueror' – This trade mark was applied for in February 1914 and granted in April 1914
'Pilot' – This trade mark was applied for in February 1914 and granted in April 1914

In September 1915 Mr Wills, an employee of Schultze sent to *Arms & Explosives* specimens of their cartridges for examination. The subsequent examination revealed that:

'Schultoid' brand cartridges were using Eley Bros Ltd Pegamoid paper cases
'Rainproof' brand cartridges were loaded with 'Lightning' powder
'Eyeworth' brand cartridges used buff cases loaded with 'Schultze' powder
'Conqueror' brand cartridges were loaded with 'Lightning' powder
'Rufus' brand cartridges were loaded with 'Popular' powder

The following proved to be shallow base cartridges:
    'Albion' loaded with 'Lightning' powder
    'Yeoman' loaded with 'Popular' powder
    'Pickaxe' loaded with 'Popular' powder

13.12 Examples of the company's cartridges

 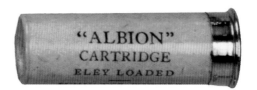

Although the Albion cartridge brand was short lived at least two variants exist.
The Albion brand refers to the fact that 'Albion' was a name formerly used to define Great Britain

At the time of examination by Mr Wills the 'Captain' and 'Pickaxe' brands had been temporarily withdrawn owing to the pressure from Government orders.

The 'Pilot' brand name was issued but I have yet to locate a specimen bearing this name.

A specimen of the 'Pickaxe'. It bears the headstamp shown where the J above London indicates the case was made by Joyce of London

It is perhaps worth mentioning that the brand name 'Captain' was clearly linked to Captain Schultze and due to the problems concerning the public perception of Schultze being a company linked to Germany, very few specimens of this brand remain; there is good reason to believe its production numbers were low although specimens do exist in both 12 and 20 bore

THE SCHULTZE GUNPOWDER COMPANY, LIMITED

SOLE MANUFACTURERS OF

SCHULTZE and LIGHTNING

GUNPOWDER

The Company desire to inform the Sporting Public that the constitution of the Company is entirely British. There are no alien shareholders, and all the Directors and employees are British. The Schultze Powders were the first smokeless sporting powders made in this country and have been manufactured since 1869 at the Company's Works in Hampshire. Sportsmen may therefore continue to use the Schultze Gunpowder Company's products with the knowledge that by so doing they are supporting a purely British industry.

Works:
EYEWORTH and REDBRIDGE, HANTS.

HEAD OFFICES : 40, New Broad Street, London, E.C.

Above is one of many adverts taken out by the company to impress its readers that the company was not German. This one appeared in Sporting Goods Review *on 26 April 1917*

The name Conqueror relates to William the Conqueror who converted the New Forest into a royal hunting ground and the Schultze site was in the heart of this former Royal chase

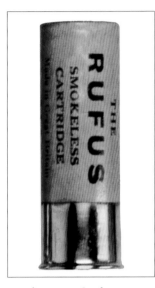

Rufus was the favourite son of William the Conqueror and was killed by a stray arrow whilst hunting in the New Forest at Brockenhurst. It was believed that the arrow in question was fired by one of his entourage, a Walter Tyrrell and a stone, entitled the Rufus Stone marks where he died

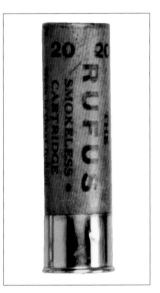

Examples of the Rufus cartridge are seldom encountered

The Rufus Stone which is believed to mark the point at which King William II (better known as Rufus) died and which was to result in his name being given to one of Schultze's cartridges is situated about three miles as the crow flies from their former factory site at Fritham

Following the takeover by Nobel's the one name which continued for some time was the 'Westminster' brand. A Schultze loaded Westminster cartridge appears in the Explosives Trades Ltd 1920 catalogue and Westminster specimens will be encountered bearing ICI headstamps right through to the end of their production in 1940.

This specimen was made in Australia by ICIANZ for the Australian market. It bears the usual ICIANZ headstamp shown below

Before Schultze loaded their own cartridges in 1899, Eley Brothers Ltd used Schultze powder as one of the list of powders they would offer their customers.
Left shows examples of case markings both on cartridges loaded by Eley Bros Ltd together with cases supplied by them to Schultze to load themselves at their premises in Westminster

The Yeoman introduced in 1905 and the Eyeworth which was first marketed in 1907

13.13 Examples of headstamps encountered on shotgun cartridges loaded with Schultze powders

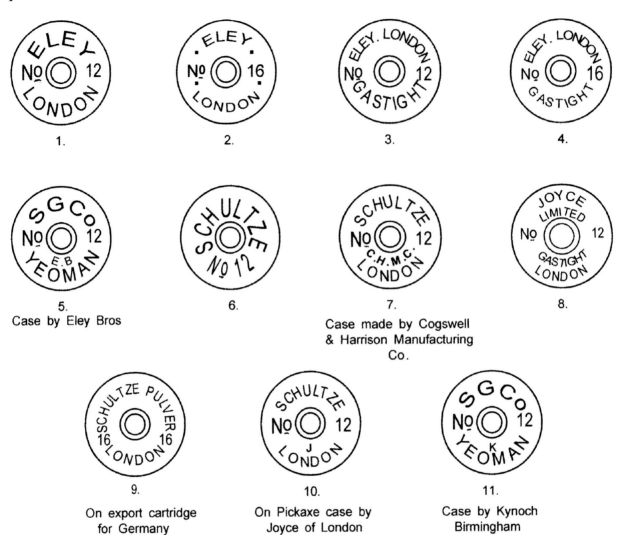

1.

2.

3.

4.

5.
Case by Eley Bros

6.

7.
Case made by Cogswell
& Harrison Manufacturing
Co.

8.

9.
On export cartridge
for Germany

10.
On Pickaxe case by
Joyce of London

11.
Case by Kynoch
Birmingham

CHAPTER 14
John Hall & Son Ltd

14.1 The company's history

John Hall & Son operated a gunpowder factory at Faversham. The site was one of the oldest gunpowder works in the country, having been opened in the reign of Queen Elizabeth I, and in the 18th century it became a royal factory. In 1812 Mr John Hall purchased a private gunpowder works in Faversham and in due course acquired from the Government the whole of the adjacent former royal factory and renamed the site 'The Oare Works'. The company commenced to manufacture gun cotton in 1847 but a major explosion terminated production. An important party in the management of the company was Mr D.J. Metcalfe. He joined the company in 1878 and on the retirement of the original partners and with the formation of the limited company in 1896, he took over as joint Managing Director together with Mr C.L. Watson-Smith, the son of one of the former company partners.

The entrance to the Oare Works of John Hall & Son Ltd in 1896

The site, when visited by the shooting press in 1896, was described as consisting of a number of important separate units. These included Marsh Mills where blasting cartridges were produced, a chronograph house and adjacent proving ground for rifle and shotgun cartridges, a large engine house and a whole group of buildings used in the manufacture of various types of black powder. The report also mentioned the recent addition of a cartridge loading unit for sporting purposes.

This unit consisted of several houses where they loaded shotgun cartridges with both black powder and a smokeless powder called 'Cannonite'. The report also stated that Halls supplied to the trade, shotgun cartridge cases pre charged with correct powder loads to prevent the potential for gunsmiths and iron-mongers loading excess powder charges when retailing their own loads.

The Hon. A.C. Ponsonby was a pioneer in smokeless powders and Cannonite smokeless powder was the product of a syndicate which Ponsonby formed entitled 'The War and Sporting Smokeless Powder Syndicate Ltd'. The powder was invented by a Mr H.M. Chapman, who also acted as the chemist to the syndicate. The syndicate members included many famous names of the day

The engine house at Marsh Works

including Lord Raglan (The Chairman), Sir Ralph Payne-Gallwey, a Yorkshire baronet, and Earl Cairns whilst Ponsonby was the Company Manager. The success of this powder was recognised by Halls and in 1894 they formed a very close relationship with the syndicate, whereby all the Cannonite powder it produced was taken by them. In due course the syndicate's works at Trimley were taken over by John Hall & Son who commenced producing this powder on a commercial scale. The first version of Cannonite smokeless powder was supplied to both Eley Bros Ltd and F. Joyce & Co., who in 1892 were using it to load shotgun cartridges. It was also being loaded into metallic rifle cartridges which produced extremely good results in competitions held at Bisley.

In 1896 the public registered company John Hall & Son Ltd was formed and on 9 November that year an explosion occurred at their Faversham works. No one was killed, however it did considerable damage to a large portion of the gunpowder works.

In June 1897 it was announced that the company were about to introduce a new variety of Cannonite on the market resulting in their Trimley works being extended in the following August to produce the new powder. Based on reports which appeared in the *Sporting Goods Review* in November 1898, it was clear that problems had occurred with loading the original Cannonite powder. Some users had wrongly assumed they could use equivalent volumes of the original Cannonite powder as a direct substitute for black powder. In reality coned based cartridges were required to reduce the internal case volume to make up the difference between the two differing volumes which many had sought to ignore, thereby generating unacceptable and dangerous breech pressures through overloads.

Trimley Works where the Cannonite power was manufactured

The company's Cannonite 2 smokeless powder incorporated new waterproof granules which burnt with little residue and it could be used on an equivalent volume for volume basis as black powder, thereby eliminating the need to use coned based cases. It did not supercede the previous version of Cannonite 1 and both powders were available on the market at the same time, however from that point onwards the company was only prepared to supply Cannonite 1 in loaded cartridges or cases pre-loaded with powder.

In April 1899 the *Sporting Goods Review* mentioned that John Hall & Son Ltd had been incorporated within Messrs Curtis's & Harvey and that both companies had offices at 3 Gracechurch Street, London EC with Hall's old offices at 79 Cannon Street now vacant. Following their take over by Curtis's & Harvey, Mr Chapman, their chemist, continued to work for C&H and it was he who invented Smokeless Diamond powder. Smokeless Diamond powder was to remain associated with shotgun cartridges right through until the ICI period of its production as one of the all-time great shotgun cartridge propellants.

The Hon. A. C. Ponsonby, the pioneer in smokeless powders, died in May 1918. He was the individual who highlighted the 'Cordite' scandal when the artillery authorities imposed on the infantry the use of Cordite in small arms cartridges when much better alternative qualities of Nitroglycerine and nitro-cellulose powders existed. He laboured manfully to do the nation a service to change that decision but he retired from the unequal combat, broken in spirit, health and in fortune.

14.2 Company adverts

1898 advert

14.3 Powders produced by the company

The following brands of powders were both produced by the company and loaded into cartridges at their works in Faversham:

'Field B', 'F.F.F.',
'Brilliant Glass',
'Southern Cross',
'Cannonite 1' and
'Cannonite 2'.

14.4 Specimens of the cartridges loaded by the company

Tube marked Hall's Southern Cross Course Grain Gunpowder for Breech Loading Cartridges

12 bore Eley Bros Ltd case for use with Hall's Cannonite

CHAPTER 15
The EC Powder Company Ltd

15.1 The company's history, its sites and management

This company's history is inextricably linked to the history of the New Explosives Company of Stowmarket which is dealt with in Chapter 16. However this chapter concentrates on the period when it was operating as an independent entity producing EC powders.

During 1881 the factory at Stowmarket was extended and in November that year it changed names to 'The Explosive Company Limited' and in the subsequent year, the company introduced what was to become one of the best known English sporting powders namely 'EC powder', where the initials indicate its company of origin. This powder was patented on 8 February 1882 (Patent No. 619) by a W.F. Reid and a D. Johnson and production of EC powder continued at the Stowmarket factory until 1883, when a separate company named the EC Powder Company Ltd was formed. Its production moved to a new factory which was to be sited about midway between Dartford and Gravesend in Kent with offices at Bucklersbury, London, leaving the former site at Stowmarket to be run by the New Explosives Co. Ltd.

In 1891 an American subsidiary was formed which was titled the Anglo American EC Powder Co. of New Jersey.

The *Sporting Goods Review* in January 1896 revealed that a Mr W. D. Borland had invented a new powder titled EC2 and also designed the machinery plant and testing equipment both for the English works and those of the American EC Powder Co. at Oakland, New Jersey. He also invented rifle powders and amongst others the rifle powder made by the American EC Powder Co.

The new EC factory was sited in 1896 between Dartford and Gravesend and about 25 miles from London

In March 1897 the company moved offices from 20 Bucklersbury, London EC to 40 New Bond Street, London and in May 1897 Mr Borland was listed as the Works Manager and Managing Director. He became to be known as a renowned expert in the testing of caps in relation to their flame size and shape, temperature generation, burn duration, their total energy generation and sensitivity. In July 1897 the company Chairman Mr H.D. Browne revealed that the company now employed its own salesmen who were dealing directly with the trade.

In January 1898 discussions took place in the shooting press over an improved EC powder which would charge by volume the same as EC2 but only weigh ⅕th of weight of a comparable volume of EC2. That new powder was to become entitled EC3.

In August 1899 it was announced that the EC Powder Co. Ltd had started to load and retail their own cartridges.

Clearly the EC3 powder became a highly sought after commodity since at least one European cartridge company produced an imitation version which they listed in their catalogue; however this came to the notice of the company and they took action against the company concerned.

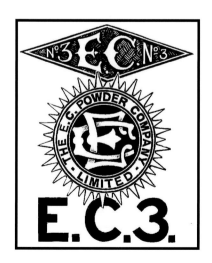

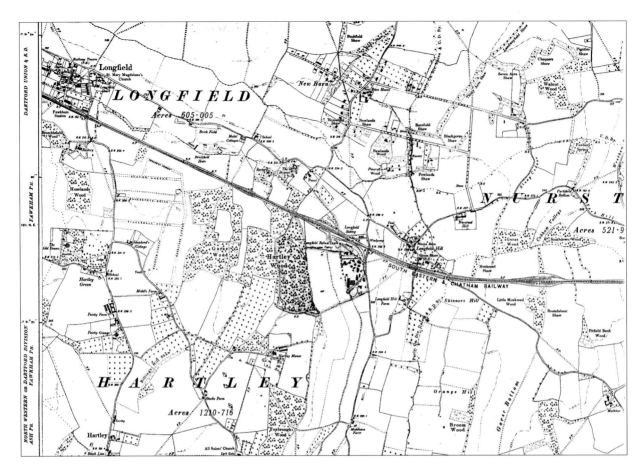

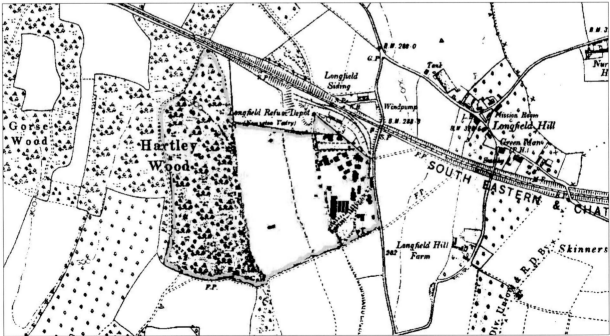

Their site at Longfield, Kent close to Dartford

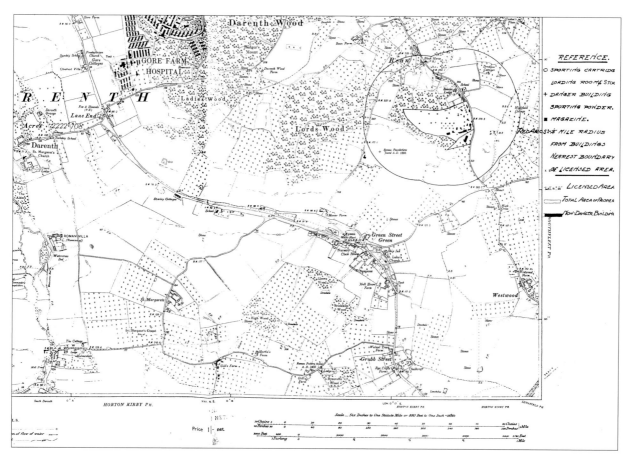

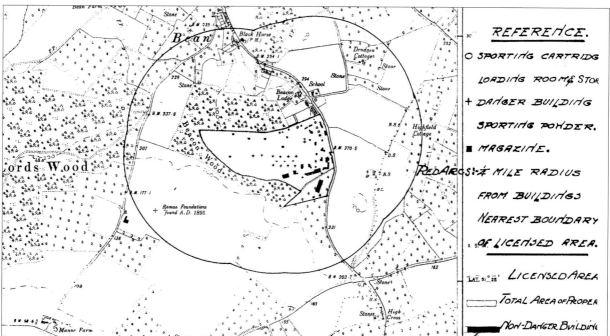

Their site at Darenth, Kent close to Dartford

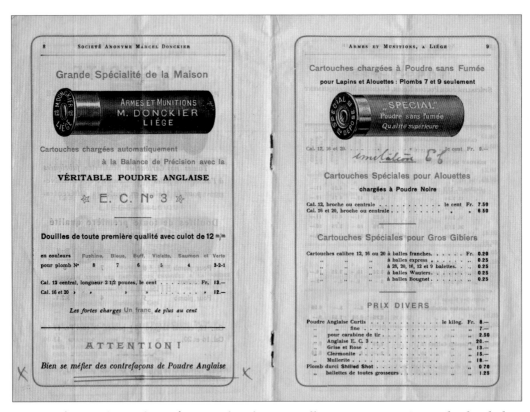

1904 catalogue of Marcel Donckier of Liege when he was selling imitation EC powder loaded cartridges

In 1907 the EC Powder Co. Ltd was acquired by Nobel's and absorbed into the management of the New Explosives Co., however their powders continued to be produced for a considerable time after this date.

15.2 Cartridges loaded by the company

It would appear from remaining specimens that the company loaded their various grades of EC powder into Eley Bros Ltd cases and specimens of their Ejectors, Gastight and Pegamoid cases will be found with EC powder loadings. The common examples bear their trade marks shown below on their paper loaded tubes.

In March 1908 the company registered the trade mark 'EConomic' sited within a flag motif Reg. No. 310466 and presumably specimens will be found bearing this insignia.

15.3 Examples of headstamps on cartridges used by the company

1.   2.   3.   4.

CHAPTER 16
The New Explosives Company Ltd

16.1 The history of the company and its management

This company's works date back to 1862–3 when the Prentice family of Stowmarket created a factory for manufacturing gun cotton. In due course the company's attention turned to the production of a propellant for sporting shotgun cartridges and on 3 April 1866 Eustace Carey Prentice, a member of the family, took out Patent No. 953. Details of the patent are shown here.

953. Prentice, E. C. April 3.

Explosives. — The rate of combustion of gun cotton is regulated by combining it with un-nitrated cellulose, in the shape of rovings or yarn, in weaving, braiding, or knitting machines. The two descriptions of yarn may be formed into ropes and cut into lengths, or the fibres may be cut into short lengths and well mixed. The two fibres may be mixed before being woven, and rovings so formed are cut into short lengths and used to fill cartridges, or the fibres may be converted into pulp, and mixed and formed into paper. When used as a propellant, the unconverted cellulose must not exceed 30 per cent.; 15 per cent. forms an explosive suitable for sporting purposes.

I have been unable to locate specimens of cartridges loaded with this substance, however they were made shortly afterwards by a company named T. Prentice & Co. The propellant used consisted of about 30 grains of paper made from a mix of approximately 85% converted gun cotton fibre and 15% uncovered fibres rolled into a plug the same width as the inside of the cartridge tube which was then loaded with one ounce of shot.

Clearly the demand for gun cotton was sufficiently high for the company to expand and in 1870 a new factory was built at Stowmarket and the company was retitled to 'The Patent Safety Guncotton Company Ltd'. In addition to their production of gun cotton they continued producing shotgun cartridges for which they claimed greater penetration, no smoke emissions, little recoil or noise generation, and failure to foul or injure the gun in which they were used. How accurate these claims were, however, is unknown. The company title nevertheless appears to have been an exaggeration, since during the afternoon of 11 August 1871 about a dozen staff were killed when 14 tons of gun cotton exploded. This was followed by two more explosions which occurred during the rescue mission killing further staff and by the end of the day 24 people were dead, half of whom had not reached the age of 17.

During 1881 the Stowmarket factory was extended and in November that year it changed names to 'The Explosive Co. Ltd'. In the subsequent year, the company introduced what was to become one of the best known English sporting powders namely 'EC powder', where the initials indicate its company of origin. This powder was patented on 8 February 1882 (Patent No. 619) by a W.F. Reid and a D. Johnson and production of EC powder continued at Stowmarket until 1883, when a separate company named the EC Powder Company was formed and its production moved to a new factory at Dartford in Kent.

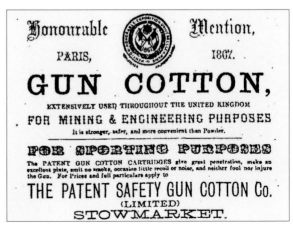

Honourable Mention, PARIS, 1867.

GUN COTTON,

EXTENSIVELY USED THROUGHOUT THE UNITED KINGDOM

FOR MINING & ENGINEERING PURPOSES

It is stronger, safer, and more convenient than Powder.

FOR SPORTING PURPOSES

The PATENT GUN COTTON CARTRIDGES give great penetration, make an excellent plate, emit no smoke, occasion little recoil or noise, and neither foul nor injure the Gun. For Prices and full particulars apply to

THE PATENT SAFETY GUN COTTON Co.
(LIMITED)
STOWMARKET.

In 1887 the company changed names again to the New Explosives Company. On 14 September 1888 two of the company's employees I.M.T. Anderson and A. Anderson took out a patent for a new form of nitro-cellulose based propellant (Patent No.13,308) which, based on its finishing methods was designed for use in military and commercial cartridges. Innes M.T. Anderson, the Works Manager, died in late 1896 to be replaced by Robert B. Pollitt A.M.I.C.E., F.C.S. In the autumn of 1898 the company started to produce Cordite at their Stowmarket factory but this was but one of several factories involved in its manufacture and although rapidly adopted by the military, competition to gain large orders was stiff.

In the February 1903 issue of the *Arms & Explosives* an interesting statement appeared relating to the company and I quote 'In the preceding 8 years the company occupied a derelict site and the old factory had been closed down.' It was at this point that the company was taken over by a new directorate. The former company Chairman, C.W.A. Goodfellow, was succeeded in 1903 by Mr F. Marchell Smith with the profits for 1902 quoted as £21,656. In November 1903 L. G. Duff Grant moved to the company from the Smokeless Powder & Ammunition Co. Ltd with 15 years experience in the trade and took over the role of General Manager replacing Mr F. Marten Hale, who resigned.

At the company's AGM held on 29 February 1904, Mr F. Marchell Smith presiding stated that only a few orders for Cordite had been received from the Government and their net profits for the year were £16,000. He advised the shareholders that the Government now required more drying time for Cordite and as a result the company was forced to buy more land and drying sheds. The company Chairman died in November the following year and was replaced at the spring 1906 AGM by a Mr E.H. Hindley. The annual report again reported poor Government orders for Cordite, and the annual accounts for the former showed a loss of £1,346.

In early 1906 the gun trade journals indicated that the company was about to introduce a new series of sporting powders to add to their production of Cordite and gun cotton and in July the company announced that they were to manufacture smokeless shotgun and rifle powders. Three brands of shotgun powder were named, namely 'Red Star', 'Felixite' and 'Neonite' for cone base shotgun cartridges. 'Neonite' was also to be produced for use in rifle, revolver and blank metallic cartridges. The trade journals also revealed that Mr F.W. Jones, who was later to be regarded as one of the two best British ballisticians,would provide all the necessary technical backup having recently joined the company from the Smokeless Powder & Ammunition Co. Ltd.

Clearly the expansion in terms of these new powders created financial difficulties for the company which resulted in yet another company being formed, namely The New Explosives Co. (1906) Ltd which was registered on the 30 June that year with a capital of £100,000 in £1 shares. The new company acquired the undertakings and assets of the former company and on 11 July a voluntary winding up of the old company occurred with Mr L.G. Duff Grant acting as liquidator. Once this transition had been completed it reverted back to the old company name removing the '1906' suffix.

In 1907 the company was bought out by Nobel's Explosives Co. Ltd, a subsidiary of Nobel Dynamite Trust, who by then had started to buy up all its main small competitors involved in explosives manufacture. The change of ownership resulted in the company establishing a new company address at 62 London Wall, London EC.

On 1 October 1907 Mr A.R. Berry was appointed Assistant Secretary of New Explosives Co. Ltd to work alongside Mr L.G. Duff Grant their Secretary and at this time Mr J.C. Ody was the Works Manager at Stowmarket. Berry had started his career with the Smokeless Powder Co. as office boy to Mr Duff Grant, however when this company was absorbed by the Schultze Powder Co. he worked with Schultze and since 1905 had been their Assistant Secretary. In June 1909

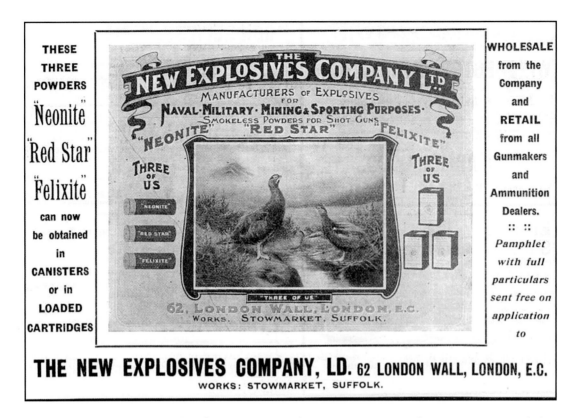

Berry was promoted to the role of Secretary and in January 1918 he was appointed Assistant Manager whilst retaining his role as Company Secretary.

At the company AGM in June 1912 the Chairman, Mr E.H. Hindley declared company profits of £4,715 5s 7d, mainly based on producing Cordite orders for the Government. In September 1912 Mr F.M. Wharton was appointed Works Manager at Stowmarket, a post he held until August 1919 when he resigned his position and was replaced by a Mr J.A. Carter. Wharton stated that his resignation was based on reduced demands for production by the company.

In January 1920 a company advert stated that the company's sales department was being transferred to Explosives Trades Ltd premises sited at Angel Road, Edmonton, London N18 and this was to mark the end of the former company's cartridge production.

Mr F. M. Wharton was educated at Mason College, Birmingham later to become Birmingham University. He gained the senior chemistry prize and was awarded the Foster & Priestley research scholarships. After a short period as a public analyst he went as an assayer to the Imperial Mint in Nanking China for two years returning in 1902 to be an assistant chemist at the National Explosives Works at Hayle in Cornwall. Five years later he transferred to Curtis's & Harvey's Cliffe Works as their Works Manager. In 1910 he returned to the mint in Nanking as their chemical advisor but due to the political unrest in China he moved to the New Explosives Company as their Works Manager in 1912

In March 1921 the *Sporting Goods Review* advised its readers that the company had changed its name to Necol Industrial Collodions Ltd. The new company's products included collodion and nitro-cellulose solutions for industrial purposes and by 1922 they were making household cement in collapsible tubes, lacquers for wood and metal and plastic wood. The change in company title marked the final termination of this company's manufacture of sporting cartridges, propellants and military explosives.

16.2.1 Cartridge brand names used by the company and where appropriate their registered trade marks

Registered No. if known	Year Applied for registration	Cartridge name
	1901	Stowite
Reg. No. 281186	1906	Felixite
Reg. No. 293865	1907	Go Lightly
Reg. No. 244303	1907	Red Rival
Reg. No. 300658	1908	Primrose Smokeless
Reg. No. 300659	1908	Stowmarket Smokeless
Reg. No. 302219	1908	Green Rival Smokeless
Reg. No. 313453	1909	Premier Smokeless
Reg. No. 330377	1911	Jackal
	1911	NECO
	1911	Nutcracker
Reg. No. 345751	1912	NE Smokeless with circular device
	1917	Blue Rival Smokeless

16.2.2 Cartridge production

When the three new powders were introduced by the company in 1906 they were loaded into Eley Bros Limited Gastights, Nitro, Smokeless and Pegamoid cartridge cases which were printed with the names of the powders in question. The company were also prepared to sell these powders in tins to potential customers.

The October 1906 issue of *Arms & Explosives* stated that the company had

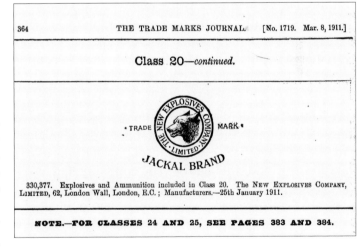

issued a trade leaflet which stated that the powders in question should be loaded as follows:

Felixite for 12 bore cartridges required 42 grains of powder with 1oz or 1⅛th oz shot and therefore 1lb of this powder would load 166, 12 bore cartridges

Red Star for 12 bore cartridges required 33 grains of powder with 1oz or 1⅛th oz shot and therefore 1lb of this powder would load 112, 12 bore cartridges

Shotgun Neonite for 12 bore cartridges required 30 grains of powder with 1oz or 1⅛th oz shot and therefore 1lb of this powder would load 233, 12 bore cartridges solely for use with coned based cases.

The circular also pointed out that the company offered supplies of nitro-cellulose rifle powders for use with rifles in calibres from .236" to .315" and also for use in rook or rabbit rifles and revolvers which were obtainable from the company in powder canisters or in loaded cartridges.

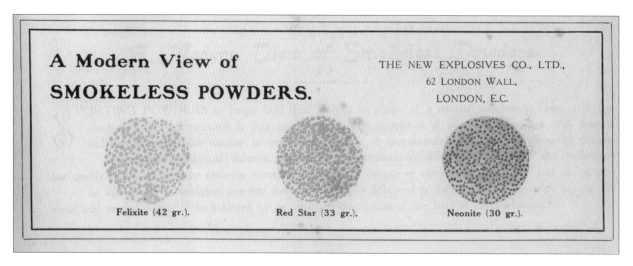

By 1907 the trade journals indicated that the company's powders were being offered loaded in a variety of cases namely:

Gastight Cartridge – Crimson ⅝" deep shell case for Felixite, Red Star and Neonite
Nitro Cartridge – Orange case for Felixite, Red Star and Neonite
Smokeless Cartridge – Brick Red case for Felixite, Red Star and Neonite
'The Go Lightly' Cartridge for Light Guns (Gas Tight) Crimson ⅝" deep shell case
'The Go Lightly' Cartridge for Light Guns (Nitro) Orange case
'The Go Lightly' Cartridge for Light Guns (Pegamoid) Special waterproof quality case
    (All the Go-Lightly cartridges were loaded with ⅞ to 1 oz shot and Neonite smokeless powder and designed as low recoil cartridges)

In July 1908 the company extended its range by offering two new second grade proprietary cartridges, namely the 'Stowmarket Smokeless' loaded with 33 grains of powder and the 'Primrose Smokeless' loaded with 42 grains of powder plus two better quality items bearing the titles of the 'Green Rival' and 'Go Lightly'. The company had also extended its range of loads for metallic rifle cartridges using Neonite which they now offered for use in .450", .303", .250" and .22" rifles as well as Neonite cartridges for revolver and in blanks.

In 1909 the company further extended the range with their 'Premier' cartridge and in March 1911 the company introduced the 'NECO' brand cartridge loaded into a green case with 1¹⁄₁₆ oz of shot. The same year they registered two further brand names, 'Jackal' and 'Nutcracker,' however to date I have yet to find evidence that either of these cartridges went into production.

By 1912 'NE Smokeless' had been added to their range, which at this point consisted of the 'Green Rival', 'Red Rival', 'NECO', 'Premier', three types of 'Go-Lightly', Ejectors in 12 bore and 16 bore, Pegamoid Waterproof, lined and unlined Gastights plus Nitro and Smokeless cases loaded with the three powders, Neonite, Felixite and Red Star.

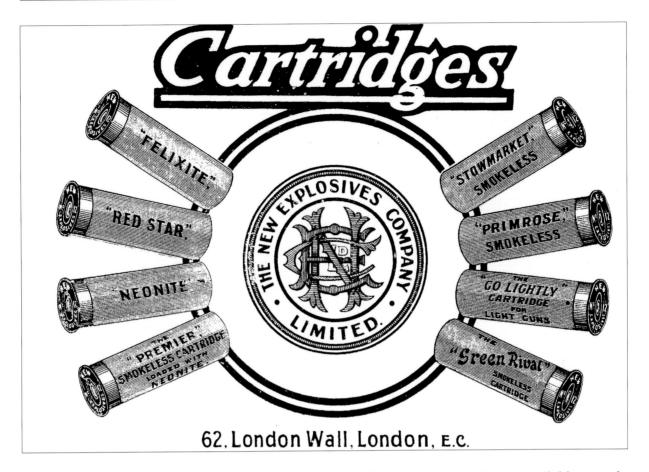

The company trade catalogue for 1914 listed the following cartridges being available namely the 'Premier', 'Red Rival', 'NECO', 'Green Rival', 'NE Smokeless' and 'Go Lightly', 'Red Star', 'Stowmarket Smokeless', 'Felixite' and 'Premier Smokeless'. However WWI demands for the company's propellants soon took their toll on shotgun cartridge manufacture and this, linked to availability of cartridge cases, was to result in a drastic reduction in their manufacture. *Arms & Explosives* in September 1915 was advised by a Mr Berry, a company spokesman, that current production had been reduced to the following brands, the 'Premier' at 11s per 100, 'Red Rival' at 10s per 100 with the 'NECO', the 'Green Rival' and the 'NE Smokeless' all out of stock with no date quoted for recommencement, and supplies of 'Red Rival' approaching the same state. The company's final shotgun cartridge registered trade mark was granted in April 1917 for the name 'Blue Rival Smokeless' but I have yet to locate a specimen bearing this brand name and it seems unlikely that many or indeed any were made, since by December 1917 all their shotgun cartridge production had ceased.

With the formation of Explosive Trades Ltd in 1918 only the 'Red Rival' and 'Green Rival' brands were still listed in the ETL catalogue for 1920/1921 as being made by the company, and by 1924 Nobel's Industries Ltd catalogue indicated that these two remaining brands were being made by Eley and bore the Eley Nobel headstamps. By 1928 both these brands had disappeared from Nobel's Industries catalogue, thus ending a chapter in the company's production of cartridges.

Finally it is perhaps worth adding that the vast majority of the cartridges loaded by the company were loaded into 12 bore Eley cases. However a few will be encountered in 16 bore loaded into Eley Ejectors, Pegamoid, Gastight and Nitro cases and Primrose Smokeless brand were also made in .410". I have also encountered an 'NE Smokeless' cartridge loaded into a Remington UMC Nitro Club case which must date after 1912 and may have been used when the company had difficulties getting cases from Eley during the early part of the WWI period.

Sporting Goods Review 16
April 1917

Advert in Sporting Goods
Review *15 March 1919*

Advert in Sporting Goods
Review *16 June 1919*

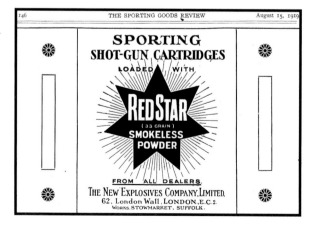

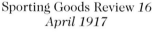

16.2.3
Examples of
the company's
shotgun
cartridges

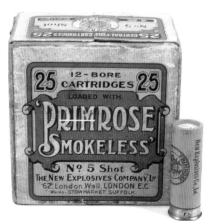

LEFT TO RIGHT: *'Premier', 'Primrose Smokeless', 'Felixite' early version, 'Green Rival', 'Red Rival', 'NE Smokeless'*
LYING DOWN: *Felixite later version*

16.3 Examples of headstamps encountered on cases loaded by the company

1.

2.

3.

4.

5.

Found on factory dummies

6.

On 12 bore loaded by New Explosives Co. with N E powder

CHAPTER 17

The Smokeless Powder Company and Smokeless Powder & Ammunition Co. Ltd

17.1 The companies' histories

The Smokeless Powder Company was formed in 1888 but it was not until 1890 that their smokeless powder was placed on the market. During the intervening period the company sought a suitable manufacturing site out of the 182 sites they examined. The problem they faced was trying to locate a site which was of adequate size which the Inspector of Explosives was prepared to license. The final choice was at Barwick in Hertfordshire, five miles from Ware, some 30 miles north of London and within 2¼ miles from a local railway station which was needed for transport. It was also some 5 miles away from the river Lea and a canal which afforded a further trade route into London for export of its wares. The site extended to some 126 acres on which the company secured a 99 year lease. The factory consisted of around 40 different buildings scattered over about 33 acres and enclosed within a 6 foot ring fence.

The photograph on the following page shows the mill where the fibre used to produce the smokeless powder granules was torn apart and disintegrated by a revolving ball in a metal drum. The resultant product was dried in these sheds and then subjected to being nitrated by being submerged in nitrating vats. The nitrated fibre was then placed in earthenware pots and left standing in running water, after which it was subjected to the removal of the remaining nitric acid which was achieved within a centrifugal drum rotating at 1,200 revolutions per minute, which contained small perforations to allow the acid to exit the material. It was then rewashed and finally boiled to remove all remaining traces of the acid. Finally it was moved to the mill where the substance was ground up into small granules by 5 ton edge running rollers.

The company was founded by Mr J.D. Dougall Junior of the firm of J.D. Dougall & Sons. It was his father, a well known Scottish gunmaker, who was the person who brought the British public's attention to the smokeless powder invented by Captain

A view within the works

Pulping mill, nitrating tanks and washing unit

Schultze. Both Dougall Senior and Junior had devoted their lives to the investigation of all aspects of gunpowder manufacture, composition and testing and therefore it was a natural progression to enter the world of smokeless powder production. Acting in the role of Technical and Managing Director he was joined by the chemist Mr F.W. Jones, who during his career was to become Britain's leading ballistician in relation to metallic cartridge production. Jones was an extremely conscientious and meticulous chemist who subjected the company's products to the most stringent tests before their release to the public. Without doubt the company's success in relation to the powders they produced revolved around his work.

The May 1893 issue of *Arms & Explosives* reported that the company was supplying Martini Henry smokeless powder ammunition to the Indian Government and was making smokeless powder for revolvers. Later that same year the company sold ½ million rounds of .577"/.450" Martini Henry ammunition to the Bengal Presidency and ¼ million rounds to both Madras and Bombay which had apparently found satisfaction with the recipients.

In January 1896 the Managing Director, James Daniel Dougall Junior died and his role was taken over by Mr Claude Bishop, a member of the Institute of Secretaries, with the aid of two further Directors, Mr M.S. Vanderbyl and Colonel Mackinnon, an Indian Army Officer. Mackinnon had previously held the roles of Assistant Adjutant-General for Musketry, Army H.Q. India and Chief Instructor at the School of Musketry at Hyde and at the time of gaining the post of Director he was the Secretary of the National Rifle Association at Bisley. Given his background it was believed that he was an ideal choice for his ability to advise the company on military matters.

Mr F. W. Jones held an early interest in science and spent four years at Nottingham University College, finishing his initial course in 1887. Whilst there he gained the Ossington Scholarship and a National Scholarship qualifying entry to the Royal College of Science. Here he studied no less than 28 separate subjects including science, higher maths, physics, chemistry, agriculture and natural history gaining passes in 19. After two years at the College he left, since he felt he would be better employed in industry and entered the Smokeless Powder Company as a chemist whilst still in his early twenties. Sixteen months after entering the company the Manager died and Jones took on his role. He initially concentrated on the production of the rifle powders for use in Martini Henry and Lee Metford rifles, rook rifles and revolvers, for which the company gained considerable demand. He left in 1902 to join Eley Bros Ltd during which time he was involved, alongside Mr R.W.S. Griffith, developing proof loads for the two Proof Houses in relation to metallic cartridges

The *Sporting Goods Review* in February 1896 reported that a new Chairman had been appointed to the company, namely Lt.Col. J. A. S. Colquhoun, late Royal Artillery with connections with the Indian Ordnance Dept and former Officer in Charge of the Dum Dum small arms ammunition factory in India, whilst Mr L. G. Duff Grant was nominated General Manager and Secretary of the company with his Assistant Secretary being Mr A. R. Berry. The other Directors at this point were E. S. Bishop and S. Vanderbyl who replaced Mr M. S. Vanderbyl. In the same year the AGM minutes reported that the company's Riflelite .303" cartridges used at Bisley had won the top score of 48 out of 50 at 900 yards, having been shot by a Private Hay 2nd Volunteer Battalion Liverpool, and that during the previous 12 months the company had developed Shot Gun Riflelite powder. It also revealed that shotgun cartridges loaded with SG Rifleite powder were available direct from themselves or from Eley Bros Ltd, F. Joyce or G. Kynoch & Co. Ltd.

In July 1896 the company reported receiving a letter from Messrs Bircham & Co., Solicitors, acting for Mr J.N. Heideman, the Managing Director of United Cologne Rottweil Gunpowder Mills of Cologne and owner of Angel Patent 6022 of 1887, stating that Riflelite contravened their patent. The subsequent court proceedings resulted in a major decrease in trade and in a protracted court case which lasted 11 days but with a final outcome that The Smokeless Powder Company won their case in April 1898. The Nobel Trust were the owners of the Cologne factory and had originally unsuccessfully brought an action against the British Government over the production of Cordite and having failed, sought to uphold a virtually forgotten patent relating to the manufacture of rifle powders by use of completely gelatinised nitro-cellulose. F.W. Jones was the company's primary witness and the case was lost when Jones pointed out to the court that their company had sought to avoid using completely gelatinised nitro-cellulose and left in their products a large part of the original fibre mixed up with that part which had dissolved. Nobel's lost their case but the cost of defending this case bore into the company's finances, at a cost they could ill afford.

On 10 December 1896 at the General Meeting of the Smokeless Powder Company the shareholders agreed to a proposal from the Schultze Gunpowder Co. Ltd for their acquisition by the Schultze Gunpowder Co. owing to the pending litigation between themselves and Mr Heideman of the Rottweil Powder Co. over alleged infringements of the Engel patent.

It will be noted that when the New Schultze Gunpowder Co. Ltd was formed on 22 March 1897, it only took over from the old company the whole staff and works connected with Schultze powder, leaving in the hands of the old company i.e. Schultze Gunpowder Co. interests in the Smokeless Powder Co., so the Barwick site retained a separate Board of Directors, L.G. Duff Grant, as General Manager and Secretary, F.W. Jones as the Works Superintendent and the chemist R.W.S. Griffith, where they continued to produce SS powder and 'Shotgun Riflelite' powder. In June 1897 the company introduced a new improved version of SS powder and by November that year the sporting press reported them offering a new '.450 Riflelite' powder designed to do away with special linings necessary with the former .450 Rifleite, with Eley Bros Ltd making suitable caps and cases for the new powder. The new powders were reported to be excellent and in 1900 the company was selling .303" Eley cartridge cases loaded by themselves with 'Rifleite'.

In August 1898 the company's name changed to The Smokeless Powder & Ammunition Co. Ltd and their offices transferred to 28 Gresham Street, London.

During April 1900 the company announced a new powder called 'Blue Rival', supplying it in tins or loaded in three qualities of 12 bore cases, their cheapest quality cases designed solely for export. By June their new catalogue list included 'Blue Rival' powder being available in tins, in pre-charged cases without shot or in fully loaded shotgun cartridges, and also revealed that 'Rifleite' was offered for use in punt gun cartridges, ball loaded cartridges and standard shotgun cartridges.

Shortly after 1900 the company's offices moved to Dashwood House with Mr J. D. Dougall appointed MD, Mr L. G. Duff Grant acting as the Company Secretary with Mr Pepper and Mr Berry members of the administrative staff. Clearly at this point the company had failed to gain any real size military orders and remained reliant on other companies for the supply of metallic cases. Mr L. G. Duff Grant saw the writing on the wall and left the company in November 1903, moving to the New Explosives Co. Ltd having been preceded by Mr F. W. Jones, who left the previous year to join Eley Bros of London.

On 15 April 1905 reports in the trade press indicated the failure of the rifle powder business of the Smokeless Powder & Ammunition Co. and no further reference is made subsequently to it until 1912 when the Schultze company was being wound up and a liquidator wrote to the registrar of joint stock companies stating that the S. P. & A. Co. had no assets, had not conducted business for several years and the name had been retained solely for commercial value.

17.2 Specimens of company adverts

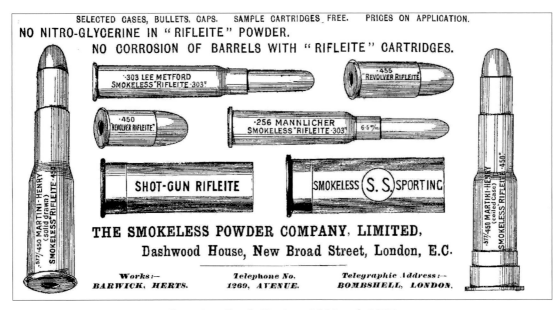

Sporting Goods Review 15 March 1897

17.3 Copy of the company's 1900 sales catalogue

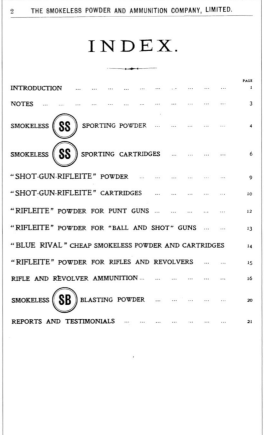

6 THE SMOKELESS POWDER AND AMMUNITION COMPANY, LIMITED.

SMOKELESS (SS) SPORTING CARTRIDGES.

No. 1 Best Quality.—Grey Colour Central Fire Gastight Cases.

Gauge.	Length.	Powder.	Shot.	Cartridges, per 100.			Cartridges with Powder only, per 100.			Cartridge Cases, per 1,000.		
	Inches.	Grs.	Ozs.	£	s.	d.	£	s.	d.	£	s.	d.
10	$2\frac{5}{8}$	44	$1\frac{1}{2}$	—	16	4	—	13	—	2	17	6
12	$2\frac{3}{4}$	41	$1\frac{1}{4}$ to $1\frac{3}{8}$	—	13	9	—	11	6	2	10	—
12	$2\frac{1}{2}$	38	1 to $1\frac{1}{8}$	—	12	3	—	10	—	2	2	6
16	$2\frac{1}{2}$	35	$\frac{7}{8}$ to 1	—	11	9	—	9	6	2	2	6
20	$2\frac{1}{2}$	32	$\frac{3}{4}$ to $\frac{7}{8}$	—	11	3	—	9	—	2	2	6

No. 2 Quality.—Orange Colour Central Fire Gastight Cases.

Gauge.	Length.	Powder.	Shot.	Cartridges, per 100.			Cartridges with Powder only, per 100.			Cartridge Cases, per 1,000.		
	Inches.	Grs.	Ozs.	£	s.	d.	£	s.	d.	£	s.	d.
12	$2\frac{1}{2}$	38	1 to $1\frac{1}{8}$	—	10	9	—	9	—	1	14	2
16	$2\frac{1}{2}$	35	$\frac{7}{8}$ to 1	—	10	9	—	9	—	1	14	2
20	$2\frac{1}{2}$	32	$\frac{3}{4}$ to $\frac{7}{8}$	—	10	6	—	8	9	1	14	2

THE COMPANY GUARANTEE ALL CARTRIDGES LOADED AT THEIR OWN FACTORY.

THE SMOKELESS POWDER AND AMMUNITION COMPANY, LIMITED.

SMOKELESS (SS) SPORTING CARTRIDGES.

GROUSE OR EJECTOR CASES.

Standard length of Brass $2\frac{1}{4}$ inches.

Gauge.	Length.	Powder.	Shot.	Cartridges per 100.			Cartridges with Powder only, per 100.			Cartridge Cases per 1,000.		
	Inches.	Grs.	Ozs.	£	s.	d.	£	s.	d.	£	s.	d.
10	$2\frac{5}{8}$	44	$1\frac{1}{2}$	—	19	4	—	16	—	4	7	6
12	$2\frac{3}{4}$	41	$1\frac{1}{4}$ to $1\frac{3}{8}$	—	16	3	—	14	—	3	12	6
12	$2\frac{1}{2}$	38	1 to $1\frac{1}{8}$	—	14	3	—	12	—	3	2	6
16	$2\frac{1}{2}$	35	$\frac{7}{8}$ to 1	—	13	9	—	11	6	3	2	6
20	$2\frac{1}{2}$	32	$\frac{3}{4}$ to $\frac{7}{8}$	—	13	3	—	11	—	3	2	6

"EXTRA GAS-TIGHT" CASES.

Gauge.	Length.	Powder.	Shot.	Cartridges per 100.			Cartridges with Powder only, per 100.			Cartridge Cases per 1,000.		
	Inches.	Grs.	Ozs.	£	s.	d.	£	s.	d.	£	s.	d.
10	$2\frac{5}{8}$	44	$1\frac{1}{2}$	—	17	1	—	13	9	3	3	4
12	$2\frac{3}{4}$	41	$1\frac{1}{4}$ to $1\frac{3}{8}$	—	14	6	—	12	—	2	15	—
12	$2\frac{1}{2}$	38	1 to $1\frac{1}{8}$	—	12	9	—	10	6	2	7	6
16	$2\frac{1}{2}$	35	$\frac{7}{8}$ to 1	—	12	3	—	10	—	2	7	6
20	$2\frac{1}{2}$	32	$\frac{3}{4}$ to $\frac{7}{8}$	—	11	9	—	9	6	2	7	6

THE COMPANY GUARANTEE ALL CARTRIDGES LOADED AT THEIR OWN FACTORY.

8 THE SMOKELESS POWDER AND AMMUNITION COMPANY, LIMITED.

SMOKELESS (SS) SPORTING CARTRIDGES.

SPECIAL WATERPROOF CASES.

Gauge.	Length.	Powder.	Shot.	Cartridges per 100.			Cartridges, with Powder only, per 100.			Cartridge Cases, per 1,000.		
	Inches.	Grs.	Ozs.	£	s.	d.	£	s.	d.	£	s.	d.
10	$2\frac{5}{8}$	44	$1\frac{1}{2}$	—	18	1	—	14	9	3	13	4
12	$2\frac{3}{4}$	41	$1\frac{1}{4}$ to $1\frac{3}{8}$	—	15	—	—	12	9	3	2	6
12	$2\frac{1}{2}$	38	1 to $1\frac{1}{8}$	—	13	—	—	10	9	2	10	—
16	$2\frac{1}{2}$	35	$\frac{7}{8}$ to 1	—	12	6	—	10	3	2	10	—
20	$2\frac{1}{2}$	32	$\frac{3}{4}$ to $\frac{7}{8}$	—	12	—	—	9	9	2	10	—

These prices are subject to Discounts of 30 per cent. and 5 per cent. at settlement, six months' journey account. Packing cases extra. Full price allowed for packing cases returned in good condition, Carriage Paid, to the Company's works at Barwick, Herts (Hadham Station, G.E.R.).

Cartridges of the nett value of £10 and upwards delivered free to any Railway Station in the United Kingdom.

All Cartridges are loaded with Patent Shot unless otherwise ordered, and are packed in boxes containing 100 each. Cartridges loaded with chilled shot 3d. per hundred extra.

THE COMPANY GUARANTEE ALL CARTRIDGES LOADED AT THEIR OWN FACTORY.

THE SMOKELESS POWDER AND AMMUNITION COMPANY, LIMITED. 9

"SHOT-GUN-RIFLEITE"

FOR CONE BASE CASES.

Size of Tins	Price per 100 lbs.	Trade Discount.	Extra Discount for Cash within One Month.		Net Price per lb.
$\frac{1}{2}$ or **1** lb.	**700/-**	**$33\frac{1}{3}$%**	**5%**	=	**4/5**
5, 25 or **50** lbs. ...	**670/-**	,,	,,	=	**4/3**

Or $33\frac{1}{3}$ per cent. and $2\frac{1}{2}$ per cent. for Cash within Three Months.

1 lb. weight of this Powder is equivalent to about $2\frac{1}{4}$ lbs. of the best Black Gunpowder, and will load **189** 12-bore Cartridges charged with 37 grains "Shot-Gun Rifleite."

Carriage free in cylinders to any Railway Station in the United Kingdom on minimum quantities of 15 lbs. or F.O.B. Thames in quantities of not less than 100 lbs. Packing Cases extra.

Full price allowed for packing cases returned in good condition, Carriage Paid, to the Company's Works at Barwick, Herts (Hadham Station, G.E.R.).

For Reports and Testimonials see Page 21.

LOADING INSTRUCTIONS.

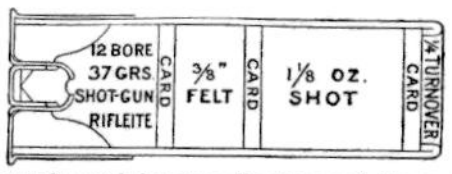

As the charge of this powder occupies much less space than the usual charge of Black Powder, SPECIAL CONE BASE CASES should be used.

The charge for a $2\frac{1}{2}$ inch 12-bore cone base case is 37 grs., the wadding giving the best results, being as follows:—

1st Wad—A Card.
2nd Wad—Felt $\frac{3}{8}$ inch or of suitable thickness for correct turnover.
3rd Wad—A Card and $1\frac{1}{8}$ oz. of shot.
4th Wad—A Card $\frac{1}{4}$ inch of the case being left for the turnover.

Where smaller charges of shot are used, the Felt should be thicker, or the card next the powder replaced by a cloth or "Field" Wad of suitable thickness so that when shotted ¼ inch of the case is left for turnover.

The charges for different bores in special cases when wadded on the above lines are:—

10-bore, **44** grs. or about $2\frac{5}{8}$ drs. by volume.
12 ,, **37** ,, ,, **2** ,, ,,
16 ,, **32** ,, ,, $1\frac{3}{4}$,, ,,
20 ,, **29** ,, ,, $1\frac{1}{2}$,, ,,

When loading by volume, in every instance the machine should be set by weighing a few charges.

As this powder throws very high patterns, the charge of shot may with advantage be $\frac{1}{16}$ oz. less than is usual in different bores, with the consequent decrease in recoil and increase of penetration.

The above page is of particular interest since it illustrates why coned based shotgun cartridges were constructed

10 THE SMOKELESS POWDER AND AMMUNITION COMPANY, LIMITED.

"SHOT-GUN-RIFLEITE" CARTRIDGES.

No. 1 Best Quality.—Red Central Fire Gas-tight Cases, with Cone Base.

Gauge.	Length.	Powder.	Shot.	Cartridges. per 100.			Cartridges with Powder only, per 100.			Cartridge Cases, per 1,000.		
	Inches.	Grs.	Ozs.	£	s.	d.	£	s.	d.	£	s.	d.
12	$2\frac{3}{4}$	41	$1\frac{1}{4}$	—	14	9	—	12	6	2	15	—
12	$2\frac{1}{2}$	37	$1\frac{1}{16}$ to $1\frac{1}{8}$	—	12	9	—	10	6	2	6	—
16	$2\frac{1}{2}$	32	$\frac{7}{8}$ to 1	—	12	3	—	10	—	2	6	—
20	$2\frac{1}{2}$	29	$\frac{3}{4}$ to $\frac{7}{8}$	—	11	9	—	9	6	2	6	—

No. 2 Quality.—Terra Cotta Cases, 12-bore only.

Gauge.	Length.	Powder.	Shot.	Cartridges per 100.			Cartridges with Powder only, per 100.			Cartridge Cases, per 1,000.		
	Inches.	Grs.	Ozs.	£	s.	d.	£	s.	d.	£	s.	d.
12	$2\frac{1}{2}$	37	$1\frac{1}{16}$	—	11	—	—	9	6	1	17	0

THE COMPANY GUARANTEE ALL CARTRIDGES LOADED AT THEIR OWN FACTORY.

11 THE SMOKELESS POWDER AND AMMUNITION COMPANY, LIMITED.

"SHOT-GUN-RIFLEITE" CARTRIDGES.

GROUSE OR EJECTOR CASES.

Standard length of Brass $2\frac{1}{4}$ inches.

Gauge.	Length.	Powder.	Shot.	Cartridges, per 100.			Cartridges with Powder only, per 100.			Cartridge Cases, per 1,000.		
	Inches.	Grs.	Ozs.	£	s.	d.	£	s.	d.	£	s.	d.
12	$2\frac{3}{4}$	41	$1\frac{1}{4}$	—	17	—	—	14	9	3	17	6
12	$2\frac{1}{2}$	37	1 to $1\frac{1}{8}$	—	14	9	—	12	6	3	7	6
16	$2\frac{1}{2}$	32	$\frac{7}{8}$ to 1	—	14	3	—	12	—	3	7	6
20	$2\frac{1}{2}$	29	$\frac{3}{4}$ to $\frac{7}{8}$	—	13	9	—	11	6	3	7	6

SPECIAL WATERPROOF CASES.

Gauge.	Length.	Powder.	Shot.	Cartridges, per 100.			Cartridges with Powder only, per 100.			Cartridge Cases, per 1,000.		
	Inches.	Grs.	Ozs.	£	s.	d.	£	s.	d.	£	s.	d.
12	$2\frac{3}{4}$	41	$1\frac{1}{4}$	—	16	—	—	13	9	3	7	6
12	$2\frac{1}{2}$	37	1 to $1\frac{1}{8}$	—	13	6	—	11	3	2	15	—
16	$2\frac{1}{2}$	32	$\frac{7}{8}$ to 1	—	13	—	—	10	9	2	15	—
20	$2\frac{1}{2}$	29	$\frac{3}{4}$ to $\frac{7}{8}$	—	12	6	—	10	3	2	15	—

THE COMPANY GUARANTEE ALL CARTRIDGES LOADED AT THEIR OWN FACTORY.

12 THE SMOKELESS POWDER AND AMMUNITION COMPANY, LIMITED.

"SHOT-GUN-RIFLEITE" CARTRIDGES

—Continued.

SHORT CARTRIDGES LOADED WITH "SHOT-GUN RIFLEITE," 12-BORE ONLY.

Gauge.	Length.	Powder.	Shot.	Cartridges per 100.			Cartridges with Powder only per 100.			Cartridge Cases, per 1,000.		
	Inches.	Grs.	Ozs.	£	s.	d.	£	s.	d.	£	s.	d.
12	$2\frac{1}{4}$	35	1	—	10	9	—	9	—	1	14	2

These prices are subject to Discounts of 30 per cent. and 5 per cent. at settlement, six months' journey account. Packing cases extra. Full price allowed for packing cases returned in good condition, Carriage Paid, to the Company's works at Barwick, Herts (Hadham Station, G.E.R.)

Cartridges of the nett value of £10 and upwards delivered free to any Railway Station in the United Kingdom.

All Cartridges are loaded with patent shot unless otherwise ordered, and are packed in boxes containing 100 each. Cartridges loaded with chilled shot 3d. per hundred extra.

"RIFLEITE" SMOKELESS POWDER FOR PUNT GUNS.

PRICES AS UNDER:—

Size of Tins.	Price per 100 lbs.	Trade Discount.	Extra Discount for Cash within One Month.		Net Price per lb.
½ or **1** lb.	**800/-**	**33⅓%**	**5%**	=	**5/1**
5, 25 or **50** lbs. ...	**770/-**	,,	,,	=	**4/10½**

Or 33⅓ per cent. and 2½ per cent. for Cash within Three Months.

Carriage free in cylinders to any Railway Station in the United Kingdom on minimum quantities of 15 lbs., or F.O.B. Thames in quantities of not less than 100 lbs. Packing cases extra.

Full price allowed for packing cases returned in good condition, Carriage Paid, to the Company's Works at Barwick, Herts (Hadham Station, G.E.R.).

FOR REPORT OF "FIELD" TRIALS ON THE ABOVE, SEE PAGE 23.

THE SMOKELESS POWDER AND AMMUNITION COMPANY, LIMITED. 13

"RIFLEITE" SMOKELESS POWDER

FOR

BALL AND SHOT GUNS, "COSMOS," "PARADOX," &c.

PRICES AS UNDER:—

Size of Tins.	Price per 100 lbs.	Trade Discount.	Extra Discount for Cash within One Month		Net Price per lb.
½ or **1** lb.	**800/-**	**33⅓%**	**5%**	=	**5/1**
5, 25 or **50** lbs. ...	**770/-**	,,	,,	=	**4/10½**

Or 33⅓ per cent. and 2½ per cent. for Cash within Three Months.

Carriage free in cylinders to any Railway Station in the United Kingdom on minimum quantities of 15 lbs., or F.O.B. Thames in quantities of not less than 100 lbs. Packing Cases extra.

Full-price allowed for Packing Cases returned in good condition, Carriage Paid, to the Company's Works at Barwick, Herts (Hadham Station, G.E.R.).

BALL AND SHOT GUN CARTRIDGES.

LOADED WITH "RIFLEITE" POWDER, 12-BORE ONLY.

Cartridges for Ball, Powder only ... ... 13/9 per 100.
,, for Shot, Powder only ... ... 10/6 per 100.

These prices are subject to the usual trade discounts of 30 per cent. and 5 per cent. at settlement, six months' journey account.

FOR REPORT OF "FIELD" TRIALS ON THE ABOVE SEE PAGE 22.

14 THE SMOKELESS POWDER AND AMMUNITION COMPANY, LIMITED.

"BLUE RIVAL"

CHEAP SMOKELESS POWDER.

In order to meet the requirements of a large number of their customers who have been using cheap powders, chiefly of foreign make, for lower grade cartridges, the Company have decided to put a Cheap Smokeless Powder on the market. The price in **5, 25** or **50** lb. tins will be **2s. 8d.** per lb., subject to a discount of **5** per cent. only for cash monthly account, or **2½** per cent. quarterly. In ½ or **1** lb. tins **3d.** per lb. extra.

This Powder is also supplied loaded in Cartridges **12**-bore only.

PRICES AS UNDER:—

No. 1 Quality.—Light Orange Case.

Gauge.	Length.	Powder.	Shot.	Cartridges, per 100.	Cartridges with Powder only, per 100.	Cartridge Cases, per 1,000.
	Inches.	Grs.	Ozs.	£ s. d.	£ s. d.	£ s. d.
12	2½	42	1⅛	— **9 9**	— **8 3**	**1 14 2**

No. 2 Quality.—Red Case.

Gauge.	Length.	Powder.	Shot.	Cartridges, per 100.	Cartridges with Powder only, per 100.	Cartridge Cases, per 1,000.
	Inches.	Grs.	Oz.	£ s. d.	£ s. d.	£ s. d.
12	2½	42	1⅛	— **9 0**	— **7 6**	**1 9 6**

These prices are subject to the usual trade discounts on Cartridges of **30** per cent., and **5** per cent. at settlement, **6** months' journey account.

16 THE SMOKELESS POWDER AND AMMUNITION COMPANY, LIMITED.

RIFLE AND REVOLVER CARTRIDGES

LOADED WITH

"RIFLEITE" SMOKELESS POWDER

SELECTED CASES, BULLETS, CAPS.

·303 "RIFLEITE" CARTRIDGES.

·303 BRITISH GOVERNMENT.
SMOKELESS "RIFLEITE" ·303.

	Per 1,000 £ s. d.
British Government Pattern Cartridges for Rifles or Machine Guns, loaded with "·303 Rifleite" Powder and Nickel Covered Bullets, Mark II....	**9 0 0**
Military Pattern Bullets, 215 Grains, Mark II.	**3 3 4**
Cartridge Cases, Capped and Necked (or Capped only)	**3 11 8**

·303 SPORTING CARTRIDGES

LOADED WITH "·303 RIFLEITE" AND ANY OF THE FOLLOWING PATTERNS OF BULLETS.

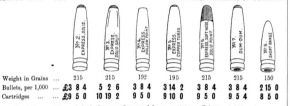

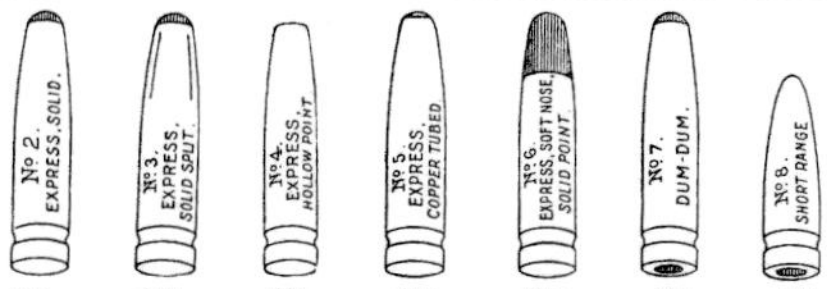
No. 2. EXPRESS, SOLID.
No. 3. EXPRESS, SOLID SPLIT.
No. 4. EXPRESS, HOLLOW POINT.
No. 5. EXPRESS, COPPER TUBED.
No. 6. EXPRESS, SOFT NOSE, SOLID POINT.
No. 7. DUM-DUM.
No. 8. SHORT RANGE.

Weight in Grains ...	215	215	192	195	215	215	150
Bullets, per 1,000 ...	**£3 8 4**	**5 2 6**	**3 8 4**	**3 14 2**	**3 8 4**	**3 8 4**	**2 15 0**
Cartridges	**£9 5 0**	**10 19 2**	**9 5 0**	**9 10 0**	**9 5 0**	**9 5 4**	**8 5 0**

Cartridges with weighed charges for special competitions **£1** per 1,000 extra.

THE COMPANY GUARANTEE ALL CARTRIDGES LOADED AT THEIR OWN FACTORY.

THE SMOKELESS POWDER AND AMMUNITION COMPANY LIMITED. 17

RIFLE CARTRIDGES, MILITARY AND SPORTING.

Description.	Bullet.	List Price per 1,000. £	s.	d.
·297/·230 Short, for Morris Tubes and Cadet Rifles	**38** grs.	**2**	**1**	**8**
·297/·230 Long, for Morris Tubes and Cadet Rifles	**38** grs.	**2**	**4**	**2**
·297/·250 for Rook Rifles	**56** grs.	**2**	**14**	**2**
·256 Mannlicher (**6·5** m/m)	**156** grs. military	**9**	**0**	**0**
" " "	**156** grs. soft nose, solid point...	**9**	**5**	**0**
" " "	**156** grs. hollow pointed ...	**9**	**5**	**0**
Clips for above, extra	... ...	**1**	**10**	**0**
·275 Spanish Mauser (**7** m/m)	**173** grs. military	**9**	**0**	**0**
Clips for above, extra	... ...	**1**	**10**	**0**
·295 or **·300**, for Rook Rifles	**80** grs.	**3**	**5**	**0**
·300 U. S. A.	(See American ammunition, page 18).	**9**	**0**	**0**
·301 Belgian Mauser (**7·65** m/m)	**219** grs. military	**9**	**0**	**0**
·315 Mannlicher (**8** m/m)	**244** grs. military	**9**	**0**	**0**
·360 Express, solid drawn, 2¼ inch case ...	**155** grs.	**6**	**15**	**0**
·380 Long, for Rook Rifles	**124** grs.	**3**	**5**	**0**
·450/·400 Express, solid drawn, 2⅜ inch case	**230** grs. express	**9**	**12**	**6**
" " " " " " ...	**255** grs. solid	**9**	**12**	**6**
" " " " 3¼ inch " ...	**230** grs. express	**11**	**0**	**0**
" " " " " " ...	**255** grs. solid	**11**	**0**	**0**
·450 Martini-Henry, solid drawn	**480** grs. military	**9**	**12**	**6**
" " coiled	**480** grs. military	**8**	**12**	**6**
·450 No. 1 Carbine	**380** grs. solid	**7**	**17**	**6**
·450 No. 2 Musket	**310** grs. solid	**8**	**17**	**6**
" " "	**480** grs. solid	**8**	**17**	**6**
·450 Taper Express, solid drawn, 3¼ inch case	**270** grs. express	**11**	**2**	**6**
" " " " " " " ...	**310** grs. solid	**11**	**2**	**6**
" " " " " " " ...	**325** grs. express	**11**	**8**	**6**
" " " " " " " ...	**365** grs. solid cannelured ...	**11**	**8**	**6**
·500/·450 No. 1 Express, 2¾ inch case ...	**270** grs. express	**11**	**2**	**6**
" " " " " ...	**310** grs. solid	**11**	**2**	**6**
·500/·450 Magnum Express, 3¼ inch case ...	**325** grs. bullet	**13**	**0**	**0**
" " " " " ...	**365** grs. bullet	**13**	**0**	**0**

18 THE SMOKELESS POWDER AND AMMUNITION COMPANY, LIMITED.

RIFLE CARTRIDGES, MILITARY AND SPORTING.

Description.	Bullet.	List Price per 1,000. £	s.	d.
·500 Taper Express, solid drawn, 3 inch case	**340** grs. express	**11**	**12**	**6**
" " " " " " " ...	**380** grs. solid	**11**	**12**	**6**
" " " " " 3¼ inch " ...	**440** grs. express	**12**	**12**	**6**
" " " " " " " ...	**480** grs. solid cannelured ...	**12**	**12**	**6**
·577 Taper Express, solid drawn, 2¾ inch case	**520** grs. express	**13**	**0**	**0**
" " " " " " " ...	**560** grs. solid	**13**	**0**	**0**
" " " " " 3 inch " ...	**570** grs. express	**14**	**0**	**0**
" " " " " " " ...	**610** grs. solid cannelured ...	**14**	**0**	**0**
·577/·500 No. 2 Express	**340** grs. express	**11**	**12**	**6**
" " "	**380** grs. solid	**11**	**12**	**6**
·577 Snider, solid drawn	**480** grs. military	**8**	**5**	**0**

SPECIAL AMMUNITION FOR AMERICAN ARMS.

Description.	Bullet.	£	s.	d.
·22 W. C. F.	**45** grs....	**3**	**7**	**6**
·25 20	**85** grs....	**3**	**7**	**6**
·25 36	**117** grs....	**6**	**7**	**6**
·30 U. S. A.	**215** grs....	**9**	**0**	**0**
·32 20	**115** grs....	**3**	**7**	**6**
·32 40	**165** grs....	**6**	**2**	**6**
·38 40	**180** grs....	**4**	**5**	**0**
·38 55	**255** grs....	**6**	**15**	**6**
·38 56	**255** grs....	**7**	**7**	**6**
·40 65	**260** grs....	**7**	**17**	**6**
·40 82	**260** grs....	**9**	**0**	**0**
·44 40	**200** grs....	**4**	**5**	**0**
·45 70	**405** grs....	**8**	**12**	**6**
·45 90	**300** grs....	**9**	**0**	**0**
50 Winchester Express	**300** grs....	**10**	**0**	**0**

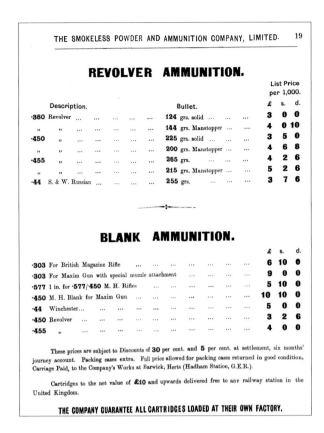

17.4 Examples of the company's shotgun cartridges

Two examples of cartridges loaded with SS powder. The case on the left was made by Eley Bros Ltd of London and the one on the right was manufactured by Frederick Joyce

17.5 Examples of the company's loaded metallic cartridges

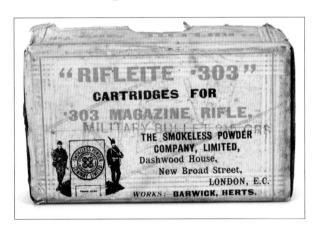

A packet of the company's .303" cartridges. They bear the headstamp Eley .303

This is the only type of specimen I have encountered of a shotgun cartridge bearing the company's initials. These initials date it between 1898 and 1905

CHAPTER 18

The Normal Powder Syndicate Ltd, Normal Powder Co. and the New Normal Ammunition Co.

18.1 The companies' histories

Normal Powder was invented about 1888 by a Swiss Government chemist named Herr E. Schenker. It consisted of a gelatinised nitro cotton powder. Following several years of extensive trials it was finally adopted as the official Swiss Government powder for use in the Schmidt Rubin cartridge and was manufactured at the Federal Powder factory at Worblaufen near Berne. The Swiss Government allowed Schenker to sell the secrets of the powder to the Swedish company named Aktiebolaget Svenska Krutfakorierna, from which the Normal Powder Syndicate Ltd acquired the rights to sell the powder in Britain, its Colonies and Dependencies, and also in Turkey, China, Persia, Egypt and Japan. The powder was manufactured at the Swedish company site at Landskrona in southern Sweden.

The first major reference to the company appeared in *Arms & Explosives* in May 1895. The article outlined the comparative facets of the powder in relation to its contemporaries and these included the following claimed benefits based on extended Swiss Government tests:

a. It generated 40% less barrel temperature when trialled against a Nitroglycerine powder thereby reducing the potential for cook-off in automatic small arms.

b. A comparative test of firing 40,000 rounds through a rifled barrel produced no major injurious effects whilst 3,000 rounds of Nitroglycerine based cartridges rendered the related rifling useless.

c. It proved to be stable across a range of climatic conditions, and cartridges loaded with it were found to be perfectly useable after being stored for up to 3½ years.

d. It was claimed to be virtually flameless and therefore difficult to spot where fired from at night.

e. It produced no injurious gases to affect the user.

f. It was found to be capable of use in both rifles and field guns up to 4.72".

A sequence of trials was conducted with the powder which had been loaded by Eley Bros Ltd, G. Kynoch & Co. Ltd and Messrs Greenwood & Batley Ltd into .303" rounds and then independently tested, which produced the following average results:

	At Eley Bros Ltd 21/3/1895	At Greenwood & Batley 26/3/1895	At G. Kynoch & Co. 2/3/1895
Powder weight	31 grns	30 grns	30 grns
Bullet weight	215 grns	215 grns	215 grns
Muzzle Velocity	2,153 ft/sec	2,026 ft/sec	2,106 ft/sec
Mean variation in velocity	12.5 feet	13 feet	23 feet
Breech pressure	16 tons/sq inch	15.8 tons/sq inch	16 tons/sq inch

Similar tests conducted by Armstrong Whitworth & Co. on large calibre guns also produced extremely favourable results. In theory it would therefore have been reasonable to assume that the British Government would have shown interest in the powder since it was clearly superior to Cordite as a propellant. Cordite however had been introduced into British small arms ammunition in 1891 and therefore numerous factors were against Normal powder receiving a favourable reception. Perhaps one of the strongest factors against its acceptance was that it was a foreign product. Since no English factory existed, in the event of war the Government could not rely on the overseas powder manufacturer supporting their policies; furthermore during this period Britain was the major industrial nation where 'Made in Britain' and 'Buy British' were very much the order of the day and therefore this powder never stood a chance of gaining any real political backing.

The initial capital of the syndicate was some £10,000 in £5 shares, half of which were held by the Swedish company and the remainder were open to allocation, with preference being given to parties capable of influencing its acceptance in the right circles. It was not surprising therefore that its initial listed Directors were Major General M. Tweedie RA, (selected as the Chairman), Count F.A. Posse CE, Lt. General G.H. Fraser RA. and Mr Gustaf Ross. Ross was also the Managing Director and a Captain C.B. Norman was given the role of Manager of the colonial and foreign business sections.

In February 1896 this advert appeared in *Sporting Goods Review* which indicated that the powder was available for use in rifle cartridges in the English market place.

THE SWISS GOVERNMENT POWDER.

NORMAL POWDER.

The "Field" Trials
PROVE
NORMAL is the best non nitro-glycerine Rifle Powder at present in the English market.

WHOLESALE ONLY OF

The Normal Powder Syndicate, Ltd.,

38 and 39, Parliament Street,

LONDON, S.W.

15 February 1896 Sporting Goods Review

In March 1896 the syndicate raised further capital of £7,500 to acquire the patent rights to the Ohman cartridge loading machine. This invention included powder fillers for both sporting and military cartridges, a shot/powder filler for sporting cartridges, wad and bullet seating machines, a gauging machine for rifle cartridges, a gauging machine for the height of the anvil inside the ignition cap, a pressure gauge and a bullet weigher. It is interesting to note that the machine was subject to British Patent No. 17133 taken out jointly by L.G. Ohman and G. Ross. No doubt you will recall that Ross was the company's Managing Director. The syndicate then entered into an agreement with Mr B.T. Moore of the Thames Ammunition Works at Erith for filling the cartridges for them using the Ohman machines. One month later the trade journals reported the syndicate were selling a new 'Telescopic' cartridge loader to gunsmiths to enable them to load their own cartridges.

Although I would never claim to have a real knowledge of good or bad commercial practices it seemed illogical for the syndicate to use a separate company to load their cartridges, since to do so was likely to incur greater costs than if the process was under the direct control of the parent company. The same trade journal in April 1896 reported that Col. P. Fitz G. Gallwey, late RA, formerly Inspector General of Ordnance in Bengal and Bombay, had joined the Board of Directors of the syndicate and that their offices were sited at 38 and 39 Parliament Street, London SW.

June 15, 1896. THE SPORTING GOODS REVIEW. 123

THE SWISS GOVERNMENT POWDER.

NORMAL POWDER.

The "FIELD" TRIALS Prove that

NORMAL IS the best Non-Nitroglycerine Rifle Powder at present in the English Market.

·303 Service Ammunition and ·256 Manlicher. Ammunition loaded with NORMAL POWDER by first-class English Houses.

Nearly 20% Lower Price than Cordite Ammunition.

Ballistics equal Cordite.

No Erosion of the Rifling.

NORMAL SPORTING POWDER IS NOW READY.

A Blasting Powder under the name of "NORMALITE" will soon be brought on the Market.

OHMAN'S Cartridge Filler.

(PROVISIONALLY PROTECTED.)

In Use at the Swedish Government Factories.

TELESCOPIC Cartridge Filler.

(PROVISIONALLY PROTECTED.)

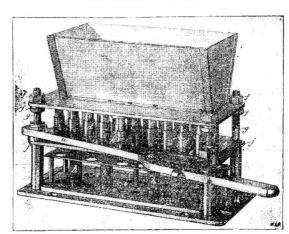

For Governments and Large Private Ammunition Factories.

For Gunmakers and Private Sportsmen.

WHOLESALE ONLY OF

THE NORMAL POWDER SYNDICATE, Ltd., 38 & 39, Parliament Street, London, S.W.

By July 1896 the company was loading their own green coloured shotgun cartridges cases (these were to change to pink in October 1896) which they were supplying to the trade either fully loaded or powdered without shot in gastight cases of English manufacture, and in August 1896 their price list included .303" & .256" Mannlicher rifle cartridges, the case and projectile manufacturers being Eley, Kynoch and Greenwood & Batley.

In January 1897 the Normal Powder Syndicate acquired new premises at 8 King Street, Westminster to act as its distribution centre for London. In February 1897 it was reported that the syndicate intended to increase their capital by £100,000, allegedly with a view to manufacturing there own powders in this country. By March a prospectus had been issued for the Normal Powder & Ammunition Co. Ltd which had been formed to take over, as a going concern, the business of the Normal Powder Syndicate Ltd. The capital hoped to be raised was £70,000 divided into 40,000 shares of £1 each and 30,000 deferred shares at £1 each.

The new Directors were identified as Major General Alex A.A. Kinloch, CB, The Earl of Westmorland, The Earl of Eva, Mr Cecil F.W. Fane, Capt. E.W. Fosester Leighton, C.A. Osborne, Count F. Arvidson Posse, CE, Col. P. Fitz G. Gallwey late RA, and Gustaf Ross Esq. Ross was nominated Managing Director, the Earl of Westmorland Chairman with Major General Kinloch taking on the role of Vice Chairman. The aim of the reconstruction was subsequently stated to provide an additional £100,000 working capital and no further mention of the powder being manufactured in Britain was made.

At the company's AGM on 8 July 1897 it was reported that the Erith factory produced range of cartridges had been improved and that steam power was now being used for producing turnovers on the shotgun cases. A warehouse had been opened at 8 King Street, Westminster, which had been licensed to store 100,000 cartridges. The licence at King Street also authorised the company to load 10,000 cartridges per day. It also stated that the company proposed to acquire a new factory about five miles from Marble Arch, where it intended to erect three good sized sheds capable, together with the Erith site of turning out 10 million sporting cartridges per year. In December 1897 the company had an issue of a further 18,262 ordinary shares. The new factory at Hendon was now fully working and capable of turning out 250,000 sporting cartridges per week and export agencies had been established in Bombay, Calcutta, Lahore, Rawal Pindi, Karachi, Srinagar, Colombo, Rangoon, Johannesburg and Sydney and the shares in question were to provide the extra working capital required.

One year later on 17 December 1898, the company moved their offices to 2 Bank Buildings, Cricklewood, London, NW and at the company's AGM on the 29 December 1898 the Directors stated that in 1897 they had produced 2,486,055 cartridges but had experienced problems with flooding at the Erith site.

In January 1899 the *Sporting Goods Review* reported that the company, following the floods at Erith, had moved their works and offices to Hendon. In June that year a reporter from this journal visited the company's loading plant at Hendon where they discovered that an Erskine machine was being used with a 2½ dram tray and Normal Powder. They took some samples out and weighed the powder contents which came to 31 grains ± ½ grain. An Erskine machine was also being used to load the ¹¹⁄₁₆ oz shot load.

During 1900 it was clear the company was facing major financial problems and this was reflected by the fact that for some 18 months the Directors had not issued a balance sheet. The *Financial Times* on 19 May had issued an article on the company entitled 'Shooting Backwards'. In it, it referred to a balance sheet issued to a shareholder who had demanded its issue, which in the previous 18 months showed a company loss of some £6,348 which, when added to the identified loss on the balance sheet issued on 30 September 1898 of £9,592, indicated an overall trading loss of some £16,000 with its remaining assets standing at only £6,164. In the summer of that year it was stated that although the turnover in cartridge numbers had been considerable the cost of production was not sufficient to cover working expenses and the Directors were seriously considering amalgamating the business with the London Sporting Park, Hendon, London, which was a member of the Inanimate Bird Shooting Association. Presumably the company's assumption was that this clay shooting ground would boost their sales of shotgun cartridges. It appeared that their Hendon loading factory and this shooting ground were adjacent, both were leasing the ground they occupied and their recommendation was to jointly purchase the site, which in theory would have been to the benefit of both parties. Unfortunately I have been unable to ascertain if the company finally purchased the site, however it was quite clear that it did not receive the support of the sporting press.

In February 1902 rumours in *Arms & Explosives* outlined agitation for the reconstitution of the Normal Powder & Ammunition Co. Ltd, one remedy suggested as a means of solving the company's difficulty being to extinguish the capital which at that time was unissued. During the company's four and a half years of existence it had lost £19,000. In February 1903 the same journal reported that a debenture holder, namely Mr Gustaf Ross, was taking over control of The Normal Powder & Ammunition Co. Ltd and that Mr J. H. Thomas has been appointed Works Manager at the Hendon factory. Previously Thomas had been employed by the company as a sales representative.

Irrespective of the financial difficulties faced by the company the quality of their shotgun cartridges was not lost on the sportsman of the day and the company was honoured by the grant of a warrant of appointment as purveyors of Normal Powder cartridges to His Majesty the King of Portugal in March 1905, later to be extended to the King of Spain. In October 1908 the company was appointed warrant purveyors of cartridges loaded with Normal powder to H.M. King Gustav V of Sweden.

On 3 September 1910 the New Normal Ammunition Co. Ltd was registered which took over the former company. The new Company Directors were H.C.K. Rogers and J.H. Thomas. A notice in the *Sporting Goods Review* on 15 January 1914 stated 'Notice has been given of the intention to dissolve at the expiration of three months the old limited liability company known as the Normal Powder & Ammunition Co. Ltd which was the predecessor of the present Normal Ammunition Co. Ltd'. It appeared from this statement that the name of the new company which had added the word 'New' to its title had reverted to its former title and this appeared to be common practice during this era.

From this point onwards I can find no further references to the company and no further adverts appeared for its products after February 1919. Clearly the advent of WWI would have severely restricted the company importing foreign made cases from Belgium and the British cartridge case manufacturers would have been concentrating their efforts on the production of war materials, so almost certainly its ability to expand would have been curtailed. In contrast however to this statement the headstamps encountered on New Normal Powder Company cartridges indicate production occurred well after this date, since specimens bearing ICI headstamps, those used by Fiocchi of Italy, Gevelot of Paris and Baikal of Russia will be encountered. I have also established from the Hull Cartridge Company that they also loaded cartridges for this company during the later period of their existence.

18.2.1 Cartridges loaded or supplied by the company

In April 1897 the company were supplying .303" & .256" Mannlicher rifle cartridges which they were getting Eley Bros, Kynoch Ltd and Greenwood & Batley to load for them with Normal powders. They were also offering Pegamoid cases, Brass Ejectors, 'Nimrod' brand and best pink quality cases which were being made for them by Joyce, Kynoch, Eley and Bachmann. By July 1897 they had orders for 300,000 shotgun cartridge cases, some of which they loaded whilst others were to be supplied empty, together with powder for gunsmiths and ironmongers to load at their own premises. They stated that shotgun cartridge cases of different bore sizes were being obtained by the syndicate for re-sale to the trade from suppliers in England, the USA and Europe. In March 1903 it was revealed that the syndicate had entered into a very favourable contract to obtain three types of shotgun cases for nitro loads all of which would bear no names and would be available at 15s per 1,000 cases. Their quality would be equal to their existing 'Keepers' Normal'.

In October 1914 the *Sporting Goods Review* reported that the company's supply of 'Keepers' Normal' cartridges has been exhausted since supplies of its Belgian made cases has dried up and they had substituted a light blue 12 bore case which were being made in Britain.

The brand names encountered on this company's products include:

Hendon

Nimrod

Nomalis

Special Twenty

Keepers' Normal

Superior Nimrod

Normal 'Light Blue'

They also loaded .410" in 2½" cases, full brass ejectors, half brass Hendons which were pink cased together with Eley Pegamoid cases. They initially produced their shotgun cartridges in 12 bore and 16 bore and in October 1896 they extended the range to include 20 bore.

Their use of Winchester Rifle Ammunition Company cases appears to be restricted to a short period of supply during the late 1890s.

18.2.2 Examples of the companies' shotgun cartridges

LEFT TO RIGHT: *Unnamed, Kynoch 'Grouse Ejector', 'Keepers' Normal' , 2 Normal 'Light Blue', and 3 versions of 'Nimrod'*

LEFT TO RIGHT:
*Light Blue lying down at back, 'Hendon',
'Hendon',
'Normalis', unnamed using WRA case*
AT FRONT LYING DOWN: *unnamed*

18.3 Examples of adverts used by the companies

"NORMAL" SPORTING POWDER. SMOKELESS-WATERPROOF

EXTRAORDINARY

SUCCESS.

NORMAL POWDER "NIMROD" CARTRIDGE

NORMAL SPORTING POWDER.

3s. per lb.

ONE POUND LOADS ABOUT 220 12-BORE CARTRIDGES.

N.B.—CAN BE LOADED BOTH IN CONE AND GOOD ORDINARY NITRO POWDER CASES

PRICES OF SPORTING AMMUNITION.

12 Bore (Eley's, Joyce's, or Kynoch's Cases) **8/3** per 100	12 Bore (Eley's Brass Ejector Cases) ... **10/-** per 100
16 ,, ,, ,, ,, ,, **8/-** ,,	12 ,, ("Nimrod" Waterproof Cases) ... **7/6** ,,
20 ,, ,, ,, ,, ,, **7/9** ,,	
12 ,, (Eley's Waterproof Pegamoid Cases) **9/-** ,,	12 ,, (Eley's or Joyce's 2¾in. Pigeon Cases) **9/-** ,,

NORMAL RIFLE POWDER

2s. per lb.

ONE POUND LOADS ABOUT 220 ·303 CARTRIDGES.

PRICES OF RIFLE AMMUNITION.

·303 Cartridges for the Lee-Metford, Martini-Metford, or Machine Guns, with Service Bullet ... ... **12/6** per 100	Do., with Bullets with Split-jacket ... **14/6** per 100
	·256 Mannlicher ... ... **15/-** ,,
Do., with Tubular or Soft-nosed Bullets ... **14/6** ,,	Do., packed in Clips ... ... **15/6** ,,

PRICES OF AMMUNITION ARE SUBJECT TO TRADE DISCOUNTS.

Sample Cartridges sent Gratis.

THE NORMAL POWDER SYNDICATE, LIMITED,

38 & 39, PARLIAMENT STREET, LONDON, S.W.

December 15, 1897.   THE SPORTING GOODS REVIEW.   271

Normal Sporting Powder.

☞ MOST PERFECT NITRO. ☜

SEE NEW PROSPECTUS AND NEW PRICE LIST.

Special Advantages to Gunmakers and Dealers being holders of one £1 Share or upwards:

FIRST.—Orders for 500 Cartridges and upwards will be executed carriage free in London, or to any Railway Station in the United Kingdom.

SECONDLY.—If a minimum quantity of 1,000 Cartridges are ordered, $2\frac{1}{2}$ per cent. discount **extra** will be allowed off the **special trade prices.**

THIRDLY.—5 per cent. discount on Normal Powder on 10 lbs. or upwards, and free delivery to any Railway Station in the United Kingdom.

FOURTHLY.—5 per cent. discount on empty Cartridge Cases specially made for Normal Sporting Powder, at prices from 20/- per 1,000 and upwards, and carriage paid on quantities of 5,000 to any Railway Station in the United Kingdom.

WRITE FOR PARTICULARS TO

THE NORMAL POWDER AND AMMUNITION CO., LIMITED,

38 & 39, PARLIAMENT STREET, LONDON, S.W.

NORMAL SPORTING POWDER.

☞ NEW ISSUE PERFECT. ☜
Superior to all other Nitros.

SPECIAL OFFER OF CARTRIDGES TO THE TRADE.

NORMAL POWDER, charged in superior metal lined cases :

							Absolutely Nett Price.					
In Quantities of							Per 1,000 Cartridges, powdered only with 3 wads.			Per 1,000 Cartridges, completely loaded.		
							£	s.	d.	£	s.	d.
1,000 and upwards...	...	...	...	...	...	...	2	7	0	3	4	6
5,000 ,,	...	...	...	...	...	...	2	5	9	3	3	3
10,000 ,,	...	...	...	...	...	...	2	4	6	3	2	0
20,000 ,,	...	...	...	...	...	...	2	3	3	3	0	9

N.B.—*These prices are for 12 bore. The price for 16 bore will be 2/6 per 1,000 less. 20 bore cannot be supplied in these cases.*

10 SAMPLE CARTRIDGES GRATIS.

NORMAL SPORTING POWDER.

This is a pure Gun-Cotton Powder without any mixture of Nitro Glycerine, and from recent trials it has been found to possess the following qualities :—

It is practically Smokeless!
It is absolutely Waterproof!
Leaves no Residue in the Barrel!
No unburnt Grains blown out of the Barrel!
High Velocity combined with Low Pressures!
Good Pattern and Hard Hitting!
Quick Ignition and Easy Shooting!

PRICES OF SPORTING AMMUNITION.

All Sporting Ammunition sold by the Syndicate will be in Gas-tight Cases made by the well-known firms of Kynoch, Eley or Joyce, unless otherwise ordered.

In all cases Soft Shot will be used unless Hardened is specially Ordered.

Bore.	Charge.	Shot.		Cartridges, complete, per 100.	Cartridges, with Powder only.
12	32 grains.	1⅛ oz.	-	**8s. 3d.**	**6s. 6d.**
16	29 ,,	1 ,,	-	**8s. 0d.**	**6s. 3d.**

1,000 of the above Cartridges, or upwards, sent Carriage Paid to any Town in the United Kingdom (by Goods Train).

N.B.—*Sample Boxes of Five Cartridges sent Gratis, but Receiver to pay the Carriage.*

PRICES OF AMMUNITION ARE SUBJECT TO TRADE DISCOUNTS.

The NORMAL POWDER SYNDICATE, Ltd.,
Offices: 38 & 39, Parliament Street, London, S.W.
Powder Stores and Ammunition Factory: ERITH, KENT.

NORMAL
SPORTING POWDER.
——(New Issue).——

This is absolutely uniform, giving the highest penetration and velocity with the least recoil. It can be confidently recommended to all who object to the unpleasant jar and concussion caused by most other Nitro Powders.

THE NIMROD CARTRIDGE, 8/- per 100,
is perfectly waterproof, and is therefore, for use in Ejector Guns, equal to an expensive brass case.

THE NORMAL POWDER Co. are so confident in the unequalled shooting of their present issue that they will send sample Cartridges, gratis, to any sportsman willing to give them a fair trial.

Advert from Sporting Goods Review *15 December 1899*

18.4 Examples of headstamps encountered on Normal and New Normal Ammunition Company shotgun cartridges

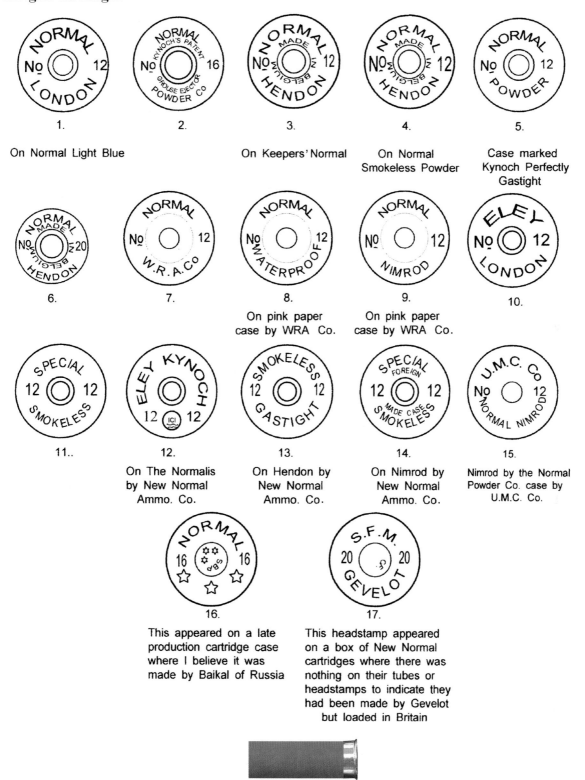

1.

On Normal Light Blue

2.

3.

On Keepers' Normal

4.

On Normal
Smokeless Powder

5.

Case marked
Kynoch Perfectly
Gastight

6.

7.

8.

On pink paper
case by WRA Co.

9.

On pink paper
case by WRA Co.

10.

11..

12.

On The Normalis
by New Normal
Ammo. Co.

13.

On Hendon by
New Normal
Ammo. Co.

14.

On Nimrod by
New Normal
Ammo. Co.

15.

Nimrod by the Normal
Powder Co. case by
U.M.C. Co.

16.

This appeared on a late
production cartridge case
where I believe it was
made by Baikal of Russia

17.

This headstamp appeared
on a box of New Normal
cartridges where there was
nothing on their tubes or
headstamps to indicate they
had been made by Gevelot
but loaded in Britain

CHAPTER 19

Luck's Explosives Ltd and Henrite Explosives Ltd, London

19.1 The company history

The company of Luck's Explosives Ltd was registered in November 1898 with a capital of £80,000 in £1 shares. The company was formed to carry into effect an agreement between Mr A. Luck, Mr L. Henry and the New Industrial Contract Ltd to manufacture gunpowder and explosives.

The trade name 'Henrite' was registered in the *Trade Marks Journal* on 1 September 1901 to Messrs Luck's Explosives Ltd. The original trade mark consisted of two circles, one inside the other, with the words Luck's Explosives Ltd written between them. The middle circle contains a cross with 'Henrite' written across it.

Less than two years later in April 1903 *Arms & Explosives* reported that Luck's Explosive Ltd had gone into liquidation. The related news extract stated that their chief product was the 33 grain Henrite shotgun cartridge favoured by pigeon shooters.

On 11 April 1906 Henrite Explosives Ltd was registered with a capital of £30,000 in £1 shares to adopt an agreement with Luck's Explosives Ltd to carry on the business of manufacturers and dealers in explosives, arms and ammunition. No initial public issue of shares was offered and the registered office was located at Salisbury House, London EC. Following on from this announcement on 9 July 1906, Luck's Explosives Ltd voluntarily wound up its business.

An entry in *Sporting Goods Review* on 15 January 1909 refers to the sale of the works, goodwill patents and other property of Henrite Explosives Ltd and I quote '*we are informed that it is intended to carry on the business under new proprietorship. We are requested by the purchasing syndicate that the company will be carried on under new proprietorship and Mr Robertson who was employed by the old company is in no way connected to the new syndicate*'. On 7 January 1909 Messrs Foster & Cranfield at the Mart, Tokenhouse Yard sold by auction for £700 the leases, huts, plant, machinery patent interests and goodwill of the Henrite Explosives Co. Ltd. It consisted of buildings and land held on lease at Powder Mills Lane, Dartford including interests of the vendors in a number of British, Belgian, French, Italian and Spanish patents bearing dates from 1898 to 1906.

Three months later in May 1909 the same journal reported that the plant at their Dartford Works, now greatly enlarged, was operating under the direction of the new management and had the capacity to turn out greater quantities of powder, resulting in the trebling of cartridge production. It stated that Mr C.E.C. Luck was in charge of the manufacture of Henrite and had been so for some years and remained as its Manager. Its Managing Director was a Mr Henry with an Assistant Manager Mr S.D. Smith. The article also stated that the company's shotgun cartridges were solely sold to trade customers.

When these snippets of data were first extracted I was totally confused but it all falls into place when you consider they reflect a mirror image of events which occur in today's society namely an example of a phoenix company which arises from the dead, a legal although totally unethical means of shedding outstanding debts and rendering former shares worthless, whilst the value to the key owners remains intact.

In June 1912 Mr S. D. Smith was promoted to the role of General Manager and in August 1913 the London offices of the company moved to 97 Wilton Road, Euston from their former ones sited at 18 St. Swithin's Lane, London EC.

On 2 January 1920 a meeting was held to examine the liquidation report on the company and the disposal of its remaining assets. This then marked the end of the company.

19.2 Cartridge production

The vast majority of remaining specimens bearing either the Luck's or Henrite headstamps were made in Austria and if you examine the edges of their turnovers you will see the words 'CASE MADE IN BAVARIA' running radial around the top edges. The company used both brass cases and paper cases, where on the specimens examined, the paper tubes or the paper liners in brass cases have been yellow. In the October 1911 issue of *Arms & Explosives* the company stated that they had now standardised their production using English made cases unless foreign made cases were specifically asked for and that the English made cases loaded with their powder were giving good results. Three types of named paper cased cartridge have been seen namely 'The Pigeon' which I have seen with a Luck's Explosives headstamp, 'The Rabbit' which bore a Henrite headstamp and the more common example which consists of the name Henrite written vertically and horizontally in the centre of the tube intersecting using the common letter R.

19.3 Company adverts

The company regularly advertised their shotgun cartridges in trade journals of the period however unlike most they never registered to my knowledge any names applied to these cartridges other than 'Henrite'.

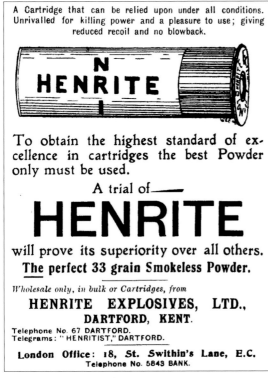

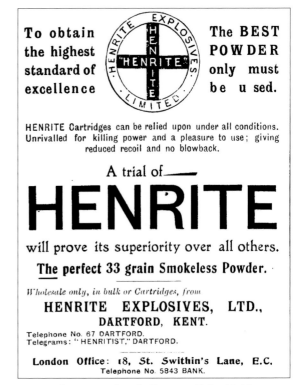

Sporting Goods Review *August 1909*   Sporting Goods Review *July 1910*

19.4 Cartridge headstamps used by Luck's Explosives Ltd and Henrite Explosives Ltd

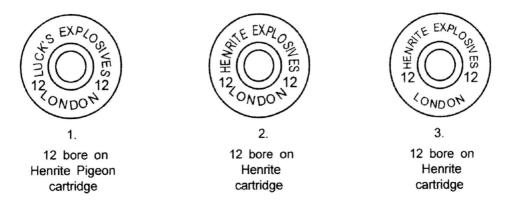

1.

12 bore on
Henrite Pigeon
cartridge

2.

12 bore on
Henrite
cartridge

3.

12 bore on
Henrite
cartridge

CHAPTER 20
Messrs Curtis's & Harvey

20.1 The company's history

This company was originally formed in 1822. It initially acquired the Hounslow works and shortly afterwards an adjacent factory at Bedfond. In due course the company expanded further purchasing works in Tonbridge in 1869 and in 1876 they acquired the Kames Gunpowder Co. at Millhouse near Glasgow.

In 1871 the company's TS No.6 black powder was adopted as the standard load for use in the British Boxer primed Henry cartridge which was retitled RFG. 2 powder.

In 1893 the Clyde Mills Company placed a new smokeless powder called 'Amberite' on the market. In 1895 this company was acquired by Curtis's & Harvey and in due course 'Amberite' became one of its most well known and profitable propellants. The Clyde Mills were sited in a deep and well wooded glen at the head of Holy Loch and the Firth of Clyde alongside the river Little Echaig Glenlean. It started life as a black powder mill and in 1891 was rebuilt to manufacture 'Amberite' smokeless powder.

A view within the boundaries of the Curtis's & Harvey factory at Hounslow alongside the river Colne

In March 1896 a visit was made to the Hounslow factory which was reported in the sporting press of the period and a copy of that report is shown below.

62   THE SPORTING GOODS REVIEW.   March 16, 1896.

Presenting ourselves at the lodge gate, and giving up matches and cigar-case, we pass the belt of trees, and make our way to the offices, whence under the courteous guidance of Mr. J. R. Knights, the manager of the factory, we commence our round of inspection.

Although, of course, the fact is known to readers, it may be well here to premise that the manufacture of black powder is by no means so complicated as that of nitro-compounds in their present state, owing in great part to the simplicity of the ingredients used, which consist essentially of saltpetre, sulphur, and charcoal.

We make our way first to the ovens, where alder, willow, and dogwood, are reduced to charcoal, the first two for export and the latter for best sporting powders. These ovens consist of large cylinders, arranged, some horizontally, others vertically, in which the wood is charred to the required state. Outlets are provided for the escape of the tar and acid, which are collected in receptacles provided for the purpose, and the progress of the charring is judged by the colour of the smoke there issuing. A building is next visited, where the double-refined saltpetre is being carefully powdered and sifted through fine sieves. Here is also to be seen the plant for refining crude saltpetre, a process no longer carried on at the works. Passing on we reach the brimstone mill, which we enter in a pair of overall boots, henceforth our constant companions. Here the pure sulphur is ground under heavy stone runners, and subjected to a sifting process, by means of a powerful fan, at the end of which it is found reduced to the finest powder. The motive power for this, and many of the other mills, is furnished by a water wheel driven from the river Colne, which runs through the grounds. Attention is next directed to the mixing house, where charges of either fifty or sixty lbs. of the correct proportions of the three constituents are thoroughly mixed. The mechanism employed consists of a series of hollow revolving drums, into which the mixture is introduced, together with a number of lignum-vitæ balls. At the expiration of a given period, the drum being opened, the balls drop on a grating beneath, and are received in a leather lined receptacle, the mixture falling through, and being collected in bags each containing a charge. Visiting the incorporating mills, we see the charges being ground beneath heavy metal runners, inner and outer ploughs being provided to keep the mixture always in the path of the revolving edges. A number of groups of these mills were visited, each consisting of six, three on either side of an engine house, and all driven from overhead shafting. We were afforded an opportunity of inspecting the group where the recent accident occurred, which it will be remembered was unattended by any loss of life or limb. The cause was plainly to be seen in a fractured spindle, flawed from the inside, an unfortunate mishap, against which all precautions are powerless to guard. It is surmised that the washer between the boss of the spindle and the boss of the runner fell amongst the powder when the spindle came out, causing the explosion. It is just possible that had the accident occurred in the daytime, the increasing looseness of the washer might have been noticed, but at night so slight an alteration in its position was most unlikely to attract attention. It is recorded that the only man who was injured when the explosion happened, took the occurrence with the utmost *sang froid*, and was one of the first to render assistance with the hose and pumps. It speaks well, too, for the construction of the mills, that only three out of the six in the group exploded.

But to resume. The finished charge is now conveyed in leather covered barrows from the incorporating mill to the hydraulic press house, where it is first carefully sieved, and then pressed. This process is effected by placing layers of powder, carefully guaged as to quantity, between plates of ebonite, and submitting them to steady pressure in a hydraulic press, from which they emerge in the form of hard cakes. The hydraulic power here is provided by pumps contained in an adjoining pump-room, and the building is surrounded by an earth mound. The next process to be performed, is that of forming the powder into grains. The pressed cake being received in the granulating house, passes through teethed rollers and on through smooth rollers until the requisite degree of fineness is obtained, when the resultant meal is sifted by means of a sifting frame; thence it is conveyed to one or other of the series of glazing houses, and submitted to a glazing process. These houses contain a series of large wooden cylinders, all revolving steadily on an axis, much after the fashion of glorified churns. In these, the powder remains for ten, twelve, or fourteen hours, and is transformed into one or other of the familiar forms of black or brown sporting compounds. The motive power at the glazing houses is provided by a large water wheel. The powder is now subjected to a drying process in the stove house, which is kept at a temperature of 100 to 150 deg. F. by steam from the boiler houses, the explosive being spread out on trays which are contained in racks almost filling the house. After inspecting these, we walk some little distance to the dusting house, noting on the way the elaborate precautions taken against fire or explosion. Embankments and earth traverses abound, plantations of trees yet further isolate the erections, the river is diverted in all directions, hose-pipes and stands are met with everywhere, and lightning conductors, frequently tested, are fitted to most of the buildings.

In the dusting house, the powder is passed through a series of screens kept constantly agitated ; each screen is of different mesh, and as the process proceeds, the powder is fed into bags, each containing a stated quantity of a given size, according to the screen from which it was received. In this part of the factory, there is no water power immediately available, but the force is transmitted from a water wheel by means of a teledynamic rope. Returning towards the office, we visit a house where the bags of powder are being headed up in casks and boxes ready for transit ; and inspect also the two large storage magazines almost hidden behind a high, tree-crowned embankment, which surrounds them on all sides.

At this point, having inspected the main process from start to finish, and visited just half the factory, our guide proposes luncheon, and accordingly we betake ourselves to a region where the temperature is no longer subject to such violent fluctuations, as perforce attend the visitor to a powder factory on a frosty February morning.

After luncheon, a profitable half hour is spent in looking over the samples of the various productions of the works, ranging from S.B.C. for 100 ton guns, to the finest sporting powder, and all the familiar intermediate compounds. Pebble powders, black and brown prismatic, blasting pellets, diamond grain, basket, &c., are inspected, and afterwards we see some specimens of various spurious labels, imitations of those issued at the factory. " Cubtis's & Marvey, of Hounslom," are presumably a firm " made in Germany." " Cortis's & Hadvey " we seek for in vain at " Hounslom and London ; " whilst the various firms who are *the only makers* of Diamond Grain Powder, seem in number as the sands of the sea. Ingenuity worthy of a better cause has been displayed in imitating both canisters and labels, but Messrs. Curtis's & Harvey can scarcely be expected to appreciate the subtle flattery conveyed. Dealers in explosives, more particularly abroad, should take special care, in the first place that the flasks and canisters are genuine, and secondly that the seal above the cork is unbroken, when handling powder purporting to come from these works.

Resuming our round, we make our way to the pellet press house, where the circular blasting pellets are pro-duced in one operation. The pressure here is provided by a hydraulic accumulator. Next the labelling house is visited, where a large staff is constantly employed affixing various labels to the tins and canisters, ranging in capacity from an ounce to twenty-five pounds. At the packing house we see the tins filled with powder, sealed down, packed in boxes, and made ready for transit, or for storage in the magazine. Next we visit the large steam cooperage (so far as we know the only one attached to a powder factory), and the box making establishment, where the familiar white wood cases are being rapidly turned out.

Passing on, we are conducted to the canister department, where sheets of thick tin are being transformed into canisters, flasks, and bottles of various shapes. In the next house these receive several coats of paint—blue, red, yellow—are varnished carefully, and then stored. In the stores adjoining, they remain packed on shelves until required for issue.

One or two other stores are visited, we look in at the large well-appointed stables, see the proof ground, pass some of the workmen's dwellings, and so bring our visit to a conclusion. At the office, we bid farewell to our courteous and obliging cicerone, and as we take our last glance round the wide expanse of the factory, a place almost historic, by virtue of its long association with the favourite pursuit of sportsmen, we feel that the high expectations we had formed of it have been most fully realised.

The illustration at the head of this article represents only a very small portion of the factory, as no complete view of it could be obtained owing to the wide area its buildings are distributed over. To attempt a general photograph would be merely to reproduce a picturesque expanse of well-watered and well-wooded landscape, a park-like scene which the various mills and buildings can scarcely be said to mar It is, indeed, only upon close inspection that one realises the huge extent of the industry carried on within the boundaries of the factory, which has for years past provided employment for a very considerable staff of workmen and others, and the output from which in all the various classes of explosives manufactured, has associated the name of Hounslow with that of Messrs. Curtis's & Harvey in every country of the world.

In September 1897 the *Sporting Goods Review* revealed that Curtis's & Harvey had started loading cartridges with 'Smokeless Diamond' powder for supply to the trade.

In 1898 the public registered company of Curtis's & Harvey Ltd was formed which incorporated the old gunpowder company of John Hall & Son, Pigou Wilkes & Lawrence, Hay Merricks & Co., Ballincollig Gunpowder Works, Kennall Vale Gunpowder Works, East Cornwall Gunpowder works and the War & Sporting Smokeless Powder Company.

Following the formation of the limited company Curtis's & Harvey moved in 1899 to new offices sited at 3 Gracechurch Street, London EC having vacated their former offices at 74 Lombard Street, London EC.

In November 1899 it was reported that Curtis's & Harvey Ltd had shut down their old Midlothian Gunpowder works at Camily West Calder and in the subsequent March *Arms and Explosives* reported that Cannonite production, then made at Trimley near Felixstowe was to be moved at the end of the year to the Tonbridge Gunpowder Works, which were also owned by Curtis's & Harvey Ltd.

In February 1906 it was stated that the company had recently erected at their Cliffe factory, the necessary magazines, building and other facilities for loading Government ammunition under an arrangement reached with the Coventry Ordnance Works Ltd.

The July 1911 issue of *Arms & Explosives* reported that Curtis's & Harvey Ltd had decided to open a subsidiary in Canada in order to overcome the 'tariff wall' imposed on imports into Canada from Britain, which since their inception had affected a considerable amount of its trade. It was entitled Curtis's and Harvey (Canada) Ltd and operated from a new factory at Rigaud, a few miles from Montreal. It opened in 1911 and closed in 1917 when a fire destroyed the whole plant.

In January 1920 an advert stated that the former company's sales department had transferred to Explosives Trades Ltd, Angel Road, Edmonton, London N18 following its takeover by Nobel's.

20.2 The company's management structure

The company was founded by Sir William Curtis in 1822 as a partnership between Mr Harvey and Sir William Curtis, his son C. W. Curtis and a nephew. In 1881 T. R. Curtis, the great grandson of the founder Sir William Curtis, commenced a long apprenticeship with the company in their offices in Lombard Street, when his father C. W. Curtis was the sole proprietor. In 1894 T. R. Curtis became a partner in the company and when the limited company was formed he became a Director and Vice-Chairman, the Chairman of the Board being his elder brother Col. C. H. Curtis. On the retirement of his brother Col. Curtis in December 1918, T. R. Curtis took on the role of Chairman and following amalgamation with Nobel's became a Director of Nobel's.

D. J. Metcalfe entered the service of John Hall & Son at Faversham in 1878 and on retirement of the partners in this company in 1896 a private limited company was formed, of which he became Managing Director. Two years later in 1898, Halls amalgamated with Curtis's & Harvey Ltd and Metcalfe joined the Board of Directors, a post he retained until it was acquired by Nobel's.

In May 1913 Mr E. D. Metcalfe (the son of D. J. Metcalfe, a Director of Curtis's & Harvey Ltd) was appointed Company Secretary after serving as Assistant Secretary for some years.

C. L. Watson-Smith MA JP was the son of one of the partners in the firm of John Hall & Son of Faversham. In 1896 J. Hall & Sons was registered as a limited company and he joined D. J. Metcalfe as a Director. He continued as a Director for Curtis's & Harvey Ltd when Halls were amalgamated with them in 1898 and died aged 54 years on 5 November 1915.

On 5 May 5 1905 the death of Charles W. Curtis, former President of Curtis's & Harvey Ltd was reported. He died at his residence Kearsney Manor in Dover.

In August 1919 Colonel C. H. Curtis, the former Chairman of Curtis's & Harvey Ltd, retired precipitated by the amalgamation with Nobel's.

20.3 Accidents at the company premises

During the period that Curtis's & Harvey manufactured powders they were to experience a number of explosions with related deaths and serious injuries at their sites. A summary of the most devastating follow:

On 2 February 1904 an explosion occurred at their gunpowder factory at Hounslow and two men subsequently died. Two days later an explosion occurred at their Cordite works at Cliffe killing one man and seriously injuring a second.

In February 1906 a serious explosion occurred at their gunpowder mills at Hounslow which wrecked several sheds and injured a George Rider and a W. Bye.

A further incident occurred at the Cordite factory at Cliffe when it caught fire on 1 April 1908 and although no one was injured it generated £1,000 of damage. The fire had started in the drying house.

On 15 June 1909 an explosion occurred at their West Calder Factory. There were two groups of mills on this site, each group consisting of three incorporating mills. The explosion virtually destroyed one group of three mills but with no loss of life.

On 26 July 1911 three staff were killed and 11 injured in an explosion at the Cliffe factory near Rochdale. The seat of the explosion was in the Nitroglycerine washing and filtering houses. A Law Hawkins and a man named Walkinshaw were killed whilst carrying nitrating paste on a bogie. The explosion destroyed both the building and bogie and created deep craters under it.

On 9 July 1915 an explosion occurred at the Hounslow factory killing a man named Marks whilst other employees received minor injuries. It caused a considerable amount of damage to the factory

20.4 Trade marks registered by the company and introduction dates for their shotgun cartridges and powders

Date	Trade name of shotgun cartridge or powder
1899	Tom Thumb (2" case)
1899	Cannonite – in production however before 1894
1899	Ruby powder introduced but not registered until December 1904
May 1900	Fusilite
January 1902	Mastiff for cartridge cases
January 1902	Bulldog motif for cartridge cases
March 1902	Amberite with Winged Dragon
January 1903	Smokeless Diamond powder introduced
May 1905	Feather Weight – designed as a light load to reduce recoil and headaches
May 1905	Registered the Smokeless Diamond triangle trade mark
April 1900	Jewel and Rampant Dragon become trade marks
November 1911	Marvel and Crystal Smokeless Sporting Gunpowder and Marvel cartridges registered
April 1913	Albion and Fulmen smokeless powders

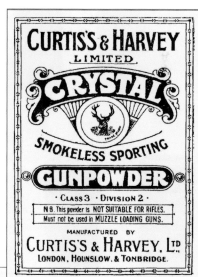

No claim is made to the exclusive use of the word " Crystal."

334,165. Gunpowder. CURTIS'S & HARVEY, LIMITED, 3, Gracechurch Street, London, E.C., and Hounslow, Middlesex, and Tonbridge, Kent ; Explosives Manufacturers.—6th June 1911. (*To be associated. Sect. 24.*)

20.5.1 Examples of the company's shotgun cartridges

LEFT TO RIGHT: *Eley Bros Ltd case loaded with Amberite at Hounslow factory, Eley Bros Ltd case loaded with Ruby powder at Hounslow factory, Eley Bros Co. Ltd case loaded at Eley's with Smokeless Diamond, Eley Ejector loaded at Hounslow with Smokeless Diamond (lying down), C&H 'Marvel' cartridge case by Eley Bros Ltd, Amberite in an Eley Bros Ltd case with printing reversed in relation to first specimen*

Hounslow loading in an Eley Bros lined Nitro case and a Kynoch factory loaded Smokeless Diamond cartridge

ABOVE:
LEFT TO RIGHT:
Early Amberite loaded in a George Kynoch Co. case, Kynoch loaded Smokeless Diamond, Hounslow loading in an Eley Bros Ltd lined Nitro case, Hounslow loading in an Eley Bros Ltd, unlined Nitro case, Hounslow loading in a Nobel's case made at Joyce factory, ICIACZ Australian factory loading
LYING DOWN:
Eley Bros Ltd Gastight case loaded with Smokeless Diamond

During the 1908/09 season the company's catalogue indicated they were retailing the Eley Bros Ltd, Ejector, Gastight, Pegamoid ⅝" lined and unlined or ⅜" lined and nitro lined or unlined cases with Smokeless Diamond, Amberite or Ruby powders.

In September 1915 *Arms & Explosives* reported that Ruby and Marvel cases could not be delivered by the manufacturers for some time to come due to Government demands and that they were only loading their proprietary cartridges with Smokeless Diamond and Amberite powders.

Following the takeover by Nobel's the majority of the Curtis's & Harvey trade names vanished within a short period of time. One however was to last into the ICI period, namely 'Smokeless Diamond' powder and specimens of ICI manufactured Grand Prix cartridges will be encountered with the wording on their tubes:

'Eley Loaded ◇ Smokeless Diamond'.

20.6 Examples of adverts by the company

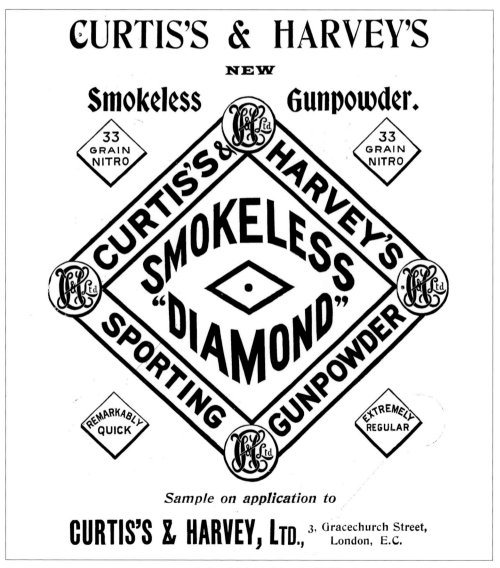

Arms & Explosives *March 1905*

CURTIS'S & HARVEY'S
SMOKELESS CARTRIDGES.

PRICE MAINTAINED.　　　　　　　　**GOOD PROFITS.**

There is a big demand
for these Cartridges.

"MARVELLOUSLY
QUICK."　　　　　　　THE BEST
　　　　　　　　　　　　OBTAINABLE.

AVOID FOREIGN AND UNRELIABLE CARTRIDGES.

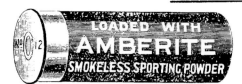

A GREAT FAVOURITE.

Has a world-wide Reputation for Game
and Pigeon Shooting.

Contains no Nitro-Glycerine.

Contains no Nitro-Glycerine.

Contains no Nitro-Glycerine.

☞ All Curtis's & Harvey's Cartridges are PRICE MAINTAINED.

REGULAR !　　　　　**RELIABLE !**

Memorandum Books and Game Registers sent on application.

Write for List at once to—

CURTIS'S & HARVEY, Ltd., 3, Gracechurch St., LONDON, E.C.

Advert in Sporting Goods Review *15 November 1911*

Curtis's & Harvey, Limited.

SPORTING CARTRIDGES.

HOUNSLOW LOADING.

Nitro Case.
Unlined or lined.

Nitro Case.
Unlined or lined.

5/8in. Deep Shell.
Unlined or lined.

5/8in. Deep Shell.
Unlined or lined.

"Smokeless ◇ Diamond" Pegamoid.

"Amberite" Pegamoid.

"Ruby."

"Marvel."

Card Boxes contain-
ing 25 Cartridges
supplied without ex-
tra charge if specially
ordered.

Brass Ejector.
Loaded with "Smokeless ◇ Diamond," "Amberite,"
or "Ruby" Powder.

Card Boxes contain-
ing 25 Cartridges
supplied without ex-
tra charge if specially
ordered.

All Curtis's & Harvey's Sporting Cartridges are "Price Maintained."

20.7 Examples of the types of powder manufactured by the company

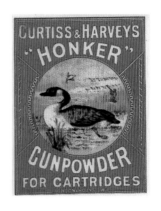

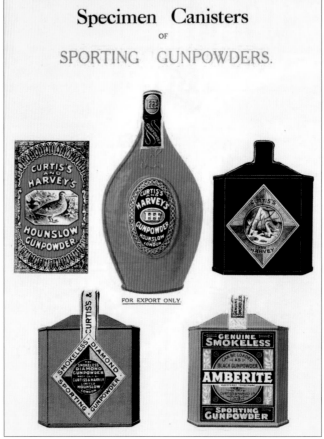

20.8 Examples of headstamps found on cartridges loaded by them or on those of other companies who used their powders

1.

On Eley Bros Ltd case
Marvel brand loaded at
Hounslow

2.

Amberite loading in
an Eley Brass Ejector

3.

On a best quality case
made by Nobel at the
Joyce works

4.

On best Gastight
case made by Kynoch
& Co. Ltd loaded at
Houslow

5.
On Eley Bros Ltd
Gastight quality case

6.
On early Amberite loading
Case by George Kynoch
& Company

7.
On Kynoch & Co. Ltd
Gastight case loaded
by Kynoch

8.
On Eley Bros Ltd
Gastight case

9.
On Amberite loading
by ICIANZ

10.
On Eley Bros Ltd
case loaded with Ruby
powder

11.
On Eley Bros Ltd
lined Nitro case

12.
On Eley Grand Prix cases
in red, cream, blue and two
types of green.

13.
On Eley Bros Ltd
unlined Nitro case

14.
On Nobel case loaded
with Ruby powder

15.
On REM-UMC
case. Marvel

CHAPTER 21

Charles Hellis, Charles Hellis & Sons Ltd, Charles Rosson, Rosson & Son, C. S. Rosson & Co. Ltd, Hellis-Rosson Ltd and The Anglia Cartridge Co.

21.1 History of the companies

Charles E. Hellis began trading as a London gunmaker in 1884. He moved premises to 119 Edgware Road, London in 1897 and in 1902 he was joined by his two sons Clifford and Charles resulting in the company title initially changing to Charles Hellis and Sons. In 1928 the limited company of Charles Hellis & Sons Ltd was formed. Exactly when Hellis commenced cartridge loading is unknown but specimens exist which were made before he was joined by his two sons so pre date 1902. A leaflet produced by the company after 1928 when the limited company was formed and before 1935 when they moved to their new premises in 121–123 Edgware Road, indicated that the family had been hand loading for 40 years, so their commencement date must have been either before or during 1895.

Charles Rosson was a gunmaker in Derby and had premises at 4 Market Head. He is first recorded as a gunmaker in 1886 and was later joined by his son when the company was renamed Rosson & Son. Exactly when Charles Rosson commenced loading shotgun cartridges has not been established. It is known that he patented one of the first English large scale loading machines in 1892 and cartridge cases exist which were manufactured by Eley Bros Ltd before 1918 bearing tube marking 'Loaded by Rosson's Patent Machinery', so it is reasonable to assume they were actively loading shotgun cartridges from the early 1890s.

In 1905 Charles Rosson acquired the premises of 13 Rampant Horse Street, Norwich, Norfolk, previously occupied by a gunmaker named Edwin Wilson. In 1913 C.S. Rosson & Co. was formed and traded from the Norwich address, whilst as an apparent separate entity Rosson & Son continued to trade through the ICI cartridge production period as Rosson & Son from the address of Market Head, Derby.

In 1953 Hellis-Rosson Ltd was formed to manufacture shotgun cartridges at a new factory at Taverham near Norwich. The factory was sold in 1956 to P. Darlow and the cartridge loading continued, producing shotgun cartridges under the name of The Anglia Cartridge Company until the mid 1960s when the Rosson business was sold to Gallyon & Sons. Also in 1956 Charles Hellis & Sons Ltd was taken over by Henry Atkin Ltd. Following the takeover by Henry Atkin Ltd in 1956 the Hellis name continued to be used on cartridges; however if you examine those made by Atkin you will notice the address reads 7 Bury Street or 27 St James's Street and the name Hellis is printed on a slant similar to the late production of Charles Hellis & Sons Ltd cartridges using a non standard font.

8813. Rosson, C. May 10.

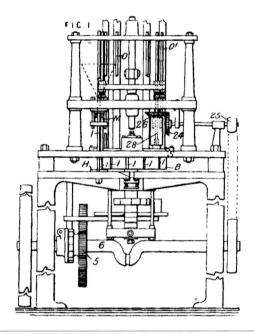

Cartridge-loading machines.—Fig. 1 shows a front elevation of the machine. The shaft 6, driven by foot or power, carries a pinion 5 which drives the main driving-shaft parallel to the shaft 6. The table B receives a step-by-step movement of rotation from the main driving-shaft, and is provided with locking-notches I which are successively engaged by a bolt to keep the table rigid during the loading operations. As the table B rotates it turns the star-wheel H, which, through its shaft I, rotates the telescopic powder-measuring tubes M, and delivers a charge. The next step in the rotation of the table brings the cartridge cases into position for receiving one or more wads from the horizontally-moving wad plate S, which is operated from an eccentric on the main driving-shaft, while at the same time the wad rammers O¹ are depressed by a second eccentric on the main driving-shaft. A second star-wheel similar to H then delivers the charge of shot, and a further wad is delivered. At the next stage the bobbin 28 (which is rotated by the mitre-wheels 24, 26 from the pulley 25) is depressed while the loaded cartridge is raised and the end is thereby crimped. The finished cartridge is finally marked and ejected from the machine.

Rosson, with whom Charles Hellis were later to combine, was a patentee of one of the early English shotgun cartridge loading machines and the patent shown was registered in 1892

21.2 Photographs inside the Hellis-Rosson factory at Taverham

Note the cases are being loaded with powder, wads and shot with Dixon's Climax machines

In addition to using rolled turnovers the demand for crimped cartridges had resulted in the company's acquisition of a crimping machine

Running alongside the star crimping machine was a roll turnover machine where the loaded cases were hand fed onto the loading ramp

Crimp break testing gauge. Specimens were continually tested to ensure regular crimps had been applied

Shot testing. The counter was used to take test samples of shot to ensure the correct number of pellets in a given charge was exact. E.g. No. 6 shot 270 pellets per oz

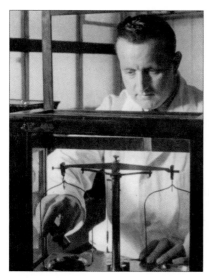

Checking wad weights, powder and shot volumetric throws

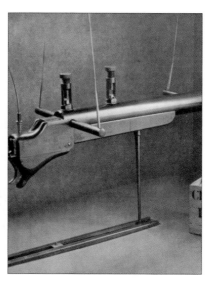

Webley & Scott pressure and recoil test gun constantly used to test samples using crusher gauges for pressure measurement

Waterproofing by dipping the cartridges in a thin cellulose using a slow conveyor belt system to dry them

Final inspection and packing

21.3 Cartridges produced by the companies

21.3.1. Brands produced by C.Hellis, C. Hellis & Sons and C. Hellis & Sons Ltd

The following brand names are known to have been used or loaded by the company:

12 x 2 inch	The Falcon
Aladix Astra	Pheasant (cases bear a drawing of a
Aladix Ventura	pheasant but without the name)
Damp-Proof	The Service
The Economist	The Standard
Economy	The Kestrel
The Burwood	Woodcock (cases bear a drawing of a
The Championship	woodcock but without the name)
The Edgware	

21.3.2 Brands produced by Hellis-Rosson Ltd

The Eclipse	The Sixteen
Burwood	The Twenty
The Kuvert	The Economist

21.3.3 Brands produced by the Anglia Cartridge Company

Anglia
Red Rival
Viking

21.3.4 Brands produced by Rosson, Derby

Monvill – Eley Bros Ltd cases
Eclipse – Eley Bros Ltd cases

21.3.5 Brands produced by Rosson & Son, Derby

Monvill – ICI period and Kynoch Nobel cases	Kuvert – ICI period cases
Vipax – ICI period cases	Roeditch – ICI period cases

21.3.6 Brands produced by C. S. Rosson & Co. Ltd, Norwich

Roeditch and Lowrecoil both in ICI period cases
Monvill – Eley Bros Ltd, Eley Nobel and ICI period cases
Eclipse – Eley Bros Ltd cases
Crown and Kuvert both in ICI period cases
Star and Ektor both in .410"

21.4 Examples of advertisements by Hellis

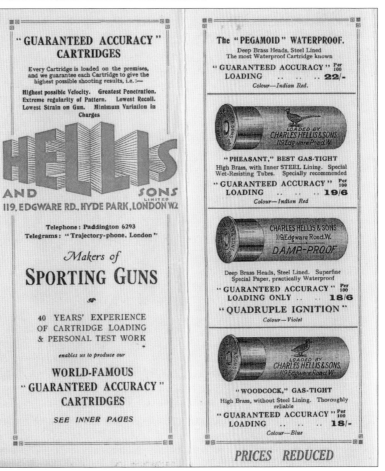

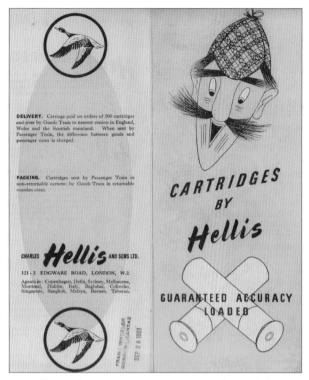
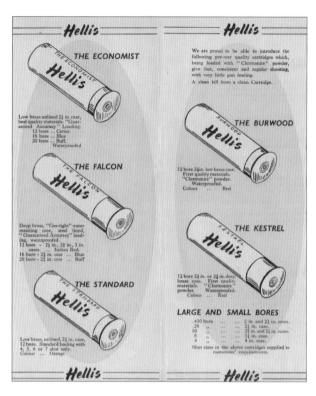

This advertisement was issued in 1951

21.5 Examples of these companies' shotgun cartridges

LEFT TO RIGHT STANDING: *Charles Hellis & Son Ltd 'Kestrel', 'Falcon', 'Falcon', 'Economist' before the limited company formed, and a 16 bore 'Economist' after the limited company was formed*
LYING DOWN: *'Aladix Ventura' by Charles Hellis & Son Ltd and an untitled specimen bearing a pheasant motif made using an Eley Nobel case*

STANDING LEFT TO RIGHT: *'Championship' made before the limited company was formed, 20 bore and 12 bore 'Economist' both by Charles Hellis & Sons Ltd, a 20 bore and 12 bore both untitled and by Chas Hellis & Son using Belgian made cases*
LYING DOWN: *A 2" and an untitled 12 bore bearing a snipe motif by Charles Hellis*

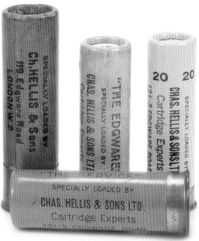

LEFT TO RIGHT STANDING: *These were all products of Charles Hellis & Sons Ltd. Untitled 12 bore, 'The Economist', 2", untitled 3", 'The Edgware', untitled 20 bore*
LYING DOWN: *Untitled and 'The Service'*

LEFT TO RIGHT: *All specimens by C.S. Rosson & Co. The 'Crown', 'Monvill', 'Kuvert', 'Roedich', unnamed and 'Lowrecoil'*

'Aladix Astral'. It bears the headstamp
Hellis London England and was made by
Hellis Rosson Ltd

ABOVE:
Hellis & Rosson products.
LEFT TO RIGHT STANDING: 'Eclipse', 'Burwood', and the
'Twenty'
LYING DOWN: The 'Sixteen'

Specimens loaded by the Anglia Cartridge Co.
LEFT TO RIGHT:
'Viking', 'Anglia' and
'Red Rival'

Examples of Anglia Cartridge
Co. boxes

21.6 Examples of headstamps used by these companies

Examples of headstamps on C. Hellis cartridges

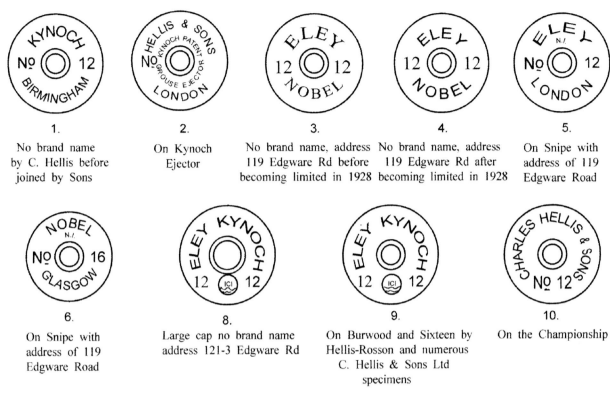

1.
No brand name
by C. Hellis before
joined by Sons

2.
On Kynoch
Ejector

3.
No brand name, address
119 Edgware Rd before
becoming limited in 1928

4.
No brand name, address
119 Edgware Rd after
becoming limited in 1928

5.
On Snipe with
address of 119
Edgware Road

6.
On Snipe with
address of 119
Edgware Road

8.
Large cap no brand name
address 121-3 Edgware Rd

9.
On Burwood and Sixteen by
Hellis-Rosson and numerous
C. Hellis & Sons Ltd
specimens

10.
On the Championship

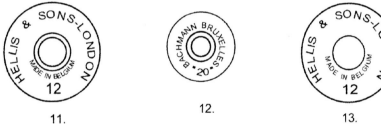

11.

12.

13.

Headstamps 11, 12 and 13 appear on specimens made by C. Hellis & Sons whilst at 119 Edgware Road

Examples of headstamps on Hellis marked cartridges after C. Hellis & Sons Ltd were taken over by Henry Atkin Ltd in 1956 to form Hellis-Rosson Ltd

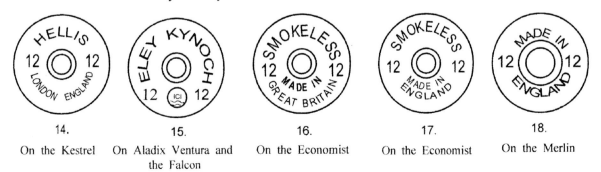

14.
On the Kestrel

15.
On Aladix Ventura and
the Falcon

16.
On the Economist

17.
On the Economist

18.
On the Merlin

Example of headstamps on Anglia Cartridge Company specimens in operation
between 1956 and the mid 1960s

1.

2.

3.

4.

These two headstamps appear on both the Eclipse and
Monvill by Charles Rosson whilst occupying premises
in both Derby and Norwich. The case have printed on
them 'Loaded with Rosson's Patent Machinery'

These two headstamps appear on various
brands loaded by Rosson & Son with the
Derby address

5.

This is the headstamp used by
C.S. Rosson & Co. Ltd, Norwich

CHAPTER 22
The smaller and lesser known cartridge manufacturers and loaders of the UK, together with brief notes on the more recent cartridge loading companies

22.1 The Nitrokol Powder Co.

This company is listed as having its main offices in 39 Victoria Street, London SW between 1908 and 1917 and certainly operated between 1903 and 1921. The powder was used by Eley Bros Ltd in .300" Rook Rifle cartridges. An advert in *The Argus*, Melbourne dated 4 June 1921 stated it was still being used as a load in rook rifle cartridges. In 1903 Greenwood & Batley loaded 1,000,000 .303" MkV cartridges with Nitrokol powder for Curtis's & Harvey and Nitrokol also placed their own orders for a further 1,000,000 .303" MkIIC in 1905 with Greenwood & Batley. On the 14 October 1909 the *Victoria Government Gazette*, Australia lists it as a nitro-cellulose Gelatised powder with a suitable solvent coated with or without graphite.

At least two known brand names for this company's shotgun cartridges exist, namely the 'Redskin' and 'Rover'. The company headstamp is shown alongside

22.2 The Abbey Improved Chilled Shot Co. Ltd

This company was sited at 22 Dean Street, Newcastle on Tyne and at the turn of the 1900s it was one of the large shot manufacturers. On 7 November 1908 it registered the trade mark 'Abbeyrite' Reg. No. 3077555 for use on shotgun cartridges.

It was acquired by Eley Bros Ltd in 1912 thus terminating cartridge production.

22.3 Latimer Clark Muirhead & Co.

This company operated in Millwall in London during the 1880s and made solid cased .577"/.450" Martini Henry ammunition in both carbine and rifle loads, all of which were housed in drawn brass cases. The company also owned the manufacturing rights to the Lorenz Company of Karlsruche in Austria and in 1887 the proprietor of that company, Herr W. Lorenz, purchased this company and it was renamed the Lorenz Ammunition & Ordnance Co. Lorenz was one of the three major cartridge manufacturers in Europe and the company was later renamed D.W.M. Deutsche Waffen und Munitionfabrik.

LYING DOWN:
A .577".450" Martini Henry rifle cartridge
STANDING:
A red patched specimen indicating for use in the same calibre carbine

'Dagger' brand cartridges are identifiable by an impressed dagger mark in their headstamps together with a dagger motif printed on the case wall as illustrated in this cartridge drawing from the factory of the Belgian producer of the case

22.4 The Arms and Ammunition Manufacturing Company Ltd

22.4.1 The company's history

This company was formed in the autumn of 1893 when the existing partnership between Messrs A.C. Argles and William Ward, which bore the title Argles, Ward & Co. was dissolved by mutual consent. Mr A.C. Argles agreed to carry on the London branch under the company name of The Arms & Ammunition Manufacturing Co. at 143 Queen Victoria Street, London EC and Mr Ward was to carry on his business at the Victorian Gun Works, 35 Whittall Street, Birmingham under the name Thomas Wild & Company.

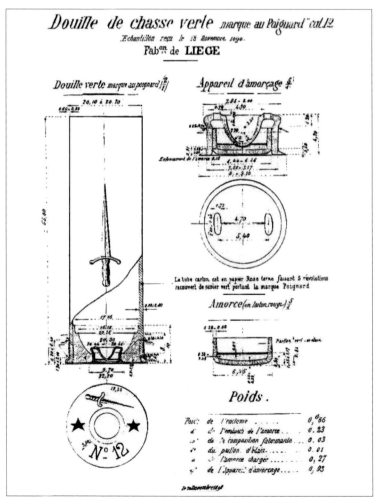

In January 1894 the company was experiencing problems with debts of £3,669 with assets being valued at £1,075, resulting in the company registering as a limited company on 5 February 1894 with a capital of £5,000.

The company produced a number of named shotgun cartridges and these included the 'Britannia' and green 'Dagger'. In 1900 they registered the trade mark 'Hercules' in relation to their cartridges (Registration No. 233316).

In September 1901 the company moved addresses from 143 Queen Victoria Street, London to 140 Southwark Street, London SE and in December that year applied to register the trade mark 'Nipper'. This was granted to them in February 1902.

Drawing of 143 Queen Victoria Street, London

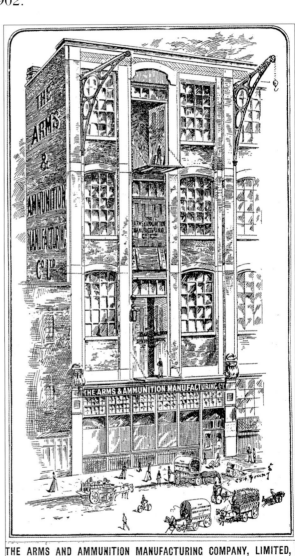

Drawing of 140 Southwark Street, London SE

22.4.2 Company adverts and extracts from an undated price list whose contents date it between 1901 and 1902

SPORTING CARTRIDGES.

No. A91.

The "Britannia" (TRADE MARK.)

This Cartridge is METAL-LINED.　Made and Loaded in ENGLAND.

SPORTING CARTRIDGE.

12" Gauge.　　12" Gauge.

WILL NOT SPLIT.　METAL LINED.　WILL NOT MIS-FIRE.

'16 and '20 Bores, same Prices.

A SOUND, GOOD **ENGLISH** CARTRIDGE CASE,

Loaded at our London Factory by Experienced Loaders.

☞ BEST MATERIALS ONLY USED.

42 grains Best Selected Smokeless Powder, 1⅛ oz. Best English Shot, and four Wads.

Imitations of this well-known "Britannia" Cartridge have been sold by others. Sportsmen should see that each Cartridge is marked, "Made in England."

per 6s. 10d. 100.

CASH WITH ORDER.

If loaded with either Schultze, E.C. or Amberite, **7s. 6d.** per 100. No. A92.

1,000 Cartridges sent CARRIAGE PAID to any Railway Station in Great Britain.

We are the SOLE MAKERS of the "BRITANNIA" CARTRIDGE.

Each Cartridge is stamped with our Trade Mark "BRITANNIA." No others are genuine.

BEWARE OF IMITATIONS.

We should be grateful to any Person informing us should any other Firm offer to supply "Britannia" Cartridges.

THE ARMS AND AMMUNITION MANUFACTURING COMPANY, LIMITED,

Telegraphic Address: "BULLSEYE, LONDON."

74

No. A89.

CARTRIDGES.

TRADE MARK.　　TRADE MARK.

THE

GREEN

"DAGGER" (REG.)

(Treble Strong) **T S** *(Black Powder)*

CARTRIDGE.

This Cartridge has been sold for many years with great success. '12 & '16 Bores, Central Fire.

Loaded at our London Factory by competent Loaders with 3 drms. Best Treble Strong Black Powder, 1⅛ oz. Best English Shot, and 4 Wads.

A SOUND and RELIABLE CARTRIDGE for every day Shooting.

5s. 2d. per 100.

1,000 sent Free any Railway Station in Great Britain.

CASH WITH ORDER.

CANNOT BE BOUGHT ELSEWHERE.

Every Cartridge Case bears our Trade Mark, "A DAGGER."

No others are genuine.

BEWARE OF IMITATIONS.

THE ARMS AND AMMUNITION MANUFACTURING COMPANY, LIMITED,

Telegraphic Address: "BULLSEYE, LONDON."

SPORTING.

No. 259.
A MARVELLOUS CARTRIDGE AT THE PRICE.

— THE —

GOOD MATERIALS.

GOOD LOADING.

GOOD SHOOTING.

"MONKEY"

Smokeless

Cartridge.

'12 Bore, Central Fire.

NEW SMOKELESS CARTRIDGE FOR THE MILLION.

This Cartridge is loaded at our London Factory, by experienced loaders, with 3 dms. of best Smokeless Powder, 1⅛ oz. best English Shot, and 4 Wads.

An Eminent Firm of Gunpowder Manufacturers who have tested these Cartridges write as follows:—

"Your 'Monkey' Smokeless Cartridges are wonderful value, and deserve to be popular."

6s. 2d. per 100.

CASH WITH ORDER.

1,000 sent FREE any Railway Station in Great Britain.

THE "MONKEY" CARTRIDGE (Red).

The paper tube of each Cartridge Case bears our "Monkey" Trade Mark. No Others are Genuine.

140, SOUTHWARK STREET *(close to Blackfriars Bridge)*, **LONDON, S.E.**

OUR WELL-KNOWN SPORTING CARTRIDGES.

GOOD QUALITY.

No. A92.

THE

☞ "X L" ☜

Smokeless Cartridge.

'12 Bore only.

IVORY.

Brass Covered.

Loaded 42 grains Best Smokeless Powder, 1⅛ oz. Best English Shot, and 4 Wads.

CAREFULLY LOADED BY HAND.

Per 7s. 8d. 100.

Carriage paid on orders of 1,000 to any Railway Station in Great Britain.　*CASH WITH ORDER.*

THIS CARTRIDGE CANNOT BE EQUALLED AT THE PRICE.

TEST IT FOR YOURSELF.

THE ARMS AND AMMUNITION MANUFACTURING COMPANY, LIMITED,

Telegraphic Address: "BULLSEYE, LONDON."

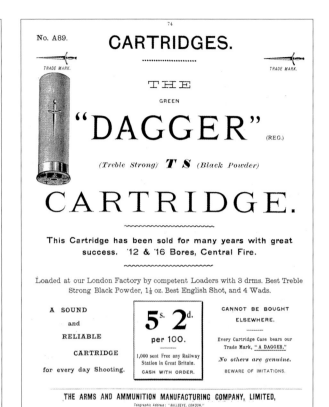

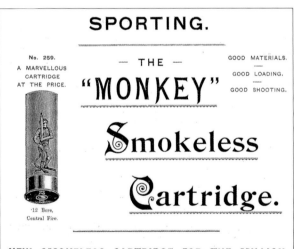

SPORTING AMMUNITION (for Breech-loading Guns).

DAGGER BRAND.

Trade Mark.   Trade Mark.

OUR WELL-KNOWN CARTRIDGE CASES
FOR THE MILLION.

No. B100.   GREEN, ·12° and ·16° bores, Central Fire ...   2ˢ· 4ᵈ· per 100.
No. B101.   SALMON, ·12° and ·16° bores, Central Fire ...   2ˢ· 4ᵈ· per 100.

SUITABLE FOR BLACK OR NITRATE POWDERS.

NITRO BRAND.

With Interior Lining.

CAPPED WITH SPECIAL LARGE PERCUSSION CAP.

No. 224.   RED, ·12° and ·16° bores, Central Fire ...   ... 2ˢ· 6ᵈ· per 100.

BEST CARTRIDGE CASES.

Maroon, Green and Blue.

No. 225.

GAS-TIGHT.

12 gauge, 2ˢ· 9ᵈ· per 100.

THE ARMS AND AMMUNITION MANUFACTURING COMPANY, LIMITED,

Telegraphic Address: "BULLSEYE, LONDON."

OUR WELL-KNOWN SPORTING CARTRIDGES.

No. 243.

LOADED

SMOKELESS, E.C., AMBERITE OR SCHULTZE.

·12 bore.

42 grs. Powder, and 1¼ oz. Best English Shot, and 4 Wads.

BEST QUALITY.

THE ARMS & AMMUNITION MFC. CO.'S

BEST GAS-TIGHT CARTRIDGE.

LOADED

SMOKELESS, E.C., AMBERITE OR SCHULTZE.

·12 bore.

42 grs. Powder, and 1¼ oz. Best English Shot, and 4 Wads.

BEST MATERIALS ONLY USED.   LOADED AT OUR LONDON FACTORY.

You may pay a higher price, but you cannot get a Better Cartridge.

THE CARTRIDGE CASE IS METAL LINED INSIDE, AND PERFECTLY GAS-TIGHT.

Carriage paid on orders of 1,000 to any Railway Station in Great Britain.

HIGH-CLASS ENGLISH MAKE,
If loaded with Selected Smokeless Powder,

per 8ˢ· 3ᵈ· 100.
CASH WITH ORDER.

If loaded with Schultze, "E.C.," Amberite, or Kynoch Powder,

per 8ˢ· 9ᵈ· 100.
CASH WITH ORDER.

BRASS COVERED.

Usually sold at

10s. 6d. and 11s.

per 100.

FOR STRENGTH OF SHOOTING THEY ARE UNSURPASSED.

140, SOUTHWARK STREET (close to Blackfriars Bridge), LONDON, S.E.

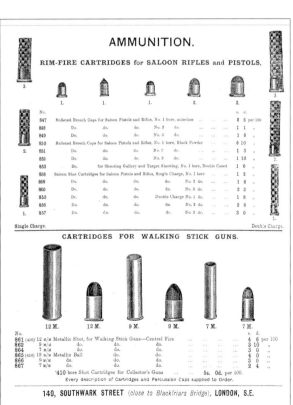

AMMUNITION.

RIM-FIRE CARTRIDGES for SALOON RIFLES and PISTOLS.

No.			s.	d.	
847	Bulleted Breech Caps for Saloon Pistols and Rifles, No. 1 bore, noiseless	...	0	6	per 100
848	Do. do. do. No. 2 do.	...	1	1	,,
849	Do. do. do. No. 3 do.	...	1	6	,,
850	Bulleted Breech Caps for Saloon Pistols and Rifles, No. 1 bore, Black Powder	...	0	10	,,
851	Do. do. do. No. 2 do.	...	1	3	,,
852	Do. do. do. No. 3 do.	...	1	10	,,
853	Do. for Shooting Gallery and Target Shooting, No. 1 bore, Double Cased	...	1	2	,,
858	Saloon Shot Cartridges for Saloon Pistols and Rifles, No. 1 bore	...	1	2	,,
859	Do. do. do. do. No. 2 do.	...	1	8	,,
860	Do. do. do. do. No. 3 do.	...	2	2	,,
855	Do. do. do. Double Charge No. 1 do.	...	1	8	,,
856	Do. do. do. do. No. 2 do.	...	2	6	,,
857	Do. do. do. do. No. 3 do.	...	3	0	,,

Single Charge.   Double Charge.

CARTRIDGES FOR WALKING STICK GUNS.

12 M.   12 M.   9 M.   9 M.   7 M.   7 M.

No.					s.	d.	
861 (410)	12 м/м Metallic Shot, for Walking Stick Guns—Central Fire	...	...	...	4	6	per 100
862	9 м/м do. do. do.	...	...	...	3	10	,,
864	7 м/м do. do. do.	...	...	...	3	0	,,
865 (410)	12 м/м Metallic Ball do. do.	...	...	...	4	0	,,
866	9 м/м do. do. do.	...	...	...	3	0	,,
867	7 м/м do. do. do.	...	...	...	2	4	,,

·410 bore Shot Cartridges for Collector's Guns ...   5s. 0d. per 100.

Every description of Cartridges and Percussion Caps supplied to Order.

140, SOUTHWARK STREET (close to Blackfriars Bridge), LONDON, S.E.

In March 1904 Messrs Jas. R. Watson & Co. of 35 Queen Victoria Street, London EC purchased the goodwill and trade marks of the Arms and Ammunition Manufacturing Co. Ltd following it becoming bankrupt.

22.5 Dyer & Robson

This company had premises in Woolwich Road, London and loaded Very light cartridges into both 12 bore and 4 bore cases made by Eley Bros Ltd. They were listed as a Wad manufacturer.

The cartridge owes its existence to the introduction of the 'Very Pistol' by the United States naval officer Edward Wilson Very which was used for signalling by the United States Navy. Very was granted an American patent for his Very signal cartridges in 1877 and Dyer & Robson acted as the UK retailer for his brass framed model 1882 signal pistol and related cartridges. Dyer & Robson was taken over by the Henry Rifled Barrel Engineering & Small Arms Company in 1890 so I assume cartridges bearing these markings date from between 1882 and 1890 unless the rifle company retained and used the former company's trading name, following its acquisition.

22.6 Frank Dyke & Co.

This company can be traced back to the 1880s when it appears to have commenced trading manufacturing and selling gun wadding. It occupied various premises in London and by 1900 was selling shotgun and metallic cartridges. The company loaded imported shotgun cases from Europe and their brand names included 'Shamrock', 'Yellow Wizard', 'Rabbit Cartridge' and 'Dykes Supreme'.

On 1 January 1908 an explosion occurred at the company's premises at 5 St George's Avenue, Aldermanbury, London which killed a John Cocker aged 21 years. The report in *Arms & Explosives* described the company as wholesale guns and ammunition dealers, managed by a Mr E.R. Reeve. The subsequent inquest on Cocker revealed that the basement of these premises was used to store and load ammunition from a safe which was licensed to hold 50 lbs maximum. The premises had been licensed for safety cartridges but what exploded were in fact pin-fire cartridges.

Sporting Goods Review *15 August 1923*

The business became a limited company after WWII and continued to trade from 1–7 Ernest Avenue, West Norwood, London, SE 27 through to the early 1990s.

What I find interesting is the fact that the registered trade mark 'Shamrock' was previously used by Thomas McCarthy & Co. in the 1890s which poses the question did Dyke purchase this company to acquire the Shamrock Trade Mark?

When the company's residual stock was disposed of in 1996 the collector who acquired it was able to ascertain that the company had mainly been using cases made in Germany, which they loaded in Britain. For orders of 2,000 or more they would print the name and address of the gunsmith or ironmonger on the cartridge tube, often in conjunction with their brand name in vivid and eye catching colours.

This action was in total contrast to the budget end of their market, where they loaded 12 bore S.F.M. cases (S.F.M.'s full title was Societe Francaise des Munitions which in 1950 was renamed Gevelot S.A.) which they then retailed at the prices below:

$\frac{1}{16}$"	brass headed green case	13s 3d per 1,000
$\frac{1}{4}$"	brass headed pink case	18s 0d per 1,000
$\frac{3}{8}$"	brass headed red case	19s 6d per 1,000
$\frac{1}{2}$"	brass headed mauve case	23s 9p per 1,000

This related residual company stock was in boxes dated 14 April 1913. The headstamps on these French cases consisted of the numerals 12 appearing either side of the primer pocket, whilst their tubes were devoid of all markings.

The last brand names used by Dyke I have been able to locate were the 'Matchless' and 'FD' brands which appears in the company's July 1973 catalogue.

LEFT TO RIGHT STANDING: 'Supreme', 'The Rabbit', rare version of the 'Yellow Wizard' in black, standard 'Yellow Wizard', 'The Rabbit' and Special Smokeless LYING DOWN: 28 gauge and .410" both 'Shamrock' brand

BETTER VALUE THAN EVER BEFORE

BIGGER DISCOUNTS FOR QUANTITY

KEEN RETAIL PRICES

AS MANUFACTURERS WE CAN OFFER IMMEDIATE DELIVERY

FOR ANY SPECIFICATION

Loaded with regular, reliable COOPPAL Powder, Non-corrosive, non-erosive primers.

"MATCHLESS"				Trade price per 100		Retail price inc. V.A.T.	
				1,000 lots	Less than 1,000 lots	Per 100	Per 25
†12 bore 2½" Case	1	oz. Shot	LIGHT LOAD	£2.82	£2.88	£4.28	£1.08
†12 bore 2½" Case	1¹⁄₁₆	oz. Shot	STANDARD	£2.88	£2.94	£4.36	£1.09
†12 bore 2½" Case	1⅛	oz. Shot	GAME LOAD	£2.94	£3.00	£4.46	£1.12
†12 bore 2½" Case	1³⁄₁₆	oz. Shot	LONG RANGE	£3.15	£3.21	£4.78	£1.20
†12 bore 2½" Case	1⅛	oz. Shot	TRAPSHOOTING & SKEET	£2.94	£3.00	£4.46	£1.12
16 bore 2½" Case	1⁵⁄₁₆	oz. Shot	STANDARD	£2.88	£2.94	£4.36	£1.12

(RED PAPER CASE)

"F.D." PLASTIC				Trade price per 100		Retail Price inc. V.A.T.	
				1,000 lots	Less than 1,000 lots	Per 100	Per 25
†12 bore 2½" Case	1	oz. Shot	LIGHT LOAD	£2.82	£2.88	£4.28	£1.08
†12 bore 2½" Case	1¹⁄₁₆	oz. Shot	STANDARD	£2.88	£2.94	£4.36	£1.09
†12 bore 2½" Case	1⅛	oz. Shot	GAME LOAD	£2.94	£3.00	£4.46	£1.12
†12 bore 2½" Case	1³⁄₁₆	oz. Shot	LONG RANGE	£3.15	£3.21	£4.78	£1.20
†12 bore 2½" Case	1⅛	oz. Shot	TRAPSHOOTING & SKEET	£2.94	£3.00	£4.46	£1.12

(Red Ribbed Case)

FRANK DYKE & CO. LTD.

WATERPROOF — RED RIBBED PLASTIC CASE

The cases and powder are specially imported and loaded by

FRANK DYKE & CO., LTD   **LONDON, S.E.27**

"ELEY-KYNOCH"				Trade price per 100		Retail price inc. V.A.T.	
				1,000 lots	Less than 1,000 lots	Per 100	Per 25
12 bore 2½" Case	1¹⁄₁₆	oz. Shot	STANDARD	£3.00	£3.15	£4.55	£1.16
16 bore 2½" Case	1⁵⁄₁₆	oz. Shot	STANDARD	£3.00	£3.15	£4.55	£1.16
20 bore 2½" Case	1³⁄₁₆	oz. Shot	STANDARD	£3.00	£3.15	£4.55	£1.16
410 bore 2½" Case	⁷⁄₁₆	oz. Shot	STANDARD	£2.75	£2.90	£4.18	£1.06

† Denotes Crimp Closure.

22.7 Modern Arms Co. Ltd

The Modern Arms Co. Ltd operated from Marco House, 28 Marshalsea Road, Southwalk, London SE1 and was responsible for a cartridge of which specimens exist in 16, 12, 20 and 28 bore. They appear to have been ammunition dealers rather than loaders and the printing appearing on the cartridge tube indicates the case was produced in Germany. A company letterhead dates their existence to the 1930s.

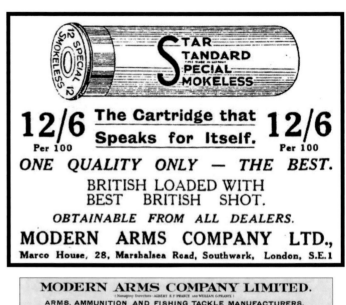

22.8 Hercules Arms Co.

This company operated as cartridge dealers during the 1950s from a corner site in Leicester Square, London which housed E.J. Churchill on one side and this company on the other. The illustrated specimens state on their tubes that they were hand loaded by this company; however at some stage the Hull Cartridge Company loaded them on their behalf.

Examples of two headstamps used on Hercules cartridges

22.9 The Practice Cartridge/Syndicate Ltd, The Miniature Ammunition Co. Ltd, The Morris Aiming Tube & Ammunition Co. Ltd and The Re-loading Miniature Ammunition Co. Ltd

This group of companies was involved in the manufacture of training ammunition before the advent of the general usage of .22" rim-fire ammunition for training purposes, particularly by the military forces.

The Practice Cartridge Co. Ltd was registered with a capital of £5,000 in September 1896 to take over the business of the **Practice Cartridge Syndicate Ltd** to make a miniature rifle cartridge adapted for use in the .303" Lee Metford rifle and other service rifles. The company was struck off on 23 July 1901.

The Miniature Ammunition Co. Ltd was reported in the July 1907 issue of *Arms & Explosives* as using the Kings Norton Metal Company to act as their distibuting agents for their miniature and mid-range ammunition. In October 1909 this company moved premises from 48 Dover Street to 11 Pall Mall, London SW.

The Morris Aiming Tube & Ammunition Co. Ltd. This company was registered on 12 March 1900 with capital of £50,000 in £5 shares. The object was to adopt a certain agreement with **Morris Tube Ammunition and Safety Range Co.** and its liquidator and to manufacture and deal in Morris tubes, ammunition, ordnance and firing appliances. (The Morris Tube Ammunition and Safety Range Co. were certainly in existence in May 1894 and had ranges at Ilford.)

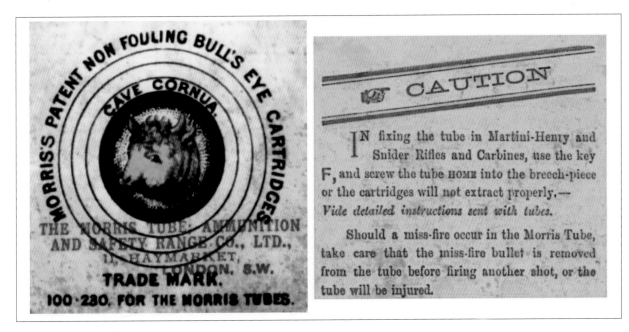

At the May 1902 AGM, with Captain J.W. Reid presiding, General Sir John Stokes KCB and Mr G.H.M. Batten retired from the Board and Mr Waymouth and Mr Webster became the company's new Directors and the company moved from its former premises in Haymarket to 17 Charing Cross Road, London WC. The *Sporting Goods Review* on 15 January 1907 reported the voluntary winding up of this company following Captain J. W. Reid stating he was unable to raise new capital. Mr E. J. Husey and Walter C. Luff were appointed liquidators and the company's final meeting was held in 1910.

In May 1907 **The Morris Tube & Rifle Clubs Accessories Co.** of 11 Hart Street, Mark Lane, London EC was formed by Mr Walter C. Luff, Mr West and Mr Steniford to supply the class of goods previously supplied by **The Morris Aiming Tube & Ammunition Co. Ltd.**

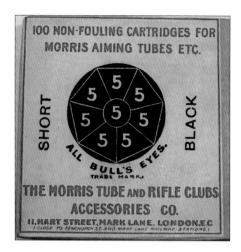

In June 1907 the War Office sanctioned the fitting of new barrels to .303" rifles for use with .22" rim-fire, following problems being encountered when Morris tubes were fitted into .303" rifles. They had been originally designed for use in .577"/.450" Martini Henry rifles and proved to be too flimsy when fitted in the smaller calibre .303" rifle. This decision marked the end of the military use of the .297"/.230" Morris cartridge but it was to live on for many years as a cartridge for use in rook rifles and for use in adaptors fitted into .455" Webley & Scott revolvers

The Re-loading Miniature Ammunition Co. Ltd was registered on 11 July 1906 with a capital of £3,000 in £1 shares with no initial public issue. The idea behind the company was to acquire from Mr P.E.V.G. Plater the benefits of the licence for inventions relating to miniature cartridges for rifle practice and to carry on business as manufacturer of such arms and ammunition.

22.10 William Soper of Reading

William Soper was one member of a family involved in gun and rifle making, the other parties being John, Richard and Elizabeth. Collectively they span the period from about 1823 to 1883, occupying various addresses in Reading (Berkshire) and Basingstoke (Hampshire). William Soper appears to enter the trade with his brother Richard in 1862, initially operating from 138 Friar Street, Reading and later from 23 Friar Street. In 1878 he moved to 22 Friar Street with the manufacturing base being close to the railway station. In 1865 and 1868 William took out two interesting rifle patents numbers. Patent No. 2151 of 1865 relates to a falling block rifle without an external hammer and with a thumb activated trigger located on the side of the action. Clearly this was not a success and subsequent remaining specimens incorporating the patent have normal triggers placed within a trigger guard.

It appears that William started rifle manufacture hoping to be successful in

designing a rifle for use by the British military. This came about when the Ordnance Board issued an advertisement to the gun trade (No. 7669/534 on 22 October 1866) asking them to design and submit for trial a suitable army replacement rifle. As a result Soper submitted a specimen based on the 1865 patent in .577" Snider calibre. The special sub-committee rejected his design stating it was too complicated, although it was deemed satisfactory in terms of rapidity of fire and accuracy.

On 31 August 1868 William took out a further patent No. 3327 for a military trials rifle which utilised a side lever, operating in essence a snider type hinged action. This was also entered into the military trials but arrived one day too late on 13 November 1868. Although tested it was not adopted and the Ordnance Board selected the Martini Henry. Although Soper failed to gain acceptance of his rifles by the British military his adverts in the 1870s indicate he had made weapons for the German Emperor William I, the Sultan of Turkey Abdül Azîz and William III, King of the Netherlands and indicated that he used ammunition manufactured by the best makers of the day. Recently I have had opportunity to examine the packet of cartridges shown in the accompanying photograph and was amazed by its contents. The related .500"/.450" No. 1 Express cartridges bore three different headstamps which are shown at the top of the related headstamp drawings. Two bore Westley Richards Arms & Ammunition Co. headstamps and the third one was from the National Arms & Ammunition Company. In my earlier book I established that Westley Richards Arms & Ammunition Company operated from Holford Mills, Birmingham between 1870 and 1872 and in January 1872 the National Arms & Ammunition Company took over this company and continued to occupy Holford Mills, so it appears that N.A. & A. Co. made this packet of cartridges for Soper shortly after their takeover in 1872 and made use of residual stock from the former company.

Although Soper was unsuccessful in obtaining acceptance of his rifles for British military use, they were accepted for civilian usage and many were made in other calibres, some of which were solely made for use by Soper, namely the 2½" and 2 5/16" .450" cartridges.

Examples of headstamps found on Soper rifle cartridges

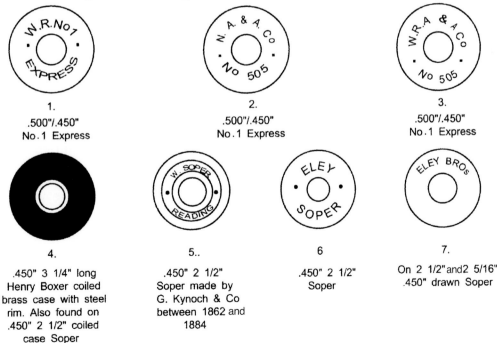

1.
.500"/.450"
No.1 Express

2.
.500"/.450"
No.1 Express

3.
.500"/.450"
No.1 Express

4.
.450" 3 1/4" long
Henry Boxer coiled
brass case with steel
rim. Also found on
.450" 2 1/2" coiled
case Soper

5..
.450" 2 1/2"
Soper made by
G. Kynoch & Co
between 1862 and
1884

6
.450" 2 1/2"
Soper

7.
On 2 1/2" and 2 5/16"
.450" drawn Soper

22.11 The Progressive Cartridge Company Chandler's Ford, Hampshire

I have been unable to establish information concerning this company, however shotgun cartridges exist which bear this company's name.

22.12 The Cornwall Cartridge Works, Liskeard, Cornwall

This company was formed to load and retail shotgun cartridges. It sold the following branded products: 'Cornubia', 'Cornwall', 'Tamar' and 'Trelawny'. They used ICI cases and therefore date between 1930 and October 1963

22.13 Kent Cartridge Co.

This company loaded shotgun cartridges at East Peckham, Kent. It produced the 'Kent', 'Topmark' and 'Tru-Tracer' brands during the 1980s. The East Peckham factory has closed. This company is now owned by Kent Cartridge America which in turn is an amalgam of Kent Cartridge Co. Activ of West Virginia and Gamebore of Hull. Gamebore was established in 1973 by a Mr A.J. Dales.

22.14 Club Cartridge Company Ltd

The company occupied premises at 2 Pickering Place, London and retailed shotgun cartridges brand named 'Clubs are Trumps'. It is believed they both loaded and retailed shotgun cartridges but I have been unable to establish their period of production.

22.15 Eskdale Gun & Cartridge Co.

It is known that this company was located in High Street, Longtown, Cumberland and its proprietor was a Mr J.J. Graham. The company was established in November 1909 to load shotgun cartridges.

22.16 Thames Ammunition Works Ltd

In January 1900 *Arms & Explosives* reported the death of B. T. Moore MA, M.I.C.E., F.R.A.S. who died on 18 November 1899 aged 69 from a heart disease. For the previous 20 years he had been involved in the manufacture of fuses and ammunition at the Thames Ammunition Works at Crayfordness, Kent, during which period he had established two factories. Following his death Mr H. G. Ticehurst took over the management of the company.

On 8 May 1902 it was registered as a limited company with a capital of £25,000 in £1 shares, and operated as a manufacturer and dealer in ammunition, gunpowder, lyddite, explosives, shot, bullets and cartridges with registered offices at Elswick Works, Newcastle on Tyne.

CHAPTER 23
Brands of shotgun cartridges which once originated from gunmakers, gunsmiths, ironmongers and other retailers in the UK

23.1 An overview of their activities

Several shotgun cartridge case manufacturers both in Great Britain and on the continent were prepared to supply gunmakers, gunsmiths, ironmongers, cycle shops, agricultural suppliers and large stores with cartridges bearing their respective names. This action started from about 1880. The case makers were prepared to sell to these outlets primed cases, powder loaded cases or fully loaded cartridges and this resulted in the emergence of literally hundreds of retailers' brand names or alternatively cartridges merely bearing just the name of the retailer.

From remaining specimens the most common name used by ironmongers is the 'Rabbit' brand; however the spectrum of names applied to these cartridges reflects a vast sequence of subjects which include the names of many species of game, the names of local rivers, colours, local land marks, town crests or seals, town, county or district names, reflections of local former events and on many examples their claimed objectives e.g. 'Best of All', 'Invincible', 'Superior', 'Utility', 'Reliable' and 'Clay Bird'. It is believed that one brand used by an ironmonger even named a cartridge after the black Labrador belonging to Guy Gibson, the famous bomber pilot who led the Dambuster raids against the German dams during WWII. Below is a reflection of the various motifs applied under these groups.

LEFT TO RIGHT: *'The Scottie' by J.S. Sharpe, Aberdeen, 'The Four Best' by F.W. Lightwood, Practical Gunmaker & Cartridge Loader, Brigg, Grimsby & Market Rasen, 'The Dreadnought' by A.E. Ringwood, Gunmaker, Banbury, 'The Referee' by A.W. Gamage Ltd, Holborn, London, 'Sign of the Knife & Fork' by John Collins Ltd, Drogheda, Ireland, 'Sure Killer' by Bowerbanks, Gunmakers, Penrith*
LYING DOWN: *'The Sunset' by Lewis, Ironmongers, Wells, Somerset – a typical example of a cartridge made for an ironmonger by Frank Dyke*

Large numbers of these gunsmiths, gunmakers and ironmongers used their own equipment to load the cartridges which enabled them to profit from their endeavours and allowed them to favourably compete with the price of the factory loaded cartridges. In due course a number of companies designed and retailed small machines to speed up the former process of individually hand loading each case. Perhaps the best known of these was the Climax Cartridge Loader manufactured by James Dixon of Sheffield. It consisted of a number of parts which are illustrated.

Town and City crests
LEFT TO RIGHT:
'Bailey Special', Gaolgate St, Stafford, 'Bradford Cartridge' by Smith Midgley & Co., 16 bore 'City of Newcastle' by P. Smalls and unnamed by C. Hall & Co., Practical Gunmakers, Knaresboro

Game animals and birds
LEFT TO RIGHT: *Unnamed by Joseph Pleas Ltd, Gunmakers & Sports Outfitters Darlington, 'Otter Vale' by H.P. Roberts, Ottery St Mary, 'The Monnow Cartridge' by Taylor & Jones, Monmouth & Ross, unnamed by Howard Bros, 240 St Ann's Rd, Tottenham, London*
LYING DOWN: *'The Falcon' by John Tyler Ltd, Gunmakers, Highbridge, Somerset*

Many collectors have restricted their interest to paper tubed rolled turnover shotgun cartridges achieved either with a hand tool, or a foot or electrically operated lathe. Perhaps they need reminding that star crimped paper case cartridges were first introduced in 1933, so early specimens of star crimp cartridges are now 78 years old. It is also worth mentioning that certain companies continued to produce both rolled turnover and star crimp cartridges right the way through until the mid 1960s, so certain rolled turnover cartridges are of less age than their star crimped counterparts.

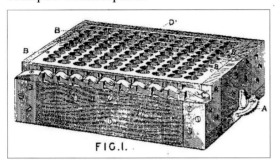

The Loading Trays
The machine was supplied with one or more trays as shown. To load with cases the block was inverted and the plate marked 'A' was pulled out and 100 empty cases were inserted mouth first in the holes. The plate was then replaced and this unit was ready to be inserted into the powder loading machine

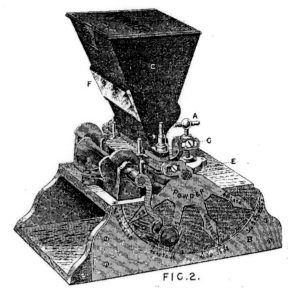

The Powder Loading Machine
The required quantity of powder can be set using the adjustable pointers on the end of the machine. The loading trays are now inserted into the right-hand end of this machine and the handle on the side rotated slowly. Each complete revolution of the handle causes an equal volume of powder to drop into each row of ten cases and the ratchet in the loading tray engages with an internal rack and moves it forward onto the next row

The Wadding Machine
The loading tray having been moved from the powder machine had a plate fitted onto its top which was carefully aligned with a sequence of vertical pegs in the brass plate which engaged in corresponding holes in the wooden top of the tray. This brass plate has attached to it 100 flared top tubes to allow easy initial entry of felt wads. As the arm is pulled down the row of rammers pushes the wads down into the cases and compresses them over the powder. Each time the handle is raised the ratchet moves the loading block onto the next row of cases

The above statement, I believe gives rise to an obvious question, 'why was the old rolled turnover cartridge replaced by the star crimped version?' The answer lies in the patterns produced by the two systems. The overshot wad encountered in the rolled turnover variant often deflected and dispersed the shot on leaving the barrel, whereas the crimped cartridge did not which resulted in better patterns.

The Shot Loading Machine
The required weight of shot can be set using the adjustable pointers on the end of the machine. The loading trays are now inserted into the back of the machine and the handle rotated slowly. Each complete revolution of the handle causes an equal volume of shot to drop into each row of ten cases from the black hopper and the ratchet in the loading tray engages with an internal rack and moves it forward onto the next row

Cartridge loading in premises such as gunsmiths and ironmongers across the UK started to wane as the effects of the licensing inspectors started to impose ever increasingly stringent conditions on their loading and storage areas, until finally they gave up and terminated their activities. According to one gunmaker I have discussed this subject with, his company's termination date for cartridge loading occurred during the 1950s.

Based on the knowledge that many cartridge collectors are interested in these retailers and, where appropriate their branded products, the residual text within this chapter has been split into two lists. The first list consists of companies who did not apparently use brand names and the second lists retailers who did, together with examples of their related brands. It should be noted that these lists are incomplete and merely give a reflection of some of the many hundreds or indeed perhaps thousands of companies involved together where appropriate with some of their branded cartridges. The list does not include entries covered by my former two books and is restricted to entries relating to paper cased cartridges.

23.2 Examples of the names of companies which appear on paper tube shotgun cartridges which did not apparently use related brand names

Key to class field

AUCT =	Auctioneer	ED =	Explosives dealer	GS =	Gunsmith
AD =	Ammunition dealer	ENG =	Engineer	IRN=	Ironmonger
AM =	Agricultural merchants	GD =	Gun dealer	SA =	Sporting association
AS =	Agricultural supplies	GFM =	Game food manf.	SS =	Sports supplier
CD =	Cartridge dealer	GM =	Gunmaker	ST =	Shop or stores
CL =	Cartridge loader	G&RM =	Gun & rifle maker	UK =	Unknown trade
CT =	Cutler	GRO =	Grocer	WM =	Wine merchants

Key to headstamp field

CHMC =	Cogswell & Harrison Manf. Co.	Nobel =	Nobel's pre 1919
EBL =	Eley Brothers Ltd pre 1919	Own HS =	Bears its own retailer's headstamp
G&B =	Greenwood & Batley	REM-UMC =	Remington Arms & Union Metallic
ICI =	Imperial Chemical Industries		Cartridge Co.
Irish M.I. =	Irish Metal Industries	SG =	Smokeless Gastight
Kynoch =	George Kynoch, B'Ham pre 1919	SS =	Special Smokeless

Name & Address	Class	Comments/headstamp
ABBOT & BAKER, Newport	UK	Kynoch
ADAMS J.H. & Sons, Littleport, Cambs	IRN	EBL Gastight
ADSETT T. & Son, Guildford	GM	ICI & G&B
ALEXANDER & DUNCAN Ltd, Leominster & Hereford	AM/ENG	EBL
ALPASS & BAKER, Wiveliscombe, Somerset	IRN	EBL
AUSTIN T.C., Ashford	CL	EBL
BAKER F.T., London	GM	EBL & Kynoch
BAKER J.T., Darlington	GD	Own HS & ICI
BARNARD & LEVET, Lichfield	IRN	CHMC
BARNES W., Ashbourne	IRN	Kynoch
BATES A.T., Canterbury	UK	Eley-Nobel
BAYS & Co., Swindon	IRN	Nobel
BEESLEY, London	GM	EBL & Kynoch
BENIGNO A., Peebles	GD	SS
BLANCH John & Son,London	GM	ICI & Own HS
BLAND T. & Sons, London	GM	Own HS
BOND & Sons, Thetford	GM	EBL
BOSS & Co., London	GM	Early to late
BOWTELL C., Bungay, Suffolk	UK	SS
BRAKENBURY G., Framlingham	UK	SS
BRASSEY'S, Eastgate St.,Chester	UK	Own HS & CHMC
BROMLEY John & Co., several shops in Shropshire	IRN	ICI
BROWN J., Morpeth	UK	EBL
BUCKMASTER & WOOD, Wokingham	IRN	Kynoch
BULLMORE George G., Newquay & St Columb	IRN	Kynoch
BURT'S STORES, Devises	ST	SS
CARR & Co., Nottingham	GD	Kynoch
CARR Bros, Huddersfield	UK	EBL
CASSWELL F.G., Bradstock	IRN	EBL
CHAMBERLAIN E., Andover	GM	EBL & Kynoch
CHAMBERS R., Bath	GM	Kynoch
CHAMBERS, Dunstable	UK	Own HS
CLATSWORTHY COOKE & Co., Taunton	UK	ICI
CLAYTON & Son, St Neots	SS	SG
CLOUGH R.H., West Hartlepool	UK	EBL

Name & Address	Class	Comments/headstamp
COCK J.H. & Co., Cirencester	IRN/GS	EBL
COOK G. & Co. Ltd, Leigh	UK	Kynoch
COONEY George, Kells	IRN	Kynoch
CORDEN, Warminster	UK	Kynoch
COSTER G. & Son, Glasgow	UK	Eley Nobel
CREIGHTON G., Carlisle	GM	EBL
CROSS S.B., Birkenhead	ED	Kynoch
DAINTITHS Ltd, Warrington	GM	G&B & SS & Kynoch
DAWSON W., Settle, North Yorkshire	UK	EBL
DENBY, Eastbourne	Saddler	EBL
DOE Ernest & Sons Ltd, unknown address	AM	ICI & SS
DOUGALL, Glasgow	GM	Own HS
DUDDINTON C.E., Whitchurch, Hampshire	UK	SS
DYKES A.H., Stowmarket, Suffolk	UK	SG
ENTWISTLE S., Blackpool	GM	ICI
EVANS John Golby, Carmarthen	IRN	Eley & Nobel
EVANS T.J., Welshpool	UK	Own HS
FIRTH A.H., Alfreton	UK	SS
FLETCHER E., Gloucester	GM	EBL
FOX Cecil, Canterbury	G & RM	EBL
FRASER Daniel, Edinburgh	GM	EBL & Own HS
FULLER S.C., Dorking, Surrey	UK	Nil
GALBRAITH W., Lancaster	UK	EBL
GARDINER T.M. Ltd, Hoddeston,Herts	AD	ICI
GEORGE W.J., Dover	GM	Kynoch
GILMAN J. & Son Ltd, Birmingham	GM	Kynoch
GODFREY W. & Sons, Yeovil	UK	EBL
GOLD G.E., Bristol	UK	Own HS
GOLDEN Charles, Bradford	GM	EBL
GRAHAM G.P., Cockermouth, Cumbria	UK	Own HS
HADDEN J.B., Penzance	IRN	Own HS
HALL Hugh, Wetherby	ST	Kynoch
HALL John & Son, London	UK	EBL
HAND Brothers,Odiham,Hants	UK	SS
HARKOM & Son, Edinburgh	GM	Kynoch
HARRIS G.A., Uttoxeter	UK	REM-UMC
HART Ernest Frederick	IRN	EBL
HAYWARD & Sons, Tewskesbury & Upton on Severn	UK	EBL
HEMING W., Wickham, Hants	IRN	SS
HEPPLESTONE T., Manchester	GM	Kynoch & EBL
HILL C.A., Ashford, Kent	UK	Own HS
HOCKNELL A .S., Eccleshall, Staffs	IRN	EBL
HOLTOMS, Lowestoft	UK	SS & SG
HOWARD Bros, London	UK	SG
HOWE William & Sons Ltd, Shrewsbury	IRN	EBL

Name & Address	Class	Comments/headstamp
INMAN MORROW & Co., Leeds	GM	Kynoch
IRVING George, Penrith	IRN	Kynoch
JACKSON Alfred, Abergavenny	IRN	ICI
JACKSON J., Nottingham	UK	Own HS
JOHNSON E.M., Tenterden, Kent	UK	Eley Nobel
JONES H., Wrexham	GM	Own HS & Kynoch
JONES, Newtown	GM	EBL
KEMPTON H., London	UK	SG
KNIGHT J.N., Wells, Somerset	IRN	Kynoch
KYNASTON Brothers, Wem & Ellesmere	IRN	Eley Nobel
LACEY Arthur, Strafford on Avon	IRN	Own HS
LAKER Henry & Son, Billingshurst	SS	SS
LANE Frank & Co., Faringdon	IRN	ICI
LANG Joseph & Son Ltd, London	GM	EBL
LAST R.G.F.	UK	SG
LAWN & ALDER, London	ST	REM-UMC
LEGGETT Herbert E., Eye, Suffolk	IRN	SG
LINCOLN JEFFRIES, Birmingham	GM	EBL
LONDON SPORTING PARK Ltd, Hendon	UK	EBL
LONG Henry & Sons Ltd, Whitney, Hants	UK	SS
MACNAUGHTON & Sons, Edinburgh & Perth	GM	Kynoch, Kynoch Nobel
MALCOMSON & Co., Lugan, NI	AUCT	Own HS
McCOLL & FRASER, Dunfermline	GM	ICI
McCRIRICK & Sons, Kilmarnock	GM	ICI
METCALFE W., Richmond, Yorkshire	UK	ICI
MITCHELL F.C., Inverness	UK	ICI & Kynoch Nobel
MORGAN, Wem & Whitchurch	IRN/GRO	EBL
MORRIS H.M., Burgess Hill, West Sussex	UK	Loaded by Midland Gun Co.
MORTIMER & Son, Edinburgh	GM	EBL
NEWLAND & STIDOLPH, Stratford on Avon	IRN	EBL
NORTON C.W., Newtown, Montgomery	IRN	Kynoch
NOTT J.E. & Co. Ltd, Brecon & Llandridodwells	UK	EBL
ODELL Brothers, Newport Pagnell	IRN	EBL
ORPIN'S Stores, Bradbourne	ST	Trent Cart. Co.
PARKER Hugh Estates, West Country	Estate	ICI
PARKINSON Tom, Ulverston	UK	Kynoch
PARSONS C., Nuneaton & Coventry	IRN	Own HS
PARSONS SHERWIN & Co. Ltd, Nuneaton & Coventry	IRN	Own HS & EBL
PEASE Joseph Ltd, Darlaston	GM	ICI
PERROTT S., Knightsbridge, Devon	IRN	EBL
PHILLIPS & POWIS, Reading	UK	SG
POTTER & Co., High Wycombe	UK	EBL
POTTER R. & E., Thame	GS	ICI & Eley Nobel
RAY M., Dartford, Kent	GM	Kynoch

Name & Address	Class	Comments/headstamp
RIGBY John & Co., London	GM	ICI
ROBERTS E., Birmingham	GM	Own HS
ROWELL & Sons, Chipping Norton	UK	EBL
ROWLATTS, Wellingborough, Northants	UK	Nobel
RUSSELL James, Elgin	IRN	ICI
RUTHERFORD W.M. & E.E., Berwick on Tweed	UK	SG
RUTT Alfred H., Northampton	GM	Own HS
SAMPLE W. Amble, Northumberland	GD	Kynoch
SCOTT & SARGEANT, Horsham	SS	SS
SEPTIMUS CHAMBERS, Bristol, Cardiff, Shepton Mallet	GM	Kynoch & Own HS
SIMPSON, London	ST	SS
SMITHSON G.J., Doncaster	UK	EBL
SMYTHE J.F. Ltd, Darlington	GM	Eley Nobel
Southern Counties Agriculture Trading Soc., Salisbury	AM	SS
Southern Counties Agriculture Trading Soc., Winchester	AM	SS
SPENCER Alfred L., Richmond	GM	ICI
STEBBINGS & Son, Attleborough, Norfolk	GD	SS
STOCKER A.J. & Son, Chulmleigh	IRN	ICI
STREET J.& Sons, Christchurch & Boscombe	IRN	EBL
STRONG J. & Son, Carlisle	GD	ICI & Kynoch Nobel
SYKES Bros, Ossett	GM	Own HS + Eley
SYKES Robert & Sons Ltd, Oldham & Stalybridge	UK	Own HS
TAYLOR, Newbury	Barber	SG
TAYLOR S. R. & Sons Ltd, Penzance & St Ives	IRN	Own HS
TETT H.G. Ltd, Coventry	GS	Eley Nobel
THAIN E.W. & R., Bramfield, Suffolk	UK	SG
THRASHER F., 49 Coventry Rd, B'Ham	UK	Kynoch
TILBURY G.S. & F.A. Jeffries, Worthing	Garage	SS
TILL William C. Ltd, Battle, Sussex	IRN	Kynoch
TILY M.J., Farnham, Surrey	UK	Nobels
TINNING John Longtown, Cumbria & Newcastleton	UK	Kynoch
TROUGHTON S., Blackpool	GM	Kynoch
TRULOCK & HARRIS, Dublin, Ireland	GM	Nobels, Kynoch & Own HS
TULLOCK W. & Co. London	UK	Eley Nobel
TURNBULL, Bridgnorth	IRN	Own HS/Joyce
TURNER H.A., Marlborough	GM	Nil
VARLEY Wm., Hull	UK	Own HS
WADDEN H.J., Wedmore	UK	Foreign case
WALES D., Great Yarmouth	GM	EBL
WALLAS D.H., Wigton & Carlisle	GM	Kynoch Nobel
WARD THOMPSON A., Middlesborough	GS	ICI
WARING Edwin, Leamington Spa, Warks	GS/IRN	ICI
WARNERS, Bantry, County Cork, Ireland	UK	Irish M.I.
WATKINS & Co., Banbury	GM	EBL

Name & Address	Class	Comments/headstamp
WATSON Bros, London	GM	Kynoch & EBL
WEEKS F., Lymington	UK	SS
WELLS H & Son, Ware	GD	SS
WEST E., Retford	GM	EBL
WHITNEY H.H., Newtown	GM	EBL
WILD Thomas, Birmingham	GM	REM-UMC
WILDMAN H.W., Ledbury	GS/IRN	Eley Nobel
WILLIAMS Harry, Isle of Wight	IRN	Kynoch
WILLIAMS J.S., Pontypridd	IRN & Exp Expert	Own HS
WILLIAMSON D., London	GM	Own HS
WILSON F.H. & Co., Stokesley	IRN	EBL
WILSON G.H., Horncastle	UK	Kynoch
WILSON James & Sons, York	GM	EBL
WREN G., Hungerford & Ramsbury	IRN	Kynoch
WRIGHT Randall, Spalding	GS	EBL

23.3 Examples of the names of companies which appear on paper tube shotgun cartridges together with some of their related brand names

Key to the class field

AUCT = Auctioneer	ED = Explosives dealer	GS = Gunsmith
AD = Ammunition dealer	ENG = Engineer	IRN = Ironmonger
AM = Agricultural merchants	GD = Gun dealer	SA = Sporting association
AS = Agricultural supplies	GFM = Game food manf.	SS = Sports supplier
CD = Cartridge dealer	GM = Gunmaker	ST = Shop or stores
CL = Cartridge loader	G&RM = Gun & rifle maker	UK = Unknown trade
CT = Cutler	GRO = Grocer	WM = Wine merchants

Name of company	Class	Brand names	Town/City/County
ADAM H. R.	IRN	Yeo Vale	Crediton/Devon
ADGEY	UK	Universal, Deluxe Special	Belfast/NI
ADGEY R.J.	UK	De Luxe, De Luxe Special, Favourite	Belfast/NI
ADKIN H.	GM	Ajax, Demon, Reliance	Bedford/Bedfordshire
ADKIN H. & Sons	GM	Demon, Exon Smokeless, 20 Gauge	Bedford/Bedfordshire
AGNEW & Son	GM	Devonia, Exon Smokeless	Exeter/Devon
AGNEW J.	UK	Special Smokeless	Colchester/Essex
AKRILL H. Esau	GM	Collector, Holderness, Universal	Beverley/Yorkshire
ALDRIDGE E.	UK	Anglian, Crown, Hyde Park	Ipswich/Suffolk
ALEXANDER Bros	IRN	Fordingbridge	Fordingbridge/Hants
ALLAN Arthur Ltd	IRN/GM	Three Star, Super AA, Imperial	Glasgow/Lanarkshire
ANDERSON J. & Son	GS	Derwent, Eclipse, Rabbit, Malton	Malton/Yorkshire
ARMSTRONG & Co.	ST	Pressure & recoil reducing case	Newcastle upon Tyne

Name of company	Class	Brand names	Town/City/County
ARMY & NAVY Co-op Ltd	ST	Victoria, Reliable, Nitro, Services	London
ARNOLD A.G. & Son	UK	Arnolds Club	Newport
ARNOLD S.R.	GS	Express Special	Louth/Lincs
ARNOLD'S	UK	Club	Reading/Hampshire
ATKIN Henry Ltd	GM	Ever Ready, Gem, Covert, Jermyn	London
ATKIN, GRANT & LANG	GM	Raleigh, Gem	London
ATKINSON	SS	Grand Finale, Special	Swansea/Glamorgan
ATKINSON & GRIFFIN	GM	Reliable	Kendal/Cumbria
ATKINSON T. & Sons	GM	Ajax, Kendal Castle, Reliable, Kent	Kendal/Cumbria
ATKINSON W.	GM	Lancaster Castle	Kendal/Cumbria
AVERILL & Son	GS	Averill's Express	Evesham/Worcs
BAGNALL & KIRKWOOD	GM	Setter, Pointer, Tyne	Newcastle upon Tyne
BAILDHAM E. & Son	IRN	Extra, Standard	Stratford on Avon/Warks
BAILEY	UK	Bailey's Special	Stafford
BAILEY W.R.	IRN	Somerset Velocity	Congresbury/Somerset
BAINBRIDGES	UK	The Best	Boston/Lincs
BAKER F.T.	GM	Bakerite, Harovian	London
BAKER J.C	IRN/ENG	Baker's Special Bull's Eye	Worcester/Worcs
BAKER Joseph & Son	IRN/GM	Baker's Special, West Norfolk	Fakenham/Norfolk
BAKER S.W.	ST	Deadsure	Crowcombe Station/Somerset
BAKER W.E.	UK	Special Bull's Eye	Tavistock/Devon
BALMFORTH J.J.	IRN	Balmforth's Special	Ormskirk/Lancs
BAMFORD H. & Sons	AS	Plough, Mow-em-down	Uttoxeter/Staffs
BANFIELD J.G. & Sons Ltd	IRN	Unitro	Tenbury
BARFORD H.W. & Co Ltd	UK	Special Imperial Smokeless	Coventry/West Mids
BARHAM H. then C.H.	GM	The Herts, Comet, Challenge	Hitchen/Hertfordshire
BARKER Bros	UK	Mullerite Smokeless	Grantham/Lincs
BARKERS	UK	Barkers S.S. De Luxe	Huddersfield/Yorkshire
BARNES A.	GM	Lonsdale, Referendum	Ulverston/Lancs
BARNES John	GM	Chieftain, Challenger, Garrick	Ayr/Ayrshire
BARNES John & Son	UK	Challenger, Garrick	Ayr/Ayrshire
BARNES W.	IRN	Special Red	Ashbourne/Derbyshire
BARNETT T.W.	IRN	Crown	Sturminster Newton/Dorset
BARNITTS Ltd	UK	Barnitt's Special	York/Yorkshire
BARNWELL H. & Sons Ltd	Garage	Hartley Special Smokeless	Hartley Wintney/Hants
BARTRAM G.T.	GM	Bartram's Hard Hitters	Braintree/Essex
BASSETT G.J.	IRN	Champion, Butser	Petersfield/Hants
BATE G. Ltd	GM	Leader, Imperial, Game	Birmingham
BATES A.	GM	Challenge, Imperial, Rabbit	Canterbury/Kent
BATES E.R. & Sons	UK	Challenge	Canterbury/Kent
BATES G.	GS	Mallard, Reliable, Eastbourne	Eastbourne/Sussex
BEARE H. & S.	IRN	Sharpshooter	Newton Abbot/Devon
BEDDOW James	IRN	The Castle	Pembroke
BEESLEY	GM	The Feathers & unnamed	London

Name of company	Class	Brand names	Town/City/County
BELLOW & Sons	UK	Special cartridge	Several addresses – Worcs
BENNETT Arthur W.	IRN	West Country	Bideford/Devon
BENNETT G.W.	GS	Yellow Seal Mullerite	Blackpool/Lancs
BENTLEY J.	UK	Croft	Liversedge/Yorks
BEVAN & EVANS	UK	Abergavenny Ace	Abergavenny/Monmouthshire
BEVAN & PRITCHARD	UK	Ace	Abergavenny/Monmouthshire
BEYTON R. Rous	UK	Eclipse	Suffolk
BIDMEAD R.M.	UK	The Mayhill	Newent/Gloucestershire
BLACK J.	GD	Bollin	Macclesfield/Cheshire
BLACKADDER C.G.	UK	Black Douglas	Castle Douglas/ Kirkcudbrightshire
BLAKE Bros	IRN	Wye Valley	Ross on Wye/Herefordshire
BLAKE James	UK	Roxburgh	Kelso/Roxburgshire
BLAND T. & Sons	GM	Bee, Farm	London
BLANTON R.	GM	Competitor, Imperial	Ringwood/Hants
BOLE H.W.	UK	Kyrle	Hereford/Herefordshire
BOND G.E. & Son	GM	Invincible	Thetford/Norfolk
BOSS & Co. Ltd	GM	Special, Regent	London
BOSWELL C.	GM	Special Express	London
BOWEN John	UK	Myrddin	Carmarthen
BOWERBANKS	GM	Sure Killer	Penrith/Cumbria
BRADDELL J. & Son Ltd	GM	Victory, Braddells Special, Meteor	Belfast/NI
BRETT & Sons	UK	Sureshot	Horsham/Sussex
BRITT W. & Sons	IRN	Sydenham	Chesterfield/Derbyshire
BROADWAY S. & Co.	UK	Dunkeries	Worksop/Notts
BROMLEY John & Co.	IRN	The Rabbit	Wellington/Salop
BROWN E.W. & Co. Ltd	UK	White Horse	Calne/Wilts
BUGLER J.U.	IRN	National	Ashford/Kent
BULPIN A.C.	UK	Bulpin's Straight Shot	Newton Abbot/Devon
BUNTING W.	UK	Yellow Seal Mullerite	Cromford/Derbyshire
BURGESS F.H. Ltd	AS	Champion	Several addresses – Shropshire
BURROW J.	GM	Paragon, Challenge, Economic	Preston/Lancs & Carlisle
BUTLER A.R.	IRN	Special	2 addresses/Devon
CALDER E.	GM	Dog & Duck	Aberdeen/Aberdeenshire
CAMBRIDGE & Co.	IRN/GD	Antrim, Ulster	Carrickfergus/NI
CAMERON W. & Co.	GS	Cameronian	Ballymena/NI
CAMPBELL & Sons	UK	Wensleydale	Leyburn/Yorkshire
CAPELL R.L.	IRN	Capella	Northampton/Northamptonshire
CARSWELL W.C.	GM	Banshee, Carswell's Special	Liverpool/Lancs
CAWDRON H.	AD	Holkham	Wells next the Sea/Norfolk
CHAMBERLAIN A.	GM	Wessex, Special Loading, AC County	Salisbury/Wiltshire
CHAPLIN B.E.	GM	Ideal, Winton	Winchester/Hants
CHITTY R.S.	UK	Chichester Cross	Chichester/Sussex
CHURCHILL E.J.	GM	Gem, Premier, Utility, Prodigy	London
CLARKE C.	GS	Original JWG Special	Salisbury/Wiltshire

Name of company	Class	Brand names	Town/City/County
CLARKE F.	IRN	Crafton, Invincible	Thetford/Norfolk
CLARKE H. & Sons	GM	Express, Alma, Midland, Keeper	Leicester/Leicestershire
CLEMITSON T.	IRN	Langley Castle, Special	Haydon Bridge/Northumberland
CLIMIE & Son	GM	Special Smokeless	Greenock
CLOUGH T. & Son	GM	Sandringham, Practical	Kings Lynn/Norfolk
COLE & Son	GM	Crown, Globe, Signature	Several addresses – Wiltshire
COLE F.J. Ltd	GM	County Favourite, Champion	Cirencester/Gloucestershire
COLLINS John	UK	Knife & Fork	Drogheda/ Ireland
COLLIS J. Ltd	UK	Nulli Secundus, All Round	Several addresses – Kent
COLTMAN & Co.	GM	Marvel, KC, Smithfield, Burton, Rabbit	Burton on Trent/Staffs
COLTMAN R.H.	GM	The Cartridge	Burton on Trent/Staffs
CONWAY Roy	IRN	Humber Duck & Goose	Grimsby/Yorkshire
CONYERS Arthur	GM	Express, Dorset County, Marvel	Blandford/Dorset
CONYERS Arthur & Sons	GM	Express	Blandford/Dorset
COOMBS William	UK	Eclipse, Champion	Frome/Somerset
COOPER Geo	UK	Noted Ryedale	Pickering/Yorkshire
CORDEN S.L.	IRN	Quickfire	Warminster/Wilts
CORDING J.C. & Co.	GM	Cording's Beater	Newbury/Berkshire
CORNISH J.	IRN	Okement	Oakhampton/Devon
CORY A.C.	GD	Champion	Diss/Norfolk
COTON Walter	GS	Special Keepers	Coventry/West Mids
COULSON	AD	Special Smokeless, Border	Bellingham/Northumberland
COUNTY GENTLEMENS Assoc.	SA	CGA Improved Waterproof	Letchworth/Hertfordshire
COX & CLARKE	GM	Southampton	Southampton/Hampshire
COX & MACPHERSON	GM	Special	Southampton/Hampshire
COX & Son Ltd	GM	JWG, Popular	Southampton/Hampshire
COZENS & SHAW Ltd	IRN	Reliable	Wolverhampton/West Mids
CROCKART D. & Sons	GM	Crockart, Stirling	Sterling/Stirlingshire
CROCKART D.B.	GM	Spotfinder, Perth	Perth/Perthshire
CROCKART J. & Son	G&RM	J.C. & S.	Blairgowrie/Perthshire
CROSS Bros Ltd	SS	Cardiff	Cardiff/Glamogan
CRUDGINTON I. Bath Ltd	GM	Spa	Bath/Somerset
DANIEL & MORRIS	IRN	Victor	St Clears/Wales
DARLOW W. Ltd	IRN	Big Bag, Orford, Buff Orford	Norwich/Norfolk
DATE & Bros	SS	Fur & Feather	Frome/Somerset
DAVIDSON J.A.	WM	New Era	Wells next the Sea/Norfolk
DAVIES H.A.	GM	Flight, Winton	Winchester/Hants
DAVIES T.	UK	Instanto	Llandyssul/Ceredigion
DAVIS A.	GM	Bishopgate	London
DEABILL J.G.	UK	Partridge	Nottingham/Notts
DEAN G.E.	UK	The Bicester	Bicester/Oxon
DENNIS A.	UK	Demon	Dunmow/Essex
DESBOROUGH & Son	UK	Dovedale	Derby/Derbyshire
DEVON & SOMERSET STORES	ST	Red Deer	Exeter/Devon

Name of company	Class	Brand names	Town/City/County
DICKSON J. & Son Ltd	GM	Capital, Horton, Special Blue Shell	Edinburgh/Midlothian
DISTIN E. & Son	IRN	Demon	Totnes/Devon
DIXON & Co.	CL	Pigeon	Birmingham
DIXON & Scott	IRN	Champion	Sudbury/Suffolk
DODD G.	UK	Dodd's Calthorpe Cartridge	Birmingham
DOLBY G.	UK	Long Range	Mould/Wales
DONALSON W.G.	UK	Triumph	Grantown on Spey/Morayshire
DORSET FARMERS Ltd	AM	Unity & Special Smokeless	Dorchester
DUBBEN A.G.	UK	Damar	Dorchester
DUDDINGTON C.E.	UK	Countryside	Whitchurch/Hants
DUGDALE R.L. Ltd	UK	Champion	Preston/Lancs
DUNCAN C.V. & Co.	GM	Ducan's Special Load	Hull/Yorkshire
DYMOND M.	UK	Kit-Hill	Callington/Cornwall
EARLE G.A.	IRN	Special	Bridgnorth/Shropshire
EDGAR F.R.	UK	Eskdale	Longtown/Cumbria
EDMONDS R.E.	GM	Stalham Superior, Stalham Gold	Stalham/Norfolk
EDWARDS & MELHUISH	UK	See previous book	Birmingham
EDWARDS A. & Co. Ltd	UK	Gower, Eclipse	Swansea/Glamorgan
EDWARDS C.G. & Son	UK	Eddystone, Smeaton	Plymouth/Devon
EDWARDS H. Ltd	GM	Newport	Newport/Monmouthshire
EDWARDS John	UK	Kerry Blue	Tralee/Ireland
ELDERKIN & Son	GS	Premier	Spalding/Lincs
ELLICOTT	UK	Ellicott Cartridge	Cardiff/Glamogan
ELLIOTT H.C.	GM	Smasher	Dartford/Kent
ELLIS J.	ST	Regal Special Smokeless	Oswestry/Shropshire
EMSLIE D.	UK	Sniper, Glen Moral	Elgin/Murrayshire
ERSKINE	GM	Erskine	Newton Stewart/Scotland
EVANS Ben & Co.	UK	Special	Swansea/Glamorgan
EVANS C.A.	IRN	Cotswold Special Smokeless	Burford/Oxfordshire
EVANS Dan	IRN	TY-GWYN	Whitland/Carmathenshire
EVANS William	GM	Markover, Sky High, Pall Mall	London
EWEN J.W.	UK	Ewen Special	Aberdeen/Aberdeenshire
FARMER R.	GM	Excel	Leighton Buzzard/Bedfordshire
FARRELL G. F. & Sons	UK	Champion Special Smokeless	Chippenham/Wiltshire
FARRELLY Bryan & Sons	UK	Kenlis	Kells/ NI
FAWLEY H. & Son	UK	Special	Manchester/Lancs
FIDDIAN Samuel	UK	Enville	Stourbridge/Worcs
FINCH B. & Sons	UK	Lone Flyer	Reigate/Surrey
FITCHEN'S A.T.	UK	Excel	Ramsgate/Kent
FLETCHERS Sports	ST	Gloucester	Cirencester/Gloucestershire
FLINT H.A.	IRN	Primrose Smokeless	Hemel Hempstead/Herts
FOLLETT	UK	Eclipse	Colyton & Seaton/Devon
FOORT & Son	UK	Dead Shot	Oxford
FORD William	GM	Eclipse, Ford's Patent Ignition-Tube	Birmingham
FORREST & Sons	GM	Tweed	Kelso/Roxburgshire

Name of company	Class	Brand names	Town/City/County
FOSTER A.J.	GS	Quickhit, Field, Empire	Kidderminster/Worcs
FOX Isaac	GM	County Favourite, Castle	Canterbury/Kent
FRANCIS C. & Son	GM	Demon, Reliable	Peterborough/Northamptonshire
FROST E.	UK	Devon Smokeless	Exeter/Devon
FROST George	Blacksmith	Special Smokeless	Bakewell/Derbyshire
FRY J.	GM	Derby	Derby/Derbyshire
FUSSELL'S Ltd	GM	Club	Newport/Monmouthshire
GALBRAITH W.	IRN	Primrose Smokeless	Lancaster/Lancashire
GALE E.	GM	XL, Hawk, Flag	Bideford/Devon
GALLYON & Sons Ltd	GM	Kilham, Camroyd, Granton	Cambridge/Cambridgeshire
GAMAGE A.W. Ltd	ST	W.W.G., Corona, Referee, Holborn	London
GAMBLE John G.	AD	Swift	Magherafelt/NI
GARDEN W.	GM	Granite City, Competitor	Aberdeen/Aberdeenshire
GARNETT M.	CL	Retriever, Kilquick, Sure Death	Dublin/Ireland
GARRETT Frank	GM	Blue Flash, Crimson Flash, Tempest	Birmingham
GIBBS G. Ltd	GM	Bristol, Field, County, Intermediate	Bristol/Gloucestershire
GILL John	UK	Sproxton	Leeming Bar/N. Yorks
GLIDDON & Sons	AM	Exmoor	Minehead/Williton/Somerset
GOLDING C.E.	IRN	Watton	Watton/Norfolk
GOW John R. & Sons	GM	Tayside, Excel	Angus/Dundee
GRAHAM G.P.	GM	Skiddaw	Cockermouth/Cornwall
GRAHAM J. & Co. Ltd	GM	Bon-Ton, Highland, Primo	Inverness/Invernesshire
GRANT & LANG	GM	Grantbury, Velogrant, Curzon, Gem	London
GRAY & Co.	GM	Autokill, Wetproof, Mors	Inverness/Invernesshire
GRAY R.	SS	Don	Doncaster/Yorkshire
GREEN Edwinson & Son	GM	Cotswold, Fur & Feather, Maxim	Cheltenham/Gloucestershire
GREENER W.W.	GM	See previous book	Birmingham & London
GREENFIELD H.S. & Son	GM	County	Canterbury/Kent
GREGSON James	UK	Special	Blackburn/Aberdeen
GRIFFITHS Charles S.	UK	Craven	Skipton/Yorkshire
GRIFFITHS W.	UK	TWM Speedwell	Manchester/Lancs
GRIMES S.J.	GS	Champion Special Smokeless	Stamford/Lincs
GROOM A.	UK	Monarch	Lincoln
HALL C.	GM	Hall's Smokeless Castle	Knaresborough/Yorkshire
HALL Frank	GS	Hallrite-Special	Chesterfield/Derbyshire
HALL Hugh	AM	Express	Wetherby/Yorks
HALLIDAY B. Co. Ltd	GM	Express	London
HAMMOND Brothers	GM	Winton, Trustee Servant	Winchester/Hants
HANDSCOMBE F.G.	UK	Victor	Bishops Stortford/Herts
HARDING Bros Ltd	UK	Rabbit Brand	Hereford/Herefordshire
HARDY & HOLGATE	IRN	York	York/Yorkshire
HARDY Brothers Ltd	GM	Northern, Hotspur, Reliance	London, Manchester, Alnwick etc.
HARPER P.J.	IRN	Invincible	Crewe/Cheshire
HARPUR Brothers	UK	Sure Shot	Waterford/Ireland
HARRISON & HUSSEY Ltd	GM	Abermarle, Curzon, Grafton	London

Name of company	Class	Brand names	Town/City/County
HARRODS	ST	Knightsbridge, Kill Sure, Hurlingham	London
HART F.W.	GM	Crackshot, Express, Marvel	Scarborough/Yorkshire
HARTWELL J.T.	UK	Mayfair	London
HAWKES & Sons Ltd	IRN	Hawk Brand	Taunton/Somerset
HAYGARTH C.H.	GS	Economax	Dunnet/Caithness
HAYMAN C.	GD	Setter	Weymouth
HAYWARD S.E. & Co. Ltd	UK	New Special Smokeless	Crowborough/Tunbridge Wells
HEAL W.E.	IRN	Tivvy	Tiverton/Devon
HELLIS & Sons Ltd	CL	See related chapter	London
HELLIS Chas & Sons	CL	See related chapter	London
HELLIS-ROSSON Ltd	CL	See related chapter	Norwich/Norfolk
HELSON J.	UK	Victor, Demon	Exeter/Devon
HEMING W.	IRN	Meon Valley Special Smokeless	Wickham/Hants
HENRY Alexander & Co.	GM	Clan, Club	Edinburgh/Midlothian
HESFORD C.M. & Co. Ltd	AS	Hesford Special	Ormskirk/Lancs
HEWETT & Son	IRN	Express	Alton/Hants
HEYWOOD & HODGE	UK	Reliable	Torrington/Devon
HIGGINS Harry	UK	Dead Shot	Tenbury Wells/Worcs
HIGHAM G.G.	GS	Hios, Velox	Oswestry/Shropshire
HILL & Son	GM	County, Champion, Reliable, Challenge	Horncastle/Lincs
HILLSDON Russell	GS	Sussex Express, Goodwood	Horsham, Chichester/Sussex
HILTON GUN Co.	GS	Hilton Cartridge	Hilton/Derbyshire
HINTON G.	GM	Standard	Taunton/Somerset
HINTON G. & Sons	GM	Taunton, Standard	Taunton/Somerset
HOBSON J.	GM	Challenge	Leamington Spa/Warks
HODGSON	GM	Reliance	Bridlington/Yorks
HODGSON A.A.	UK	Luda	Louth/Lincs
HODGSON Henry	GM	Perfect, Special, Eclipse, Suffolk	Ipswich, Bury St Edmonds
HODGSON Jesse P.	UK	Express	Louth/Lincs & Bridlington
HODGSON R.C.	GS	Rapido	Ripon/Yorkshire
HODGSON R.T.	IRN	Harrogate	Harrogate/Yorks
HODGSON W.	GM	Special, Rapido	Ripon/Yorkshire
HOLLAND & HOLLAND	GM	Royal, Northwood, Dominion etc.	London
HOLLAND C.R.	GM	Nonsuch Smokeless	Cirencester/Gloucestershire
HOLLIS Isaac	GM	Special Blue, Special Green	Birmingham
HOME	UK	Home's Special Loading	Reading/Berkshire
HOOKE T.J. & Son	GM	Eclipse, Ebor	York/Yorkshire
HOOTON & JONES	GM	Smokeless Cartridge	Liverpool/Lancs
HOOTON Wm	UK	Sleaford	Sleaford/Lancs
HOPKINS H.G.	UK	Mark II Game	Sandbach/Cheshire
HOPKINS J.J.	IRN	Golden Pheasant	Leighton Buzzard/Bedfordshire
HOPPING E.A.	IRN	Rabbit Special	Lostwithiel/Cornwall
HORRELL & Son	IRN	Electric	Crediton/Devon
HORSLEY T. & Sons Ltd	GM	Rabbit	York/Yorkshire
HORTON W.	G&RM	Extra	Glasgow/Lanarkshire

Name of company	Class	Brand names	Town/City/County
HOWES & Son	IRN	Champion	Wymondham/Norfolk
HULL T.L. & Co.	IRN	Shaston	Shaftesbury/Dorset
HUNTER & Son	GM	Long Shot, Ideal, Reliable, De Luxe	Belfast/NI
HUNTER & VAUGHAN	UK	Special Smokeless	Bristol/Gloucestershire
HUSSEY Ltd	GM	Times	London
HUTCHINSON ROE & Co.	UK	The Rabbit	Cranbrook/Kent
INGRAM Charles	GM	Ingram	Glasgow/Lanarkshire
JACKSON & Son	GM	Dead Shot, Woodcock Brand	Gainsborough/Lincs
JACKSON Alfred	IRN	Pheasant	Abergavenny/Monmouthshire
JACKSON S.	GM	Nottingham Cartridge	Nottingham/Notts
JAMES & Co.	GFM	Marlborough, Kennett	Hungerford/Berkshire
JAMES M. & Sons	IRN	Gwalia	Newcastle Emlyn/Carmathenshire
JEFFREY A.R. & H.V. Ltd	GM	Empire, Eddystone	Plymouth/Devon & Yeovil/Somerset
JEFFREY C. & Sons	GM	Royal Game, Empire, Club	Doncaster/Yorkshire
JEFFREY S.R. & Son (Ltd)	GM	Champion	Guildford/Surrey
JEFFREY W. & Son	GM	Sky High	Plymouth/Devon & Yeovil/Somerset
JEFFREY W.J. & Co. Ltd	GM	Club, XXX, Sharpshooter, Vimite	London
JEWSON A.J.	CL & SS	Crown, Leader, Champion, Practical	Halifax/Yorkshire
JOBSON G.	UK	Milford	Milford/Surrey
JOHNSON & WRIGHT	IRN	County	Northampton/Northamptonshire
JOHNSON Thomas & Son	GM	Anglian, Reliable	Swaffham/Norfolk
JONES & Son	IRN	Abbey	Malmesbury/Wiltshire
JONES Bros	UK	Knockout	Cardigan/Lancs
JONES Robert	GM	Liver Smokeless	Liverpool/Lancs
JONES Tom	IRN	Majestic	Carmarthen
JONES W.Palmer	GM	Accuratus, Priority	Birmingham
KAVANAGH W. & Son	GM	Ideal, Mirus, Clay Pigeon	Dublin/Ireland
KEEGAN L.	GM	Emerald Isle	Dublin/Ireland
KENT & Son	IRN	Wantage	Wantage/Berkshire
KERR Charles	GM	Royal	Stranraer/Dumfries & Galloway
KERRIDGE H.E.	GS/IRN	East Anglian	Gt Yarmouth/Norfolk
KINGDON T.M. & Co. Ltd	IRN	The Hampshire	Winchester, Olton etc.
KIRK J.	GM	Land of Burns, Blue Rock Pigeon	Ayr/Ayrshire
KNIBBS S. & Co.	IRN	County Life	Badcox, Frome/Somerset
KNIGHT P.	GM	Castle, Thurland, Invincible	Nottingham/Notts
LACE	UK	Lace's Smokeless Cartridge	Wigan/Lancashire
LACEY J. & H.	IRN	Imperial	Long Eaton
LAKER Henry & Son Sports Ltd	ST	XL Special	Billingshurst
LANCASTER C. & Co. Ltd	GM	Leicester, Norfolk, First Class	London
LANE	AM	Cheddar Vale	Cheddar
LANE Bros	IRN	Eclipse	Faringdon/Oxfordshire
LANE Charles L.	IRN	Lane's Champion	Bridgewater/Somerset
LANGDON J.	GS	Langdon	Truro/Cornwall
LANGLEY & LEWIS	GM	Blue Rock	Luton & Malden
LANGLEY James John	GM	Blue Rock	Luton/Bedfordshire

Name of company	Class	Brand names	Town/City/County
LAW Tom	GM	Galloway	Castle Douglas
LEATHAM G.H.	UK	Durham	Durham
LEECH & Sons	GM	Standard, Club	Chelmsford/Essex
LEESON W.R.	UK	Invicta	Ashford/Kent
LEMON John & Son Ltd	UK	Killem	Inniskillen
LEONARD C.	GM	Glanford	Brigg/Lincs
LEWIS	IRN	Sunset	Wells/Somerset
LEWIS Aubrey	GM	Severn, Chelt, Prizewinner	Luton/Bedfordshire
LIGHTWOOD F.W.	GM	Woodcraft, Dog & Gun	Brigg, Grimsby, Market Rasen
LIMMEX S.J. & Co.	IRN	Pheasant	Swindon/Wiltshire
LINDSAY	IRN	Clayking	Perth/Perthshire
LINES A.G.	AD	Supershot	Stevenage/Herts
LINSLEY Bros	GM	Nomis, Swift, Standard	Leeds/Yorkshire
LISLE Robert	GM	Victa, Field, Tiger	Derby/Derbyshire
LITTLE H.C. & Son	GM	Blackmore Vale, Sparkford Vale	Yeovil/Devon
LLOYD & Son	GM	County, Improved Imps, Imperial Crown	Lewis/Sussex
LOCK C.H.	UK	Lock's Special	Atherstone/Warks
LONG Henry & Sons	IRN	Witney	Witney/Oxfordshire
LOVERIDGE & Co.	IRN	Royal County	Reading/Berkshire
LUCKE	IRN	Demon	Taunton
LYON & LYON	GM	Gamester & Midlong	London
MacKAY Alex & Son	IRN	Argyll	Tarbert
MACKENZIE & DUNCAN	UK	Dunmax	Brechin/Tayside
MACPHERSON John	GM	Barrage, Royal, Clack, Challenge	Inverness/Invernesshire
MACPHERSON Robert	SS	Badenoch	Kinguissie
MALEHAM C.H.	GM	Wing, Wizard	Sheffield & London
MALLINSONS	UK	Shamrock	Driffield/Yorskhire
MALLOCH P.D.	UK	Standard, Matchless, Triumph	Perth/Perthshire
MANBY A.	IRN	Suffolk Champion	Southwold/Suffolk
MANBY F. & Bros	IRN	Manby's Special	Skipton/Yorkshire
MARK J. Stewart	UK	Markmore	St Andrews/Scotland
MARSHALL & PEARSON	UK	Lochaber	Fort William/Invernesshire
MARTIN Alex	GM	Age, Club, Velm, Thistle, Caledonian	Aberdeen/Aberdeenshire
MATHERS J. & Co.	IRN	Britannia	Bingham, Southwell,& Newark
MATTHEWS Bros	UK	Excelsior	Honiton/Devon
MATTHEWS James	GD	Swift	Ballymena/NI
MAYES Bros	AS/IRN	Farmer's Favourite	Wickford/Essex
McBEAN Robert	GM	Challenge	Stafford
McCALL W. & Co.	GM	Border, Popular, Tally Ho, Keepers	Dumfries/Dumfries & Galloway
McDOUGALL Duncan	UK	Lorne	Oban
McEWAN James & Co.	UK	Loch	Unknown location
McSORLEY J.	Garage	Abercorn	Omagh/Ireland
MELLARD & Co.	UK	Yellow Champion	Denbigh & Abergele
MEREDITH H.L.	IRN	Meredith Special	Bideford/Devon

Name of company	Class	Brand names	Town/City/County
METCALF	UK	Champion	Burton on Trent/Staffs
METCALFE R.	GM	Swaledale, Richmond	Richmond/Yorkshire
METCALFE W.	GM	Metcalfe's Special, Demon	Catterick Camp/Yorkshire
MIDLAND GUN Co.	GM	See previous book	Birmingham
MILBURN & Son	GS	MSB, Noxhall, Rex	Brampton/Cumberland
MITCHIE	UK	Unequalled	Stirling
MOGG B.D. & Son	UK	Mendip	Wells/Somerset
MONK H.	GM	Straight, Popular, Imperial	Chester/Cheshire
MOODY W.F.	GM/CT	Ranger	Romsey/Hants
MOOR T.H.	UK	Special Rabbit	South Molton/Devon
MOORE & GREY	GM	Special	London
MORELAND S.	AD	Special	Northwich/Cheshire
MORRELL & Son	IRN	Electric	Crediton/Devon
MORREY	UK	Morrey Special	Holmes Chapel/Cheshire
MORRIS P. & Son	GS/IRN	Hereford, Lightning, Imperial	Hereford/Herefordshire
MORROW & Co.	GM	Challenge	Halifax/Yorkshire
MORTIMER	UK	Club	Barnstable/Devon
MORTIMER & Son	GM	Rabbit	Edinburgh/Midlothian
MORTON G.P. & Son	IRN	Killer	Whittlesley/Cambridgeshire
MULLERITE Cartridge Co.	CL	See previous book	Birmingham
MUMFORD R.C.	UK	Stopper, Rabbit	Southwold/Suffolk
MURRAY T.W. & Co. Ltd	GM	Wildfowler, Special Blue, Reliable	Cork/Ireland
NAUGHTON T. & Son	UK	Blazer	Galway/Ireland
NAYLOR C.	GM	Naylor's Cannot be Beaten	Sheffield/Yorkshire
NEEDHAM J.V.	GM	See previous book	Birmingham
NELSON Francis	UK	Reliable	Sligo/Ireland
NEWHAM & Co.	GM	Special Game	Portsmouth/Hampshire
NEWNHAM Ltd	GM	Special Game	Landport/Hants
NEWTON T.	GM	Lightning	Manchester/Lancs
NICHOLSON E.	GS	Eddnick Game	Preston/Lancs
NICKERSON John	UK	Special	Grimsby/Yorkshire
NIGHTINGALE & Son	IRN	Moonraker	Salisbury/Hants
NOBBS S.A.	IRN	Sureshot	Lincoln
NORMAN & Sons	GM	Standard	Woodbridge/Suffolk
OAKES	UK	Premier	Unknown/UK
OAKEY F.C.	UK	The OK	Stafford
OLBY	UK	Cantium	Ramsgate, Ashford etc./Kent
ORPIN'S STORE	ST	Cert	Bradbourne/Kent
OSBORN J.P.	AD	Danetre	Daventry/Northamptonshire
OTTON'S	UK	Devon	Exeter/Devon
PALMER Edward	GS/CT	Swift	Strood/Kent
PALMER G.	GM	Champion	Sittingbourne/Kent
PALMER W. & H.E.	GM	Century	Rochester/Kent
PAPE W.R.	GM	Beryl, Heather	Newcastle upon Tyne
PARAGON GUN SPECIALISTS	GS	Invincible	Belfast/NI

Name of company	Class	Brand names	Town/City/County
PARSON	AM	Special loading	Nuneaton, Hinkley/Warks
PARSONS F.	IRN	High Down	Worthing/W. Sussex
PARSONS SHERWIN & Co. Ltd	AM	Special loading	Nuneaton, Hinkley/Warks
PATSTONE & COX	GM	Pheasant, Reliable	Southampton/Hampshire
PATSTONE & Son	GM	Renown, Precision	Southampton & Winchester
PATTERSON J.C.	IRN	Smokeless Cartridge	Lisburn/Ireland
PENNY & Son	UK	The Times	Frome/Somerset
PITTS H.B.	IRN	Premier	Trowbridge/Wiltshire
PLAYFAIR C.	GM	Keepers	Aberdeen/Aberdeenshire
PLUMBERS Ltd	GD	Velocity, Original	Gt Yarmouth/Norfolk
POLLARD H.E. & Co.	GM	Keepers, Our Game, Long Shot	Worcester/Worcs
POWELL William & Son	GM	General, Marshall, Our Game	Birmingham
POWELL W. J.	GM	Lightning	Leiston/Suffolk
PRATT Albert	CD	Fysche	Knaresborough/Yorkshire
Preston & District Farmers Trading Soc.	AM	Farmers General Purpose	Preston
PUGH C.F.	IRN	Rabbit	Knighton/Radnorshire
PULLAN H.	GM	V.W.H.	Unknown location
PUNTER A.F.	IRN	Minimax, Shamrock	Basingstoke/Hampshire
PURCELL C.	UK	High Velocity	Gloucester
PURDEY George	IRN	Chevin	Otley/Yorkshire
PURDEY James & Sons	GM	Large Cap Special	London
PURVIS & Co.	UK	Sure Shot	Alnwick/Northumberland
RAINE Bros	GM	Irresistible, Border	Carlisle/Cumbria
RAMSBOTTOM	SS	Sudden Death	Manchester/Lancs
RANDELL F.	UK	Special Smokeless	North Walsham & Cromer
RATCLIFFE K.D.	SS	A True Fit, All Over the World	Colchester/Essex
REGENT GUN Co.	GM	Regent	Birmingham
REILLY E.M.	GM	Harewood	London
REYNOLDS E.G.E.	SS	Champion	Saxmundham/Suffolk
RICHARDS C.C.	IRN	Wivey	Wiveliscombe/Somerset
RICHARDS W.	GM	R.P., Castle, Mark Down, Express	Liverpool & Preston/Lancs
RICHARDSON & CLINCEN	SS	Killem	Enniskillean
RICHARDSON G.M.	UK	Buccleuch, Ideal	Dumfries/Dumfries & Galloway
RICHARDSON W.G.	GM	Barnite, Barnoid, Nulli Secundus	Barnard Castle/Durham
RIGGS C. & Co. Ltd	GM	Mitre, Bishop	London
RINGWOOD A.E.	GM	Dreadnought, Ideal, Ringer	Banbury/Oxfordshire
ROBERTS Augustus John	IRN	The Roberts	Ludlow/Shropshire
ROBERTS H.P.	IRN	Otter Vale	Ottery St Mary/Devon
ROBERTSON Alex & Son	IRN	Expert	Wick/Caithness
ROBINSON H.	UK	Burlington, Lightning Express	Bridlington/Yorks
ROBINSON H. & Co.	GS/IRN	Castle	Bridgenorth/Shropshire
ROBINSON R. Ltd	GM	Magnet, Humber, Kingston	Hull/Yorkshire
ROLANDS R.H.	UK	Marl Special	Woodbridge/Suffolk
ROPER R.Son & Co.	GM	Hallamshire	Sheffield/Yorkshire

Name of company	Class	Brand names	Town/City/County
ROYS	IRN	Roys Rabbit Cartridge	Wroxham/Norfok
RUDD A.J.	GM	Star, X.L., Standard	Norwich & Yarmouth/Norfolk
RUSSELL A.J. & Sons	GM	Reliance	Maidstone/Kent
RUTHERFORD Alex Ltd	UK	Champion, Premier	Darlington/Co Durham
SALT H. & Son	UK	Dreadnought	Church Stretton/Shropshire
SANDERS A.	GM	Long Tom, Medway	Maidstone/Kent
SAUNDERS E.F.	UK	Golden Pheasant	Chichester/Sussex
SAYER	UK	Bulzi	Watton/Norfolk
SCOTCHER John A. & Son	GM	Invincible	Bury St Edmonds/Suffolk
SCOTT & SARGEANT	IRN	Horsham Special	Horsham/Sussex
SHARP F.A.	IRN	Sharps Express	Dorset
SHARPE J.S.	GM	Scottie	Aberdeen/Aberdeenshire
SHUFFREY Ltd	IRN	Beacon	Walsall/West Mids
SKINNER & Co.	UK	Champion	Leek/Staffs
SLINGSBY Bros	UK	Stump, Swift, Fen	Boston/Lincs
SMAIL John & Sons	IRN	Best Smokeless	Morpeth/Northumberland
SMALL P.	UK	Burnand	Newcastle Upon Tyne
SMALLWOODS S.	GS	Kleankiller, Challenge	Shrewsbury/Shropshire
SMITH A.F.	UK	Yellow Boy	Hailsham & Heathfield/East Sussex
SMITH C. & Sons	GM	Castle, Universal, Keeper	Newark, Nottingham/Notts
SMITH C.H. & Sons	GM	Invincible	Birmingham
SMITH MIDGLEY	GM	Bradford	Bradford/Yorkshire
SMITH Steve	UK	Special, Trap & Game	Newcastle under Lyme
SMYTHE J.F. Ltd	GM	Field, Durham Ranger, Champion	Darlington/Co Durham
SNEEZUM H. & R.	GM	Sneezum's Special	Ipswich/Suffolk
SOWMAN J.W. E. Ltd	IRN	Sureshot Smokeless	Olney/Buckinghamshire
SPENCER F.P.	IRN	Vectis	Newport/IOW
SPILLER G.	IRN	Blackmore Vale	Sherborne/Dorset
STANBURY & STEVENS	CL	Monocle, Red Flash, Game	Exeter/Devon
STANBURY P.	CL	Stanby	Exeter/Devon
STENSBY T. & Co.	GM	All British, Club, Champion, Victory	Manchester/Lancs
STERLING	UK	Extra Primer	London
STOCKER A.J. & Son	IRN	Chulmleigh	Chulmleigh/Devon
SYKES Brothers	UK	Safety	Ossett/Yorkshire
TARR W. & Sons	UK	Exmoor	Minehead/Somerset
TAYLOR & JONES	UK	Monnow	Monmouth & Ross
TAYLOR J.	IRN	Lightning	Bromsgrove/Worcs
THACKER & Co.	GM	Long Shot	Worcester/Worcs
THIRKETTLE W.E.	Garage	Kilhemall	Darsham, Ipswich
THRASHER F.	UK	Special	Birmingham
TICKNER W.J.	IRN	Sportsman	Waltham/Hampshire
TILNEY R & Son	GS	Beccles	Beccles/Suffolk
TISDALL John	GM	Chichester	Chichester & Arundel/Sussex
TISDALL W. Ltd	UK	The Retriever	Wellington/Salop

Name of company	Class	Brand names	Town/City/County
TOLLEY J.& W.	GM	Altro	Birmingham
TOWY TIVY FARMERS	Co-op	Reyward	Several Welsh towns
TUCKER J.	GS	Oswestrian	Oswestry/Shropshire
TURNER Arthur	GM	Wizard, Clay Bird, Steeltown	Sheffield/Yorkshire
TURNER Henry	UK	Kennett	Marlborough/Wilts
TURNER Thomas & Sons	GM	Fillbag, Craven, Midget	Reading & Newbury/Berkshire
TYLER John Ltd	GD/CD	Falcon	Highbridge/Somerset
URQUHART C. & J.	IRN	Ardross	Dingwall/Highlands
URTON William Ltd	UK	Spire	Chesterfield/Derbyshire
USHERS	UK	Stuffit	Unknown
VENABLES J. & Sons	GM	County, Oxford	Oxford/Oxfordshire
WAGSTAFF & Co.	AD	A1	Basingstoke/Hampshire
WALKER James B.	GD	Northumbria, Newgate	Newcastle upon Tyne
WALKINGTON H.	GD	Reliable	Bridlington/Yorks
WALLIS Bros	GM	Big Tom of Lincoln, Licoln Imp	Lincoln
WANLESS & Co.	GM	Long Range	South Shields/Tyne & Wear
WARD THOMPSON Bros	GM	Boro	Middlesborough/Cleveland
WARNER H.P. & Son	IRN	General Service, High Velocity Special	Newton Abbot/Devon
WARREN	IRN	The Warren	Horncastle and Spilsby
WARREN A.E.	GM	Windsor Special	Windsor/Berks
WARRILOW J.B.	GS	Badminton, Electric Long Shot	Chippenham/Wiltshire
WATSON BRACEWELL	UK	Yellow Seal Mullerite	Peebles
WATSON Bros	GM	Reliance	London
WEBBER & SAUNDERS	IRN	The Pheasant	Tiverton/Devon
WEBBER J. & Son	SS	ISCA	Exeter/Torquay
WEBBERS	UK	Ottervale	Honiton/Devon
WEBSTER A.F.	UK	Globemaster, Vampax, High Velocity	Hull/Yorkshire
WEBSTER G.R.	UK	Field, Favourite, Snipe, Wellford	Boston/Lincs
WEBSTERS	IRN	Axe Valley	Axminster/Devon
WELSH William	UK	Queen of the South	Dumfries/Castle Douglas
WEST & Son	GM	Sherwood, Grand National	Retford/Notts
WEST & Son Ltd	GD/CD	Norfolk Hi Velocity	Gt Yarmouth/Norfolk
WESTLEY RICHARDS	GM	See previous book	Birmingham
WESTON C.& A.	GM	Brighton Special	Brighton/East Sussex
WHALEY T.H. & Son	IRN	Mullerite	St Ives
WHEATER J.	GM	Humber	Hull/Yorkshire
WHITEHOUSE J.E. & Sons	GM	Cottesmore, Rutland, Quorn	Oakham/Rutland
WHITEMAN Bros Ltd	UK	Rapid, Warren	Worcester/Worcs
WHITEMAN F.S.	GS/IRN	Fordian	Wallingford/Oxfordshire
WHITLOCK J.P. & Son	IRN	Nigger	Holsworthy
WILKES John	GM	Doughty, Tom Tom	London
WILKINSON	SS	Beacon	Penrith/Cumbria
WILKINSON'S	GM	Special, Regal	London
WILLIAMS T.M.	IRN	The Rabbit	Llandilo/Wales
WILSON Fred	IRN	Champion	Clitheroe/Lancs

Name of company	Class	Brand names	Town/City/County
WILSON G.	GM	Wilkill	Skipton/Yorkshire
WILSON Geoff	GS	Nomis	Carlisle
WISE Richard	IRN	Lightning	Kidderminster/Worcs
WOOD Arthur	GS/IRN	Demon	Newport/IOW
WOOD G.L. & Sons	GM	Woods Supreme	Orvington/Norfolk
WOODROW R.J.	IRN	Champion	Brandon/Suffolk
WOODWARD J. & Sons	GM	The Automatic	London
WRIGHT	UK	What Ho	Maldon/Essex
WYLIE A.B.	IRN	Killklean	Warwick/Warks

23.4 Examples of these companies' shotgun cartridges

LEFT TO RIGHT: *'Demon' by H. Adkin & Son, Bedford, 'Devonia' and 'Special Smokeless' by Agnew & Son, 'Holderness' and 'County' by H.S. Akrill and 'Three Stars' by Arthur Allan Ltd*
LYING DOWN: *'Fordingbridge' by Alexander and 'Malton' by J. Anderson & Son*

LEFT TO RIGHT: *'Club' by Arnold's, unbranded by J.H. Adams & Sons, Ironmongers, Littleport, unbranded by T. Adsett & Son, Guildford, unbranded by Alexander & Duncan Ltd, Leominster & Hereford, 'The Hyde Park' by Aldridge, Hyde Park Corner, Ipswich*

LEFT TO RIGHT: *'Gastight' by Armstrong, unbranded and 'Ever Ready' both by Henry Atkins Ltd,*
'The Gem' by Atkins Grant & Lang, 'The Raleigh' by Henry Atkins Ltd, 'Express' by Averill's
LYING DOWN: *Armstrong's 'Pressure Reducing', 'Reliable' and 'Castle' both brands by Atkinson's of Lancaster*

*All specimens by
the Army &
Navy Stores*

LEFT TO RIGHT:
*'Nitro', 'Nitro',
'Reliable',
'Service',
'Victoria' and
'Victoria'*
LYING DOWN:
*'Everyday Nitro'
and 'Victoria'*

LEFT TO RIGHT:
*'Bailey's Special' by
Bailey, Stafford, 'Hard
Hitters' by Bartram,
Braintree, 'The
Champion' by G.J.
Bassett, 'The Mallard' by
G. Bates Gunsmith,
Eastbourne, 'The
Castle' by James Beddoe,
Pembroke, 'The West
Country' by Arthur
W. Bennett, Ironmonger,
Bideford*
LYING DOWN:
*unbranded by J. Bentley,
Liveridge*

303

LEFT TO RIGHT:
'West Norfolk' by Joseph Baker & Son, 'Bull's Eye' by Bakers of Worcester, 'Balmforth's Special' by J.J. Balmforth, 'Unitro' by J.C. Banfield & Sons Ltd, 'Barnitts' Special' by Barnitts Ltd, 'Black Douglas' by C.G. Blackadder
LYING DOWN:
'Baker's Best Special Loading' by F.T. Baker

ABOVE:
LEFT TO RIGHT: *'Ace' by Bevan & Pritchard, Abergavenny, 'Black Douglas' by C.G. Blackadder, Castle Douglas, 'The Imperial', R. Blanton, Gunmaker, Ringwood, 'Myrddin' by John Bowen, Carmarthen, 'Sure Killer' by Bowerbanks, Gunmakers, Penrith, unbranded by John Bromley & Co. (Wellington) Ltd*
LYING DOWN:
'National' by Bugler, Ashford, Kent

RIGHT:
LEFT TO RIGHT:
'Game' by George Bate, 'The Challenge' by E.R. Bates & Son, 'Special Cartridge' by Bellow & Son Ltd, The 'Challenge' by A. Bates
LYING DOWN:
'Wye Valley' by Blake Bros

LEFT TO RIGHT:
'The Challenge' by C.H. Barham, 'The Pointer' by Bagnall & Kirkwood, 'Special Imperial Smokeless' by H.W. Barford & Co. Ltd, 'Barkers De Luxe', 'The Garrick' by John Barnes
LYING DOWN:
George Bates's 'Game', 'Leader' and 'Imperial'

LEFT TO RIGHT: *Unbranded Boss, 'Special Express' by Charles Boswell, 'Braddells Special' and 'Victory' by Braddell & Son, 'The Sydenham' by Wm Britt & Son, unbranded by Buckmaster & Wood*
LYING DOWN:
'Cameronia' by W. Cameron & Co., pin-fire by W. Burgess Malvern Wells, and 'Banshee' by W.C. Carswell

LEFT TO RIGHT: *The 'Cardiff' by Cross Brothers Ltd, Sports Outfitters, Cardiff, 'Reliable' by Cozens & Shaw Ltd, Wolverhampton, 'Wonder' by R.S. Chitty, Chichester, 'Sandringham' by T. Clough & Son, Kings Lynn, 'Noted Ryedale' by Geo. Cooper & Sons (Pickering) Ltd, 'Invincible' by Frank Clarke, Castle St, Thetford*
LYING DOWN: *'Wensleydale' by Cambell & Sons, Leyburn and 'County Favourite' by E. Calder, Gunmaker, Aberdeen*

LEFT TO RIGHT:
*'Wessex' by
A. Chamberlain,
unbranded by
E. Chamberlain, 'Special
Smokeless' by Septimus
Chambers, 'Ideal' by
B.E. Chaplin, 'J.W.G.' by
Chas Clarke*
LYING DOWN:
*Unbranded by Septimus
Chambers, 'Midland' and
'Express' both by
H. Clarke & Sons*

All specimens by Churchill
of London

LEFT TO RIGHT:
*'Utility', 'Premier',
'Waterproof' and 'Field'*
LYING DOWN:
'Express' and 'Imperial'

LEFT TO RIGHT: *'Champion' and 'County Favourite' both by F.J. Cole, unbranded by Crown Squire,
'Nulli Secundus' by J. Collis Ltd, 'The Cartridge' by R.H. Coltman, 'Marvel' by Coltman & Co.*
LYING DOWN:
*'Humber Duck and Goose' by Roy Conway, 'The Express' by Arthur Conyers & Sons and
'Dorset County' by Arthur Conyers*

LEFT TO RIGHT: *Unbranded by Daintiths Ltd, 'Triumph' by W.G. Donaldson, 'Eddystone' by C.G. Edwards & Son, 'Smasher' by H.C. Elliott, unbranded by John Colby Evans and unbranded by S. Entwistle.* LYING DOWN: *'Dovedale' by Desborough & Son*

LEFT TO RIGHT:
'Special Smokeless' by A.H. Dykes, Stowmarket, 'Demon' by E. Distin & Son, Totnes, 'The Triumph' by W.G. Donaldson, Grantown-on-Spey, unbranded by W. Dawson & Co., Ironmongers and Agricultural Merchants, Settle & Bentham
LYING DOWN:
'Victor' by Daniel & Morris, Agricultural Ironmongers, St Clears

LEFT TO RIGHT: *'Cording's Beater' by J.C. Cording & Co. Ltd, unbranded by Walter Coton, 'Special Keeper's Cartridge' by Walter Coton, 'Perth Cartridge' by D.B. Crockart, 'Orford' by Darlow & Co. and 'The Flight' by Howard A. Davies*
LYING DOWN: *Unbranded by Alfred Davis and 'Winton' by Howard A. Davies*

LEFT TO RIGHT:
'Duncan's Special Load'
by C.V. Duncan & Co.
unbranded by Ernest
Doe, 'The Partridge' by
J.D. Deabill, unbranded
by J. Dickson & Son and
'Special Blue Shell' by
J Dickson & Son
LYING DOWN:
Unbranded by Ernest Doe
and unbranded by
J. Dickson & Son Ltd

LEFT TO RIGHT: *'Premier' by Elderkins, 'Special Cartridge' by Earle's, 'Mark Over', 'Pall Mall' and*
'Sky High' all by William Evans and 'Newport' by Edwards Ltd
LYING DOWN: *'Cotswold' by Edwinson Green & Sons*

LEFT TO RIGHT:
'The Eskdale' by F.R.
Edwards successor to J.J.
Graham, Longtown, 'Ty Gwyn' by Dan
Evans, Whitland, unbranded
by Entwhistles late Troughton,
Gunmakers, Blackpool, 'Kerry
Blue' by John Edwards, Tralee,
Ireland and unbranded by Ben
Evans & Co. Ltd
LYING DOWN:
Unbranded by Eskine, Newton
Stewart and 'Ewen Special' by
J.W. Ewen, Aberdeen

LEFT TO RIGHT:
*Unbranded by Farmer,
'The Gloucester' by
Fletchers (Sports) Ltd,
'Eclipse' by William Ford,
'Quick Hit' by A.J. Foster,
'Demon' by C. Francis &
Son and 'The Club' by
Fussell's*
LYING DOWN:
*'Eclipse' by William Ford
and 'The Devon' by
E. Frost*

LEFT TO RIGHT:
*Unbranded by H. Fawley
& Son, Newton Moor,
Hyde, 'Follett's Eclipse',
Colyton, 'Kilquik' by
M. Garnett & Son, Dublin,
unbranded by W.J. George,
Dover and unbranded by
T.M. Gardiner Ltd,
Hoddesdon*
LYING DOWN:
*'Champion Special' by
S.J. Grimes, Stamford*

LEFT TO RIGHT: *Unbranded by G.E. Gold, Castle Mill Street, Bristol, 'Cumberland' by G.P. Graham,
Gunmaker, Cockermouth, 'The Referee' by A.W. Gamage Ltd, London, 'Primrose Smokeless Cartridge'
by W. Galbraith, Lancaster and 'Exmoor' by J. Gliddon & Sons, Williton*
LYING DOWN:
'The Watton Waterproof' by C.E. Golding, and 'The Monarch' by A. Groom, Lincoln

LEFT TO RIGHT:
*'Competitor' by Garden,
unbranded by T.M. Gardiner,
'Exmoor' by J. Gliddon &
Sons, 'Swift' by John G. Gamble and unbranded by Charles
Golden*
LYING DOWN:
'Enville' by Samuel Fiddian

LEFT TO RIGHT: *'Camroyd' by Gallyon & Sons, 'Camroyd' by Gallyon & Sons Ltd, 'X.L.' by Gale, two
'Crimson Flash' by Frank Garrett and unbranded by J. Gilman & Son Ltd*
LYING DOWN:
'County' and 'Bristol' both by George Gibbs Ltd

LEFT TO RIGHT:
*'Tayside' by John R. Gow &
Sons, 'Bon-Ton' by
J. Graham & Co. Ltd,
'Grantbury' and 'Velogrant'
both by Grant & Lang,
'Autokill' and 'Wetproof'
both by Gray & Co.*
LYING DOWN:
'Curzon' by Grant & Lang

LEFT TO RIGHT:
'Fur & Feather' by Green, 'The County Cartridge' by H.S. Greenfield, 'Hallrite Special' by Frank Hall, 'The Express' by B. Halliday & Co. Ltd, 'Trusty Servant' by Hammond Bros and 'Hardy's Reliance' by Hardy Bros Ltd

LYING DOWN:
'Beaufort' by Harrods Store, 'New Special' by S.E. Hayward & Co. Ltd and 'Economax' by C.H. Haygarth

LEFT TO RIGHT:
Unbranded by Hugh Hall, 'Rabbit Brand' by Harding Bros Ltd, 'Curzon' by Harrison & Hussey Ltd, unbranded by J. Harkom & Son and 'Hawk Brand' by Hawkes & Sons Ltd

LYING DOWN:
Unbranded by Hayward & Sons and 'Reliable' by Heywood & Hodge

LEFT TO RIGHT: *'Tivvy' by W.E. Heal, 'Dead Shot' by Harry Higgins, 'Victor' & 'Demon' both by Helson, unbranded by G. Hinton & Sons Ltd, 'Velox' by G.G. Higham, unbranded by E. & G. Higham*
LYING DOWN: *'Sussex Express' and unbranded .410" both by Russell Hillsdon*

All specimens by Holland & Holland

LEFT TO RIGHT: *Unbranded, 'Dominion', 'Northwood', 'Badminton High Velocity', 'Royal' and 'High Velocity'*
LYING DOWN: *'Badminton' & 'Twelve Two'*

LEFT TO RIGHT: *'Meon Valley' by W. Heming, 'Eclipse' by T.J. Hooke & Son, 'Rabbit' by Horsleys, 'Special Smokeless' by Hunter & Vaughan, unbranded by William Howe & Sons Ltd and unbranded by Hooton & Jones*
LYING DOWN: *Unbranded by A.S. Hocknell*

LEFT TO RIGHT: *'Harper's Invincible', Crewe, 'Hooke's Imperial' by T.J. Hooke & Son, Gunmakers, York, 'Hall's Smokeless' by C. Hall & Co., Knaresboro, 'Express' by J.P. Hodgson, unbranded by Howard Bros, Tottenham, London, unbranded by C.S. Hudson, Stockport*
LYING DOWN: *Unbranded by Holtom's, Lowestoft and 'The Setter' by C. Hayman, Weymouth*

LEFT TO RIGHT:
Unbranded by George Irving, Ironmonger, Penrith, 'The Gwalia' by M. James & Sons, Newcastle Emly, 'Anglian' by T. Johnson & Son, Swaffham, unbranded by Jackson & Son, Gunmakers, Gainsborough and 'The Majestic' by J. Tom Jones, Ironmongers, Carmarthen
LYING DOWN:
Unbranded by H. Jones, Gunmaker, Wrexham

LEFT TO RIGHT:
'Eddystone' by A.R. & H.V. Jefferies Ltd, 'Empire' by C. Jeffrey & Sons, 'Club Smokeless' and 'Sharpshooter' both by W.J. Jeffery & Co. Ltd, 'Special Smokeless' by S.R. Jeffrey & Son Ltd, and 'Sky High' by W. Jeffery & Son
LYING DOWN:
'Champion' by W.J. Jeffery & Co. Ltd

LEFT TO RIGHT: *'Best Pheasant Loading' by Jackson & Son, unbranded by Alfred Jackson, 'County' by Johnson & Wright, 'Liver' by Robert Jones and 'Accuratus' by W. Palmer Jones*
LYING DOWN: *'The Milford' by G. Jobson and 'Champion' by A.J. Jewson*

LEFT TO RIGHT:
Unbranded by H. Kempton, Plumstead, London, 'Mirus' by W. Kavanagh & Son, Dublin, 'The Marvel' by Herbert Kirkman, Ironmonger & Gunmaker, Scunthorpe, unbranded by Kent & Son, Wantage, and 'The Emerald Isle' by L. Keegan, Gunmaker, Dublin

LEFT TO RIGHT: *'The Sunset' by Lewis, Wells, 'Champion' by Lane, Bridgwater, 'Standard' by Lloyd & Son, Lewes, 'Sparkford Vale' by H.C. Little & Son, Gunmakers, Yeovil and unbranded by Frank Lane & Co. (Faringdon) Ltd, Faringdon*
LYING DOWN: *'The Four Best' by F.W. Lightwood, Gunmaker & Cartridge Loader, Brigg, Grimsby etc., .410" 'The Durham' by G.H. Leatham, Durham and 'Imperial' by J. & H. Lacey, Ironmongers, Long Eaton*

LEFT TO RIGHT:
Unbranded by Frank Lane & Co., 'Lace's Smokeless' by Lace, Wigan, unbranded by Joseph Lang & Son Ltd, 'Langdon' by John Langdon and 'The Killem' by John Lemon & Son Ltd
LYING DOWN:
'Sunset' by Lewis, Wells and unbranded by Leech & Sons, Chelmsford

LEFT TO RIGHT:
*'Victa' by R. Lisle,
'Blackmore Vale' by H.C.
Little & Son, unbranded
by London Sporting Park
Ltd using an Eley
Gastight Pegamoid case,
'Lock's Special' by
C.H. Lock, and
'Woodcraft' by
F.W. Lightwood*
LYING DOWN:
*'Galloway' by Tom Law
and 'High Velocity' by
Linsley Brothers*

LEFT TO RIGHT: *'Border' by Wm McCall & Co., 'Keepers Cartridge' by Wm McCall & Co., Dumfries, 'Argyll'
by Alex MacKay & Son, 'The Lorne' by Duncan McDougall, Oban, 'Badenoch' by Robert MacPherson
and unbranded by P.D. Malloch*
LYING DOWN: *'Markmore' by J. Stewart Mark and 'Swift' by James Matthews*

LEFT TO RIGHT:
*'Mendip' by B.D. Mogg &
Son, 'Bradford Cartridge'
by Smith Midgley,
unbranded by
W. Metcalfe, 'Wildfowler'
by Murray & Co. Ltd and
'Challenge' by Morrow
& Co.*
LYING DOWN:
*Unbranded by H.M.
Morris and 'Special
Rabbit' by T.H. Moor*

LEFT TO RIGHT:
'Club' by Mortimer, Barnstable, 'Yellow Champion' by Mellard & Co., Denbigh, 'Meredith Special' by H.I. Meredith, Bideford, 'Special Loading' by J.S. Mark, St Andrews, unbranded by C.H. Morgan, Wem & Whitchurch and 'Challenge' by Robert McBean, Stafford
LYING DOWN:
'The Killer' by G.P. Morton & Son, Whittlesey and 'Stopper' by R.C. Mumford, Kent

LEFT TO RIGHT:
'Special Game' by Newnham & Co., 'Moonraker' by Nightingale & Son, unbranded by J.E. Nott & Co. Ltd, 'Eddnick Game' by E. Nicholson, 'Special' by Norman & Sons and 'Lightning' by T. Newton
LYING DOWN:
'Lightning' by T. Newton

LEFT TO RIGHT:
'The Sureshot' by S.A. Nobbs, Lincoln, 'Reliable' by Francis Nelson & Son Ltd, Sligo, unbranded by C.W. Norton, Newtown, 'Premier' by Oakes, Madras, 'The O.K.' by F.C. Oakey, Stafford and 'Devon' by Otton's, Exeter
LYING DOWN:
Unbranded by J.E. Nott & Co Ltd, Brecon & Llandrindod

LEFT TO RIGHT: 'Sureshot' by Purvis & Co., 'Champion' by G. Palmer, unbranded by Potter & Co., unbranded by R. & E. Potter and unbranded by Joseph Pease Ltd
LYING DOWN: unbranded by Tom Parkinson

LEFT TO RIGHT: Unbranded by Joseph Pease Ltd, Gunmakers & Sports Outfitters, Darlington, 'Fysche' by Albert Pratt, Ironmonger & Ammunition Dealer, Knaresborough, 'High Velocity' by C. Purcell, Gloucester, 'Crown' by Paragon Gun, Belfast, 'Highdown' by F. Parsons, Littlehampton and unbranded by J.C. Patterson, Lisburn

LEFT TO RIGHT: Unbranded by John Rigby & Co., 'Nulli Secundus' by Richardson, Barnard Castle, 'Wivey' by C.C. Richards, 'Dreadnought' by A.E. Ringwood, 'Regent' by Regent Gun Co., 146 Corporation Street, Birmingham and 'Border' by Raine Bros
LYING DOWN: 'Mitre' by C. Riggs & Co. Ltd, 'Ideal' by A.E. Ringwood and 'Otter Vale' by H.P. Roberts

LEFT TO RIGHT:
*'The Roberts' by
Augustus J. Roberts,
'Expert' by Alexr
Robinson & Son, 'The
Castle' by H. Robinson &
Co., 'Burlington Express'
by H. Robinson ,
'Hallamshire' by
R. Roper Son & Co., and
unbranded by James
Russell*
LYING DOWN:
*'Star' and 'Standard'
both by A.J. Rudd*

LEFT TO RIGHT:
*Unbranded by James
Russell, Ironmonger, Elgin,
unbranded by J. Rowlatt &
Sons Ltd, Gunsmiths,
Wellingboro, 'The Castle'
by H. Robinson & Co.,
Ironmongers &
Gunsmiths, Bridgnorth,
'The Champion' by Alex
Rutherford Ltd, Sportsman
Repository, Darlington and
'Roy's Rabbit', Wroxham*

LEFT TO RIGHT:
*'The Dreadnought' by A.E. Ringwood,
Banbury, 'Border Cartridge' by Robert
Raine, Sportsman's Depot, Carlisle,
'Otter Vale' by H.P. Roberts, Ottery St
Mary, 'Stalham Superior' by Redmonds,
Stalham, Norfolk, unbranded by
R. Rous, Heyton, Suffolk*
LYING DOWN:
*'The Towcester' by H.E. Robedson,
Towcester*

LEFT TO RIGHT: *'Medway' by A. Sanders, 'Dreadnought' by H. Salt & Son, 'Best Smokeless' by John Smail & Sons, unbranded by J.F. Smythe Ltd, 'Sneezum's Special' by H.&R. Sneezum and 'Sureshot' by J.W. & E. Sowman Ltd*
LYING DOWN: *'Invincible' by Scotcher and unbranded by Alfred L. Spencer*

LEFT TO RIGHT:
'Bulzi' by Sayers, 'The Scottie' by J.S. Sharpe, Gun & Fishing Tackle Maker, Aberdeen, 'The Standby' by Stanbury & Stevens, Exeter, .410" by Chas Smith & Son, Newark, 'The Bradford' by Smith Midgley & Co., Bradford, 'Burnand' by P. Small, Newcastle, and 'Sharpe's Express' by F.A. Sharp & Son, Poole
LYING DOWN:
'The Blackmore Vale' by George Spiller, Ironmonger, Sherborne

LEFT TO RIGHT:
'Victory' by T. Stensby & Co., 'Game' by Stanbury & Stevens, unbranded by Robert Sykes & Sons Ltd, 'Universal' by Chas Smith & Son, 'Stump' by Slingsby, 'Invincible' by C.H. Smith & Sons
LYING DOWN:
Unbranded by Smallwood, 'Best Smokeless' by John Smail & Sons & 'Monocle' by Stanbury & Stevens

319

LEFT TO RIGHT: 'Reynard' by Towy-Tivy Farmers, Llanwrda etc., 'The Oswestrian' by J. Tucker, Gunsmiths & Sports Outfitters, Oswestry, 'The Falcon' by John Tyler (Highbridge) Ltd, Somerset Gun & Amunition Specialists, unbranded by H.A. Turner, Gunmaker, Marlborough, 'The Monnow' by Taylor & Jones, Monmouth and Ross and 'Special' by W. Tulloch & Co., Bishopgate Churchyard, London EC

ABOVE:
LEFT TO RIGHT: 'Monnow' by Taylor & Jones, unbranded by H.G. Tett Ltd, 'Chichester Cartridge' by John Tisdall, 'Falcon' by John Tyler and 'Special' by W. Tulloch & Co.

RIGHT:
LEFT TO RIGHT: Unbranded by William Varley, Gunmaker, Hull, 'The Ulster' by an unknown maker and 'Stuffit' by Usher

LEFT TO RIGHT: *'Champion' by G.H. Wilson, Gunmaker, Horncastle, 'Northumbria' by James B. Walker, Gun & Fishing Tackle Dealer, Newcastle on Tyne, 'The Warren', Warren, Ironmongers, Horncastle & Spilsby, 'The Rabbit' by T.M. Williams Ironmonger, Llandilo, 'The Champion' by Theo. Wilson & Sons Ltd, Ironmonger, Clitheroe*
LYING DOWN: *'The Nigger' by J.P. Whitlock & Sons, Ironmongers, Holsworthy*

LEFT TO RIGHT: *Unbranded by Watson Bros, 'Long Range' by Wanless & Co., 'Northumbria' by James B. Walker, 'Special' by H.J. Waddon, 'Quorn' by Whitehouse & Son, 'Champion' by Woodrow of Brandon*
LYING DOWN: *Unbranded by Thomas Wild & unbranded by H.H. Whitney*

Index